PRAISE FOR
MANAGING AND
LEADING PEOPLE THROUGH
ORGANIZATIONAL CHANGE

Managing and Leading People through Organizational Change is a brilliant book packed with information that delivers immediate benefits to both practising professionals and management students. This clearly structured book connects theoretical concepts with timely practical examples and compelling case studies and provides valuable recommendations. This is a must-read for every professional leader and manager and is inspirational also for those dealing with people on a day-to-day basis.

Jeanny Paren, Client Development Manager EMEA, Thomson Reuters

All too often the people aspect is ignored in both organizational change practice and theory. Not so with this book. This is a refreshing read for practitioners, scholars and students alike based on the simple philosophy that change is all about people. This book will enable everyone with an interest and drive for leadership and management responsibilities to better engage with those we work for: our people. Because it is only through our people that we will ever deliver successful change.

Professor Rune Todnem By, Editor-in-Chief, *Journal of Change Management*, Co-founder, the Public Leadership Foundation

Despite them being a growing field of focus, we still see organizational change initiatives undertaken without regard given to possible people impacts and responses. This book is comprehensive in its deliberation of people responses to change and the role of those supporting, leading and managing the change process from planning through implementation and review. It effectively combines theoretical and practical approaches to deliver an insightful and comprehensive consideration of the people aspects of change management in the context of accelerating global change and disruption.

Elizabeth Strong, Regional Manager Asia & EMEA, Human Resources, Qantas Airlines

This book explains and articulates that managing change cannot be done without understanding human emotion. It is the combination of this understanding with practical tools and guidance that makes this book so relevant and so effective for individuals, leaders, HR managers and organizations alike.

Tom Woolgar, Director, Corporate Banking, Scotia Bank

In this valuable book Hodges moves beyond the technical aspects of change and the focus on overcoming resistance from individuals. Instead she focuses on people, providing practical recommendations based on frameworks and theories from the academic literature as well as comprehensive examples from practitioner experiences. In this way readers from industry, academics, and students will all deepen understanding about how to engage individuals collaboratively in transformational processes as organizational change is implemented.

Deirdre Anderson, Senior Lecturer in Organizational Behaviour, Cranfield School of Management

For change managers and people leading organisation change, *Managing and Leading People through Organizational Change* is a great reminder of existing theories and concepts with real life examples from the author and professionals. Additionally it seeks to examine the latest innovations and research and their relevance in the workplace. This book successfully translates theory into practise with realistic scenarios for reference. The insights into the experience of others is invaluable. A must for executives and managers!

Christine Hartridge, Commercial Manager, Philips UK

Julie Hodges has built her experience both by practicing and researching change in organisations. In this new book, Hodges puts people at the heart of organisational change. People need to be understood enough and included to be engaged and committed. Change can be complex and misunderstood – just like human beings. This book can help greatly: it provides insights on people's emotions and decision making process without falling into overly complex considerations or debate. Furthermore it equips the people who need to lead or manage change with some very practical tools and techniques.

Cyril Lebel, Client Service Partner, Customer Presales and Service – Americas Vodafone Global Enterprise

Managing and Leading People through Organizational Change

Managing and Leading People through Organizational Change

The theory and practice of sustaining change through people

Julie Hodges

KoganPage

LONDON PHILADELPHIA NEW DELHI

First published in Great Britain and the United States in 2016 by Kogan Page Limited

2nd Floor, 45 Gee Street	1518 Walnut Street, Suite 1100	4737/23 Ansari Road
London	Philadelphia PA 19102	Daryaganj
EC1V 3RS	USA	New Delhi 110002
United Kingdom		India

© Julie Hodges 2016

The right of Julie Hodges to be identified as the author of this work has been asserted by her in accordance with the Copyright, Designs and Patents Act 1988.

ISBN   978 0 7494 7419 5
E-ISBN   978 0 7494 7420 1

British Library Cataloguing-in-Publication Data

A CIP record for this book is available from the British Library.

Library of Congress Cataloging in Publication Control Number

2015050911

Typeset by Graphicraft Limited, Hong Kong
Printed and bound by CPI Group (UK) Ltd, Croydon CR0 4YY

CONTENTS

Introduction 1

PART ONE Understanding organizational change 11

01 The context and nature of change 13

Introduction 13
Context 14
Drivers of change 15
Definitions 21
The nature of change 27
Recognizing the need for change 39
Summary 42
References 42
Further reading 45

PART TWO Individual responses to change 47

02 The impact of organizational change on emotions 49

Introduction 50
Emotions at work 51
Definition of emotions 52
Types of emotions during organizational change 52
Impact of emotions on work performance 54
Emotion perspectives 54
Emotions and culture 59
Suppressing and expressing emotions 61
Emotional contagion 63
Emotional balancing 63
Emotional intelligence 64
The role of emotions during organizational change 66
Summary 69
Implications for managers and leaders 70
References 72
Further reading 74

133098

03   Individual sense-making processes 75

Introduction 76
Motivating people to change 89
Resistance to change 93
Perceptions of justice and fairness 98
How change affects the psychological contract 99
Building trust 101
Helping people to make sense of change 103
Summary 104
Implications for managers and leaders 104
References 108
Further reading 109

PART THREE The role of leaders and
managers 111

04   Leading people through change 113

Introduction 113
Change management or change leadership 115
The transformation of leadership 116
Leadership enablers of change 120
Power and politics 135
Challenges of leading change 136
Change and people-centred leadership 140
Summary 142
Implications for leaders for leading change 143
References 144
Further reading 147

05   Fostering commitment and ownership 148

Introduction 148
Change management 150
How change is mismanaged 150
The role of managers 152
Managing people's health and well-being 154
Commitment or compliance 157
Ownership of change 158
Implementing change with impact 166
Managing conflict 166
Stakeholder analysis 172
Impact analysis of change on people 179
Summary 181
Implications for managers in the change process 182
References 184

Further reading 184
Appendix 5.1 – Change readiness assessment template 185
Appendix 5.2 – Managing people through change: a checklist for managers 189
Appendix 5.3 – Stakeholder management plan 192

06 Engaging people through dialogue 193

Introduction 193
Communicating change 195
Addressing rumours 199
The human dimension of communication 200
The art of dialogue 203
Using social media to communicate 211
ZOUD – the zone of uncomfortable debate 212
Summary 214
Implications 214
References 215
Further reading 216
Appendix 6.1 – Template for a stakeholder communication plan 217

07 Understanding and carrying out culture change 218

Introduction 219
Organizational culture 220
The management of organizational culture 223
Challenges of culture change 232
Patterns breaks 234
Creating a culture for change 236
Delivering sustainable culture change 240
Summary 243
Implications for managers and leaders 243
References 249
Further reading 250

PART FOUR Building capabilities 251

08 The role of HR in transitioning people through change 253

Introduction 254
The importance of HR during change 255
The strategic role of HR 257
Key HR activities 258
Managing performance 266
Working across global borders 267
The role of HR during restructuring 268

Retaining staff   271
Employee assistance programmes (EAPs)   272
Internal and external HR consultants   272
The capability of HR for transformations   276
Summary   277
Implications for HR   278
References   279
Further reading   280
Appendix 8.1 – Framework for initial discussions with HR about change   281
Appendix 8.2 – Using external HR consultants   282

09   Building capabilities for change   283

Introduction   284
Learning and reflection   284
Capabilities for change   286
Resilience   293
Intelligences for leading people through change   295
Building capabilities   303
Leadership development   313
Summary   320
Implications for leaders and managers   321
Note   322
References   322
Further reading   324
Appendix 9.1 – High-level training and development audit: training needs analysis template   325
Appendix 9.2 – Structuring action-learning group meetings   326

PART FIVE   Ethics, sustainability and change   329

10   Sustaining change   331

Introduction   331
Ethical standards of behaviour   333
Ethical aspects of managing change   334
Ethical aspects of leading change   336
The ethics of culture change   339
Sustaining change   340
Moving forward   344
Summary   345
Implications for managers and leaders   346
References   347
Further reading   348

Glossary   349
Index   353

Introduction

At the beginning of the 21st century, Ray Kurzweil, futurist and chief engineer at Google, predicted that 20,000 years of progress would be crammed into the next 100 years. If anything, progress and change have accelerated even faster than that, as tremendous forces for change are radically reshaping the world to the extent that we are living and working in an era of exponential change. Economic shifts are redistributing power, wealth, competition and opportunities around the globe. Disruptive innovations, radical thinking, new business models, shifting social and demographic trends and resource scarcity are impacting every sector. As a result, industries are facing varying levels of turmoil, including being disintermediated, out-Googled, or otherwise made irrelevant. Charles Handy (2015) in his book *The Second Curve* refers to such transformation as a major new curve, the implications of which are slowly dawning on us. Handy says: 'we have no choice but to ride that new curve... confident that we will adapt and survive' (2015: 47). The pervasive nature of change and its accelerating pace and magnitude are a ubiquitous reality of organizational life.

Disruption penetrates every aspect of business. Take, for example, the way that the competitive landscape has changed. In the past, industries were disrupted when rivals swooped in to attack large pieces of the value chain. Now, however, according to an IBM (2014) survey more than two in five chief executive officers (CEOs) expect their next competitive threat to come from companies outside their industries. These new competitors are not just set to steal market shares, they are turning whole industries upside down.

The challenge for companies is how they create and implement successful change in a competitive environment that is driven by a global marketplace, demanding customers and evolving technology. The constant reinvention and innovation is pushing the boundaries of many organizations and opening up opportunities for increasing collaboration, flexibility and creativity. The magnitude, speed, unpredictability and impact of change are greater than ever before.

A state of continuous change has become almost routine and an ever-present feature of organizational life, both at an operational and strategic level. Change is a dynamic force that constantly seeks opportunities, identifies initiatives that will capitalize on them, and completes those initiatives swiftly and efficiently. It is an ongoing process of searching, doing, learning and modifying, and has become both pervasive and persistent. Whether we like it or not, organizational change plays a significant role in our lives. It affects the nature of our jobs, or even if we have a job. In our everyday life, it impacts on the cost, quality and availability of the services and goods we rely upon. No longer can companies have the luxury of expecting day-to-day operations to fall into static or predictable patterns that are interrupted only occasionally by short bursts of change. In reality, the new normal is continuous change – not the absence of change.

Despite the fact that change will not disappear nor dissipate, we do not seem to be getting any better at leading and managing it successfully. There is a widely held view in the literature on organizational change that attempts to implement organizational change are predominantly unsuccessful, and fail to achieve their intended outcomes and sustain the benefits required. Even though the variable criteria and measures typically used make it difficult to draw definitive conclusions about the failure rates and their causes, the continuing consistent and accumulated evidence from CEOs, project and change managers through a wide range of sources does point to the reality that many change efforts do fail. Yet this is not a new phenomenon. As far back as the 1940s Kurt Lewin pointed out that all too often change is short-lived. He emphasized that after a 'shot in the arm', life returns to the way it was before (Lewin, 1947). This has significant implications for organizations because troubled or failed change incurs significant expense in terms of wasted resources, lost opportunities and a lack of accrued benefits.

The ability to lead, manage and sustain change is often the difference between market leadership and extinction. There is a long trail of companies that have not adapted to change and have declined swiftly or agonizingly slowly over a long period of time. The decline of Blockbuster, Comet, Phones4U, Borders, Habitat and Woolworths are just a few examples. To many this may seem paradoxical. On the one hand, the failure rate of change initiatives is immense. On the other hand, there is now more advice on how to manage change than ever before.

Academics and practitioners are continually producing studies of change, and offering supposedly new approaches. Some of these do offer new and useful insights into organizational change, others stress academic rigour but lack relevance (and vice versa), whilst others appear to contain neither. Many of the books on organizational change are dedicated to describing what change looks like, what instigates it, how it develops over time, and how it can and should be managed. The perspective in these books tends to be that of management, with little attention being given to what change looks and feels like for employees in the organization, or how they can be effectively engaged in change initiatives. Yet change is all about people, as all change affects someone. Activities such as preparing, planning, implementing and sustaining change in organizations are all done by people and, in turn, impact on individuals who are doing the work.

People play a key role in determining the potential for change to succeed. Yet they also represent the greatest challenge to the mastery of change. IBM's *Making Change Work* report (2008) concludes that success depends on people-related factors rather than technology-related factors, which are typically easier to identify and measure. Indeed structures, systems, processes and strategies tend to be fairly straightforward to redesign and change, whereas people are more complex. Individuals have different backgrounds, capabilities, personalities, dispositions, 'hang-ups', interests, motivations and aspirations, so change has the potential to have a different impact on each of them and cause different emotions, attitudes and reactions. Some people will be optimistic and react positively to change, some may be cynical, some may feel stressed and unable to cope, while others may overtly or covertly oppose what is being proposed.

The literature on organizational change tends to focus on how and why people resist change in organizations. This body of research has increased our understanding of employee responses to organizational change and has offered insights to scholars and practitioners alike on how to implement change for the best possible results. However, it tends to focus on an analysis of negative reactions to change and to neglect what affects individual orientation towards change initiatives. In practice, there is also a tendency to neglect and even to ignore the important people dimension of change. According to Sally Woodward and Chris Hendry (2004: 164), one-third of senior managers acknowledge that the people aspects are ignored in their change programmes. This is quite a shocking statistic, for any organization that believes change can be implemented and sustained without considering the impact, reaction and involvement of people is in deep delusion. The vast majority of organizational change is managed from a technical viewpoint without recognizing or understanding how the people element influences the success or failure of change. It is often easier for managers to focus attention on, and to become preoccupied with, the technical side of change, dealing with quantifiable and predictable issues such as developing strategies and action plans, calculating profitability and rationalizing resources.

Change efforts often falter because leaders and managers overlook the need to understand how individuals perceive change and to engage people in the change effort. Instead their focus is often on the process rather than the people element of change. However, companies can no longer justify or afford to ignore leading and managing people through change. Improving the outcome of change initiatives requires attention to the people dynamics, as it is human behaviour that ultimately will sustain change in organizations.

Leading and managing people through change requires an understanding and respect of how change affects individuals. No organization can institute change if its employees will not, at the very least, accept the change. No change will work if employees are not involved in the effort, as change is not possible without people changing their behaviours and the way that they work.

This book therefore focuses on understanding how managers and leaders can guide people through change so that they emerge at the other end of the transformation with a return on their investment and benefits achieved that are sustainable.

Aim of the book

The aim of this book is to inform the practice of managing and leading people through change in organizations. It goes beyond what is already known and sets out frameworks, perspectives and practical approaches and recommendations for current and future managers and leaders in organizations. This is done in the following ways. First, the book focuses on what has been learnt about change by considering existing theories and concepts. Second, the book includes a practical perspective: practising managers, leaders, human resource (HR) and organizational development (OD) professionals and consultants have provided their personal experiences of managing and leading people through change in organizations. Third, the author contributes her own experiences from the business and academic worlds. Fourth, the book covers some of the latest thinking and innovative ideas in the field of organizational change that can help achieve sustainable benefits from the change. There is often a gap between the latest thinking in organizational change and translation into practice in organizations. This book seeks to close the gap by drawing on relevant academic literature, examples from companies across the globe, as well as practitioner publications and experience. From this platform of knowledge, advice for managing and leading people through change is developed. This gives the book a unique perspective in being crafted from theory as well as practice. By providing practical examples and recommendations, the book focuses on the importance of understanding the impact of change on individuals and how to engage them collaboratively throughout the change process. The book's distinctive feature is that it focuses on the people dimension of change in organizations. It provides a theoretical overview of the key issues as well as a focused practitioner orientation.

Learning outcomes of the book

As well as providing inspiration this is a practical book and, after reading it, you will be able to:

- appreciate the importance of managing and leading the human dynamics of change;
- be more effective in managing and leading people through change in organizations;
- use the practical skills mentioned throughout the book to manage the emotional aspects of change;
- achieve the benefits from sustaining change through people in your organization.

Audience

The book is aimed at anyone who needs to know how to manage and lead people through organizational change. It will be of benefit for practising managers and leaders who are responsible for identifying the need and readiness for change as well as implementing, evaluating and sustaining change in organizations. It will also be a helpful resource for line managers, internal and external consultants and specialists in human resources, organizational development, project management, and other related disciplines responsible for facilitating change and transformations. It is also meant for students of organizations (undergraduate and postgraduate), in particular those who strive to assess and understand change and transformation in organizations.

How the book is structured

The book is divided into five parts. *Part 1 – Understanding organizational change –* places the issues of the book in the wider context of socio-economic and techno-political change experienced by organizations in the 21st century. It also presents the core concepts of the book and the relevance for managers and leaders engaged in organizational change. *Chapter 1 – The context and nature of change –* examines how the wider external context in which organizations operate is changing and the impact on organizations. It discusses how external and internal factors trigger, stimulate and drive organizational change. The chapter also reviews some of the contemporary debates that populate the literature on the nature of change, including a brief critical examination of some of the theories relating to change and an exploration of the different types of change, such as planned and emergent. The chapter concludes by looking at how leaders and managers can recognize the need for change. The chapter addresses key questions such as: what triggers change? How can change in organizations be classified? What happens when organizations ignore the need for change? Should change be process driven or people driven?

In *Part 2 – Individual responses to change –* the impact of change on individuals is explored and how they may react to change. Since change is a process that involves emotions, *Chapter 2 – The impact of organizational change on emotions* illustrates how organizational change emotionally affects an individual. The chapter begins by examining the nature and meaning of emotions in the workplace. Theoretical perspectives on emotions are firstly considered and how they relate to change; the positive and negative emotions to change are then highlighted. The role that an organization's culture plays in influencing the expression or suppression of emotions is explored, along with factors such as 'emotional contagion' and 'emotional labour'. How managers and leaders recognize and cope with their own emotions is also discussed, including 'emotional balancing' and 'emotional intelligence'. The chapter concludes by providing practical advice. Key questions are addressed such as: what drives emotions towards change? What might be the anticipated emotional and attitudinal reactions of individuals facing change? What responses can be expected from different people? What are the concerns of employees about change? How are emotions spread amongst individuals during change? What impact does culture have on emotions and how might changing a culture impact on people's emotions?

The transition of people through change is the focus of *Chapter 3 – Individual sense-making processes*. This chapter examines how individuals make sense of change and how this relates to the way that they behave. The chapter begins by considering how change is interpreted. Transition models are critically evaluated, such as those by Elisabeth Kübler-Ross (1973), William Bridges (2004) and Lynn Isabella (1990). The energy and willingness of individuals for change and how this affects their response to change is then explored. The importance of how motivation affects individuals' willingness to embrace change is also discussed. The chapter goes on to consider how people react to and make sense of change. In particular, it examines the concept of 'resistance' to change and critically evaluates whether or not opposition to change can be viewed as a positive or negative attribute. The heightened sensitivity to justice and fairness, and how this can affect levels of trust, are explored. The chapter concludes by providing practical approaches to help people to make sense of change. Some key questions are addressed such as: what pattern of emotions do people typically progress through in response to change in organizations? How effective are transition models and how can they be used in practice? How can trust be developed and sustained during times of change? What motivates people to embrace or resist change?

Part 3 – The role of leaders and managers – focuses on the approaches to managing and leading people through change that are likely to be the most effective. Practical suggestions are offered as to how best to work with people before, during and after a change initiative is implemented. In *Chapter 4 – Leading people through change* – begins by exploring the difference between leading and managing people through change. The different styles of leadership are then explored and how they can help to lead people through change. The benefit of leadership philosophies is emphasized, as well as the right approach and attitude from leaders. The chapter critically reviews models of leadership and change and illustrates what has worked in organizations, using examples from a number of companies. Particular attention is paid to what leaders can do to gain commitment from people to change and transformation. The chapter concludes by advocating a people-centred approach to leadership. Key questions are addressed such as: what is the role of leaders in the change process? What approach to leading change is likely to be the most effective? What are the implications of different leadership styles for organizational change? What leadership behaviours tend to be associated with effective change? What are the different leadership enablers of change? What is the impact of power and politics on change and how should leaders deal with them? What do leaders need to do to nurture people through the change once it is on its way?

Leading change is a necessary but alone not a sufficient condition to sustain change through people. Change must also be managed – it must be planned, organized, directed and controlled. Managing people through change is therefore the focus of *Chapter 5 – Fostering commitment and ownership*. In the first part of this chapter the role of managers in relation to managing people through change is examined. In the second part, the focus is on the importance of engaging employees collaboratively throughout the transition journey. Specific approaches are considered on how to gain commitment and ownership from individuals such as: ensuring readiness for change; involvement in the decision-making process; creating a sense of shared ownership; and enabling individuals to actively contribute to the shaping of the change intervention. The chapter also examines key factors such as stakeholder engagement and management. How to resolve conflicts is also considered and some practical advice is suggested. The chapter concludes by considered how managers can identify the impact of change on people. The chapter addresses several questions including: what are some of the key principles underpinning the way that change is managed? How can individuals be supported through change? What can be done to build ownership of change? How can managers identify whether or not people are ready for change? How can stakeholders be identified and managed?

Chapter 6 – Engaging people through dialogue focuses on using communication to enable a greater understanding of and commitment to change. The chapter reviews the importance of dialogue on eradicating uncertainty about change, gaining commitment and building trust among individuals and teams in an organization. In particular, the chapter explores how to engage employees in conversations about change. The chapter begins by reviewing the importance of communication as a change practice. It then goes on to discuss how dialogue is at the heart of communications. The key aspects of successful dialogue are outlined. The chapter concludes by describing an approach for discussing the difficult issues of change by getting into the ZOUD (zone of uncomfortable debate).

Key questions are addressed such as: what are the most appropriate communication approaches to use during transformation? How can managers and leaders encourage effective dialogue during times of uncertainty? What affects the quality of dialogue? How should rumours be addressed? How should difficult conversations be managed? Practical tools are included to help you to develop an approach for dialogue.

Chapter 7 – Understanding and carrying out culture change – reviews the challenges of attempting to manage culture. It queries whether or not culture can be changed and, if so, how this can be done. The importance of creating a culture for change is emphasized, with examples of what some companies have done to achieve this. A diagnostic model is provided for describing and understanding the current and desired culture of an organization, and the challenges of changing a culture are explored. The chapter also introduces the concept of 'pattern breaks' and how they can impact on changing a culture. Key questions are addressed such as: can the culture of an organization be changed? If so, how can this be done? What are the challenges of attempting to change a culture? How can a culture of innovation be developed?

Part 4 – Building Capabilities – focuses on the skills, knowledge and abilities required for sustaining change through people. In *Chapter 8 – The role of HR in transitioning people through change* – the focus is on the role of HR professionals managing and leading people through change. In particular, attention is paid to how HR can act as facilitators, strategists, pastors and/or consultants. Attention is given to HR's strategic and operational role in the diagnosis, planning, implementation, monitoring and sustaining of the benefits of change through people. The chapter also discusses the importance of performance management in helping to embed changes to work activities and behaviours. Examples are provided about HR's approach to change, as well as the challenges they face and how they address them. In particular, the role of HR during restructuring is examined. The chapter concludes by discussing the consultancy role that HR can play, as well as considering the benefits of employing external and internal HR consultants. Key questions are addressed such as: what role can and should HR play in organizational change? How can the proposed benefits of change and their measures be integrated into performance management systems? How should HR support restructuring? How can key employees be retained during transformation? What are the benefits of using internal versus external HR consultants?

Chapter 9 – Building capabilities for change – examines the importance of building change capabilities across an organization. The chapter begins by focusing on organizational learning – what it is and why it is important in the context of change. The importance of learning and reflecting on the success and failure of change is also discussed, as well as the capabilities for change – what they are and how they can be developed. In particular, the multiple intelligences for leading people through change are reviewed and how suggestions for enhancing them are considered. Key questions are addressed such as: how can the learning from change be developed? How can organizations learn from the failure as well as the success of change and transformation? How can organizations harness and apply the knowledge and lessons learnt from transformations? What are the key capabilities for change? How can an organization build such capabilities?

In *Part 5 – Ethics, sustainability and change* – the key concepts of ethics and sustainability are explored: *Chapter 10 – Sustaining change* – focuses on these two key factors. The first part of the chapter discusses the importance of the ethical dimension of change as a means of ensuring that managers and leaders act in the interests of the people within the organization. The key ethical issues in carrying out change, especially culture change, are explored. The implications for leaders and managers and what they need to do in order to pursue an ethical approach to change are also considered. The second part examines how change can be sustained and the benefits realized from it, focusing on the leadership, management and individual influences on sustaining change. The chapter concludes by reviewing the traditional approach to change and the emerging people approach. Key questions are addressed such as: what do we mean by ethical and sustainable change? How can we ethically lead and manage people through change and transformation? How can managers implement change in a way that is both effective and ethical? What are the key influences for sustaining change?

Each chapter has an introduction and a list of the key points covered; there is also a summary at the end of each chapter. This will help you to navigate through the book. Each chapter also includes: learning outcomes, principal theories, relevant research, tools and frameworks, business examples and further reading. There are also recommendations at the end of each chapter that provide you with some of the practical implications of the issues discussed.

You are encouraged to take time to reflect on your learning and personal approaches to managing and leading change as you go through the book – through various case studies, exercises and questions for discussion.

When considering using any of the tools or frameworks presented in this book it is important to adapt them to meet the context of your organization. Warnings about best-practice traps and management-theory fads should be adhered to. As Capozzi, Kellen and Smit (2012) point out when reviewing so-called 'best practice' companies, practitioners and management theorists assume that everything these companies do be regarded as best practice – often without examining the context in which they derive their success or without parsing the true nature of accomplishments. The danger with best practice is that the different context, the scale of the challenge as well as the business issues and risks posed, mean that even for experienced practitioners organizational change is never routine. The implications of getting it wrong can be detrimental to your organization, your people, your customers and other stakeholders. So it is important that you adapt the tools and techniques to the context of the organization/department/team or situation in which you are working, rather than attempting a cut-and-paste approach of 'one-size fits all'.

Organizational change is in transition from an art to a profession, from improvisation to a far richer approach based on empirical and practical perspectives on what works and what does not. This book is intended to help with that transition by providing theoretical and practical perspectives on managing and leading change successfully in organizations. It attempts to address some of the key issues related to sustaining change through people from a practical and realistic perspective as well as a theoretical one. The experiences that are included from individuals and organizations provide insights into what makes change successful and what makes it fail, as well as lessons learnt.

It is a privilege to share this book with you. I hope that you enjoy reading it and that it helps you to manage and lead the most important part of organizational change successfully – people.

References

Bridges, W (2004) *Managing Transitions: Making the most of change*, 3rd edn, Nicholas Brealey Publishing, New York

Capozzi, M, Kellen, A and Smit, S (2012) The perils of best practice: should you emulate Apple? *McKinsey Quarterly*, September

Handy, C (2015) *The Second Curve*, Random House, London

IBM (2008) *Making Change Work*, IBM Global Services, New York

IBM (2014) *Making Change Work... While the Work Keeps Changing: How change architects lead and manage organizational change*, IBM Institute, New York

Isabella, L A (1990) Evolving interpretations as a change unfolds: how managers construe key organizational events, *Academy of Management Journal*, 33, pp 7–41

Kübler-Ross, E (1973) *On Death and Dying*, Tavistock, London

Lewin, K (1947) Frontiers in group dynamics II: channels of group life; social planning and action research, *Human Relations*, 1 (2), pp 143–53

Woodward, S and Hendry, C (2004) Leading and coping with change, *Journal of Change Management*, 4 (2), pp 155–83

Further reading

Hodges, J and Gill, R (2015) *Sustaining Change in Organizations*, Sage, London

PART ONE
Understanding organizational change

01
The context and nature of change

KEY POINTS

- There are many driving forces that trigger the need for change. These forces arise from the external and internal environment in which an organization operates.
- Organizational change is about *content*, *process* and *context*.
- Change can be *incremental* or *transformational*. *Transition* is the process that an individual goes through in adapting to the change.
- *Planned* change is deliberate, a product of conscious reasoning and action. In contrast, change sometimes unfolds in an apparently spontaneous and unplanned way. This type of change is known as *emergent* change.
- Organizational change has traditionally been viewed as an either/or proposition: either process driven to create economic value for stakeholders (Theory E) or people driven to develop an open, trusting corporate culture (Theory O). Sustainable change is process driven and people driven.
- When an organization becomes incapable of looking outside, reflecting on success and failure, accepting new ideas and developing new insights, it decreases its customer focus, and costs increase. If unchecked, the ultimate outcome of this trap of success can be the 'death spiral'.

Introduction

The aim of this chapter is to provide an overview of the nature and the context in which change operates. The chapter begins by examining what triggers change in organizations, by reviewing some of the external and the internal drivers of change. The definitions of the key concepts that are used in the book – including change, transition and transformation – are then presented. This is followed by an overview of the theoretical perspectives of the different types of change that organizations may experience, such as planned and emergent. The chapter concludes by examining how leaders and managers can recognize the need for change. Key questions are addressed such as: what triggers change? How can change in organizations be classified? What happens when organizations ignore the need for change? Should change be process driven or people driven?

LEARNING OUTCOMES

By the end of this chapter you will be able to:

- appreciate the complex nature of change in organizations;
- critically evaluate the theoretical perspectives relating to the types of change that organizations may experience;
- evaluate the potential need for change;
- identify the most appropriate approach for change in an organization in which you work or one that you are familiar with.

Context

Organizations operate in a dynamic, diverse environment and are being transformed by a multiplicity of factors. All sizes of companies are now internet-enabled and access markets across geographical boundaries. All types of joint ventures and alliances are being created between different organizations in different countries. Private and public companies now have multiple interfaces in multiple locations. New entities are emerging with international organizations based on a combination of initiatives: non-governmental, charitable trusts and foundations, and philanthropy-based. Multinational companies are now bigger, more diverse and have multiple locations in different regions, with a diverse range of employees and customers. There is now greater reach and interdependency across geographies and cultures. Along with this there is a greater focus and scrutiny on governance, ethics and sustainability. Shifting ownership models and domicile realities are calling for different controls and legislation that challenge national taxation and corporation accountability, and different funding models are increasingly being used such as crowdfunding and crowdsourcing. All in all, organizations have become more complex whilst becoming more transparent; they have become more interconnected whilst becoming more technology driven; and they have become more democratic whilst becoming more accountable (De Haan and Kasozi, 2014).

Alongside this there is a decreasing lifespan of corporations, products and services. Since the 1950s the lifespan of large corporations has reduced by 75 per cent: the average lifespan for the S&P (Standard & Poor) 500 largest companies listed on the US stock market index was more than 60 years in 1957 and in 2014 was approximately 15 years. Looking ahead this means that by 2030 less than three-quarters of the leading companies in the S&P 500 will exist. To survive organizations need to be more adaptable in response to the global, national and local events that are driving change.

Drivers of change

As organizations face a dynamic changing environment they are required to adapt, change and in some cases totally transform in order to survive. The forces that are driving the need for change arise from the external and internal environment in which an organization operates.

External environment

External drivers of change for an organization come from many directions. They may be seen as challenges, opportunities or threats and include political, economic, social, technological, legal and environmental factors. Some of the key drivers in each of these areas are (but are not limited to): shifts in global economic power (economic); climate change and resource scarcity (environmental); demographic shifts (social); technological breakthroughs (technological); new ideologies (political); and legislation (legal).

Shift in global economic power

Economically, globalization is changing the map of consumerism. By 2030 it is estimated that the purchasing power of the E7 countries – which is the BRIC (Brazil, Russia, India and China) economies plus Mexico, Indonesia and Turkey – will overtake that of the G7 countries (Canada, France, Germany, Italy, Japan, the UK and the United States). As incomes continue to rise in the E7 markets, they are contributing to an increasing share of the global middle class and creating a radical shift in the kind of league table of economies around the world. Just below the E7 countries in size are the F7 countries that include Colombia and Peru in Latin America; Nigeria and Morocco in Africa; and Vietnam, Bangladesh and the Philippines in Asia. As these emerging economies continue to develop they will become huge consumer markets. It is predicted that the middle class in the Asia-Pacific region will be far ahead of the United States and Europe by 2030 (PwC, 2014). This will create a whole range of opportunities for other organizations to exploit these huge consumer markets.

For businesses to operate in this changing marketplace they need to focus on differentiation. The emerging markets cannot just be treated as a single block. This means being aware of the nuances, the institutional differences, the regulatory differences and the differences in social perspectives in these economies. Companies need to take a differentiated approach if they are going to be successful in these emerging markets. In an article entitled 'Going Glocal: How Smart Brands Adapt to Foreign Markets', Sylvia Vorhauser-Smith (2012) provides examples of how this is happening. For instance, KFC serves porridge for breakfast and Peking duck burgers for lunch in Shanghai. Starbucks serves green and aromatic teas in Beijing, while Coca-Cola produces carbonated fruit drinks and bottled water in Shenzhen. These brands are indisputably Western and they are carving out a market share as global businesses. But they have also learned that success in the emerging markets requires adaptation to local tastes, attitudes and values.

The shifts in economic power are causing globalization itself to change. In an article in the *Harvard Business Review* on the 'new rules of globalization' Ian Bremmer (2014) points out that following the global recession that began in 2007–08 the approach to going global changed. The governments of developing nations have since then become cautious, selecting the countries or regions with which they want to do business, picking the sectors in which they will allow capital investment and selecting the local, often state-owned, companies they wish to promote. This is a very different approach to globalization. Bremmer (2014) says that several factors have contributed to this trend, including: many governments find it risky to continue opening their markets to foreign competition, because local companies and consumers often attempt to block new entrants; some countries have built large foreign exchange reserves and boosted exports, so they are no longer trying to attract large amounts of foreign investment; and policymakers in developing countries are intervening to create uneven playing fields that give local players an advantage.

As a result of such drivers for change companies are finding it harder to sustain their presence in overseas markets. Pfizer, the biopharmaceutical company, is one such corporation. In 2013, as part of the Indian government's efforts to make medicine accessible to as many people as possible, India's Patent Office revoked Pfizer's patent for the cancer drug Sutent and granted a domestic manufacturer, Cipla, the right to produce a cheaper generic version. Such shifts are creating major risks for multinational companies such as Pfizer.

So the new era of guarded globalization is having an impact on the strategy of international companies and, for such companies, responding is not always easy.

Climate change and resource scarcity

Climate change is amplifying existing global challenges. The World Bank (2012) in its report *Turn Down the Heat* focuses on the risks of climate change to global development, especially in sub-Saharan Africa, South-East Asia and South Asia. The report spells out what the world would be like if it warmed by 4 degrees Celsius, which is what scientists are predicting will happen by the end of the 21st century, unless there are serious policy changes (2012: xi). It is a stark reminder that climate change affects everything.

The president of the World Bank Group, Dr Jim Yong Kim, is very clear in the foreword of the report about the dangers: 'The result is a dramatic picture of a world of climate and weather extremes causing devastation and human suffering. In many cases, multiple threats of increasing extreme heatwaves, sea-level rise, more severe storms, droughts and floods will have severe negative implications for the poorest and most vulnerable' (2012: xi–xii).

The solutions for organizations to address such challenges lie not only in climate projects but also in effective risk management and ensuring that all the thinking and work in organizations is designed with the threat of global warming in mind.

Demographic shifts

Demographic changes, including rapid population growth and an unprecedented ageing of the global population, will have a major impact on business in the coming years. By 2050, we are likely to see between 2 billion and 3 billion more people on the planet. In *The Age of Aging* (2008) George Magnus highlights the demographic trends shaping the world, which include:

- *The ratio of children to older citizens is declining.* By 2050 there will be twice as many older citizens as there are children.
- *There has been a sea-change in the nature of illness to non-communicable diseases.* One of the consequences of rapid aging and rising longevity is the change in the nature of illness and disease. For example, by 2030 depression is expected to become the biggest single cause of disability. This is what the World Health Organization has called the invisible epidemic of non-communicable diseases.
- *The speed of aging is rising rapidly in emerging economies.* The emerging markets are aging at an astounding pace. What this means is that emerging markets have far less time to build the financial infrastructure and social security systems to deal with the consequences of an aging population.
- *Old-age dependency ratio is rising rapidly in Japan and European countries, but at a slower pace in Anglo-Saxon economies.* The old-age dependency ratio in countries such as Germany, Japan, Italy and Spain is expected to rise rapidly. These countries are characterized as the 'hares' because of the rapid progression of old-age dependency in them, whereas the Anglo-Saxon economies such as Sweden and France are 'tortoises' by comparison, as the progression is much slower.

Due to such shifts in demographics new organizational strategies are needed. Differing work situations with greater flexibility are needed to retain older workers, who may prefer to work part-time, the ability to work from home, and/or phased retirements, where retirement occurs gradually over time. So organizations need to consider providing more flexible working options.

Not only is the population ageing but the proportion of the global population living in urban areas is also increasing. The Development Concepts and Doctrine Centre (DCDC) (2010) in a report entitled *Global Strategic Trend – Out to 2040*, predicts that by 2040 around 65 per cent, or 6 billion, of the world's population will live in urban areas, attracted by access to jobs, resources and security, with the greatest increases in urbanization occurring in Africa and Asia. Such trends are supported by the United Nations (2014) report *World Urbanization Prospects*. The report forecasts that as the world continues to urbanize, sustainable development challenges will be increasingly concentrated in cities. At the same time, cities offer opportunities to expand access to services, such as health care and education, for large numbers of people in an economically efficient manner. Providing public transportation, as well as housing, electricity, water and sanitation for a densely settled population is typically cheaper and less environmentally damaging than providing a similar level of services to predominantly rural households. Urban dwellers also have access to larger and more diversified labour markets, and enjoy healthier lives overall. The United Nations report outlines that urbanization is integrally connected to the three pillars of sustainable development: economic development, social development and environmental protection. The report highlights the need to forge a new model of urban development that integrates all facets of sustainable development to promote equity, welfare and shared prosperity in an urbanizing world. The report concludes that: 'accurate, consistent and timely data on global trends in urbanization and city growth are critical for assessing current and future needs with respect to urban growth and for setting policy priorities to promote inclusive and equitable urban and rural development' (2014: 4). In response, governments and organizations must implement policies to ensure that the benefits of urban growth are shared equitably and sustainably.

Technological breakthroughs

Technology represents new and different ways of doing things. It also causes disruption, supplanting traditional ways of doing things and rendering skills and organizational approaches obsolete. Disruptive technologies include the automation of knowledge work, the 'internet of things', cloud technology, advanced robotics, autonomous and near-autonomous vehicles, next-generation genomics, energy storage, 3D printing, advanced materials, advanced oil and gas exploration and recovery, and renewable energy. Such technologies are bringing advances that transform life, business and the global economy. They are relentless and far reaching, impacting on most organizations. Some of the biggest opportunities and threats for organizations will arise from technologies that have the potential to transform how work is done. An example of the impact that disruptive technologies can have is evident in the e-finance revolution. In Africa, India and Eastern Europe, a service for mobile money called M-Pesa has replaced banking for millions of people who do not have or, in fact, even need a bank account. M-Pesa can be cashed by sending a text message and receiving money immediately at ATMs, without the need for a debit card (Bershidsky, 2014).

Many technologies, including advanced robotics, next-generation genomics and renewable energy, have real potential to drive tangible improvements in the quality of life, health and the environment. For example, advanced robotic surgical systems and prosthetics may improve and extend many lives, while renewable energy sources may help to clean up the environment and lessen the deleterious health effects of air pollution. Such technologies are also changing how and what consumers buy, and altering overall consumption of certain resources such as energy and materials. They are also fundamentally changing the nature of work for many employees around the world.

As a result of disruptive technologies the nature of work is changing. Technologies such as advanced robotics and knowledge-work automation tools move companies to leaner, more productive operations, but also far more technologically advanced operations. The need for high-level technical skills is growing, even on assembly lines. In response to this, companies need to find ways to get the workforce they need, by engaging with policymakers and their communities to shape secondary and tertiary education and by investing in talent development and training to keep their corporate skills fresh (Manyika *et al*, 2013).

New ideologies

Despite the emergence of a possible 'age of convergence' due to globalization, ideologically driven conflicts are, according to the DCDC (2010) likely to continue to exist. The economic and social difficulties in some countries may lead to extremist identity and xenophobia. The DCDC (2010) report predicts that new ideologies will emerge, driven by religion, ethnic differences, nationalism, inequality or a combination of these factors. The social tensions caused by what some may see as the intrusive global culture are likely to be most acute amongst those who seek to maintain their indigenous and traditional customs and beliefs, and feel threatened by changes. This is likely to lead to an increasing number of individuals and groups, many of whom form around single issues that differentiate them from wider society, becoming marginalized and possibly radicalized. When such conditions exist, particularly when exacerbated by high levels of marginalization and social exclusion, sections of the population will develop grievances that may lead to extremism. This is already evident in some parts of the Middle East.

The emergence of such new ideologies may pose a further challenge to organizations attempting to operate across the globe, especially in terms of risk and security issues.

Legislation

A further driver for change in organizations is the implementation of new legislation and policies. For instance, the European Union (EU) VAT legislation that came into effect from 1 January 2015 had an impact on the tax affairs of many companies. It meant that an online business had to account for

VAT in the EU member country where its customer lives, and at the VAT rate applicable to the buyer's country rather than charging the seller's country VAT rate, as previously. This shift in legislation has affected anyone selling digital content or e-services, including telecommunication providers and broadcasters. Such legislation applies to businesses based inside and outside of the EU. The rationale for the rules changing were that the EU wanted to create a level playing field for all businesses that sell to consumers. The idea was to remove the unfair advantage gained by competitors undercutting rivals by geographically locating themselves in an EU state with lower taxes, or outside the EU altogether. The way in which a business can operate may therefore have to change, based on the constraints imposed by such legislation.

Such external factors as those outlined above can trigger the need for change in organizations. Drivers for change can also come from internal organizational factors.

The internal environment

Drivers of change emanating from the internal environment of an organization are often those related to people wanting to improve the things that they do, such as developing new and better ways of working to solve problems with current practices; improving operational efficiency; reducing costs; and improving the quality of products and services, as well as processes. Internal drivers for change can also include changes in ownership through takeovers, mergers or acquisitions, or the arrival of a new leader. The new owners/leaders will normally bring their own views about the company and what needs to change and, like a new owner of an old house, will be tempted to alter or remodel the existing business processes. Such drivers may result in changes to the strategy, structure, processes and behaviour of people within the organization.

Internal and external factors

Leaders and managers need to be aware of the demands of the external environment. Those who detect and anticipate external drivers of change will be ready to respond to them and view them as an opportunity, rather than a threat. At the same time the internal drivers of change should not be ignored. However, internal and external drivers do not in themselves bring about change and transformation. They simply create the need for change.

The need for change seldom arrives as single events or issues. For example, when changes in the economic environment result in interest-rate increases, the costs for an organization also rise. To deal with those increased costs the organization may decide to change working practices to improve efficiency. Changes in the rate of interest will also increase the cost of living for people working in the organization. As a result they may demand a higher salary.

The increase in interest rates is one single event that can occur at the same time as new legislation is brought in, new governmental targets are launched, or a new humanitarian aid crisis arises (Price, 2009).So leaders and managers need to be aware of the drivers for change that are internal and external to the organization.

Definitions

Three concepts appear frequently in discussions of change, including, of course, 'change' itself as well as 'transition' and 'transformation'. In this section we will clarify what these are and how they are defined in the context of this book.

Change

Change is any adjustment or alteration in an organization that has the potential to influence the organization's stakeholders' physical or psychological experience (Oreg, By and Michel, 2013). It is an opportunity to make or become different through new ways of organizing and working (Dawson, 2003). Alterations can include changes to processes, policies, procedures and systems, such as technology, performance management, reward and recognition schemes, financial payment systems and improvements to operations. They also include longer term and larger changes, which are often harder to design and implement, such as structural changes.

Changes can be planned or emergent to the whole or parts of an organization in order to improve efficiency and effectiveness. The difference can be small (incremental) or radical (transformational). Incremental change aims to provide improvements. It is change that is constant, evolving and cumulative. Nearly 95 per cent of organizational changes are estimated to be incremental (Burke, 2008). A key feature of this type of change is that it builds on what has already been accomplished and has the flavour of continuous improvement (or *kaizen*, as termed by the Japanese).

Incremental changes are the outcome of the everyday process of management and tend to be when individual parts of an organization deal increasingly and separately with one problem and one objective at a time. Incremental change can include changing a product formula in such a way that customers would not notice any difference. For example, Kellogg's might change the recipes of one of its cereals by adding more dried fruit or less sugar; a retail company might outsource a function such as pensions (providing it does not lead to roles being made redundant); or an HR department might change the format but not the content of written documents such as policies, procedures or job descriptions. Incremental changes are not, however, necessarily small changes. They can be large in terms of the resources needed and their impact on people, such as adapting bonus systems to the changing consumer markets; enhancing customer resource management (CRM) systems; introducing a new type of commission on sales for how sales people will be rewarded; developing a new product for an emerging market on the basis of local demand; or modifying the structure of a department.

Incremental changes can lead to major improvements. For example, the American shoe company Keen, since it was founded in 2003, has taken small steps towards sustainability, both in its operations and how it gives back. In 2010 the company began manufacturing some of its shoes in Portland in the United States, which created local jobs. In 2014 it designed 15 per cent smaller shoeboxes that used a folding technique rather than glue to seal the box. This was an incremental change that had a major impact on the company's sustainability agenda. Similarly, Appalatch, a small ethically driven outdoor apparel company in North Carolina uses organic cotton for its products and is incrementally transitioning all of its dyes to natural, plant-base dyes. So the potential for a business to make a difference with incremental steps can be massive.

Transition

Change is very personal and each individual will have a diverse reaction to it. In order for change to be successful and sustained, each affected individual will have to decide to transition from their current ways of working and behaving to new ways of working and behaving. *Transition* is the process or period of adapting to the change. It involves moving from the current state or phase to another – for example, an individual changing from one role to another; a team changing from one process for dealing with customer complaints to another; or an organization going from one structural arrangement to another. The impact of the transition on people needs to be understood and managed and the emotional response to transition has to be recognized. For it is often transition, not the change itself, that people react to. They may resist giving up the status quo and their sense of who they are, that is, their identity as it is expressed in their current work. Some individuals may fear the chaos and uncertainty caused by change. They might feel threatened by the risk of a new beginning, of doing and being what they have never done and been before. To sustain change it is important to help people through the transition, which involves letting go of existing patterns of behaviour and ways of working – and engaging with new ones.

The difference between transition and change is subtle but important. Change is something that happens to people, whether or not they agree with it. Transition, on the other hand, is what happens as people go through change. Change can happen very quickly, while transition usually occurs more slowly. Transition is about people adopting the change or transformation (Hodges and Gill, 2015).

Transformation

Transformation is the marked change in nature, form or appearance of something. While change involves anything that is different from the norm, a transformation involves a 'metamorphosis' from one state to another. It is similar to a caterpillar transforming into a butterfly, which involves a marked change in its form, nature and appearance. Transformational or strategic change and everyday incremental change can be viewed as different, not just in terms of their objectives but also in terms of their processes and size, scope and breadth and what they demand of individuals.

Transformational change can occur in response to, or in anticipation of, major changes in the environment in which an organization operates. In addition, these changes are frequently characterized by innovation and associated with a significant revision of the organization's strategy, which, in turn, may require modifying internal structures and processes as well as the organization's culture to support the new direction of the business. As transformational change involves a paradigm shift and completely new behaviours, it means doing things differently rather than doing things better. For example, in just a few years, internet-enabled portable devices have gone from a luxury item for a few individuals to a way of life for many people who own smartphones and iPads. The ubiquitous connectivity of such devices has transformed how users go about their daily routines, providing new ways of knowing, perceiving, interacting and even working with people across the world.

Another example of transformational change is 3D printing, which can take an idea directly from a design file to a finished part or product, potentially skipping many traditional manufacturing steps. Importantly, 3D printing enables on-demand production, which has implications for supply chains and for stocking spare parts. It can reduce the amount of material wasted in manufacturing and create objects that are difficult or impossible to produce with traditional techniques. Scientists have even bio–printed organs, using an inkjet printing technique to layer human stem cells along with supporting scaffolding. Such trends are powerful ways in which companies are transforming their business models.

Transformations involve radical changes not only in how organizations operate but also in how people perceive, think and behave at work. These changes go far beyond making the existing organization better or fine-tuning parts of it. Transformations are concerned with fundamentally altering the prevailing assumptions about how the organization functions and relates to its environment. Changing these assumptions entails significant shifts in the organization's values and norms and in its structures and processes that shape employees behaviour. Not only is the magnitude of change greater, but also the change fundamentally alters the qualitative nature of the organization (Cummings and Worley, 2014). Transformational change impacts on the deep structure of an organization, which consists of its culture, strategy, structure, business models and its people. Transformational change is therefore much more disruptive to what people do and the way in which they work.

A mix of incremental and transformational change

Rather than change being either incremental or transformational, an alternative position that has gained widespread currency is that there is an interplay between incremental and transformational change. Traditionally known as *punctuated equilibrium*, this refers to change oscillating between long periods of stability and short bursts of transformational change that fundamentally alter an organization. The inspiration for this approach arose from two sources. The first is from Stephen Gould (1978) who, as a natural historian with an interest in Charles Darwin's theory of evolution, argues that there is evidence pointing to a world punctuated with periods of mass extinction and rapid origination among long stretches of relative tranquillity. The second inspiration comes from the research of Connie Gersick (1991), who defines the punctuated equilibrium as relatively long periods of stability (equilibrium) punctuated by brief periods of intense and pervasive transformational change that leads first to the formulation of new missions and then to the initiation of new equilibrium periods. Transformational episodes may affect a single organization or a whole sector. This pattern of punctuated equilibrium is evident in the banking sector, which is traditionally cautious, and by nature more likely to implement incremental change. However, as a result of the economic crisis that hit in 2007–08 banks had to go through transformational change. This resulted in some banks, such as Royal Bank of Scotland and Lloyds in the UK, moving from being privately owned to being owned by the government and the public.

Such patterns of continuous incremental and discontinuous transformational change will vary across sectors, although in almost all industries the rate of change is increasing and the time between periods of discontinuity is decreasing. However, incremental and transformational change does require implementation at the right time, pace and level. Eric Abrahamson (2004), in his book *Change Without Pain*, cites the example of Lou Gerstner who at IBM, American Express Travel Related Services (TRS) and RJR Nabusco knew when to implement transformational change and when to stick to incremental change. In Gerstner's first nine months at TRS he launched a massive reorganization of the card and traveller's cheque businesses, which was accompanied by a widespread shift of managers across those units. A rash of new product introductions followed quickly. TRS's nine-month transformation was, in Gerstner's words, like 'breaking the four-minute mile'. But Gerstner had a genius for knowing when it was time to rest. He was alert to how people were responding to change and to the early signs of change fatigue, cynicism and burnout. He also recognized that the success of his overall change campaign depended on the stability of the units involved, and he was very thoughtful about how and when to intersperse incremental changes rather than transformational ones. At TRS no new products were launched and no new executives were brought in from outside for 18 months after Gerstner's initial blitz. But he did not sit back and do nothing. He tinkered constantly in order to prevent the company from drifting into inertia; he played with the structure, with the compensation system and with the product offerings. The unthreatening nature of such incremental changes allowed the company to be ready for the next wave of product launches and restructurings when they came.

Like Gerstner, managers and leaders must learn to manage the paradoxical tensions between incremental and transformational change. Abrahamson (2004) reminds us that it is particularly easy for companies in the hurly-burly of everyday business to forget the importance of slowing down. But being first does not necessarily mean being fastest. We would do well to remember the old story of the two unfortunate campers in the jungle who noticed a jaguar stalking them. One of them sat down and put on his running shoes. The other looked at him incredulously. 'You're crazy,' he said. 'You're never going to outrun that jaguar.' 'I don't need to,' the first replied. 'I only need to outrun you.'

Content, process and context

Organizational change and transformation is about content, process and context. The *content* is 'what' actually changes in the organization, such as the operations, structure and systems. The *process* is 'how' the change occurs, which includes the pace of the change, the sequence of activities, the way decisions are made and communicated, and how people are engaged in change initiatives and respond to transition (Barnett and Carroll, 1995). The process of change is critical not only for recipients, given that their acceptance and engagement is a key determinant of success, but also for managers and leaders, since they are responsible for shaping and implementing strategy in order to affect required changes. The *context* is about the environment in which the organization is operating and the situation in which the change is being implemented – hence the need for an awareness of the internal and external drivers for change, and for the content and process of change to be adapted to the context in which an organization is operating.

Activity

Analyse a change that you are considering introducing either at a team or organizational level. Is the change you intend to make a transformational change or incremental change, or is it a blend of both? What kind of change does the organization really need?

Organizations

An organization is 'a social arrangement for achieving controlled performance in pursuit of collective goals' (Buchanan and Huczynski, 2010: 8). This definition emphasizes that it is the preoccupation with performance and the need for control that distinguishes organizations from other social arrangements. Like the human body an organization is an open system. Open systems import resources such as people, materials, equipment, information and money. They transform these inputs into the organizations through producing services and goods. They then export those products back into the environment, as goods and satisfied customers. Unlike closed systems that maintain or move towards states of homogeneity, organizations as open systems are able to adapt to and cope with their environment and the drivers for change. Organizations as open systems are able to become more flexible and responsive in an increasingly turbulent and changing world.

Organizations can be understood from several perspectives. Gareth Morgan in his book *Images of Organizations* (2006) introduces the use of metaphors to describe organizations. His eight metaphors are organizations as:

1 *Machines*: the basic concept of this metaphor is that the organization follows the same principles as a machine. This means that each process is carefully selected and monitored in order to make sure that it is done as efficiently as possible. This is done through highly specifying and standardizing the parts and processes that make up the machine.

2 *Biological organisms*: the organismic view emphasizes growth, adaptation and environmental relations.

3 *Human brains*: this perspective depicts organizations as information processors that can learn.

4 *Cultures or subcultures*: organizations as cultures are based on values, norms, beliefs, assumptions, manifestations, artefacts and rituals.

5 *Political systems*: in political organizations it is interests, conflict and power issues that predominate.

6 *Psychic prisons*: organizations as psychic prisons are where people are trapped by certain ways of thinking, which restricts creativity.

7 *Systems of change and transformation*: such organizations can adapt and change.

8 *Instruments of domination*: organizations as instruments of domination have an emphasis on exploitation and the organization imposing their will on employees.

Morgan (2006) presents these metaphors as ways of thinking about organizations. He suggests that by understanding the complex characteristics of organizations it becomes possible to identify novel ways in which to design, change and manage organizations. Morgan says:

> My aim is not to present an exhaustive account of every conceivable metaphor that can be used to understand and shape organizational life. Rather it is to reveal, through illustration, the power of metaphor in shaping organizational management and how the ultimate challenge is not to be seduced by the power or attractiveness of a single metaphor – old or new – so much as to develop an ability to integrate the contributions of different points of view. (2006: xii)

Richard Smith (2015) points out that these, and other metaphors, can make a profound difference to the way we manage change, in particular it provides a framework for thinking about a particular change. Smith suggests that we consider which metaphor(s) provide the best insights into the current organization and how we might look at the change from other perspectives. This process is like looking through different lenses to understand change more deeply. It helps with defining the change and with understanding its potential impact.

The nature of change

The idea that we are constantly engaged in change to a greater or lesser degree is not a new phenomenon. In 1947 Kurt Lewin postulated that life is never without change. This is still true today. Organizations over time are confronted with multiple changes that occur sequentially or simultaneously. Changes involve engaging, discussing, thinking, influencing, negotiating, piloting, learning, evolving and making choices and decisions. Change can also be complex and messy. It involves tolerating ambiguity, handling uncertainty, handling the tensions and paradoxes that need balancing to identify the right interventions, making decisions, and identifying and managing benefits and risk.

Change is sustained when it becomes an integrated or mainstream way of working and behaving in an organization, rather than something added on. As a result, when we look at the process, outcomes or people's behaviour one year on, or longer ahead, we should be able to see that at a minimum it has not reverted to the old ways or previous levels of performance. They should have been able to withstand challenge and disruption, and should have evolved alongside other changes in the organization and perhaps even continued to improve.

Change aims to create financial or non-financial benefits for an organization that can be sustained and impact ultimately on the performance of an individual, team and the organization. Above all, organizational change is about people. For without the acceptance and commitment of employees change is unlikely to stick and realize its benefits.

Although change in many organizations may be a constant, the nature of it is not always the same, as change comes in a variety of shapes and sizes and can be incremental or transformational, as well as proactive or reactive, planned or emergent.

Proactive or reactive change

Organizational change is triggered by a proactive or reactive response to perceived threats or opportunities in the external environment or internally in the organization. The interaction between proactive and reactive, and incremental and transformational change, is shown in Figure 1.1.

FIGURE 1.1   The nature of change

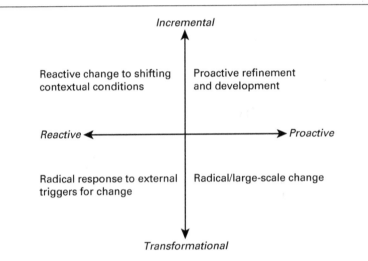

Incremental–reactive change occurs in response to shifting contextual issues; while *incremental–proactive* change involves refinement and development. In contrast, *proactive––transformational* change involves large-scale change across an organization, such as structural change or a major realignment of the strategy and purpose of the organization. For example, Apple identified an opportunity for proactive–transformational change in 2001 when the company reviewed the options for extensions of its product offering, as a result it eschewed the digital and video camera market and launched the iPod, followed by the iPhone. Such proactive–transformational change has earned the company billions of dollars in revenues. Proactive–transformational change is an opportunistic change, one in which a company creates strategic advantage because of something anticipated either internally or externally in the environment in which they operate.

Reactive–transformational change is a radical response to factors in the external environment or within the organization that has already occurred rather than those that are anticipated in the future. For example, Lego – a family-owned company based in Billund, Denmark, and best known for the manufacture of Lego brand toys – announced in 2004 losses of over US $400 million on annual sales of just over $1 billion. In a case study of the company, John Ashcroft (2014) highlights how, in response to this, Lego was forced to take a hard look at every area of its operation including costs, overheads, margins, sales, marketing and its product offering. The leadership team implemented a reactive–transformational change plan for recovery and growth, including cutting the costs of non-performing assets. This resulted in selling the company's Legoland parks. Since then company revenues have increased from $1 billion to $4.5 billion (2013) and profits have soared to $1.5 billion before tax. The company's share of the world toy market has increased from 2 per cent in 2004 to over 5 per cent in 2012. Lego has overtaken Hasbro as the second largest toy manufacturer in the world (Ashcroft, 2014). As illustrated in the case of Lego, reactive–transformational change is therefore something that has to happen in order to deal with unexpected external or internal triggers.

As well as being either reactive or proactive, change can also be planned or emergent.

Planned or emergent change

There are different approaches in how change emerges and evolves over time. Sometimes change is deliberate, a product of conscious reasoning and action. This type of change is called *planned change*. In contrast, change sometimes unfolds in an apparently spontaneous and unplanned way. This type of change is known as *emergent change*. The differences between the two are illustrated in Table 1.1.

TABLE 1.1   Characteristics of planned and emergent change

Planned Change	Emergent Change
Driven from the top	Initiated from anywhere in the organization
Structured	Flowing
Linear	Holistic
Deliberate	Open-ended
Logical	Evolving
Conscious	Unconscious

Planned change

Planned change is an intentional intervention for bringing about change to an organization and is best characterized as deliberate, structured and linear, with leaders and managers as the pivotal instigators of the change. It is usually change driven from the top of the organization once a need for change has been identified and after an analysis of the internal and external drivers for change has been conducted. Traditional planned change management strategies involve sequential steps for altering organizational and individual behaviour. This approach to change is based on the assumption that organizations are stable entities and that, in order to bring about change, an organization can be moved from its unsatisfactory current state to a desired future state, through a series of necessary stages.

Kurt Lewin (1947), the father of planned change, developed the three-stage model that has become the classic way of thinking about change in organizations and that continues to underpin many change efforts today. Lewin's model was based on field theory, group dynamics and action research, and proposes three stages for achieving change. The first stage is *unfreezing*, where the need for change is identified. The next stage is *moving*, where through trial and error the change slowly gets implemented. Once the change is implemented, the *refreezing* stage begins; the objective of this stage is to embed the change in the organization. This final stage requires behaviours to be consistent with the required changes.

Although Lewin's model is widely adopted and adapted, the idea that organizations and in particular the behaviours of individuals are frozen, much less *refrozen*, is dubious. The main criticisms raised about the model are that: first, the notion of refreezing is not relevant for organizations operating in turbulent times. Instead it is proposed that organizations need to be fluid and adaptable and that the last thing they need to be is frozen into some given way of functioning (Dawson, 2003). Second, Lewin's model is felt to ignore the views of employees, treating them as automatons (or blocks of ice) rather than active participants in the change process (Buchanan, 2003). Third, the model is very much rooted in North American assumptions of change. Robert Marshak (1993) compares the assumptions of the Lewin model with the assumptions behind an Asian model. In the Lewin model, change is linear, progressive, managed by people intent on achieving goals. In the Asian model, change is cyclical, processional, journey orientated, associated with equilibrium, and managed in a way that is designed to create universal harmony. So even if Lewin's theory is appropriate to North American organizations, it may not be appropriate to organizational change in other countries and cultures. In summary, the critics of Lewin have concerns about the relevancy, lack of focus on people, as well as the cultural assumptions embedded in his model that may limit its use across geographical and cultural boundaries. Despite such criticisms Lewin's approach has spawned a number of similar frameworks.

Models that have applied the step approach first developed by Lewin include: Shields's (1999) five steps for transforming organizations; Beer's

(1990) six steps for change; Luecke's (2003) seven steps for change; Kotter's (1996) eight-step model; Kanter, Stein and Jick's (1992) 10 commandments for successful change; and Mento, Jones and Dirndorfer's (2002) 12-step integrative framework. The process in each of these models may vary in the number of steps proposed and the order in which they should be taken (see Table 1.2). However, what unites these models is that change can be achieved as long as the correct steps are taken. John Kotter (1996) maintains that although change is full of surprises, his eight-step model will produce a satisfying result as long as the steps are followed. Similarly, Rosabeth Kanter and colleagues (1992) stress that with their 10 commandments of change it is an unwise manager who chooses to ignore any one of the steps. Such proponents of planned change argue in favour of change occurring through carefully phased or sequenced processes.

TABLE 1.2   Comparison of models of planned change

Shield (1999)	Beer (1990)	Kotter (1996)	Luecke (2003)	Kanter, Stein and Jick (1992)	Mento, Jones and Dirndorfer (2002)
Define the desired result and change plans	Mobilize commitment to the change through joint diagnosis	Create a sense of urgency	Mobilize energy and commitment through joint identification	Analyse the organization and its needs for change	The idea and its concept
Create capability	Develop a shared vision	Form a guiding coalition	Develop a shared vision	Create a shared vision and common direction	Define the change initiative
Define innovative solutions	Foster support for the new vision, competence to enact it and cohesion to move it along	Develop a vision	Identify the leadership	Separate from the past	Evaluate the climate for change
Select and deploy solutions	Spread revitalization	Empower broad-based action	Focus on results, not activities	Create a sense of urgency	Develop a change plan
Reinforce and sustain business benefits	Institutionalize revitalization through policies, systems and structure	Communicate the change vision	Start change at the periphery	Support a strong leader	Find and cultivate a sponsor

TABLE 1.2 *Cont'd*

Shield (1999)	Beer (1990)	Kotter (1996)	Luecke (2003)	Kanter, Stein and Jick (1992)	Mento, Jones and Dirndorfer (2002)
	Monitor and adjust strategies in response to problems in the revitalization process	Generate short-term wins	Institutionalize success through formal policies, systems and structures	Line up political sponsorship	Prepare target audience
		Consolidate gains and produce more change	Monitor and adjust strategies in response to problems	Craft an implementation plan	Create the cultural fit – making the change last
		Anchor new approaches in culture		Develop enabling structures	Develop and choose a change leader team
				Communicate, involve people and be honest	Create small wins for motivation
				Reinforce and institutionalize change	Constantly and strategically communicate the change
					Measure progress and integrate lessons learnt

Models of planned change (such as those in Table 1.2) provide useful checklists for managers and leaders in terms of what needs to be considered when planning change. They provide logical and sequential prescriptions for the process of change as they map out the process from the first recognition of the need for change through to the practicalities of implementation. There is, however, no one model that is sufficient to use on its own; instead, using steps from several of the models can provide a more complete checklist. You should also consider adding key elements that are missing from such models and need to run throughout a change initiative such as feedback and gaining commitment from people (we explore gaining commitment in Chapters 4 and 5). When using such models it is important to remember that change rarely happens in a linear manner and frequently there is a need to go back to a step not just once but several times. It is therefore more appropriate to see change as a cyclical process.

Kotter's accelerator model

Instead of seeing change purely as a linear process it is more advantageous to see it as cyclical. John Kotter (2014) has moved from his traditional step approach to offer a cyclical model of change. Kotter proposes that there are eight processes or accelerators that enable change to be successful. The accelerators are:

1 *Creating a sense of urgency.* According to Kotter this is absolutely critical to heightening the organization's awareness that it needs continual strategic adjustments/changes and that they should always be aligned with the biggest opportunity in sight. Urgency should start at the top of the hierarchy and leaders need to keep acknowledging and reinforcing it so that people will wake up every morning determined to find some action they can take in their day to achieve the change.

2 *Building and maintaining a guiding coalition.* The guiding coalition (GC) should be made up of volunteers from throughout the organization. The GC should represent each of the hierarchy's departments and levels, with a broad range of skills. It must be made up of people whom the leadership trusts, and must include at least a few outstanding leaders and managers.

3 *Formulating a strategic vision and developing change initiatives designed to capitalize on the big opportunity.* A well-formulated vision will focus on taking advantage of a big make-or-break opportunity. The right vision should be feasible and easy to communicate. It should be emotionally appealing as well as strategically smart. And give the GC a picture of success and enough information and direction to make consequential decisions, without having to seek permission at every turn.

4 *Communicating the vision and the strategy to create buy-in and attract a growing volunteerarmy.* A vividly formulated, high-stakes vision and strategy, promulgated by a GC in ways that are both memorable and authentic, will prompt people to discuss them without the cynicism that often greets messages about change and that cascade down the hierarchy. If done properly, with creativity, such communications will go viral, attracting employees who buy in to the ambition of the change and share a commitment to it.

5 *Accelerating movement towards the vision and the opportunity by ensuring that the network of people removes barriers.* This involves empowering people throughout the organization to remove the barriers to successful change rather than it being the sole responsibility of leaders or managers.

6 *Celebrating visible, significant short-term wins.* A change will not last long without confirmation that it is benefiting the organization. Sceptics will erect obstacles unless they see proof that the change is creating real results. As people have only so much patience, proof must come quickly. To ensure success, the best short-term wins should be obvious, unambiguous and clearly related to the vision.

7 *Never letting up.* This means that organizations should keep learning from change and not declare victory too soon. They must continue to carry out strategic initiatives and create new ones in order to adapt to shifting business environments and thus enhance their competitive positions.

8 *Institutionalizing strategic changes in the culture.* No strategic change initiative, big or small, is complete until it has been incorporated into day-to-day activities. A new direction or method must sink into the very culture of the enterprise and it will do so if the change initiative produces visible results.

This cyclical model expands on Kotter's eight-step method discussed earlier in this chapter. However, there are a number of differences between the eight steps and the eight accelerators, which are: 1) the steps are often used in rigid, finite and sequential ways, in effecting or responding to episodic change, whereas the accelerators are concurrent and always at work; 2) the steps are usually driven by a small, powerful core group, whereas the accelerators pull in as many people as possible from throughout the organization to form the guiding coalition – the 'volunteer army'; 3) the steps are designed to function within a traditional hierarchy, whereas the accelerators require the flexibility and agility of a network.

The accelerators can serve as a continuous and holistic approach and one that accelerates momentum and agility. This cyclical approach is therefore a more realistic way to view change than the traditional step approach.

Criticisms of planned change

There are various criticisms aimed at the planned approach to change. David Buchanan and John Storey argue that those who advocate planned change are attempting to impose an 'order and linear sequence on processes that are in reality messy and untidy, and which unfold in an iterative fashion with much backbreaking' (1997: 127). Similarly, Robert Paton and James McCalman (2008) say that the difficulty is that most organizations view the concept of change as a highly programmed process that takes as its starting point the problem that needs to be rectified, then breaks it down into constituent parts, analyses possible alternatives, selects the preferred solution and applies this relentlessly. So the planned approach is criticized for being based on the assumption that organizations operate under constant conditions and that they can move in a pre-planned manner from one stable state to another. These assumptions are challenged by critics who argue that the current fast-changing environment increasingly weakens this theory and that organizational change is more an open-ended and continuous process than a set of pre-identified discrete and self-contained events (Burnes, 2009). As change is a complex and dynamic process it should not therefore be solidified or treated as a series of linear events.

Critics emphasize that the planned approach is not applicable to situations that require rapid and transformational change (Senior, 2002) – for instance, political uprisings or natural disasters such as hurricanes or tsunamis. In such situations, Mary Hatch (2012) suggests that planned change can also be an unethical, fear-producing vehicle for domination that extends existing top-down power structures. Planned change is therefore criticized as slow, static and only suitable for times of stability.

These criticisms of planned change efforts are not unfounded. John Kotter (1995) identifies eight reasons that planned change efforts fail. These include failure to establish adequate urgency to change; an insufficiently powerful guiding coalition; a missing, blocked or under-communicated vision; failure to create short-term wins; declaring victory too soon; and not anchoring changes in the corporation's culture. Other factors for the failure of planned change include: difficulty negotiating conflicting group identities (McInnes et al, 2006), as well as failure to appreciate organization-environment interdependencies and connectivity (Sackmann, Eggenhofer and Friesl, 2009). Karl Weick (2000) suggests that, in the eyes of decision makers, planned change efforts often get the credit for successes in delivering new strategies for survival, but they rarely change the organization's underlying nature – and problems usually recur.

The planned approach to change is therefore not without its limitations. It represents change as a programmatic, step-by-step process with a clear beginning, middle and end, largely choreographed and controlled from the top of the organization. Change within this context is about establishing a new order. It is about setting new boundaries and putting in place new structures, systems and processes. The focus is on re-establishing order and stability. However, it tends to ignore the complexities and contradictory nature of organizations and sidesteps the concept of change as a naturally occurring, ongoing phenomenon that is prevalent in emergent change.

Emergent change

In contrast to the planned approach to change is the view that if change is truly transformational, if it breaks new ground, it cannot be predetermined. Think for a moment about how our lives have been changed by social media such as Facebook, Pinterest, Snapchat, Twitter and all the rest. No single individual or entity invented these social media sites. They emerged, in all their weird and wonderful variety, because the internet is a powerful platform for making connections and because entrepreneurs were free to develop new business models to harness that power. Emergent change, such as social media, gives everyone the right to suggest options that are diverse, radical and nuanced.

Emergent change is iterative, unpredictable, often unintentional, can come from anywhere and involves informal self-organizing groups. Advocates of emergent change emphasize that it is the uncertainty of the external and internal environment that make it more pertinent than the planned approach (Bamford and Forrester, 2003). The essential unforeseeable character of change means that the process cannot be predicted and that outcomes are often only understood in retrospect. To cope with uncertainty it is argued that organizations need to become open-learning systems where strategy development and change emerge from the way a company as a whole acquires, interprets and processes information about the environment. Bernard Burnes says that this approach stresses an:

> Extensive and in-depth understanding of strategy, structure, systems, people, style and culture, and how these can function either as sources of inertia that can block change, or alternatively, as levers to encourage an effective change process. Successful change is less dependent on detailed plans and projections than on reaching an understanding of the complexity of the issues concerned and identifying the range of available options. (1996: 13–14)

A useful illustration to consider is Wanda Orlikowski and Debra Hofman's description of how emergent change evolves the metaphor of a jazz band – how members of a jazz band do not decide in advance exactly what notes each is going to play, yet once the performance begins:

> Each player is free to explore and innovate, departing from the original composition. Yet, the performance works because all members are playing within the same rhythmic structure and have a shared understanding of the rules of this musical genre. (1997: 11–12)

Similar to how a jazz band performs, emergent change occurs through the evolution of an iterative series of steps that produces outcomes that could not have been predicted at the start. A practical example of this occurred when a small group of trainee clinicians, young leaders and improvement facilitators in the UK's National Health Service (NHS) developed and ran the first NHS Change Day in 2013, which was the biggest improvement effort in the history of the NHS. Internal activists, multiplying their impact through social media, spawned a grass-roots movement of 189,000 people who pledged to take concrete action to improve health-care outcomes. When Change Day was repeated in 2014, the number of pledges exceeded 800,000. Advocates of such emergent change, such as Patrick Dawson (2003), say that the applicability and validity of the approach is suitable for all organizations that operate in dynamic, complex and unpredictable environments.

Despite such advantages the emergent change theory does have a number of limitations. Research has found that a more emergent approach to change takes longer to deliver results and can be messy (Shaw, 2002). It has been criticized for its lack of coherence and its potential to create confusion and uncertainty in an organization due to a lack of clear objectives (Bamford and Forrester, 2003). This uncertainty can be unnerving to people in an organization. People need to be able to tolerate the unknown and to cope with the paradoxes that emergent change brings about – as some people may be incapable of *playing jazz*. In other words, not everyone will have the skills or the inclination to participate in such an unplanned, open-ended approach to change. So, as with the planned approach to change, the emergent approach has pros and cons that need to be considered.

Rather than change being either planned or emergent a number of research projects have attempted to understand the interplay between planned and emergent change. Alexander Styhre (2002) provides an example of a Swedish telecommunication company whose planned attempt to implement a new manufacturing unit was derailed by an unanticipated recession that thwarted their original plans and transformed them into a more emergent approach to change. Similarly, Miguel Cunha and Rita Cunha (2003) discuss the socialist Cuban government's planned, top-down regulatory change as being combined successfully with emergent, entrepreneurial efforts. To view the interplay between planned and emergent change requires, according to Reut Livne-Tarandach and Jean Bartunek, the reconceptualization of the role of leaders and decision makers. These authors propose that:

> Leaders should no longer be considered... solely as initiators and implementers of pre-planned organizational change; nor should they be seen... solely as reactive agents to emergent change forces. Rather they should develop the ability to connect the two to create synergy. (2009: 28)

So instead of following either a planned or emergent approach the issue for leaders, managers and others involved in change is to create synergy between the two and adopt the most appropriate approach that matches the context in which the organization is operating.

Either/or approaches

Contingency model of change

The contingency theory is based upon contextual factors determining whether a planned or emergent approach to change is adopted. As Dexter Dunphy and Doug Stace point out:

> Managers and consultants need a model of change that is essentially a 'situational' or 'contingency model', one that indicates how to vary change strategies to achieve 'optimum' fit with the changing environment. (1993: 905)

Instead of seeking a 'one best way' approach to change, the contingency approach is founded on the theory that the structure and performance of an organization are dependent on the situational variables that it faces. This approach shares with planned change the assumption that change can be directed through a series of steps. However, it parts company with the step approach in arguing that the nature of this direction depends on, or is contingent on, a range of organizational factors such as the scale of the change, the urgency of the change, and receptivity to the change. There will therefore be different types of steps that managers will need to take, depending on the confluence of various factors. The strength of the contingency theory is that it explains organizational change from a behavioural viewpoint where managers make decisions that account for specific circumstances, focusing on those that are the most directly relevant, and intervening with the most appropriate actions.

The best course of action is the one that is fundamentally situational, matched to the needs of the circumstances. The contingency approach proposes no formulas or guiding principles for organizational change, instead the focus is on achieving alignment and a good fit to ensure stability and control.

Critics of the contingency approach argue that the theory assumes that leaders and managers do not have any significant influence and choice over situational variables and structure. Instead critics argue that an organization does not necessarily have to adapt to the external environment, while organizations wishing to maintain or promote a particular approach can choose to influence situational variables to achieve this. So rather than having little choice, rather than being forced to change their internal practices to fit in with external variables, organizations can exercise some choice over these issues (By, 2005).

The flexible nature of the contingency perspective means that change can be adapted to the environment. It can be fast or slow, small or large, loosely or tightly controlled, driven by internal or external triggers, and appropriate to varying levels of uncertainty. It just depends on the situation.

Process-driven or people-driven change?

Change in organizations is often either process driven to create benefits and economic value, or people driven. Michael Beer and Nitin Nohria (2000) refer to the former as Theory E and the latter they term Theory O. The purpose of Theory E, they argue, is the creation of economic value, often expressed as shareholder value. The process approach is planned, programmatic change, based on formal structures and systems, driven from the top of an organization. This type of change usually involves the use of economic incentives, drastic layoffs, downsizing and restructuring. In contrast, Theory O focuses on the development of employees in order to implement the change as well as opportunities to learn from experience. It advocates encouraging participation from employees and in fostering employee behaviours and attitudes that will sustain change.

So which is the best theory to adopt? Unfortunately neither approach guarantees success. Theory E, which aims for rapid improvements in profitability, often succeeds in the short term but does so at the expense of future sustainability. By reducing employee roles, it often leaves survivors demoralized. Any commitment that employees have to the company can quickly evaporate, and talented employees that the company want to retain often are the first to snap up redundancy packages and look for a job in another company. Theory O is not an ideal solution either. Reorientating corporate culture around employee commitment and learning is vital but can be a long-term proposition. A successful programme may produce smarter, more adaptive employees in a few years but companies that really need change cannot wait that long for results.

Instead of an either/or approach leaders need to consider using a mix of Theory E and Theory O. General Electric (GE) is an example of a company that has employed both approaches in turn. When former CEO Jack Welsh took over he initially implemented a host of redundancies and got rid of underperforming work units through draconian Theory E methods. He then followed with Theory O change initiatives, which were designed to improve the competitiveness of the company's culture by making it faster, less bureaucratic and more customer-focused, and also to develop the capabilities and motivation of employees.

As in the case of GE, organizations can use Theory O and Theory E in sequence. However, such an approach can often take years to fully implement. Additionally, if there is a change in the senior leadership team during the change process then the sequencing may lose momentum and direction, or be stopped all together. This lack of speed and possible loss of direction can cause uncertainty and cynicism about the change. Instead of using only one theory or sequencing both theories, organizations should implement both theories at the same time. The simultaneous implementation of both Theory E and Theory O is likely to lead to a more sustainable transformation or change. As Beer and Nohria conclude:

> Companies that effectively combine hard and soft approaches to change can reap big payoffs in profitability and productivity... Those companies are more likely to achieve a sustainable competitive advantage [and]... reduce the anxiety that grips whole societies in the face of corporate restructuring. (2000: 134)

So the challenge for organizations is to combine Theory O and Theory E, as only one on its own has limitations.

Recognizing the need for change

Organizations are challenged to grow and change with the world around them. To achieve this there must first be recognition that change is desirable and feasible. Microsoft is a company that is cognizant of the changing environment in which they operate and of how they need to transform their business in order to stay ahead of the external drivers for change. In July 2013 Steve Balmer announced on the online Microsoft News Centre that, 'as the times change so must our company'. The vision that had lasted since Microsoft's inception in 1975 to have 'a computer on every desktop and in every home' seemed long surpassed in many parts of the world. The new vision is 'on creating a family of devices and services for individuals and businesses that empower people around the globe at home, at work and on the go, for the activities they value most'.

Not all companies that are successful are like Microsoft and recognize the need for change. One of the paradoxes of organizational life is that success often sets the stage for failure. This is illustrated in what David Nadler and Robert Shaw (1995) call the 'trap of success', which means that after a prolonged period of success organizations become locked into the patterns of behaviour that produced the original success. These patterns become codified or institutionalized and are rarely questioned and can lead to complacency, arrogance and an internal focus. As a result, it is taken for granted that the relation between the company and its environment will automatically be successful. This can result in an organization becoming 'learning disabled' – it becomes incapable of looking outside, reflecting on success and failure, accepting new ideas and developing new insights; it decreases its customer focus, and costs increase. If unchecked, the ultimate outcome of this trap of success can be the 'death spiral'. This spiral involves a decline in performance, denial about what is happening and more of the same behaviours and approaches that result in a negative impact on customer focus, cost and innovation. The list of companies who have entered the death spiral is long and growing and includes Borders, BlackBerry, Nokia, EMI, Time Warner and AOL. Many established companies are wrecked by complacency and hubris. While certain businesses adapt and prosper, others crumble and expire. The case study below of Kodak illustrates a company that became complacent and entered the death spiral.

Most companies die relatively slow deaths rather than suffering a sudden collapse. Sometimes extinction is inevitable because the business is so fundamentally deficient or structural changes in markets mean the business model is uneconomic. Companies can, however, be saved by transformational change if the decay is not too extensive.

CASE STUDY　Kodak

Kodak has faced an unprecedented magnitude of change. The speed with which Kodak's core market for traditional silver halide roll-film collapsed is blistering. One compelling theory is that it was not the speedy pace of the transition that undermined Kodak, which filed for Chapter 11 bankruptcy protection in January 2012, but the fact that it was drawn out over decades. In other words, Kodak first pioneered digital technologies in the 1970s and 1980s but, until relatively recently, the urgency of the challenge was never quite sharp enough to persuade its employees, investors and executives that it had to overhaul, or even sacrifice, time-honoured ways of doing business.

In 2000, with Wall Street sceptical about the promise of digital photography, Kodak was still searching for a way to bridge the gulf between its dominance of the highly profitable roll-film business and a lower-margin, highly competitive digital future. Successive chief executives talked up the opportunities, but each failed to break down the structural, cultural and strategic obstacles to change. The company's dominance of the sector and confidence in its brand and marketing also led it to rest on its strategic laurels. Fujifilm of Japan had successfully dented Kodak's roll-film dominance in the 1980s. In the 1990s, Fuji was forced to diversify simply in order to achieve the scale to compete with Kodak. It used its film expertise to create components for flat-panel LCD screens and, when the consumer roll-film market finally dropped off the cliff edge, this and other businesses cushioned Fuji's fall. For Kodak, however, by the time Antonio Pérez took over as chief executive in 2005 the company was heading down a route of intense, futile competition in the printer market. Kodak was dragged down by the alluring comfort of being on top.

Randy Ottinger (2013) reviews what has happened to Kodak since it declared bankruptcy, where it is now and if it has learnt its lessons. Ottinger points out that Kodak has emerged from bankruptcy protection as slimmer, trimmer and with a new business plan. Kodak has entered a more focused space, limited to packaging, graphic communications and functional printing. The company needs to focus on its culture and customers in order to be able to pull ahead of the competitors. In order to do this, Kodak must change its ways – going from being the behemoth in the industry to a more nimble, engaged and innovative company. Rather than looking within the organization for small changes, or even within the industry, Kodak needs to listen to the new ways that customers wish to use its products. This is the only way that they will avoid becoming 'learning disabled' again, where they failed to see the changes in consumer demands because they still had the dollars rolling in from their existing products.

The new Kodak must root out complacency at every level. It must encourage and welcome innovative ideas. If Kodak follows this approach they can avoid the dangerous place in which they found themselves in the past – the death spiral.

Discussion questions

What can today's market leaders learn from the Kodak experience, a company that saw what was coming next but still did not adapt?

What can companies like Kodak do to avoid the death spiral in the future?

Summary

We are living in an age of accelerating change and turbulence. A state of continuous change has become almost a routine. It is an ever-present feature of organizational life, both at an operational and strategic level. Against a backdrop of external and internal factors – including increasing globalization, climate change and resource scarcity, the rapid pace of technological innovation, shifting social and demographic trends, the emergence of new ideologies and increasing legislation – few would dispute that the primary task in organizations today is the leadership and management of organizational change.

Change is an opportunity to make or become different through new ways of organizing and working. Any change will involve an adjustment or alteration that has the potential to influence the experience of employees at work. Change is very personal and each individual will have a different reaction to it. In order for change to be successful and sustained, each affected individual will have to decide to transition from their old ways of working and behaving to new ways of working and behaving. Transformational change and everyday incremental change can be viewed as different, not just in terms of their objectives but also in terms of their processes and size, scope and breadth, and what they demand of leaders and managers. Transformational change is much more disruptive to what people do and the way that they work.

Change and transformation can be planned or emergent depending on the context in which an organization is operating. Planned change is an intentional intervention for bringing about change and is best characterized as deliberate, structured and linear. Emergent change is described as unpredictable and often unintentional; it can come from anywhere and involves relatively informal self-organizing.

Leaders may fail to recognize the need for change because they pay insufficient attention to what is happening in the external environment. Even if they are aware of what is happening they may fail to recognize the implications for their organization. This can lead to the trap of success and, ultimately, the death spiral. When identifying the need for change, leaders and managers need to be cognizant of how change will impact on individuals – as discussed in the next chapter.

References

Abrahamson, E (2004) *Change Without Pain*, Harvard Business Press, Boston

Ashcroft, J (2014) [accessed 16 October 2015] The Lego Case Study [Online] http://www.thelegocasestudy.com

Bamford, D R and Forrester, P L (2003) Managing planned and emergent change within an operations management environment, *International Journal of Operations & Production Management*, **23** (5), pp 546–64

Barnett, W and Carroll, G (1995) Modeling internal organizational change, *Annual Review of Sociology*, **21**, pp 217–36

Beer, M (1990) *Leading Change*, Harvard Business School Publishing, Boston

Beer, M and Nohria, N (2000) Cracking the code of change, *Harvard Business Review*, May–June, pp 133–41

Bershidsky, L (2014) [accessed 16 October 2015] The next currency killer: African e-money M-Pesa, *The Age*, 1 April [Online] Available at http://www.theage.com.au/it-pro/business-it/the-next-currency-killer-african-emoney-mpesa-20140331-zqp9j.html

Bremmer, I (2014) The new rules of globalization, *Harvard Business Review*, **1** (2), pp 103–07

Buchanan, D (2003) Getting the story straight: illusions and delusions in the organizational change process, *Tamara: Journal of Critical Postmodern Organizational Science*, **2** (4), pp 7–21

Buchanan, D and Huczynski, A A (2010) *Organizational Behaviour*, 7th edn, Pearson, Essex

Buchanan, D and Storey, J (1997) Role-taking and role-switching in organizational change: the four pluralities, in *Innovation, organizational change and technology*, ed I McLoughlin and M Harris, pp 127–45, International Thomson, London

Burke, W W (2008) *Organization Change: Theory and Practice*, 2nd edn, SAGE Publications, California

Burnes, B (1996) 'No such thing as... a 'one best way to manage organizational change', *Management Decision*, **34** (10), pp 11–18

Burnes, B (2009) *Managing Change*, 5th edn, FT/Prentice Hall, Harlow

By, R T (2005) Organizational change management: a critical review, *Journal of Change Management*, **5** (4), pp 369–80

Cummings, T and Worley, C (2014) *Organization Development and Change*, 9th edn, South-Western Cengage Learning, Ohio

Cunha, M and Cunha, R (2003) The interplay of planned and emergent change in Cuba, *International Business Review*, **12**, pp 445–59

Dawson, P (2003) *Organizational Change: A processual approach*, Paul Chapman, London

Development, Concepts and Doctrine Centre (2010) *Global Strategic Trend – Out to 2040*, 4th edn, Ministry of Defence, London

De Haan, E and Kasozi, A (2014) *The Leadership Shadow: How to recognize and avoid derailment, hubris and overdrive*, Kogan Page, London

Dunphy, D and Stace, D (1993) The strategic management of corporate change, *Human Relations*, **46** (8), pp 905–18

Gersick, C (1991) Revolutionary change theories: a multilevel exploration of the punctuated equilibrium paradigm, *Academy of Management Review*, **16**, pp 10–36

Gould, S J (1978) *Ever Since Darwin: Reflections in natural history*, Burnett Books, London

Hatch, M J (2012) *Organization Theory: Modern, symbolic and postmodern perspectives*, Oxford University Press, Oxford

Hodges, J and Gill, R (2015) *Sustaining Change in Organizations*, Sage, London

Kanter, R, Stein, B and Jick, T (1992) *The Challenge of Organizational Change: How companies experience it and leaders guide it*, Free Press, New York

Kotter, J P (1995) Leading change: why transformation efforts fail, *Harvard Business Review*, May–June, pp 11–16

Kotter, J P (1996) *Leading Change*, Harvard Business School Press, Boston

Kotter, J P (2014) *Accelerate*, Harvard Business School Press, Boston

Lewin, K (1947) Frontiers in group dynamics: concept, method and reality in social science; social equilibria and social change, *Human Relations*, **1** (2), pp 143–53

Livne-Tarandach, R and Bartunek, J (2009) A new horizon for organizational change and development scholarship: connecting planned and emergent change, in *Research in Organizational Change & Development*, ed R Woodman, W Pasmore and A Shani, p 17, Emeral Group Publishing Ltd, Bingley

Luecke, R (2003) *Managing Change and Transition*, Harvard Business School Press, Boston

Magnus, G (2008) *The Age of Aging*, Wiley, London

Manyika, J, Jacques, M, Dobbs, B, Bisson, P and Marrs, A (2013) *Disruptive Technologies: Advances that will transform life, business and the global economy*, Mckinsey Global Institute, United States

Marshak, R (1993) Lewin meets Confucius: a re-review of the OD model of change, *Journal of Applied Behavioural Science*, **24** (4), pp 393–415

McInnes, P, Beech, N, de Caestecker, L, MacIntosh, R and Ross, M (2006) Identity dynamics as a barrier to organizational change, *The International Journal of Public Administration*, **29** (12), pp 1109–24

Mento, A J, Jones, R M and Dirndorfer, W (2002) A change management process: grounded in both theory and practice, *Journal of Change Management*, **3** (1), pp 45–59

Morgan, G (2006) *Images of Organization*, Sage, London

Nadler, D A and Shaw, R B (1995) *Discontinuous Change: Leading Organizational Transformation*, Jossey-Bass, San Francisco

Oreg, S, By, R T and Michel, A (2013) Introduction, in *The Psychology of Organizational Change*, ed S Oreg, A Michel and R T By, Cambridge University Press, Cambridge

Orlikowski, W and Hofman, J (1997) An improvisational model for change management: the case of groupware technologies, *Sloan Management Review*, **38** (2), pp 11–21

Ottinger, R (2013) [accessed 16 October 2015] Kodak Is Back but Has It Learned Its Lesson?, *Forbes* [Online] www.forbes.com/sites/johnkotter/2013/09/09/kodak-is-back-but-has-it-learned-its-lesson/

Paton, R and McCalman, J (2008) *Change Management: A guide to effective implementation*, 3rd edn, Sage, London

Price, D (2009) (ed) *The Principles and Practices of Change*, Palgrave Macmillan, Basingstoke

PwC (2014) [accessed 16 October 2015] Global Annual CEO Survey, *PwC* [Online] www.pwc.com

Sackmann, S A, Eggenhofer, P and Friesl, M (2009) Sustainable change: long-term efforts toward developing a learning organization, *Journal of Applied Behavioral Science*, **45** (4), pp 521–49

Senior, B (2002) *Organizational Change*, 2nd edn, Prentice Hall, London

Shaw, P (2002) *Changing Conversations in Organizations: A complexity approach to change*, Routledge, London

Shields, J L (1999) Transforming organizations, *Information, Knowledge, Systems Management*, **1** (2), pp 105–15

Smith, R (2015) A change management perspective, in *The Effective Change Manager's Handbook: Essential guidance to the change management body of knowledge*, ed R Smith, D King, R Sidhu and D Skelsey, pp 3–74, Kogan Page, London

Styhre, A (2002) Non-linear change in organizations: organizational change management informed by complexity theory, *Leadership and Organizational Development Journal*, **23** (6), pp 343–51

United Nations (2014) [accessed 12 December 2014] World Urbanization Prospects, *United Nations* [Online] http://esa.un.org/unpd/wup/Highlights/WUP2014-Highlights.pdf

Vorhauser-Smith, S (2012) [accessed 10 December 2014] Going 'Glocal': How Smart Brands Adapt To Foreign Markets, *Forbes* [Online] http://www.forbes.com/sites/sylviavorhausersmith/2012/06/22/cultural-homogeneity-is-not-an-automatic-by-product-of-globalization/

Weick, K (2000) Emergent change as a universal in organizations, in *Breaking the Code of Change*, ed M Beer and N Nohria, Harvard Business Review Press, Boston

World Bank (2012) [accessed 10 December 2014] Turn Down the Heat: Confronting the New Climate Normal, *World Bank* [Online] www.worldbank.org

Further reading

Bell, D and Sherman, M (2011) KFC's radical approach to China, *Harvard Business Review*, **89** (11), pp 137–42

Cohan, P S (2008) *You Can't Order Change: Lessons from Jim McNerney's turnaround at Boeing*, Penguin, New York

Jarrett, M (2009) *Changeability: Why some companies are ready for change – and others aren't*, FT/Prentice Hall, Harlow

PART TWO
Individual responses to change

02
The impact of organizational change on emotions

KEY POINTS

- Leading and managing people through change involves being able to acknowledge and understand emotional responses.
- Change can trigger different emotions (positive and negative) within an individual at various times during transition depending on a range of factors, including the speed, timing and frequency of the change.
- The culture of an organization can play an important role in generating emotions during change and can influence whether individuals express or supress their emotions.
- Emotional contagion occurs when individuals react to and draw inferences from the emotions of others to change.
- The challenge in attempting to manage emotions is that emotions involve the whole person and differentiate one person from another. Emotions cannot be managed 'en masse' as different emotions require different responses.
- To lead or manage people thorough change, leaders and managers must be able to connect with, control and leverage their own emotions and be able to do the same with the people they are responsible for and who will be affected by and involved in the change.

Introduction

Organizational change can evoke a variety of emotional responses from individuals. As Robert French so eloquently says, 'merely to alter the arrangement of the furniture in a room or to appoint just one new member of staff can be enough to set the cats of anxiety and selfishness amongst the pigeons of stability and co-operation' (2001: 480). Emotional reactions to change are often viewed as a burden that leaders and managers must endure and, in some instances, even ignore. This is a misguided approach, however, as emotions are an important part of any change process in that they not only show how someone feels about change but they also have an impact on the behaviour of individuals, which can then affect the success of the change. In order to manage and lead people effectively through change it is therefore important to have an appreciation of the emotional reactions to change and understand how, in particular, negative emotions can be addressed.

The aim of this chapter is to provide a better understanding of emotions and their impact on change in organizations. The chapter begins by examining the nature and meaning of emotions. First, a definition of emotions is provided, followed by a review of some of the theoretical perspectives of emotions. The different types of emotions – positive and negative – are then examined and how they relate in practice to organizational change. The chapter also considers the influence of an organization's culture on emotions, as well as the impact that attempting to change an organization's culture can have on the emotions of individuals. The chapter goes on to review how individuals suppress, regulate and demonstrate emotions thorough concepts such as 'emotional contagion', 'emotional labour', 'emotional balancing' and 'emotional intelligence'. Key questions are addressed such as: how can we understand emotional processes in organizations during change? How is emotion socially shaped? What drives emotions towards change? What might be the anticipated emotional reactions to change? How are emotions spread amongst individuals during organizational change? What impact does culture have on emotions and how might changing an organization's culture affect emotions? The chapter concludes by providing practical advice for managers and leaders on the impact of organizational change on emotions – an especially difficult issue to address.

LEARNING OUTCOMES

By the end of this chapter you will be able to:

- evaluate the different theoretical perspectives on emotions;
- identify the impact of culture on the expression or suppression of emotions;
- define key concepts such as emotional labour, emotional contagion, emotional balancing and emotional intelligence – and how they relate to organizational change;

- appreciate the role that emotions play during organizational change;
- help people to understand and manage their emotional reactions to change in the workplace.

Emotions at work

There is comparatively little discussion in the organizational change literature on the management of the emotional side of change – that is, how individuals react to issues that impact on them personally in the work environment. Not only is there a lack of attention to emotions in the literature but there also appears to be an unwritten rule in most organizations that employees should leave their emotions at the door. In many companies only emotions that are easily controllable and can be categorized as positive are permitted. Organizations that advocate this approach fail to see the importance of emotions at work. As Noel Tichy and Stanford Sherman observe: 'work, inevitably is an emotional experience; healthy people can't just drop their feelings off at home like a set of golf clubs' (1993: 64). Emotions at work matter, because as John Elster says:

> Most simply, emotions matter because if we did not have them nothing else would matter. Creatures without emotion would have no reason for living... Emotions are the stuff of life. Emotions are the most important bond or glue that links us together. (1999: 403)

The experience of work is saturated with a variety of emotions – from frustration, happiness, anxiety or fear, to an enduring sense of dissatisfaction or commitment. Emotions influence our attitudes, behaviour and what we do and how we do it at work. For instance, research has shown that positive emotional experiences at work can lead to an improvement in an individual's performance, while negative emotional experiences can have the opposite affect (Fredrickson and Losada, 2005).

When change occurs in an organization it can create a multitude of emotions because it is so varied. Change can be a threat or an opportunity, a cause for concern or celebration, surprising or predictable, controlled or uncontrolled. It can bring growth and prosperity but it can also bring chaos and decay. It can create development and maturation or result in the sudden end of all development and progression. Change can be cyclical and reversible or one-way and irreversible. It can be superficial and spectacular, or it can be slow and far-reaching. It is not surprising, then, that change inspires an immense gamut of emotional responses, ranging from nostalgia for the status quo to hope and anticipation for what the future will be like. At one extreme, change can stretch our emotions from despondency and despair to feelings of emancipation and joy.

To succeed with change means taking time to understand the likely impact and sequence of it on not only the rational elements, such as what needs to be done, when, how and by whom, but also on the emotional elements such as how it will impact on people individually and collectively across the organization. Leading and managing people along a transformational journey demands the ability to recognize how and why people will react emotionally. To understand about the impact of change and transformation on emotions we first need to understand what is meant by 'emotions'.

Definition of emotions

Emotions are intense, short-lived reactions that are linked to a specific cause such as an event, issue, relationship or object (Frijda, 1986). For instance, you might be delighted with your birthday gift, angry with your partner for forgetting your anniversary, or happy because you are on holiday. Emotions can influence how we deal with a task at work, as well as the content of our thinking, such as what kind of information we recall, select, interpret and learn. Emotions can come and go quickly. Some are intense, such as rage; others are more subdued, such as contentment; while others are mixed, such as anger with embarrassment. Since an emotion cannot be directly seen, we communicate how we feel verbally and non-verbally. For instance, we may feel sad and show it by crying, or feel happy and show it by laughing. An individual's display of an emotion consists of 'a complex combination of [their] facial expression, body language, spoken words and tone of voice' (Rafaeli and Sutton, 1987: 33). An emotion is therefore a reaction to a person, situation, event or object, which is shown externally and has a range of possible consequences in how an individual will behave in a work situation.

Types of emotions during organizational change

Emotions can be classified as positive or negative. Positive emotions include: excitement, enthusiasm, happiness, relief, confidence, exhilaration, eagerness and hopefulness. Negative emotions include: guilt, anger, frustration, disappointment, sadness, grief, anger, worry, fear, anxiety and helplessness. Positive emotions can stimulate the desire to generate broader ways of thinking, improve decision making, increase energy and create an open mind about future possibilities. Conversely, negative emotions can create a narrow way of thinking, withdrawal from participating in meetings and decision making, criticism about future options and even result in attacking others physically and/or verbally (Barclay *et al*, 2005).

Individual reactions to organizational change can vary greatly. Some employees will react positively and view change as an opportunity for development and advancement. In a study of employees from a broad cross-section of organizations and jobs James Avey and colleagues (2008) found that positive emotions can help employees to cope with change and increase their level of commitment and engagement to it. However, not everyone will see change as positive. Some organizational members may perceive it as threatening and unfair. As a consequence they will respond with negative emotions such as anger, resentment, anxiety and/or withdraw from participating in the discussions and decisions about the change.

During organizational change individuals will experience not just negative or positive emotions but they will also experience both types of emotions simultaneously. For example, the announcement of a departmental restructure might arouse mixed emotions in some individuals, such as fear related to the uncertainty about potential job losses, mixed with hope for the improvement that the restructure might bring to the department's performance.

Emotions not only have positive and negative valence but they also have a temporal aspect. The temporal aspects of emotions are especially important, as change is a process that unfolds over time. As change progresses, employees' experiences and reactions will also change. This is evident in the study of a merger conducted by Mel Fugate and colleagues (2002). The study found that employees' emotions changed over a 10-month time period, leading to the conclusion that organizations need to be continually attentive to the concerns and emotions of employees.

The speed and frequency of change can also affect emotions. Organizations that plan and initiate changes at a quick pace may create constant anxiety for their employees about their jobs, as well as despondency and resignation as people struggle whilst trying constantly to cope with ongoing changes. The emotions of employees will therefore vary depending on a range of factors, including the speed, timing and frequency of change.

Activity

How do individuals tend to show their emotions at work during change? Reflect on your own work experience and talk to friends and relatives who have worked in organizations. Consider the following questions:

1 What emotions are permitted in the workplace during change?

2 How do individuals show negative emotions?

3 What is usually the impact of them doing so – on themselves, their colleagues and the organization?

Impact of emotions on work performance

Emotional reactions to events at work can influence an individual's attitude, performance and job satisfaction. For instance, if an employee is hassled by a demanding boss to take on extra work they might become angry and disgruntled, and therefore suffer from job dissatisfaction and begin to look for employment elsewhere. These emotions, in turn, inspire actions that can benefit or impede others at work. For example, imagine that one of your colleagues unexpectedly brings you a cup of coffee or tea to your desk. As a result of this pleasant, if unexpected experience, you may feel happy and surprised. If that colleague is your boss, you might also feel delighted and proud. Studies have found that the positive feelings resulting from work experience may inspire people to do something they had not planned (Fisher, 2002). For instance, if you volunteer to help a colleague on a project that you were not planning to work on, your action may have a positive impact on your colleague. Alternatively, if your boss has told you off for arriving late for a project meeting, the negative emotions you experience may cause you to withdraw from participating in the meeting or to act aggressively towards other people in the meeting. Over time, these tiny moments of emotion on the job can influence a person's job satisfaction. Specific events that people experience at work every day cause different individuals to feel different emotions, which subsequently affect their attitudes and behaviours at work. Emotions are therefore not something to be ignored. To understand emotions more we shall now consider some of the theoretical perspectives on emotions.

Emotion perspectives

There are various theoretical perspectives on emotion. This section will examine the following theories: emotion as biological; emotion as appraisal; emotion as social; emotion as a learned experience. Each of these perspectives offers insights into the way that emotions can arise during organizational change.

Emotion as biological

A biological perspective proposes that many of our basic emotional responses are wired into our body system through genetic heritage. In other words, we are pre-programmed to respond emotionally. This perspective was fundamental to Charles Darwin's work, which he outlined in his book *The Expression of the Emotions in Man and Animals*, published in 1872. Darwin concluded that many of our emotional reactions are rooted in prehistoric patterns of survival and are responses that have evolved to address the various challenges faced by our ancestors, and how we physically respond.

The biological perspective views emotions as being associated with physical changes in our body. This connection between emotions and the body is central to the James–Lange theory of emotions that was independently proposed by psychologists William James and Carl Lange in the 1880s. According to this theory an external stimulus – such as an event, person or situation – leads to a physiological reaction. An individual's emotional reaction is then dependent upon how they interpret those physical reactions. For example, suppose you are walking at night down a dark street and you hear a noise behind you. You begin to shake; you can feel your heart pounding and your muscles tensing. The James–Lange theory proposes that you will interpret your physical reactions and conclude that you are frightened ('I am shaking, so I am afraid'). In the context of organizational change, a proposed transformation (event) that arouses a change in an individual's body (such as muscles tensing or heart racing) may result in an individual concluding that they feel anxious about the proposed change.

Critics of the biological perspective on emotions argue that emotions are products of nurture rather than nature and that the biological perspective is inadequate, because it does not do justice to how individuals make sense of situations that stimulate emotions.

Emotions as appraisal

The cognitive appraisal perspective on emotions proposes that emotion is not there in any meaningful psychological sense until we appraise or try to make sense of what we see and hear. Richard Lazarus's (1982) research highlights that an individual's appraisal of an event at work (such as deadlines) leads to the experience of emotions, with positive events that facilitate the fulfilment of an individual's goals eliciting positive emotions such as happiness, and negative events that hinder the fulfilment of an individual's objectives eliciting negative emotions such as anger or fear.

Cognitive appraisal can be subdivided into three specific forms of appraisal:

- Primary appraisal: an event/situation is regarded as being positive, stressful or irrelevant to an individual's well-being.
- Secondary appraisal: the individual takes account of the resources that they have available to cope with the situation.
- Reappraisal: the individual monitors the stimulus situation and their coping strategies, with the primary and secondary appraisals being modified if necessary.

We can apply these three forms of appraisal to a change initiative. First, primary appraisal occurs when an individual evaluates whether the change is relevant to their well-being or personal goals. If the individual considers the change relevant, secondary appraisal follows. In this stage, an employee receives more information on the change and as the change is implemented they start to experience it in their daily work. Secondary appraisal is influenced by the degree of congruence between an individual's goals and the goals of the change initiative; an individual's degree of confidence for the success of the proposed change; an individual's psychological and actual investments and faith in the change; and the emotional ties that an individual develops with colleagues, supervisors and peers in their daily interaction. This appraisal process results in an individual's emotional response, which is then translated into a specific coping behaviour. Reappraisal may occur when an individual obtains new information about the change or re-evaluates the impact of the change. This process repeatedly occurs during a change process, as appraisal processes are initiated whenever a new stimulus event occurs. Several events may serve as stimuli for new emotional episodes during a change process, for example, when a manager communicates that the change will take longer than planned or will require more cost-cutting measures than initially announced. Whenever employees are provided with new information about the change, they will re-evaluate the proposed change and go through a new appraisal process and show different emotions. Consequently, as Klaus Scherer says, emotions are: 'rarely steady states. Rather, emotional processes are undergoing constant modification allowing rapid readjustment to changing circumstances or evaluations' (2005: 702).

The more often employees encounter certain changes, the more adept they will become at interpreting their meaning and coping with them. This enables individuals to accumulate emotional change experience at different phases of the change and across changes. Scherer (2009) defines this as individuals' emotional schemata, that is, those strongly relevant stimulus features that once they have undergone appropriate appraisal are stored in an individual's memory. The more diverse emotions an individual experiences during various changes, the more diverse such emotional schemata may become. Diverse emotional schemata may form employees' emotional experience, which through comparisons of different changes can influence their emotions about future changes.

The cognitive appraisal theory is, however, open to criticism. Stephen Fineman (2013) points out that appraisal theory tells us little about the social and cultural contexts of appraisals and emotions, the nub of much organizational emotion. Instead critics of appraisal theory argue that the emotions that people feel are heavily influenced by social conventions and the impressions they wish to convey to others. This view forms the basis of social constructivism, which provides a perspective on the social elements of emotions.

Emotion as social

According to the social constructivist theorists (such as Callahan and McCollum, 2002), emotions are social phenomena that are culturally shaped and culturally mediated. This view emphasizes that our emotions occur in the contexts of social interactions and relationships. We are subject to influences from our boss and work colleagues on how and what we feel, or pretend to feel. We might get angry at a remark from our boss, feel sad about a colleague leaving the company, or experience pride when we achieve our performance objectives. Emotions are therefore socially constructed. The idea that emotions are constructed in the moment during ongoing interactions contrasts with the biological perspective, which conceptualizes emotions as innate and pre-programmed in our heads before we express them. So in the context of organizational change, according to the social constructivist perspective the emotions that people experience, express or suppress are shaped by their social relationships.

Emotion as learned experience

Whether or not emotions are learnt is a source of debate for many of the theoretical perspectives on emotions. The biological perspective suggests that some basic emotions are innate, while the cognitive appraisal and social constructivist theories of emotion acknowledge that personal and socio-cultural factors play a part in the triggering and display of emotions.

To be emotional we need to have some knowledge that shapes our likely responses. For instance, a particular gesture made by one of our colleagues may make us angry if we interpret it as an insult, or generate contempt if we read it as an attempt at ingratiation, or perhaps compassion if we see it as pleading. According to Elena Antonacopoulou and Yiannis Gabriel (2001) our interpretation and judgement are guided by our existing knowledge, values and beliefs as well as by our prior emotional states and moods. Organizational change continuously generates emotional responses depending on the ways in which people interpret them. For example, an employee may welcome the introduction of a new online accounting system, because they understand the need for it and feel confident in using it. On the other hand, if the employee has no previous experience in using online accounting systems and is not convinced of the need for it, they are more likely to feel anxious about its introduction. Alternatively, they may welcome the new system, not realizing that it will adversely affect their work or may even cost them their job. This employee is basing their interpretation on what they have learnt. According to Antonacopoulou and Gabriel (2001) this places learning as a central aspect of emotion.

Learning informs individuals of the ways in which they relate to others, allowing them to empathize and understand their emotions and enabling them to take appropriate actions in pursuit of their aims. In effect, learning enhances an individual's understanding by allowing a reconsideration of their emotional stance towards an issue and the opportunity to reconsider that emotion. Learning in the context of emotion implies a change in position, a reconstruction of one's way of perceiving and thinking. Therefore, in the context of organizational change this means that the way in which individuals construct meaning and experience their emotions can be influenced by their learning from, and experience of, prior change initiatives.

The ABC model of emotions

The ABC model of emotions provides a practical approach to identifying how our emotions are triggered by organizational change. The roots of this model stem from Rational-Emotive Therapy (RET) developed initially by Albert Ellis in the 1950s. The 'A' of the model represents the situation (event, person, object) – it is the scene that a camera would record. The 'B' represents the interpretation that the individual gives to the scene – the story created from the situation. The 'C' represents how an individual reacts – their emotions, body sensations and impulses to act in various ways. Often during organizational change people will see the 'A' and 'C' quite clearly but will not be aware of the 'B'. They think that the change itself aroused their emotions when, in fact, it was their interpretation that did this, based on their knowledge and experience of what they learnt from past change events. So for example, you present a proposal to your manager and colleagues about a different way to implement a new performance management process, compared to the approach your manager has suggested. Your manager argues passionately and strongly against your proposal (A). You interpret this as 'she thinks I am stupid' or 'my proposals are rubbish' (B). You resent her response and consequently stay quiet in future meetings and discussions about the new process, as it reminds you of the last time you had a proposal rejected (C). It is therefore not only a change event that causes an emotional reaction but also our attitudes and beliefs based on our prior experience and learning.

We can use the ABC model to identify our beliefs about organizational change and, if necessary, challenge whether they are true. If we know what our emotional reactions are, we can identify what types of beliefs we may have such as, sadness = loss, anxiety = future threat, and anger = violation of our rights.

Activity

Using the ABC model identify a recent change in the organization in which you work, or an organization (such as a social or sports club) that you are familiar with:

1 Write down the situation (A). Describe the event objectively. Answer these questions: Who? What? Where? When?

2 Write down your thoughts about the change (B).

3 Then write down your feelings – your emotion – to the change (C).

Emotions and culture

The culture of an organization can play an important role in generating emotions and influencing whether individuals express or suppress their emotions. Edgar Schein (2004) defines an organizational culture as a set of assumptions, beliefs, values, customs, structures, norms, rules, traditions and artefacts. More commonly, culture is referred to as 'how we do things around here'.

Culture both engenders emotions and provides for their expression in socially accepted ways. The role of culture and emotion is emphasized by John Bratton and colleagues who say that:

> The most critical function of corporate culture is to generate commitment and enthusiasm among followers by making them feel they are part of a 'family' and participants in a worthwhile venture. (2005: 51)

The culture of an organization is important in signalling to staff how emotions are to be experienced, expressed and regulated. As Stephen Fineman says:

> The culture of the organization helps create and reinforce the dominant emotions of control in the workplace, such as guilt, fear, shame, anxiety, or looking happy. We have to learn what emotional 'face' is appropriate, and when to use it. (2013: 23)

So culture is an influence that informs, guides and disciplines the emotions of employees within an organization. It is therefore important in signalling to staff how emotions are to be experienced, expressed and regulated. Janie Beyer and David Nino (2001) contend that culture can shape emotions by encouraging the experience of emotions and providing ways to express them. A healthy organizational culture is one where emotional expressiveness is encouraged and value is placed on the emotional elements of work. Conversely, an organizational culture can be seen as a mechanism for the cynical manipulation of the employees' emotions, which need to be controlled for the benefit of the organization. The culture of an organization can result in emotions being harnessed, managed, controlled, sanitized, codified and commodified by organizations for their own ends, and often at the expense of the employee. As Stephen Fineman (2013) says, emotions can become 'cultural prerogatives' when some are deemed appropriate for display while others must be contained. This is evident in a study of leaders in a non-profit organization by Jaime Callahan (2002). The study found that employees were expected to hide their emotions and that the emergence of new and healthier norms was being stymied by an unresponsive organizational culture. Culture can therefore influence the experience of specific emotions and how appropriate it is to display them. So any attempt to manage culture is also an attempt to manage emotions.

Culture change

Attempts to change an organization's culture can ignite emotions. In a review of culture change at the communication company Cisco, for example, Rik Kirkland found that:

> Everyone hated the new way at first... Executives didn't like sharing resources; joint strategy setting and decision making was cumbersome... The first two years were very painful. Some of the most successful people left... Others were asked to leave. (2007: 38)

Nick Forster (2006) found a similar situation at Hewlett-Packard. Forster describes how when the strategy, structure and culture of the company all changed after the arrival of a new CEO, employees became very disaffected. The traditional family culture, which had focused on profit sharing, was replaced by a culture driven by individual performance measures. As a result of the change a number of staff resigned from the company. This example illustrates that new leaders, who are brought in specifically to change the culture, need to be mindful of the emotional reactions that will arise not only as a result of their arrival but also as a consequence of any change they decide to implement. As Edgar Schein points out:

> The infusion of outsiders inevitably brings various cultural assumptions into conflict with each other, raising discomfort and anxiety levels. Leaders who use this change strategy therefore have to figure out how to manage the high levels of anxiety and conflict they have wittingly or unwittingly unleashed.
>
> (2004: 309)

So attempting to change the culture, whether deliberately or not, can influence people's emotional reactions. Conversely, the culture of an organization can affect the way in which employees respond openly to any change on an emotional level. Leaders need to create cultures sufficiently strong to embrace change without altering their fundamental ethos and to develop an acceptance that emotions are a natural part of the culture and of change (culture change is explored further in Chapter 7).

Activity

Consider the impact of a change on an organization you are familiar with and then consider the impact on the individuals concerned. Were these impacts positive or negative? Why were they perceived that way? What emotions did individuals display towards the change? How did managers and leaders react to those emotions?

Suppressing and expressing emotions

Emotional labour

Organizations can shape and control the way that their employees display emotion. Jennifer Talwar (2002) describes how managers in McDonald's and Burger King in New York invent ways of stimulating employees' emotions so that negative feelings are suppressed. Talwar says that managers constantly remind employees to 'leave your problems at home' and to report to work in a 'good mood' (2002: 113). This shaping of emotion for commercial ends is pervasive. It has been termed the 'Disneyization' or 'McDonaldization' of organizations (Ritzer, 1993). In other words, in producing the exacting standards of the Dreamland Experience or the Big Mac, these companies also produce emotion in their staff. They shape the way that emotion is to be displayed as well as the labour that goes into making it look good – the *emotional labour*.

Arlie Hochschild first coined the term 'emotional labour' in her book *The Managed Heart* (1983). She says that people engage in emotional labour in their everyday interactions to 'create a publicly observable facial and bodily display' (1983: 7). According to Hochschild, emotional labour describes when individuals manage their emotions within an organization in exchange for a salary. It occurs when employees conform to organizational norms or display rules that dictate the kinds of emotions they should or should not express in carrying out their work. An employee is therefore regulating their emotion and emotional expression to meet the requirements of their job. Displaying what is expected of them may conflict with how they feel internally. Numerous job roles have been shown to require emotional labour, especially customer-facing roles such as waiters/waitresses, call-centre agents, supermarket staff, police officers and health-care workers such as nurses.

One of the most important aspects of emotional labour that Hochschild (1983) identifies is the difference between surface acting and deep acting. Surface acting involves suppressing the emotions that you feel, or simulating emotions that you do not feel. In the first instance, you hide the emotions you are feeling; in the second, you display emotions that you are not experiencing. For instance, a checkout assistant in a supermarket who feels cross with a rude customer will continue to smile, despite the customer's rude behaviour. In this instance, the checkout assistant is complying with display rules but faking the emotions that they are really feeling. In contrast, deep acting is the process of actually experiencing emotions based on the display rules of the organization. By developing and experiencing these inner feelings about their organizational role and the customers they serve, an employee's outward behaviour becomes automatic.

During a change initiative emotional labour may be required by managers and employees who feel the need to hide their real feelings about the change in case their expression is construed as an unwelcome form of resistance.

It may also be required by managers to inject the appropriate type of emotion to sell the benefits and rationale of the need for change to their team. In a study of middle managers and emotions Quy Huy found that many managers feel a need to 'psyche themselves up' and 'blank out negative thoughts' about organizational change (2002: 41). This is also evident in a study carried out by Sharon Turnbull (2002) into the ways in which managers respond to an organization's attempts to deliberately change its culture. Turnbull found that managers hide their feelings of mistrust, anger and embarrassment, and many of them pretend to comply with the changes, even when they are not in favour of them.

Such emotional labour can have a positive and negative impact on employees' performance and personal welfare. On the positive side, the effective management of emotional expression has been linked to an increase in sales, an improvement in the quality of team decisions and negotiations, and also an improvement in the profit and performance of an organization (Grandey *et al*, 2005). On the negative side, however, when there is a disparity between an individual's felt and displayed emotions, *emotional dissonance* can occur. When employees have to suppress their real emotions this can lead to burnout, exhaustion, low job satisfaction, a low sense of personal accomplishment, absenteeism and it can also ignite conflict (Grandey, 2000).

While Hochschild (1983) was concerned about such negative effects of emotional labour, other writers have expressed the harnessing of employees' emotional energy as a good thing. For instance, Mike Noon and Paul Blyton (2007) remind us that emotional labour is a variation on what already occurs in many work situations. These authors say that for those employees who perform service jobs, smiling at customers and interacting with them in a polite way provides meaning, pleasure and increased job satisfaction. Such employees are engaging in emotional labour but are neither acting (surface or deep) nor experiencing emotional dissonance. According to Kerry Lewig and Maureen Dollard (2003), for such individuals their felt and expressed emotions match – so they experience emotional harmony. The same can be said of change in organizations, as there will be many employees who are in favour of the change and do not need to surface or deep act – instead they are able to show their positive emotions towards the change.

Discussion questions

How important is emotional labour during change? Consider how surface and deep acting might be evident in response to a change initiative.

Describe a time when you effectively managed someone's emotions. What happened? What was the result?

Emotional contagion

Emotions can be contagious. They can spread through a department, team or a whole organization via verbal and non-verbal exchanges and shape the emotions of other people. During organizational change, individuals will react to and draw inferences from other individuals' emotions, including those of leaders and managers. Managers and leaders therefore need to be aware not only of the emotions of their staff but also their own emotions, as displayed emotions can spread to teams and other organizational members much like a virus, and this contagion can have an impact on the emotions and behaviours of employees. Similarly, the emotions of leaders and managers can influence important team outcomes such as collaboration and the amount of effort that people put into their work (Sy, Côté, and Saavedra, 2005).

Consequently, it matters what emotions are displayed by leaders and managers, and how these emotions are assessed, communicated and transferred within an organization during a change process. If a negative mood is spread throughout a team or an organization, performance and employee work-related attitudes can suffer. As Rafaeli and Worline state: 'put simply, management's job has become the management of emotion' (2001: 107). Leaders and managers therefore need to consider how they balance their emotions and those of other organizational members.

Emotional balancing

Emotions have to be addressed if operational continuity and a semblance of normal organizational service and performance are to be sustained during change. Failure to do so risks an organization sliding into paralysis or chaos. It falls upon managers to work with their own and their employees' feelings, if both change and continuity are to be achieved. Quy Huy (2002) calls this process *emotional balancing*. He illustrates the balancing principle through a study of a transformation in a large information technology company. The transformation involved closing 10 call centres located in different towns and relocating them to one site. This meant a reduction of 20 per cent of the workforce. Huy found that the company's vice president was bullish about the relocation and kept his employees in a state of uncertainty and insecurity about their jobs. Huy cites an example of one middle manager who, following the lead of the vice president, expressed her intolerance of her employees' personal worries about the change: 'We had an open line for questions. Ninety per cent of them were basically the same: how was it going to affect my work schedule, my vacation... In future should we take these calls? No!' (Huy, 2002: 500). This manager failed to restore the emotional stability of those employees who had to continue to deliver the service. In contrast, the study found a very different response from another middle manager who was sceptical about the change but hid his feelings in order to help his employees:

> I realized that one could not deal effectively with emotions when one was with a crowd. So I began to set up smaller meetings in groups of seven or eight, and I told them I would be available for private meetings after the group discussion... It was a winning formula. Every case was different. One service rep from a small town emotionally told me in a public meeting that she could not move to [Dallas] immediately. Another one was worried that her handicapped child would not find a specialized school, so I looked for a job that would suit her needs. Others have sick parents. Relocation is a very emotional thing. We addressed that by offering them paid visits to the new location a few months in advance. (Huy, 2002: 500)

This manager's empathetic actions eased the anxieties and doubts that employees were experiencing and helped to manage them through the change. In successful projects Huy (2002) found that managers addressed the emotional needs of their staff. They met with employees individually and in small groups and encouraged them to voice their concerns. Managers listened emphatically and they used company resources to ease the impact of the change when they could. Managers who strive to implement change must possess energy, enthusiasm and drive in the face of opposition, indifference, frustration and unexpected events. Managers also need to recognize their own emotional needs and support each other. This support can help to prevent the erosion of their energy. For when a manager's commitment wavers, this affects the emotions of their staff. Leading and managing people through change therefore involves leaders and managers maintaining an emotional balance. This can be done through emotional intelligence.

Emotional intelligence

The ability of managers and leaders to recognize and manage emotions in themselves and in other people is known as *emotional intelligence*. This concept, which has been popularized by Daniel Goleman (1995), was initially developed by Peter Salovey and John Mayer who define emotional intelligence as:

> The subset of social intelligence that involves the ability to monitor one's own and others' feelings and emotions, to discriminate among them and to use this information to guide one's thinking and actions. (1990: 189)

An emotionally intelligent individual is able to recognize their own and others' emotional states. In their model of emotional intelligence Salovey and Mayer (1990) identify four elements: 1) emotional awareness; 2) emotional facilitation; 3) emotional knowledge; and 4) emotional regulation:

- *Emotional awareness* refers to an individual's ability to be aware of the emotions they are personally experiencing and the emotions of others, and to express emotions and emotional needs accurately to others.

- *Emotional facilitation* refers to an individual's ability to use emotions to prioritize thinking by focusing on important information that explains why feelings are being experienced.

- *Emotional knowledge* refers to an individual's ability to understand emotional cycles and complex emotions such as simultaneous feelings of loyalty and betrayal.

- *Emotional regulation* revolves around the management of emotions. That is, an individual's ability to connect or disconnect from an emotion depending on its usefulness in any given situation. For example, when faced with what is perceived as a personal injustice during a change programme, an individual's feelings of anger may motivate or distract them from completing a specific task. An individual with high emotional intelligence would be aware of their anger and its source and be able to regulate that anger to motivate their performance. On the other hand, an individual with low emotional intelligence might allow anger to consume their thoughts and dwell on the injustice that precipitated their anger in the first place and, as a result, reduce their ability to engage with the change and maintain their performance.

This model emphasizes that emotional intelligence is a multidimensional construct and that the four elements (emotional awareness; emotional facilitation; emotional knowledge; emotional regulation) are iterative in that each of the abilities can contribute to enhancing other abilities. These abilities are based on an individual's own self-awareness. So, to lead or manage people, thorough leaders and managers must be able to connect with, control and leverage their own emotions and be able to do the same with the people they are responsible for and who will work with them to implement the change.

Emotional intelligence is not fixed for life and may be improved with suitable training. For example, coaching or training programmes can help to improve levels of emotional intelligence as well as help individuals to regulate their emotions. One way of enhancing emotional intelligence is through the practice of mindfulness.

Mindfulness

Mindfulness is an 'enhanced attention to awareness of current experiences or present reality' (Brown and Ryan, 2003: 823). Mark Williams and Danny Penman describe mindfulness as:

> Observation without criticism; being compassionate with yourself [and others]. In essence mindfulness allows you to catch negative thought patterns before they tip you in a downward spiral. (2011: 6)

Mindfulness captures a quality of consciousness that is characterized by clarity and vividness of current experience and functioning, it is in contrast to the mindless, less awake states of habitual or automatic functioning that many individuals experience. For example, an individual whose attention is focused on the sensory experience of eating chocolate will get more pleasure from it than an individual whose is engaged in doing something else at the same time, such as watching television.

The benefits of mindfulness have been identified by the Mindfulness All-Party Parliamentary Group (2015) in the UK, which conducted an eight-month inquiry into the potential for mindfulness training in key areas of public life – health, education, workplaces and the criminal justice system. The group found that mindfulness is 'a transformative practice, leading to a deeper understanding of how to respond to situations wisely' (2015: 6). Williams and Penman (2011) link the benefits of mindfulness to an increase in emotional intelligence. In an article in the *Guardian* newspaper careers blog, Mirabai Bush, who introduced mindfulness to Google writes:

> Becoming more aware of your own emotions as they arise gives you more choice in how to deal with them. Mindfulness helps you become more aware of an arising emotion by noticing the sensation in the body.
>
> (Cited in Crossland-Thackray, 2012)

Mindfulness enables individuals to take a step back and consider alternative perspectives rather than simply reacting to events. It helps to put individuals in control of their emotions, enabling them to choose an appropriate response.

As mindfulness has been found to be helpful in disengaging individuals from unhealthy thoughts, habits and unhealthy behaviour patterns (Brown and Ryan, 2003), it follows that becoming more mindful of one's thoughts and emotional response patterns can be a source for altering them and therefore be important in organizational change. For example, if an individual becomes more aware of a pessimistic thinking pattern regarding changes at work, potentially through practising greater mindfulness, this individual can use self-monitoring to identify unproductive thinking habits and choose more positive interpretations, thus reducing their negative emotions.

Mindful individuals have a greater opportunity to become aware of thinking patterns that challenge their ability to be efficacious, optimistic and resilient at work, especially during times of organizational change. Such awareness may lead employees to intentionally choose more positive and optimistic ways of dealing with change. Mindfulness can therefore influence emotions that support organizational change.

The role of emotions during organizational change

Emotions unfold in a complex way and can vary not only during change but also across changes within an organization. How individuals and teams respond to change can differ widely. Some individuals will be energized and excited by change and interpret it as an opportunity for innovation, growth and creativity. Such individuals may feel hope, anticipation and faith in what the change will create in the future, and will participate in the implementation of the change and adapt to the transformation it brings. By contrast, other people may deny the reality of the change altogether and, until it is implemented and becomes business as usual, believe that nothing can alter their ways of working. Such individuals are sometimes thought of as ostrich-like, burying their heads in the sand. There are other people for whom change unleashes acute anxieties, as they feel that the change is potentially damaging to them. Such individuals are more likely to be reluctant to embark on any change, and may resort to active or passive opposition and display emotions such as anger or fear about the transformation.

Change undoubtedly unleashes emotions. In turn, emotions form their own unpredictable mixture, which can shape, guide and inhibit change. The challenge in attempting to manage emotions is that emotions involve the whole person and differentiate one person from another. Emotions cannot be managed 'en masse' as different emotions require different responses. Furthermore, the same emotion can confer very different effects in different situations. For example, anger can spur people into action beyond the call of duty or it can disable them through fury. Fear can excite some people while terrifying others, while emotions of acute and unchecked insecurity and anxiety can paralyse any attempt to change. This can be exacerbated by organizational cultures, which, instead of recognizing emotions and their importance, ignore them.

So instead of ignoring emotions, which may occur in response to change, leaders and managers need to recognize them and take time to understand what is driving the emotional responses to change.

The following case study, written by Thomas Chambers, describes the emotions felt by employees and owners in a family firm, when it was put up for sale.

CASE STUDY   The emotions of change in a family business

Written by Thomas Chalmers, partner, Leading Figures

In 1947, my grandfather established a small family business in the form of a fresh seafood shop in west central Scotland. Over 60 years later my father and I sold the business. This case study explains how we did it in a way that preserved our sanity and maintained harmony amongst members of staff, securing their loyalty until the day we eventually stepped away from the business for good.

Having now been an executive/leadership coach for over a decade, I can see that the challenges we faced in our small business were every bit as relevant as those currently faced by much larger corporations. For example, when going through any change process, communication and transparency are vital.

Change is often fraught with mental, physical and emotional discomfort and our experience was no different. As owners of the business we wrestled with our decision to sell. What would our staff think? What would our customers think? What would our suppliers think? Were we letting down the very community in which we had lived and served all our lives? In the end, however, our decision to sell was made somewhat easier by my father's deteriorating health coupled with the fact that my wife and I had decided that we did not particularly want our sons to follow in my footsteps – nor did it seem that they wanted to. My father had followed my grandfather into the business and after a 10-year career in commercial banking I had changed direction and followed them both as the third-generation successor. But by the time we decided to sell, my grandfather had passed away, my father really needed to retire and I had decided that the business was no longer where I wanted to spend the rest of my life. However, our decision was somewhat undermined by the fact that the business was profitable, highly reputable and multi-award-winning – to the extent that we were one of Rick Stein's Food Heroes, and Tesco had even asked us to share our knowledge and experience with them. But the decision was made and my father, my mother, my wife and our sons were unanimously agreed: it was time to sell. This sounds easy but the mental challenge was compounded by the emotional turmoil of letting go, and exacerbated by the stark reality of advertising the business on the open market. However, thankfully, we were resolute as well as unanimous in our decision and such a support network is a wonderful foundation during times of change.

The next dilemma was whether to appoint an agent to advertise the business and delay telling our staff until we had secured a buyer, or to call a meeting and be completely open and transparent about our intentions – as we had close relationships with our staff and would have found it difficult to live with ourselves had they learned from any external source that the business was being sold. Even so it was by far one of the most challenging things we ever had to do in the business. We called a meeting one Monday morning, gathering everyone together, suspecting that they had an inkling of our plans and never appreciating that they were completely oblivious. And this is what we did: we told them the truth. We said that we had decided to sell the business and place it on the open market. Our reasons were that I wanted to move on and my father was eager to retire on health grounds. We advised that we were going to place the sale in the hands of an agent and that they would most likely see the business advertised in the press. However, we were quick to add that we were determined to find a buyer who would maintain the seafood quality that we had sought to deliver to our customers for more than half a century. Moreover, we advised that the business would be sold as a going concern with all employees hopefully keeping their jobs and that we would keep everyone informed of developments as they happened. Our staff left that meeting more subdued than when they arrived, but they said that they understood our reasons and would support us until a buyer was found and the sale went through. What more could we have asked from our staff? They had repaid our honesty and transparency tenfold.

In the days and weeks that followed we worked harder than ever. We maintained quality, price and service as well as a hard work ethic and the intrinsic camaraderie that had always existed between ourselves and our staff. The future was uncertain but we resolved to maintain a sense of purpose and normality. The outcome of this approach was twofold: we created a sense of optimism and enthusiasm in what was an unnerving situation and, when prospective buyers arrived to see our business as usual, they witnessed and experienced an energy and vibrancy between staff and customers that had stood the test of time – a compelling feel-good factor that underpinned our sales turnover and compelled prospective purchasers to submit their bids. In the end, we had several interested parties and were able to choose the buyer whom we thought was the most appropriate.

Our staff stood by us until the day the business changed hands. As small as our business may have been, there are I hope lessons that can be learnt from what we did, and perhaps, more importantly, how we did it. Leaders of all businesses need to drive change whilst managing that change within themselves; one is extrinsic, the other intrinsic, but both are pertinent and palpable.

My father passed away less than three years after the sale and in many respects my only regret for his sake is that we did not sell sooner. Such is the challenge of change that it probably took me three years to come to terms with the thought of selling a business that had shaped my life and provided a living for over three generations of our family.

Summary

Organizational change is an emotive event. Emotions will shape the anticipation, the experience and the aftermath of change. As Stephen Fineman says: 'Change is a process of unfolding and conflicting feelings – before, during and after the event' (2013: 121). Change can create a mix of emotions – simultaneously positive and negative. For example, the initial announcement of a change project and the communication of various issues affecting its implementation can trigger several employee emotions. Fear can coexist with exhilaration, liking with disliking, suspicion with delight. Part of leading and managing people through change is being able to acknowledge and understand emotions. There are a number of ways in which organizational change and emotions are related. First, organizational change is imbued with emotion and therefore change is especially emotional. Second, an organization's culture influences how these emotions are experienced and expressed. Third, individuals will have their own opinions about change and will experience a range of emotional responses to it, which in turn is likely to manifest in how they cope with the change and their attitudes towards the organization. Finally, emotions can affect the level of engagement of individuals with the change and, ultimately, the outcome of a change.

Managers and leaders can attempt to manage emotions through emotional labour. Emotional labour refers to the effort, planning and control needed to express organizationally desired emotions. Emotional labour can, however, be challenging for most individuals because it can be difficult to conceal true emotions and to display the emotions required by the job, as this can create emotional dissonance. Emotional intelligence can minimize this dissonance. Emotional intelligence is the ability of an individual to perceive and express emotion; assimilate emotion in thought; understand and reason with emotion; and regulate emotion in themself and others.

In order to understand emotions during change, we need to recognize them as complex and evolving. Employees may experience several emotions throughout changes. The emotions that they have experienced during previous changes may impact on their appraisal process of subsequent changes. Leaders and managers need to recognize that one change often follows after another change, or simultaneously, with multiple-orchestrated changes occurring at the same time. So individuals are often experiencing sequential and simultaneous changes and the emotions that go with them.

Despite this, acknowledging and dealing with emotions is, for many reasons, a neglected aspect of organizational change. For instance, the culture of an organization can stifle the expression of feelings and emotions. Yet, despite the common neglect of the emotional aspects of change, leaders and managers need to recognize the importance of emotions by acknowledging individual responses to change. Being able to appreciate the emotional reactions of others, as well as their own, will help leaders and managers to understand how people interpret the demands and pressures of change. Recognizing emotions, as well as creating and sustaining positive emotions, can help organizations to cope with the complexities and challenges associated with change.

Implications for managers and leaders

From this chapter there are some key practical implications to help leaders and managers to understand and cope with emotions during change:

- *Appreciate the perspectives of others*
  It is important to appreciate employees' perspectives in relation to change. Be aware of the types of conditions that produce positive emotions, and encourage a work environment that builds and maintains positive feelings that impact on how individuals think and behave. Also be cognisant of negative emotions, what triggers them and how they can be addressed.

- *Recognize and acknowledge strong emotional reaction*
  Usually this is relatively straightforward, as emotion manifests itself in verbal and non-verbal signals – but sometimes, for example, anger may be repressed, depression may be hidden, or apparent happiness may hide distress. Tactics to prevent exacerbating an already emotional situation are outlined in Table 2.1.

- *Ensure a just and fair transition process*
  Ensure that whatever process is used to transition people through the change is fair, transparent, not overly complicated and is consistently applied.

- *Provide relevant training*
  It can be helpful to provide training and coaching on the ability to accurately read the subtle social cues and signals given by others in order to determine what emotions are being expressed and to understand the perspective of other individuals.

TABLE 2.1　Managing emotions

Tactics	Appropriate Use	Inappropriate Use
To reflect on underlying emotion content, eg 'You seem upset, happy, annoyed about...'	To show awareness of emotion and to provide an opportunity to express emotion and talk about issues	When used judgementally, reproachfully, or disparagingly
Apology, eg 'I am sorry I didn't realize that...'	When used confidently and constructively to facilitate discussion	When the apology is patronizing, insincere or inappropriate
Permission, eg 'Feel free; go ahead; it's alright to...'	When a person needs to vent their emotions	When used self-piteously or to intimidate
Silence, eg sitting quietly and attentively	To encourage someone who is reticent and give someone time to compose themselves	When silence is used to control another person

TABLE 2.1 *Cont'd*

Tactics	Appropriate Use	Inappropriate Use
Conditional assistance, eg 'I will try to help you if you...'; 'If you stop... I'll be able to...'	To focus the attention of someone who is emotional and to engage them in solving the issue	When used to control rather than help someone
Normalizing, eg 'It is useful to find...'; 'People often...'	To encourage talking	When used patronizingly or when behaviour cannot or should not be normalized
Challenging, eg 'You say... [one thing] but act as if [another thing]	To raise contradictions	When the challenge is judgemental and the motive is to embarrass or punish
Asserting boundaries, eg 'Let me point out that...' 'Before you go any further...'	To indicate negative effects	When used too soon to allow the person to work through their emotions
Time-out, eg 'Let's take a break...'	When emotions are running too high to allow effective discussion	To avoid dealing with the person or the issue

SOURCE: Adapted from Ostell (1996: 542–43) and Palmer and Handy (2004: 280)

References

Antonacopoulou, E P and Gabriel, Y (2001) Emotion, learning and organizational change: towards an integration of psychoanalytic and other perspectives, *Journal of Organizational Change Management*, **14** (5), pp 435–51

Avey, J B, Wernsing, T S and Luthans, F (2008) Can positive employees help positive organizational change? Impact of psychological capital and emotions on relevant attitudes and behaviors, *The Journal of Applied Behavioral Science*, **44** (1), pp 48–70

Barclay, L J, Skarlicki, D P and Pugh, S D (2005) Exploring the role of emotions in injustice perceptions and retaliation, *Journal of Applied Psychology*, **90** (4), pp 629–643

Beyer, J and Nino, D (2001) Culture as a source, expression and reinforcer of emotions in organizations, in *Emotions at Work: Theory, research and applications for management*, ed R Payne and C Cooper, pp 173–97, Wiley, New York

Bratton, J, Grint, K and Nelson, D (2005) *Organizational Leadership*, Thomson Books, Ohio

Brown, K W and Ryan, R M (2003) The benefits of being present: mindfulness and its role in psychological well-being, *Journal of Personality and Social Psychology*, **84** (4), p 822

Callahan, J L (2002) Masking the need for cultural change: the effects of emotion structuration, *Organization Studies*, **23** (2), pp 281–97

Callahan, J L and McCollum, E E (2002) Conceptualizations of emotion research in organizational contexts, *Advances in Developing Human Resources*, **4** (1), pp 4–21

Crossland-Thackray, Gill (2012) [accessed 16 October 2015] Mindfulness At Work: What Are the Benefits? *Guardian* [Online] http://careers.theguardian.com/careers-blog/mindfulness-at-work-benefits

Ekman, P, Sorenson, E R and Friesen, W V (1969) Pan-cultural elements in facial displays of emotions, *Science*, 164, pp 86–88

Elster, J (1999) *Alchemies of the Mind*, Cambridge University Press, Cambridge

Fineman, S (2013) *Emotions at Work*, Sage, London

Fisher, C D (2002) Real-time affect at work: a neglected phenomenon in organizational behaviour, *Australian Journal of Management*, **27**, pp 1–10

Forster, N (2006) Hewlett-Packard – the new way? *Management Case Study Journal*, **6** (1), p 33

Fredrickson, B L and Losada, M F (2005) Positive affect and the complex dynamics of human flourishing, *American Psychologist*, **60** (7), p 678

French, R (2001) Negative capability: managing the confusing uncertainties of change, *Journal of Organizational Change Management*, **14** (5), pp 480–92

Frijda, N H (1986) *The Emotions*, Cambridge University Press, Cambridge

Fugate, M, Kinicki, A J and Scheck, C L (2002) Coping with an organizational merger over four stages, *Personnel Psychology*, **55**, pp 905–28

Goleman, D (1995) *Emotional Intelligence*, Bantam Books, New York

Grandey, A (2000) Emotion regulation in the workplace: a new way to conceptualize emotional labor, *Journal of Occupational Health Psychology*, **5**, pp 95–110

Grandey, A A, Fisk, G M, Mattila, A S, Jansen, K J and Sideman, L A (2005) Is 'service with a smile' enough? Authenticity of positive displays during service encounters, *Organizational Behavior and Human Decision Processes*, **96**, pp 38–55

Hochschild, A R (1983) *The Managed Heart: Commercialization of human feeling*, University of California Press, Berkeley

Huy, Q N (2001) Time, temporal capability, and planned change, *Academy of Management Review*, **26** (4), pp 601–23

Huy, Q N (2002) Emotional balancing of organizational continuity and radical change: the contribution of middle managers, *Administrative Science Quarterly*, **47** (1), pp 37–70

Kirkland, R (2007) Cisco's display of strength, *Fortune*, November, **12**, pp 34–44

Lazarus, R S (1982) Thoughts on the relations between emotion and cognition, *American Psychologist*, **37** (9), p 1019

Lewig, K A and Dollard, M F (2003) Emotional dissonance, emotional exhaustion and job satisfaction in call centre workers, *European Journal of Work and Organizational Psychology*, **12** (4), pp 366–92

Mindfulness All Party Parliamentary Group (2015) [accessed 8 February 2015] Interim Report of the Mindfulness All-Party Parliamentary Group (MAPPG) [Online] http://oxfordmindfulness.org/wp-content/uploads/mindful-nation-uk-interim-report-of-the-mindfulness-all-party-parliamentary-group-january-2015.pdf

Noon, M and Blyton, P (2007) *The Realities of Work*, 3rd edn, Palgrave Macmillan, Basingstoke

Ostell, A (1996) Managing dysfunctional emotions in organizations, *Journal of Management Studies*, **33** (4), pp 525–57

Palmer, I and Hardy, C (2004) *Thinking about Management*, Sage, London

Parkinson, B (1995) *Ideas and Realities of Emotion*, Routledge, London

Rafaeli, A and Sutton, R (1987) The expression of emotion in organizational life, in *Research in Organizational Behaviours*, vol 11, ed L Cummings and B Staw, pp 1–42, JAI Press, Connecticut

Rafaeli, A and Worline, M (2001) Individual emotion in work organizations, *Social Science Information Sur Les Sciences Sociales*, **40**, pp 95–123

Ritzer, G (1993) *The McDonaldization of Society*, Pine Forge Press, California

Salovey, P and Mayer, J D (1990) Emotional intelligence, *Imagination, Cognition and Personality*, **9**, pp 185–211

Schein, E (2004) *Organizational Culture and Leadership*, 3rd edn, Jossey Bass, London

Scherer, K R (2005) What are emotions? And how can they be measured? *Social Science Information*, **44** (4), pp 695–729

Scherer, K R (2009) The dynamic architecture of emotion: evidence for the component process model, *Cognition and Emotion*, **23** (7), pp 1307–51

Sy, T, Côté, S and Saavedra, R (2005) The contagious leader: impact of the leader's mood on the mood of group members, group affective tone, and group processes, *Journal of Applied Psychology*, **90** (2), p 295

Talwar, J P (2002) *Fast food, fast track: immigrants, big business and the American Dream*, Westview Press, Colorado

Tichy, N and Sherman, S (1993) *Control Your Destiny Or Someone Else Will*, Doubleday, New York

Turnbull, S (2002) The planned and unintended emotions generated by a corporate change program, *Advances in Developing Human resources*, **4** (1), 22–38

Williams, M and Penman, D (2011) *Mindfulness: A practical guide to finding peace in a frantic world*, Piatkus, London

Further reading

Ashkanasy, N M, Zerbe, W J and Härtel, C E (eds) (2002) *Managing Emotions in the Workplace*, Routledge, London

Koskina, A and Keithley, D (2010) Emotion in a call centre SME: a case study of positive emotion management, *European Management Journal*, **28** (3), pp 208–19

Payne, R L and Cooper, C L (eds) (2003) *Emotions at Work: Theory, research and applications for management*, Wiley, London

Shields, S A (2002) *Speaking From the Heart: Gender and the social meaning of emotion*, Cambridge University Press, Cambridge

03
Individual sense-making processes

- Every individual will experience and transition through change in a unique way. Transition models provide a framework to understand how individuals react and make sense of change.

- Resistance to change is a natural occurrence. Instead of viewing it as negative and a barrier to change, it should be viewed as an opportunity to listen to employees' concerns and to identify areas for improvement.

- Change generates a heightened sensitivity among employees to the fairness and justice of how they are treated, the processes that are employed and the outcomes of the change.

- Change has the potential to destroy trust and impact on the psychological contract that an individual has with their employer. It is vital to build and sustain trust during times of change, because once trust is violated it is not easily repaired.

- To appreciate the individual differences in how people make sense of change there is a need to understand what motivates people, as motivation can affect the attitude, energy and willingness of people to embrace change.

Consider the following scenario. You are driving along a country road with the rain hitting the car's windscreen faster than the wipers can clear it, and you are probably driving a little slower than usual. Why? Because you need to feel in control. Fear of the personal consequences of what could happen a few kilometres ahead on a slippery road slows you down. In the same way, when we hear about a proposed organizational change most of us slow down until we can make sense of it.

The aim of this chapter is to focus on how individuals seek to steer, resist and make sense of change in different ways. It begins by examining how people interpret change, with reference to some of the classic transition models such as the ones devised by Elisabeth Kübler-Ross (1973), William Bridges (2004) and Lynn Isabella (1990). The chapter then explores what motivates people to change, focusing on the expectancy theory of motivation, as well as the approach to motivation advocated by Daniel Pink (2011). The chapter then goes on to explore reactions to change, particularly resistance and whether or not resistance to change can be viewed as positive or negative. This is followed by a discussion of the importance of trust and trustworthiness. In particular, consideration is given to the impact of mistrust on an individual's psychological contract with their employer. Finally, the chapter examines the practical ways in which managers and leaders can help individuals to make sense of change and transition through it.

Key questions are addressed such as: how effective are transition models and how can they be used in practice? What pattern of emotions do people typically progress through in response to change in organizations? What responses can be expected from different people? What are the concerns of employees about change?

How do individuals make sense of change? What motivates people to embrace or resist change? How can trust be developed and sustained during times of change? What determines employees' willingness to change?

LEARNING OUTCOMES

By the end of this chapter you will be able to:

- examine what influences an individual's response to change and specifically how to address resistance to change;
- identify the attitude and energy of individuals to change and how this impacts on their response to change;
- appreciate how motivation can affect the willingness of people to embrace change and implement approaches for improving motivation;
- repair trust and build trustworthiness during times of change.

Introduction

Imagine this. You have a large family of various ages, interests and incomes, some who live with you and some who do not, some who live nearby and some who live further away. To build stronger ties and create a more cohesive family unit, you decide to organize a surprise weekend away, in a place where none of them have ever been before. You select a date, book a cottage in the countryside and arrange the travel by train. You then ask your family members to meet at your house for an important announcement. Then you surprise them with your plan and demand that everyone is ready to leave early on Saturday morning. But not everyone is happy with this announcement. Some people already have commitments that weekend. Others just hate to travel by train. They grumble, they fuss, they resist. There is crying, and a few walk away in a huff. What, you wonder, is wrong with these people? Surely, you reason, they will be more appreciative once the weekend actually begins. But when you arrive at the cottage your brother complains because he has forgotten to pack his walking boots. Your mother does not like the accommodation and finds the weather too cold; your father just wants to watch the cricket match on the TV and your partner is complaining because there is no Wi-Fi service to access e-mails. None of your relatives are taking advantage of the adventure or even the location. You decide you must have the worst, most ungrateful family in the world – and go for a long walk on your own.

Look at it another way. With perfectly good intentions, you made a well-thought-out plan. But your family became unco-operative, unhappy and resentful. Why? Because you did not involve them in the decisions about the weekend away, such as the journey or their destination. You did not ask for input. You did not share information that would have helped them to get ready. You are not even making improvements now that you are on holiday. You simply thrust everyone into unfamiliar territory without the supplies, support and clothing they need. It is not that they were unwilling to make a change. It is that you did not present the change in an appealing way. Likewise, organizational change requires people to make behavioural changes both individually and collectively, not only in the ways they perform their work but also in how they behave, interact, collaborate, learn, adjust and share.

Yet most of us are creatures of habit. We do not always appreciate changes in our daily routine, working practices and environment. We may become unhappy about any loss of freedom to do certain things, such as changes in our hours of work or ways of working. For many of us there is often a sense of security in the way things have always been done and which appear to have been done reasonably well. As a result, change when it is imposed on us can trigger a range of intense emotional reactions (as discussed in Chapter 2), which in turn can influence how we behave, depending on how we make sense of the proposed change.

To a large degree, change is in the eye of the beholder. Leaders and managers who see themselves as creating organizational change as an intentional process will have a different perspective to those who are on the receiving end of change. Change can be a cause for concern when it is done *to* us – and exhilarating when it is done *by* us. Every individual experiences change in a unique way. For some it implies a source of satisfaction, benefits or advantages, whereas for others it is a source of suffering, stress and disadvantages. One way to understand the process of change for individuals is by examining how individuals transition through change. This can help to understand how any proposed change may affect people's emotions and behaviours.

Transition models

One of the most commonly known and used transition models was originally developed by Elisabeth Kübler-Ross (1973) to show how people respond to a bereavement. According to Kübler-Ross the transition process consists of the following stages: shock and denial; anger and blame; confusion and resignation; acceptance and problem solving; and commitment. This model has been adapted to show how people react to organizational change and has become known as the 'change curve'. Each of the stages can be related to responses to organizational change and approaches developed to address them:

- *Shock and denial*
  When a change is first announced, especially if it is without any warning, individuals may be shocked by the news. As a consequence they will find it difficult to focus on their work and will feel threatened by the anticipated change. Individuals will then go on to deny the existence of the change and refuse to recognize that it is going to happen.
  During this stage it is important to:
  - Keep explaining the rationale for the change using language that individuals will understand and relate to.
  - Communicate what will change and why, and what people affected by the change will be doing differently.
  - Show individuals that you understand their situation.
  - Keep communication short and simple and allow time for it to sink in.
  - Be patient; give people time to adjust to what is being proposed.
- *Anger and blame*
  During this stage individuals will get angry at what is being proposed and at the changes they feel they are being forced to make. They will attempt to hold on to their accustomed ways of doing things while blaming management for trying to change the status quo.
  During this stage:
  - Encourage open dialogue and give people the opportunity to voice their views and issues.
  - Listen and acknowledge feelings.
  - Recognize and respond to concerns.
  - Be clear on what has to change, but highlight areas for negotiation and actively engage people in these aspects, and ask for their views.
  - Identify existing capabilities that will be of value to planning, implementing and sustaining the change.

- *Confusion and resignation*
  This is the stage when individuals reach a state of desperation and start to wonder why they should bother and what the point is of staying with the organization. During this stage some people might not be able to see a way to accept the change and move forward. As a consequence they may decide to look for a job elsewhere in the organization or even to leave the organization because they do not see themselves as having a future in it, nor do they want to be part of the change journey.
  During this stage:
  - Provide information on what is going to happen and when, and ask for feedback.
  - Reinforce the positive actions that individuals take in order to contribute to achieving the change.
  - Continue to encourage dialogue and opportunities for individuals to voice their feelings and concerns, and offer support.
  - Consider coaching or counselling for individuals, especially if they appear to be stuck in a negative state.

- *Acceptance and problem solving*
  During this stage most people start to internalize the change; begin to accept it; look for ways of doing things differently, or different ways of behaving in order to implement the change and then move forward, accepting the change and what it means for them and their job. Even if it is a grudging acknowledgement during this stage, individuals will start to consider the change for the best. In some cases, people will actively advocate what they had previously opposed. Acceptance and adaptation mean relinquishing the old ways of working and behaving, as well as the pain, confusion and fear experienced in the earlier stages of transition. It is beneficial to identify individuals who have accepted the change and involve them in the implementation. Also encourage them to act as coaches or mentors for others, especially those who are stuck in the earlier stages of the change curve.

- *Commitment*
  During this stage individuals will be committed to the change and begin to demonstrate the required new behaviours and ways of working. At this stage, identify key individuals who are committed to the change and ask them to act as role models for any new ways of working or behaving, and to help to sustain the change.

When managing people through change it is important to recognize where people are on the change curve and to respond accordingly. This is important because individuals will not always follow the prescribed sequence. There may be times when they get stuck at certain stages or move forward then back through the curve.

A similar transition process to the one developed by Kübler-Ross has been devised by Lynn Isabella (1990). Isabella's model also emphasizes that employees' reactions to change are multidimensional and multi-staged. However, it offers fewer stages than Kübler-Ross's model and instead proposes that individuals go through four stages in response to change, which are anticipation, confirmation, culmination and aftermath:

1 *Anticipation*: this stage involves uncertainty, rumours and people trying to make sense of what might be about to happen.

2 *Confirmation*: this occurs when individuals become curious about what is happening and attempt to make sense of what is proposed, based on their previous experience of change. For instance, they may confirm that, 'It is an X kind of situation' or 'It is like when Y happened'.

3 *Culmination*: this involves individuals reconciling what the change will mean and trying to understand how it will affect them, their team and the organization.

4 *Aftermath*: this happens when individuals accept the positive and negative consequences of change, once it has been implemented.

On Isabella's model, however, there are some issues that need to be raised about the transition process. First, there is a passivity to the framework that is questionable. The model does not raise how individuals might react to the change, such as delighted, angry, alarmed or frustrated. Indeed, the absence of reactions to the change contrasts with the model of Kübler-Ross, which expressly includes an anger and blame phase. Isabella's model also suffers from the same criticisms as those of Kübler-Ross's model in that there is an assumption that individuals go through the stages in a predefined way.

In an attempt to provide a different view of how individuals transition through change William Bridges (2004) describes an individual's journey as letting go of existing patterns of behaviours and engaging with new ones. Bridges's model proposes that individual reactions to change begin with an ending and then go on to a new beginning via a neutral zone. The stages of Bridges's transition process are 'ending', 'neutral' and 'beginning':

- *Ending*: this is a time when individuals let go of the current situation through disengagement and disenchantment with the organization and/or with their work. This can be painful and upsetting, but until this has happened it is difficult for individuals to engage in new roles or to change their behaviour. In this first transitional phase individuals need to be aware of how they have interpreted the change and their emotions. Managers need to be aware of how individuals are responding to the proposed change and how much of their response is emotional. The risk with people in this zone is that often managers and colleagues who have already moved on to the next stage may ignore the concerns of people or try to move them on before they are ready. According to Bridges, unless individuals move out of the ending phase under their own volition they will always be partly stuck in the old ways of doing things and will not be able to fully embrace the change – the new beginning. To help people through this stage:

- Observe and acknowledge the emotions that are being displayed and identify how they need to be addressed.
- Clearly explain the rationale for the change and the benefits of it.
- Describe what will change and how it will affect people, so that they are very clear about what will be different and what will stay the same.
- Acknowledge what people will lose as a result of the change, but also what they will gain and what will stay the same (see the Lose/Keep/Gain exercise mentioned later in the chapter in Figure 3.3).
- Discuss the successes and values of the previous ways of working and identify how they will be enhanced by the change.
- Recognize what is changing and celebrate how things used to be. For instance, an organization that is moving to a new location might hold a farewell party to the current location where people can reminisce about working in it. Alternatively, if a transformation requires a significant change of skills there may be an opportunity to reflect on the successes that the previous skill set has brought to the company.

- *Neutral zone*: although this is still a time of confusion and uncertainty, it is also a time of exploration when individuals start tentatively to build energy and enthusiasm for change. The positive side of the neutral zone is that it is an opportunity to encourage innovation and involve people in identifying new ways of working and behaving. The danger at this stage is that people may be so uncomfortable that they push prematurely for certainty and closure, and ignore any possibility of considering innovative alternatives. The aim in the neutral zone is to maintain a sense of momentum and focus on the outcomes of the change and how they will be achieved. To help people through this stage:

- Encourage individuals and teams to identify how the change will enable them to think and act differently; and also the opportunities provided by the change.
- Work with individuals and teams to provide solutions to the issues of transition as they arise.
- Encourage people to connect with others who are going through the transition and to share their hopes, fears and concerns.
- Provide opportunities to encourage and share innovative ideas about the change.

- Plan some events that bring people together and take them away from their work, such as a cake and coffee morning or an evening social event.
- Ensure that there is support and information available for individuals through communication networks or more formally from HR.
- Encourage dialogue about the change and how it will impact on individuals.

- *New beginnings*: this is a time when individuals have accepted the change and are ready to move on. The new beginning is the goal for transition, and the aim is to move people towards this and ensure that they do not slip back to their old ways of working and back to the status quo. To help encourage commitment to the new beginnings:
  - Continue to talk with teams and individuals about how they are feeling about the change.
  - Be aware of how people are adapting to the change and what organizational support they need.
  - Emphasize the benefits that will be realized from the change in order to encourage people to focus on making it work.
  - Share a picture or story that will show what will be different – what people will be saying differently, doing differently and how it will feel.
  - Give people a plan that is credible and provides a clear pathway for implementing the change.
  - Give individuals a part to play in sustaining the change and ensuring it becomes the way of working.

Throughout a change process individuals will move repeatedly between the zones of Bridges's transition model. It is therefore important to be aware of where individuals are and what will help them to move to new beginnings. Bridges (2004) notes that many organizations are often in a hurry to force employees into the third phase before they have passed through the prerequisite first and second phases. The term 'prerequisite' highlights that the transition process proposed by Bridges, as with those of Kübler-Ross and Isabella, is sequential. It is assumed that there is a linear progression that each individual must go through. This might not, however, always be the case. Some people may skip certain stages, especially if they are positive about the change or have been involved in initial discussions about it. Some employees will pass through the stages quickly; others will take more time, while others will be unable to let go and they will get stuck in certain stages. In such cases individuals may be unwilling or unable to move forward. The content of each phase, and progress through it, is subject to the individuals' willingness and capability. Some people will pass through each of the stages quickly; while others will go slowly and may even go back to stages they have already experienced. It is fundamentally a matter of employees' interpretation of the changes that determines how they react. Different individuals, because the change will affect them differently, will progress through the different stages at different rates and in different ways.

The transitional curve

None of the models that we have discussed gives a complete picture on their own of how people react to change. In my book *Sustaining Change in Organizations* (Hodges and Gill, 2015) I propose combining the Kübler-Ross and Bridges models to show a more realistic transition that individuals go through. This model, which is illustrated in Figure 3.1, has been adapted and refined further and proposes three phases:

1 Reconciliation: the letting go of current ways of working and behaving, which can be a time of uncertainty and anxiety.

2 Reorientation: exploring new ways of working and behaving, aligned to what is changing.

3 Recommitment: a time of acceptance and commitment to what is changing.

FIGURE 3.1 The transition curve

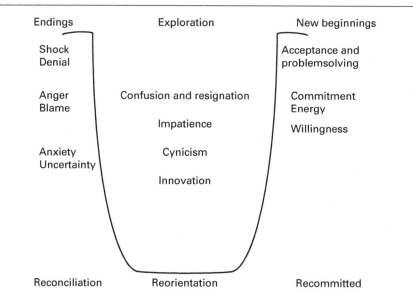

SOURCE: Adapted from Hodges and Gill (2015)

Reconciliation

This phase is aligned with the 'endings' phase from Bridges's model and the stages of shock and denial, anger and blame from the Kübler-Ross model. To this we have added anxiety and uncertainty.

Uncertainty

Organizational change is characterized by high levels of perceived uncertainty linked to the outcomes of the change. Change is not a single event with neat and tidy beginnings and endings. Instead it often comes from two or more directions at the same time, which may add to the uncertainty experienced by some individuals. Uncertainty can occur when there is lack of information about what is being proposed, such as what will change, when and how it will change and what the impact will be on jobs. Uncertainty can also relate to whether or not employees perceive that the organization is capable of implementing the change successfully. Reducing uncertainty can result in more positive employee perceptions and behaviours, and improve employee reactions and change-related outcomes. Dialogue is vital to addressing uncertainty not just downwards but up and across the organization (dialogue is explored further in Chapter 6). Ultimately, individuals need to know what the change means for them.

Anxiety

Anxiety is one of the most unpleasant feelings that an individual can experience. It can arise from perceived external threats, but will also be experienced internally by an individual. In the context of organizational change, anxiety is often caused by the surfacing of past experiences, fears or worries that an individual has experienced related to previous change/s. Russ Linden (2012) suggests that employees' anxieties about change can be assuaged by showing them how past changes and transformations were successful and how obstacles were overcome, and also by using familiar language rather than jargon. So, how can we make the new seem familiar when leading and managing people through organizational change? The following can help to reduce anxiety about organizational change:

- *Remind people of past successes.* Ask people to recall when they have done something in the past that was similar to the current change, and that was successful. What did they do? How did they achieve it? What did they learn from it that they could apply to the current change?
- *Tap a core capability.* Create a sense of familiarity by showing people how they can use their capabilities to implement the change. For instance, if an individual's core capabilities are in communications, these skills can be critical when implementing change initiatives. Ask such individuals to take key roles in the change such as drawing up and implementing a communications plan.
- *Engage familiar and experienced people.* Some organizations have brought back former (and successful) leaders to take over the reins

during a transformation. For example, Starbucks asked Howard Schultz to return as CEO when it lost its way and the company needed to transform itself. You should also engage experienced people who already work in the organization by involving them early in the change planning and asking them to take responsibility for part of the change.

- *Use familiar language.* Robert Kennedy once noted that 'everybody is in favour of improvement, but mention the word "change" and you immediately make enemies' (quoted in Linden, 2012). Language has a powerful impact on how people perceive their world, so think carefully about the language you use when describing the change.

- *Highlight what will not change.* Point out what will not be different as well as what will. For instance, if employees will have the same salary grade, use the same skills to do their work or if they will remain in the same work unit or team, let them know.

Reorientation

This is a time of exploration and innovation when staff who are optimistic about the proposed change, will want to get involved and contribute their ideas about how to make the it happen. It is also a time that can create confusion and resignation (Kübler-Ross, 1973), impatience from people who want to get on with the change, and cynicism from those who are sceptical about what is happening and who want to know more about what is going to change and how.

Cynicism

Cynicism is a negative attitude based on a belief that the organization lacks integrity. It can involve a loss of faith in the organization and in particular the leaders within it. This can occur when there is a lack of confidence in management and there is a history of changes that have not been successful, or when individuals perceive organizational change as senior management implementing the latest management fad or a quick-fix attempt to address a problem. If it is not dealt with, the price of cynicism can be high and result in low job satisfaction, a decrease in commitment to the organization, a decline in productivity, more accidents and errors, less willingness to engage in change initiatives, and the diminished credibility of leaders. It is important to identify the reasons for cynicism.

It is not just employees who can be cynical towards change. Robert Rubin and colleagues (2009) found that leaders who are highly cynical about change convey their cynicism to their employees and this in turn contributes to cynicism in employees. Cynicism can therefore be contagious and a formidable adversary for any change.

To help manage and minimize cynicism consider the following:

- Keep people involved in making decisions about changes that will affect them.

- Keep people informed of ongoing changes.
- Keep surprising changes to a minimum.
- Use positive messages that appeal to logic and consistency, and also use multiple communication channels and repetition.
- Address any previous failures. Acknowledge mistakes, apologize and make amends.
- Publicize successful changes.
- Use dialogue in order to see change from the employees' perspective.
- Provide opportunities for employees to express their feelings about proposed change.

The approach that is taken by leaders and managers in response to cynicism has the potential to counteract its negative consequences. Individuals may be much more likely to commit to organizational change if they are properly prepared for the change and given the opportunity to be involved in making decisions about it as well as in creating innovative solutions.

Innovation

Engaging people in generating and implementing innovative solutions is a key part of change. Innovation is the application of a new idea to initiate or improve a product, process or service. By definition, it is about taking time to try something that offers uncertain pay-offs, at some time in the future. The success of the TV show *Dragon's Den* over the last decade from 2005 has helped people to relate to the idea that innovation in business involves experimenting, trial-and-error and competitiveness. Creating a culture that supports experimentation is essential in encouraging innovation. Zien and Buckler say that 'the crafting of an innovative culture requires creating an environment of faith and trust that good ideas have a likely chance to become great products' (2004: 483). Innovation should be encouraged as a key part of any transformation.

Recommitted

This phase is the start of new beginnings and of employees accepting the change and recommitting to the organization. Employees' commitment for organizational change is a key determinant of successful change initiatives.

Commitment

Commitment to change is 'a force that binds an individual to a course of action deemed necessary for the successful implementation of a change initiative' (Herscovitch and Meyer, 2002: 475). This mindset can reflect an individual's desire to provide support for the change based on their belief in its benefits, recognition that there are costs associated with failure to provide support for the change, and a sense of obligation to support the change. Commitment can be shown through an individual's willingness and energy for change.

Energy and willingness

The energy and willingness of individuals for change can affect how they respond to change. The energy-investment model was originally developed by Donald Tosti and John Amarant (2005) and has been adapted here to use as a framework for identifying the attitude and energy of individuals to change. The framework, illustrated in Figure 3.2, allows you to consider different groups of people and whether they have a positive or a negative attitude, or high or low energy towards change; their willingness and ability to change; and how they invest their energy in relation to it. The framework crudely categorizes individuals into four organizational groups defined by their energy levels and their attitude towards change: the sleepwalker, the cynic, the spectator and the player.

The *sleepwalker* can be described as someone who goes to work just for the money. Sleepwalkers often act like powerless victims unable to influence change. They tend to just 'do their jobs', and no more. They may have a history of being reprimanded for mistakes or punished for trying new things. When change occurs they are likely to do as little as possible, hoping that it will go away. *They can't and won't change.* They tend to have a negative attitude towards change but expend a lot of energy in telling people about it.

FIGURE 3.2   Willingness and ability to change

Can't and Will (Spectators)	CAN and Will (Players)
● Recognizes the importance of change ● Actively supports the change ● Believes in the change as a good thing without necessarily seeing the big picture ● Doesn't have the skills/behaviours required for the change	● Focuses on end goals and means to achieve ● Recognizes how change will impact on the bottom line ● Active enthusiast for the change; enthuses others ● Role model for new vision, skills and behaviours
Can't annd Won't (Sleepers)	**Can and Won't (Cynics)**
● Does not recognize the need to change ● Shows no support for the change ● Does not want to change – is overprotective of old ways of working ● Doesn't have the skills, behaviours required for the change	● Strives for success in financial terms at expense of new behaviours ● Focus on ends at expense of means ● Shows no support for the change ● Understands the need to change but won't change ● Understands the need but disagrees with extent or process of change ● Will not change due to peer pressure

Willingness to change (vertical axis label)

Ability to change

SOURCE: Adapted from Tosti and Amarant (2005)

Sleepwalkers often feel powerless to take action or influence events. For such individuals, managers need to consider being directive in their leadership style and defining the roles of such individuals and their responsibilities clearly – and supervising them closely.

Cynics spend a great deal of time complaining about their job, management, policies and systems. Others might see them as having a bad attitude. They are often highly skilled people who have been around a long time and really know the job. When change is implemented they will spend their time and energy in making dire predictions that 'we are all doomed!' Such individuals have a low willingness to change but a high ability to do so. They *can but won't change*. They understand and could respond well to the need for the change but show no support for it. They will spend as much time describing why the changes will not work as they do taking action to make it work. However, because they have seen failed changes they also know why those changes failed. To address such reactions managers need to consider how they sell the benefits of the change to them and negotiate with them about their involvement in the change. If this fails then managers need to counsel them about why they need to change.

Spectators have a good attitude towards change but low energy levels in doing anything about it. They will speak positively about their jobs and the organization but they seldom make any effort to change anything or do anything differently. They tend to be risk-averse and will avoid doing new things until they can be sure it is safe to do so and they will not be criticized or chastised for it. When change is introduced they are likely to endorse it, talk about it positively, but not actually do anything to make it happen until they believe in its likely positive effect. They may agree in meetings, do lots of nodding, but not take action afterwards and so let other people down by not delivering on promises. Such individuals have a high willingness to change but a low ability to change: they *would change but can't* change. In other words, they recognize the importance of change and actively support it and believe that it is a positive and a necessary step forward. However, they do not have the knowledge and skills necessary for change. For such individuals, managers need to address their training and development needs. It is important to ask them for their opinions and suggestions about planning and implementing the change.

Players are usually realistic about the organization's challenges but have a positive view of how such issues can be overcome. When change is introduced they are the group most likely to support it, both verbally and through their actions. They feel they can make things better through their energy and ability and are willing to 'go the extra mile' to do so. Such individuals *can and will* change: they have considerable ability and willingness to change and they see change as a process, not an event. They recognize how change will impact on productivity and performance and are enthusiastic supporters of it. As players have the ability and willingness to change, they will quickly model the required new behaviours and skills that will help to embed and sustain change. Such individuals need to be actively involved in the change process and empowered and engaged to make decisions related to it. It is also important that they are recognized and rewarded for their performance. With players, managers need to involve them from the start of the change and delegate responsibilities to them.

It is important to caution that frameworks such as this one are not about using labels to 'brand' employees. There will no doubt be times when individuals will find themselves in each of the boxes or times when they fit into none of them. Organizations do not make a habit of recruiting sleepwalkers, cynics or spectators. When individuals join an organization they usually want to be a player. Individuals will also vary in how quickly or slowly they are willing and able to let go of the past and move to adapt to the change.

Leaders and managers need to beware that they themselves will also go through the phases at a different rate from their staff. Leaders will tend to know about the change before others and therefore may reach an acceptance of the change long before other organization members. Leaders and managers need to be sensitive to where individuals are and what they are experiencing and not just expect them to move forward. They need to consider how to address the ability and willingness of individuals to change. Ultimately, transition is a personal process and will depend on the motivations of each individual.

Motivating people to change

In the previous section we considered how people transition through change and how each individual will respond differently and at a different pace to change. To explore further these individual differences we need to appreciate what motivates people, as motivation can affect the willingness of people to embrace change.

Expectancy theory and the motivation to support or oppose change

If individuals anticipate that a change will provide them with some benefit then they may be motivated to support it, but whether or not this possibility will be translated into action will depend on their expectation that the change will deliver the promised benefits. Expectancy theorists (such as Vroom, 1964; Porter and Lawler, 1968) argue that expectations influence motivation and provide a basis for assessing whether a person is likely to support or oppose a proposed change. Whether a person is motivated to embrace or resist change will depend on their expectations about:

- their ability to deliver a satisfactory level of performance in the changed situation;
- whether a satisfactory level of performance will lead to the achievement of valued outcomes in the changed situation;

- whether the net benefits accruing to them will be equitable when compared to the net benefits accruing to comparable others in the changed situation.

From a motivational perspective, it is the expectation or belief about the relationship between effort, performance and valued outcome that will determine whether or not a person will be motivated to support or oppose the change.

Leaders and managers can use expectancy theory to assess and improve the perceived attractiveness of outcomes and build positive expectations about the relationship between effort, performance and the achievement of outcomes during a change process. This can be done by:

- being aware of the kinds of outcomes that are valued by the individuals who will be affected by the change;
- understanding the extent to which the present situation provides these outcomes;
- understanding the extent to which valued outcomes will be available once the change is implemented.

This assessment will provide a useful first indication about whether or not a person will support or oppose the proposed change. It will also indicate whether individuals are likely to be motivated to contribute through how they perform their job once the change is implemented.

Different people will value different outcomes, and even the same person may value different outcomes at different points in time. The more that leaders and managers know about this, the better they will be at understanding what motivates people during change.

Motivators for change

In his book *Drive* Daniel Pink (2011) overturns conventional wisdom about what motivates people. Pink's argument is about the tug-of-war between intrinsic and extrinsic motivation. Intrinsic motivation refers to motivation that comes from inside an individual. The motivation comes from the pleasure that an individual gets from the task itself or from the sense of satisfaction in completing or even working on a task. An intrinsically motivated person will work on a solution to a problem because the challenge of finding a solution provides a sense of pleasure. Extrinsic motivation focuses on incentives or rewards outside of an individual. These rewards can be tangible such as money, or they can be psychological such as praise. For example, if a manager informs his or her team that the first employee to design a solution to deal with one of the company's outstanding customer complaints will be rewarded with a considerable salary increase, the team members will work on the assignment based on extrinsic motivation – the increase in salary. The basis of Pink's argument, however, is that extrinsic motivation is not as potent as managers might think, nor is it effective in changing behaviour.

Instead, Pink proposes that intrinsic motivation is the main driver for individuals and suggests that there are three key motivators:

● autonomy;

● mastery;

● purpose.

Autonomy

People like to be self-directed, with a high degree of freedom to decide the direction, methods and circumstances of their work. Job autonomy is 'the degree to which the job provides substantial freedom, independence, and discretion to the individual in scheduling the work and in determining the procedures to be used in carrying it out' (Hackman and Oldham, 1980: 79). Employees who believe that the organization gives them a high level of autonomy typically achieve a higher performance because they see themselves as directly responsible for the outcomes of their work. Conversely, employees with low levels of autonomy often become frustrated with their work and are more likely to engage in cynical behaviours such as apathy, distrust of others, suspicion and contempt (Naus, van Iterson and Roe, 2007). When employees are given autonomy, job satisfaction rises as a result of a feeling of greater responsibility for the quality of their work. For example, companies such as Best Buy – an American multichannel consumer electronics retailer – have a ROWE (results-orientated work environment) programme, where employees do not have schedules and are measured only by what they achieve. Google has a 20 per cent programme where employees are allowed to use 20 per cent of their time to work on projects that interests them. While Atlassian – an Australian technology company – gives its employees a full day every quarter to work on any software issues that are of interest to them. The benefits of such approaches are illustrated in a study of 320 small companies carried out by researchers at Cornell University. The study found that the companies that encouraged autonomy grew at quadruple the rate of those who had more rigid rules (DeVaro, 2006).

Change has, however, the potential to interfere with autonomy and make people feel that they have lost control over their job, depending on how it is managed. To encourage autonomy during change, managers and leaders need to:

● Learn about employees' needs. Each individual will have different desires over what they want to control and what is important to them.

● Create decision-making opportunities. Providing people with opportunities to be involved in making decisions about change initiatives will have a powerful impact on their emotions and how they react to change.

● Establish autonomous teams. A study carried out by Yi Liu and colleagues (2012) found that granting autonomy to teams can reduce employee turnover.

- Avoid micromanagement. Autonomy is the antithesis of micromanagement. To create an autonomous environment during change, micromanagement needs to be eliminated. Managers should focus on the goals and objectives for each employee and let them decide how they will achieve them.
- Encourage and allow those affected by the change to make decisions, get involved with the planning and take ownership of implementing it.

Mastery

People like to do things well, and to get better at doing things they value, so opportunities to grow, develop and excel at their work are intrinsically motivating.

According to Daniel Pink, mastery has three laws:

- *Law 1: mastery is a pain*
  Mastery takes hard work, effort, passion and perseverance; as well as lots of repetition and practice. Pink describes it as the 'Goldilocks Tasks', in reference to the fairy story. This means finding the sweet spot for employees. If changes are too difficult, an employee will become anxious and feel they cannot cope with it. If tasks are perceived to be too easy, employees will get bored. Tasks associated with change need to be just right. The aim is not to give people tasks that fit their exact capabilities and experience, but to give them the space and support to reach a little higher and to develop so that they can achieve continual mastery and growth. It is also important to provide the resources, responsibility and decision-making powers to meet these challenges.
- *Law 2: mastery is a mindset*
  The mastery of a task or the ability associated with a change initiative requires a particular mindset – a mindset where an individual believes that they can develop their knowledge and abilities through practice and effort.
- *Law 3: mastery is an asymptote*
  Mastery is something that is always pursued but is not necessarily an arrival point or final destination. The joy is in the pursuit rather than in the realization. However, if an individual feels that they are getting nowhere, their interest might dwindle and they might even give up. Gaining a sense of progress in their work and capabilities will contribute to an individual's inner drive and to their sense that the change is beneficial.

To help individuals to develop mastery, managers and leaders need to:

- encourage individuals and teams to continually strive to gain new knowledge, skills and abilities;
- meet regularly with employees to find out where each one is in their development and if they need any support to help them to achieve their goals;

- identify ways to collaborate with team members to give them the occasional support they may need, and to provide them with the resources that will help their growth.

Purpose

People like to feel that their work has meaning and value and they will choose to invest in activities they consider worthwhile. This is illustrated in a study carried out by Adam Grant (2013) of Wharton University. The study separated employees from a call centre at a university fund-raising organization into one of three groups at random. The employees in Group 1 read stories from other employees describing what they perceived to be the personal benefits of the call-centre job. These benefits included the development of skills, the increase of knowledge and the financial gain from the job. In Group 2 the employees read stories from those who directly benefited from the fund-raising organization and how the scholarships they had obtained had positively impacted their lives. The final group (Group 3) did not read any stories. The study found that Group 3 and the employees from Group 1, who read the stories about personal benefits, raised the same amount of money. However, those in Group 2, who had read stories about what their work accomplished and how it positively affected the world, earned more than twice the number of weekly pledges and more than twice the amount of weekly donation money. This shows the power of using purpose as a motivator. To help achieve this consider the following:

- Be mindful of using purpose-orientated words in communication about the change. Words such as 'we' and 'us' need to be used in order to create an inclusive feeling. In return, employees will start to use similar language and it will make them feel part of the change.
- Ensure that the purpose of the change is communicated clearly and effectively and that everyone affected understands the purpose and the rationale for the change.
- Ensure that everyone knows how they will contribute towards achieving the purpose of the change and what the benefits will be for them, as well as their team and the organization.

Being able to understand what motivates individuals can help in appreciating their reactions to change, whether they are positive or negative.

Resistance to change

Every manager is familiar with the employee who just will not change. Sometimes it is easy to understand why – the individual fears what the change will mean for their job, whether or not they will need to learn new skills, move to another location, of if they will even have a job. With other individuals the rationale for resisting the change can be much harder to understand. Such individuals may have the capability to change – they may even be a high performer, yet they inexplicably resist the change.

Resistance to change can be defined as 'an individual's tendency to resist and avoid making changes, to devalue change generally, and to find change aversive across diverse context and types of change' (Oreg, 2003: 680). Resistance is therefore the tendency to avoid making changes and devaluing changes. It can range from apathy to aggregation, subtle acts of non-cooperation to industrial sabotage, and from verbal protest to destruction opposition. To predict what form resistance might take, managers and leaders need to be aware of the reasons that people resist change. The following organizational factors can influence an individual's response to change:

- *The nature of change.* This includes issues such as the scale of change (incremental or transformational), the perceived purpose of it, the pace and timing at which it is implemented and whether or not it is one change or a series of changes happening sequentially.

- *The consequences of change.* For many people the consequences are based on the questions of 'How will it affect me?' or 'What's in it for me?'

- *The organizational history.* Individuals will consider the history of change within the organization. What has failed and what has been a success?

On a personal level the following factors will influence an individual's reaction to change:

- *Individual history.* The way that people have individually experienced previous change will have an effect on how they respond to further changes. Some people will enhance their confidence, strength and resilience through their experiences of change, while others will feel damaged by their experiences and have concerns about future changes.

- *Personal loss.* An individual's reaction to change is dependent upon the extent to which they see change as a threat to their personal interests and the degree of their involvement in the change process. Employees typically resist change because they see it as disruptive, intrusive, threatening to the stability and continuity of their work, and likely to lead to the loss of something that they value. This can lead to challenges such as 'What's the matter with the way things are now?' or 'I don't see any reason why we should change.' Acceptance or resistance to change is therefore based on an individual's assessment of the personal costs and benefits associated with the change.

- *Lack of control and autonomy.* Individuals will resist change when they think that their autonomy is being threatened. Employees are less likely to resist change when they think that they can freely determine the way they perform their jobs. Job autonomy enhances an individual's confidence in accepting changes to their job and their willingness to adapt to new ways of working. Research by Severin Hornung and Denise Rousseau (2007) has found that employees who believe that they have greater control over their jobs are less affected by the stress associated with organizational change and develop more positive attitudes towards change.

- *A low tolerance for change.* Organizational change can inadvertently require people to change too much, too quickly. People are often unable to change their attitudes and behaviour as rapidly as required by their organizations. Even when people intellectually understand the rationale for the change, they are sometimes emotionally unable to make the transition.

- *Lack of readiness for change.* Individuals may not be ready for change. They might need more information about the rationale for the change, more time to get used to it, more support and more training. People may also be suffering from change fatigue due to too much change or too much failed change, and just do not have the energy to focus on another one.

- *A lack of communication about the change.* If there is a lack of communication about the change and how it will affect people then they may become concerned and engage in disruptive behaviours aimed at delaying or derailing the change.

- *No involvement in the decision making about the change.* This kind of resistance occurs when people feel they should have been asked for their ideas about the change, instead of it being imposed on them.

- *Lack of capabilities.* People will resist change because they fear they will not be able to develop the new skills, knowledge and behaviour that will be required of them. This can lead to 'learning anxiety'.

Learning anxiety

There are two kinds of anxiety associated with learning – learning anxiety and survival anxiety. Learning anxiety comes from being afraid to try something new for fear that it will be too difficult, or that it will make an individual look stupid, or that they will have to stop their current ways of working. Learning anxiety can be reduced by creating a safe environment for individuals to learn new ways of working, skills and/or behaving. In contrast, survival anxiety is the realization by an individual that in order to survive in the organization they are going to have to change. According to Edgar Schein (1993) learning only happens when survival anxiety is greater than learning anxiety. Survival anxiety can be increased by threatening people with the loss of their job or rewards. However, if you want people to learn new things in order to make change successful then you need to create a safe learning environment and to inform people about the rationale and benefits for the change in a way that makes your messages credible. There will always be learning anxiety, but if an individual accepts the need to learn, then the process can be facilitated by training, coaching, support from HR, feedback, and rewards and recognition.

If you were to look down on yourself as an observer and reflect on your relationship with change over the past week, month, year or years, what do you see about yourself? Are you open, positive, curious and accepting of change, or are you negative and resistant? What makes you react in that way?

Resistance as a positive reaction

Resistance is usually perceived as a negative response, a barrier to change often manifesting itself through counterproductive behaviours. Literature about organizational change often reflects this negativity, stressing how crucial it is to overcome the problem of resistance. Resistance to change is, however, a natural occurrence and therefore the prevalent negative view of overcoming or resisting resistance needs to be reconsidered, taking into account what drives people to behave in the way that they do.

Resistance actually has positive aspects, which managers should not overlook. It can play a crucial role in drawing attention to elements of a proposed change that may actually be inappropriate, not well thought through or just wrong. Resistance to change can therefore be an opportunity to identify weaknesses in the proposed change, including the purpose, approach and suggested intervention. In support of this view, Jeffrey Ford and Laura Ford describe resistance as:

> The legitimated response of engaged and committed people who want a voice in something that is important to them. It is a sign of engagement, an opening for a dialogue about the realities of the organization and the ways managers can implement their plans and strategies in coherence with those realities. (2010: 35)

So instead of interpreting resistance as something negative, it may be more accurate for us to see it as a form of productive energy for discussing what is being proposed and to explore alternative approaches. Robert Kegan and Lisa Lahey (2001) have redefined resistance as a kind of personal immunity to change. These authors have developed the following three-stage process to help managers work out what is getting in the way of change and causing opposition to it:

1 First, managers guide employees through a series of questions, including: what would you like to see changed at work, so that you could be more effective or so that work would be more satisfying? What commitments does your complaint imply? What are you doing, or not doing, that is keeping your commitment from being more fully realized?

2 Next, managers work with employees to examine these commitments in order to determine the underlying assumptions at their core. Managers can do this by asking the following question: if you imagine doing the opposite of undermining behaviour, do you detect in yourself any discomfort, worry or vague fear?

3 The final stage involves employees starting the process of changing their behaviour. Managers can help with this by asking: by engaging in this undermining behaviour, what worrisome outcomes are you committed to preventing?

This process allows managers to see what is really going on when people oppose change. It is about understanding the complexities of people's behaviour, asking them questions to bring their competing commitments to the surface, and helping them to cope with the inner conflict that is preventing them from committing to the change. This process can also help to identify aspects of a proposed change that may actually be inappropriate, not well thought through, or just wrong. In this way, resistance can be reframed to provide benefits rather than being viewed as negative and something to ignore.

Activity

Consider your experiences of being a recipient of change in an organization:

1 How did you typically respond to these changes? What were the factors that led to those responses? To help you think through these questions consider the following:

   – What was the change and how was it introduced?

   – What was the impact on you?

   – What was your initial reaction?

   – Did your attitude change over time? If so, how and why did it change?

2 Under what circumstances have you supported a change?

3 When have you resisted a change? What made you react in this way?

4 How have your earlier experiences towards change affected your feelings about change today?

Perceptions of justice and fairness

Organizational change generates a heightened sensitivity to the fairness or justice as to how individuals are treated during the process and outcomes of change. This occurs through assessments made by individuals about what they perceive as fair or unfair. In a review of the literature on fairness Mary Konovsky points out that, 'fairness judgements are salient during times of significant organizational change' (2000: 498). Individuals evaluate the fairness of change based on the following: distributive justice; procedural justice; interpersonal justice; and informational justice (Colquitt *et al*, 2006; Saunders and Thornhill, 2003):

- *Distributive justice* refers to judgements about the degree to which the outcomes are fair. This may refer, for example, to the roles that are being made redundant, and/or to redeployment and retraining opportunities.

- *Procedural justice* is the perceptions of fairness about the formal policies and/or procedures used to decide about the change initiatives. Individuals make sense of a decision to implement change based on their perceptions of procedural justice. For instance, negative responses are more likely to occur when employees perceive that the processes leading to a decision about changes are unjust, whereas procedures that allow employees to participate during the design process of a change initiative – to allow them to air their hopes and concerns, to offer new ideas, to express their opinions and appeal against any decisions – are likely to increase their commitment to change.

- *Interpersonal justice* is the interpersonal treatment that individuals receive from managers. The way in which individuals are treated can have a significant impact on their perceptions of fairness, not only about the process of how the change is implemented but also about the moral obligations to treat everyone fairly, which underpins this process. If managers and leaders treat employees with dignity, respect, politeness and honesty there is more likely to be a positive reaction from individuals.

- *Informational justice* is based on the communication that individuals receive. Effective communication is a vital part of leading and managing people through change (as discussed in Chapter 6). Communication builds trust and can address fears and uncertainty, as well as help to develop positive attitudes and a sense of fairness among individuals.

Employees are more likely to appraise organizational change as less threatening and more favourably and when they believe that it is being handled fairly. When management supports change in ways that go beyond merely selling the need for it or its benefits by visibly caring about what is needed for it to be effective, then research shows that employees tend to perceive the fairness of change more favourably (Liu *et al*, 2012). Change-related fairness provides employees with a sense that management is trustworthy, which can help to reduce the uncertainty surrounding change. The perceived fairness between employees of how they feel that their manager treats them can impact on employment relations and, specifically, on the psychological contract that an individual has with their employer.

How change affects the psychological contract

The combined effects of changes in the business environment and the necessity for organizations to implement change, often quickly, can significantly redefine employment relationships. Consequently it will have an impact on an individual's psychological contract with the organization in which they work.

The psychological contract is defined as an individual's belief about the mutual obligations that exist in their relationship with their employer (Rousseau 1989). In the workplace the psychological contract most often refers to the perceived fairness or balance usually from the point of view of the employee between how they are treated by their employer, and the effort that the employee puts into their job. For example, in addition to providing remuneration, the employer's side of the psychological contract might also include the provision of training, job security, opportunities for promotion and a focus on work–life balance, in exchange for flexibility, effort, loyalty and commitment from an employee. Empirical evidence has found that when individuals perceive they have a balanced psychological contract with their employer they have a higher level of commitment and trust in the organization. In contrast, employees who perceive they have a negative psychological contract have been found to neglect their job duties and have higher intentions to leave an organization (Turnley and Feldman, 2000).

The importance of the psychological contract in organizational change is twofold. First, the content of the contract is informal, implicit and unwritten. Consequently, employees and employers may hold different views on the content of the contract and the degree to which the employee and employer have fulfilled their obligations. For example, in a study by Jacqueline Coyle-Shapiro and Ian Kessler (2000) it was found that managers were more positive in their assessment of the employer's fulfilment of their obligations than were the employees. Second, the concept of the psychological contract is useful when thinking about organizational change in that it forces managers to consider the balance of the contract. So if an employer wants to make changes that will affect what employees are expected to give to the organiza-tion, such as an increase in the number of working hours, by implication they should also change what they will offer to the employees to maintain a work–life balance, for example increased flexibility as to when the hours can be worked.

When planning a change, it is important to consider how the psychological contract will be affected, as alterations to the ways of working can threaten an individual's psychological contract. This can result in a loss of commitment and employee engagement, which can impact on the change achieving its benefits. Nicola Busby (2014) suggests that the following activities can help mitigate threats to the psychological contract during change:

- Communicate openly and honestly about the change as early as possible.
- Build in lots of opportunities for employees to give feedback and become involved.
- Be realistic about the impact of the change – avoid overselling the benefits and be honest about what will change.
- Changes that may involve redundancies need extra care and planning. Involve HR early on and take their advice about how to communicate and handle staff issues. If the organization has a staff consultation group or is unionized, make sure you talk to everyone you need to and keep them involved from a very early stage (the role of HR is discussed in Chapter 8).

Through creating an open working environment and effective channels of communication a manager can ensure that the expectations of both employees and the employer are clear and well articulated. The manager is then well placed to address the expectations of the employees effectively. This can help to build and maintain trust in the organization.

Activity

Think about a change initiative that you have been involved in. During the change, what happened to the psychological contract that you had with your employer?

1 What was your psychological contract?

2 In what ways did the change disrupt your contract?

3 What steps did you take to manage your way through the development of a new psychological contract?

Building trust

Trust is fundamentally a judgement of confidence in either a person or an organization. Employees who perceive their leader as being able to lead change effectively, who perceive their manager as trustworthy and supportive and who feel respected are more willing to accept and support change. In a survey carried out by the Work Foundation into what leaders themselves believe leadership to be and how they practise it, trust is identified as one of the most important aspects. Good leaders, the survey found, have trust as a personal value, but outstanding leaders understand how to use trust to create the conditions for exceptional employee engagement and performance (Tamkin *et al*, 2010).

Developing or maintaining trust within changing organizations can be challenging. Svein Johansen and Marcus Selart (2014) identify the effects of trust on the formulation and the development of change initiatives. Trust can influence the quality of those decisions. It is likely to do so in two ways: first, by increasing the amount and accuracy of information that is available. People in organizations are more likely to provide information to people they trust. Not only are they likely to be more motivated to share and discuss information, they are also more likely to contribute information through formal communication channels if they trust that the information will not be distorted, or misused.

Second, trust will also influence the process of diagnosing the need for change. As strategic issues are rarely, if ever, diagnosed by a single individual, diagnosing strategic issues usually involves pulling together information held by different people in different positions and parts of an organization, internally as well as externally. In order for an organization to detect and deal effectively with diagnosing the drivers of change, members involved in the process must be able to communicate effectively while trusting the intentions and capability of each other. On the other hand, distrust between those involved in diagnosing the need for change may cause strategic issues to remain unresolved, as those involved in the process will be wary of sharing information and taking risks. Furthermore, transformational changes expose people to risk and bring attention to conflicts of interest, with some people standing to gain from the change while others lose. Thus, organizational change may easily instil organizational members with distrust.

The implication for practice is that the importance of trust may be more distinguished by its absence. Once trust is violated, it is not easily repaired and can lead to a lack of trustworthiness.

Trustworthiness

Trustworthiness means being able to be relied on as honest or truthful. The consequence of a breach of trust is disenfranchised and disengaged employees and managers. Trust is the foundation on which employee engagement is built, and employee engagement is of critical importance to organizational change. Trust therefore plays a central role in organizational change, so leaders have a responsibility to build trust by establishing their trustworthiness.

The main attributes of trustworthiness are described by Roger Mayer and James Davis (1999) as honesty, competence, fairness, benevolence and openness:

- *Honesty*: a key element of trustworthiness is honesty, because people are unlikely to look up to or follow someone whom they perceive as dishonest or who is likely to take advantage of them.

- *Competence*: people are unlikely to listen to or depend upon someone whose abilities they do not respect. Employees need to believe that the leader or manager has the skills and abilities to carry out what he or she says they will do.

- *Fairness*: it is vital that procedures, judgements and social processes associated with the change are perceived to be fair in order that individuals feel trust towards those leading and managing change.

- *Benevolence*: this denotes the extent to which a leader or manager is believed to want to do good to another individual. Benevolence includes exploring failure and accepting errors and mistakes, knowing that people will achieve great things only if they have the support and opportunity to experiment and learn from mistakes.

- *Openness*: managers and leaders exhibiting a general openness towards their followers tend to be perceived as more trustworthy than leaders keeping their thoughts and emotions close to their chest. Employees see managers as trustworthy when they take the time to explain their decisions thoroughly.

If any of these attributes are seriously called into question, then people will become wary and reluctant to engage in any risk taking and change. Ultimately it will result in trust evaporating very quickly. Such distrust can hamper collaboration, stifle innovation, damage relations and impact on the success of sustaining the change.

When people are perceived as being honest, competent, fair, benevolent and open, they are also seen as trustworthy. If, however, the perception of trustworthiness is broken then it can be difficult to repair.

Trust repair

To repair trust effectively can be challenging and take time. Nicole Gillespie and Graham Dietz (2009) propose the following four-stage approach:

1 *Provide an immediate response.* An immediate response should be given within the first 24–72 hours of the incident occurring that caused trust to be broken. This should include: a verbal acknowledgement of the incident, with an expression of regret and

an apology; an announcement of a full investigation into what caused the distrust; and a commitment of resources to prevent a recurrence of the issue.

2 *Diagnosis of the cause of distrust.* A thorough and systematic diagnosis of the causes of the failure should be conducted. This needs to include an accurate, timely and transparent diagnosis of the issue/s.

3 *Reforming interventions.* A comprehensive and targeted series of reforming interventions should be drawn up with the aim of creating an organizational system that engenders and sustains trustworthiness. This should include a verbal apology and reparations, as appropriate, and the implementation of reforms, based on the data gathered from the diagnosis stage.

4 *Evaluation.* This should include accurate, timely and transparent regular evaluations of the process. The focus should be on evaluating what has been implemented; how successful it has been; and what else, if anything, needs to be done to improve the situation and continue to rebuild trust.

Helping people to make sense of change

Reactions to change can be influenced by what an individual stands to gain or lose personally. To help people make sense of change and how it will affect them, individuals and teams need the opportunity to express how they feel about what they will lose, keep or gain. The following exercise is useful in helping people to identify the impact of the change. Using the grid in Figure 3.3, ask individuals/teams to:

1 List all the relationships/roles/work habits/methods/systems/processes/ideas that they had before the change and will still have after the change is implemented. What will they keep?

2 List all the relationships/roles/work habits/methods/systems/processes/ideas they used to have but will not have after the change is implemented. What will they lose?

3 List all the relationships/roles/work habits/methods/systems/processes/ideas they did not have before but now have. What will they gain?

4 Finally, ask individuals to identify what the benefits of the change will be to them personally and to their team/department.

This exercise can be helpful in sorting fact from fiction and helping individuals to identify the positive aspects of change, especially what they will be gaining from it.

FIGURE 3.3   Lose/keep/gain grid

What I/we will *keep* as a result of the change	What I/we will *lose* when the change is implemented	What I/we will *gain* as a result of the change	What the **benefits** of the change will be to us/me

Summary

Transition is a personal process. Individuals and teams will react very differently to change for different reasons and will vary in how quickly or slowly they will let go of the past and move to commit and adapt to the change. Reactions can range from openly embracing change to actively resisting it by attempting to undermine it. Ultimately, how people react will impact on the success of the change. Negative employee reactions can severely impede the realization of the intended benefits of change, whereas positive reactions can help to successfully embed and sustain the change.

It is therefore essential for leaders and managers to understand and appreciate employees' reactions to change in order to manage and lead people through change more effectively. When individuals demonstrate symptoms of resistance it is important to distinguish between the symptoms of resistance and the causes behind it. It may be tempting to resort to questionable techniques to overcome resistance, such as manipulation and coercion. These practices result in distrust, making change more difficult to implement.

Trust is vital for sustaining change through people. It is built up incrementally and accumulated over time but it can also be ruined in a minute. Trust also impacts on the psychological contract that an individual has with their employer. Organizations that have positive psychological contracts with their staff are rewarded with high levels of employee commitment, which normally translates into a positive impact on performance. If the psychological contract is broken, it can create a negative impact on job satisfaction, commitment, engagement and, ultimately, performance. So appreciating how individuals seek to steer, resist and make sense of change in different ways is imperative to leading and managing people effectively through change.

Implications for managers and leaders

From this chapter there are some key practical implications for managers and leaders in how individuals make sense of change:

- *What motivates you does not motivate most of your employees*
  There are various types of change stories consistently told in
  organizations. One is the 'good to great' story, which may be
  something along the lines of: 'Our position in the market has been
  eroded by intense competition and changing customer needs. If we
  change, we can regain our leadership position.' Another is the
  turnaround story, such as: 'We are performing below industry/sector
  standard and must change significantly to survive'; or 'We can
  become a top-quartile performer by exploiting our current assets and
  earning the right to grow.' These stories seem intuitively rational, yet
  they too often fail to have the impact that leaders desire. What
  leaders care about does not always tap into employees' primary
  motivators for putting extra energy into change programmes. You
  therefore need to be able to tell a change story that includes the
  things that motivate employees.

- *Monitor employee reactions*
  To determine which aspects of the changes are problematic or
  threatening it is important to monitor how people react. It is also
  important at different stages during change and transformation to
  assess individuals' reactions to change (positive and negative), since
  as change progresses individuals' reactions may fluctuate.

- *Address the reason for cynical attitudes*
  Managing cynicism about organizational change involves providing
  timely, appropriate and credible information. Cynicism can be
  minimized by admitting mistakes when they occur, apologizing and
  quickly taking appropriate corrective action. Two-way dialogue,
  whereby managers become aware of employee perceptions of change
  and their feelings about it, is critical to success.

- *Types of resistance*
  It is often difficult to determine the real reason why people resent or
  resist change. It may appear as if the individuals are just being
  stubborn or selfish, when the real reason may be entirely different
  and even fully justified. Assessing which of the many possible reasons
  there are for people resisting change will help to select the most
  appropriate way to overcome opposition to change. Table 3.1 illustrates
  the types of resistance, the symptoms and how to deal with them.

- *Embrace resistance*
  Change is resisted because it can hurt. When new technologies displace
  old ones, jobs can be lost, prices can be cut and investments can be
  wiped out. Although it is not always possible to make people feel
  comfortable with change, the discomfort can be minimized. Take the
  time before the launch of a change to assess systematically who might
  resist the change, for what reasons, and how this might be dealt with.
    Resistance should be considered as a form of feedback, often
  provided by people who know more about the day-to-day operations

TABLE 3.1 Resistance and how to deal with it

Types of Resistance	Symptoms	How to Deal with it
Unhappiness	Lots of concerns raised very publicly and vocally about people being unhappy with the change	Speak with people one-to-one to find out what is making them unhappy
		Work with people to identify any benefits there may be for them from the change
		Listen and empathize with their feedback
		Work with individuals to identify solutions to the issues they have raised
Disengagement	Lack of attendance at meetings, training events and so on	Identify the reasons for the disengagement
	Lack of participation in meetings and discussion about the change	Arrange one-to-one meetings to discuss issues
	Agreeing to proposals without questioning them	Involve people where possible, such as with pilot programmes and design sessions
Sabotage	People bring their own agenda to meetings and training events, and vocalize their agenda.	Discuss issues with the individuals concerned
	People attempt to destroy systems and processes	Give people responsibility for aspects of the change and closely monitor their performance
	Individuals spread negative rumours about the change	

SOURCE: Adapted from Busby (2014)

than managers do. It can be turned into a constructive conversation that can positively help the change initiatives. Planning and implementing change can be made smarter, faster and even cheaper by listening to the feedback embedded in resistance. If resistance is embraced, it can be used as a resource for finding a better solution. All sources of resistance to change need to be acknowledged and people's emotions validated. To assist with this, consider using information-based interventions and counselling interventions. Information-based interventions provide the individual with information to create awareness and understanding of why they are reacting in a changing environment. Information-based interventions ideally need to be supported by counselling interventions. Counselling interventions focus on activities designed to assist individuals, both singularly and collectively as a team, to analyse, interpret and understand how their own defence mechanisms influence their perceptions and motivations towards change. Such intervention strategies can help individuals to identify and interpret their own perceptions of change, thus creating greater personal awareness and understanding.

- *The process and the outcome have got to be fair*
  Proactively focusing on employees' perceptions of fairness can increase the probability of effectively implementing change. For instance, involving employees in the change process and treating them with respect and consideration can enhance employees' perceptions of fairness and thus reduce negative reactions and withdrawal.

- *Be aware of how change might impact on the psychological contract*
  Managers need to consider the nature of the psychological contract that the organization has with employees and how the changes they are introducing might alter its balance. Crucially, if the balance is altered, managers need to consider how to rebalance it if they want to avoid resistance that could undermine the process.

- *Build and maintain trust*
  Foster trust among employees by encouraging open dialogue (see Chapter 6) with emphasis on feedback, accurate information, adequate explanation of decisions, and open exchange of thoughts and ideas. Help people to answer the question 'why' and put it into context. People who have concerns about organizational change will need to hear messages that address their fears. For example, people need evidence that those leading the change are pursuing a consistent, well-thought-out strategy and really know what they are doing. People will also need reassurance that their jobs are not in jeopardy or that they will receive the training and/or development and the support they need to adjust to the changes. Providing details about the how and the why of job security, training and development interventions and support can make reassurances more believable. Trust can be built by being honest, open, benevolent and fair.

References

Bridges, W (2004) *Managing Transitions: Making the most of change*, 3rd edn, Nicholas Brealey Publishing, New York

Busby, N (2014) Change readiness, planning and measurement, in *The Effective Change Manager's Handbook*, ed R Smith, D King, R Sidhu and D Skelsey, pp 290–328, Kogan Page, London

Colquitt, J A, Scott, B A, Judge, T A and Shaw, J C (2006) Justice and personality: using integrative theories to derive moderators of justice effects, *Organizational Behavior and Human Decision Processes*, **100** (1), pp 110–27

Coyle-Shapiro, J and Kessler, I (2000) Consequences of the psychological contract for the employment relationship: a large scale survey, *Journal of Management Studies*, **37** (7), pp 903–30

DeVaro, J (2006) Teams, autonomy, and the financial performance of firms, *Industrial Relations: A journal of economy and society*, **45** (2), pp 217–69

Ford, J D and Ford, L W (2010) Stop blaming resistance to change and start using it, *Organizational Dynamics*, **39** (1), pp 24–36

Gillespie, N and Dietz, G (2009) Trust repair after an organization-level failure, *Academy of Management Review*, **34** (1), pp 127–45

Grant, A (2013) *Give and Take: A revolutionary approach to success*, Viking, London

Hackman, J R and Oldham, G R (1980) *Work Redesign*, Addison-Wesley, Massachusetts

Herscovitch, L and Meyer, J P (2002) Commitment to organizational change: extension of a three-component model, *Journal of Applied Psychology*, **87**, pp 474–87

Hodges, J and Gill, R (2015) *Sustaining Change in Organizations*, Sage, London

Hornung, S and Rousseau, D M (2007) Active on the job – proactive in change: how autonomy at work contributes to employee support for organizational change, *The Journal of Applied Behavioral Science*, **43** (4), pp 401–26

Isabella, L A (1990) Evolving interpretations as a change unfolds: how managers construe key organizational events, *Academy of Management Journal*, **33** (1), pp 7–41

Johansen, S T and Selart, M (2014) Expanding the role of trust in the management of organizational change, *New Perspectives on Organizational Change and Learning*, Bergen: Fagbokforlaget, pp 259–80

Kegan, R and Lahey, L L (2001) The real reason people won't change, *Harvard Business Review*, November, pp 85–92

Konovsky, M A (2000) Understanding procedural justice and its impact on business organizations, *Journal of Management*, **26**, pp 489–511

Kübler-Ross, E (1973) *On Death and Dying*, Tavistock, London

Linden, R (2012) [accessed 16 October 2015] Taking the Fear Out of Change, *Governing*, November [Online] http://www.governing.com/columns/mgmt-insights/col-power-of-habit-taking-fear-out-of-change.html

Liu, Y, Caldwell, S, Fedor, D B and Herold, D M (2012) When does management's support for a change translate to perceptions of fair treatment? The moderating roles of change attribution and conscientiousness, *The Journal of Applied Behavioral Science*, **48** (4), pp 441–62

Mayer, R C and Davis, J H (1999) The effect of performance appraisal on trust for management, *Journal of Applied Psychology*, **84** (1), pp 123–40

Naus, F, van Iterson, A and Roe, R (2007) Organizational cynicism: extending the exit, voice, loyalty, and neglect model of employees' responses to adverse conditions in the workplace, *Human Relations*, 60 (5), pp 683–718

Oreg, S (2003) Resistance to change: developing an individual differences measure, *Journal of Applied Psychology*, 88 (4), pp 680–93

Pink, D (2011) *Drive*, Canongate, London

Porter, l W and Lawler, E (1968) *Managerial Attitudes and Performance*, Homewood, Illinois

Rousseau, D M (1989) Psychological and implied contracts in organizations, *Employee Responsibilities and Rights Journal*, 2 (2), pp 121–39

Rubin, R, Dierdorff, E, Bommer, W H and Baldwin, T T (2009) Do leaders reap what they sow? Leader and employee outcomes of leader organizational cynicism about change, *The Leadership Quarterly*, 20, pp 680–88

Saunders, M N and Thornhill, A (2003) Organisational justice, trust and the management of change: an exploration, *Personnel Review*, 32 (3), pp 360–75

Schein, E H (1993) How can organizations learn faster? The challenge of entering the green room, *Sloan Management Review*, 34 (2), pp 85–92

Tamkin, P, Pearson, G, Hirsch, W and Constable, S (2010) *Exceeding Expectation: The principles of outstanding leadership*, The Work Foundation, London

Tosti, D T and Amarant, J (2005) Energy investment beyond competence, *Performance Improvement*, 44, pp 17–22

Turnley, W H and Feldman, D C (2000) Re-examining the effects of psychological contract violations: unmet expectations and job dissatisfaction as mediators, *Journal of Organizational Behavior*, 21 (1), pp 25–42

Vroom, V H (1964) *Work and Motivation*, Wiley, New York

Zien, K A and Buckler, A (2004) Dreams to market: crafting a culture of innovation, in *The Human Side of Managing Technological Innovation*, ed R Katz, Oxford University Press, New York

Further reading

Cameron, E and Green, M (2012) *Making Sense of Change Management: A complete guide to the models, tools and techniques of organizational change*, Kogan Page, London

Helms-Mills, J (2003) *Making Sense of Organizational Change*, Routledge, London

Wilcox, M and Jenkins, M (2015) *Engaging Change*, Kogan Page, London

PART THREE
The role of leaders and managers

04
Leading people through change

KEY POINTS

- Management and leadership are both needed for organizational change, although they have different roles to play. Leadership produces change, transformation and disruption, while management produces order and consistency.
- Leading change is complex and involves multiple forms of leadership engaged in different approaches, behaviours and activities.
- To enable change, leaders need to create a sense of purpose, provide sponsorship, build commitment and collaboration, and provide enthusiasm and energy.
- Commitment is an important enabler of change. Irrespective of how brilliant a vision may be, if employees do not buy into it then very little will change. One way to build commitment is to create an environment in which the people most affected by change have a role in shaping it.
- Innovation is important for change. Innovation is the means, at all levels of the organization, to translate the purpose and the vision that the leader has articulated into tangible business outcomes.
- Leaders need to take actions that role model the desired behavioural change and influence others to do the same.
- To understand how to lead people effectively through change, leaders need to understand the politics and power that sit at the heart of the change agenda.
- A people-centred approach to leadership involves motivating others to change, connecting with the disconnected and developing emotional ties.

Introduction

Leading 'transformational' or 'everyday incremental' change is different, not just in terms of their objectives but also in terms of their processes, size, scope and breadth. Transformations are much more disruptive to what people do and the way they work, and tend to reflect major shifts externally in the environment and internally in the organization, while incremental change happens more frequently and is more focused on fine-tuning processes, systems, policies and so on. Whether change is transformational or incremental it still demands leadership in order to make it successful.

The purpose of this chapter is to explore the leadership of people during change, while Chapter 5 focuses on the management of people through change. While change must be managed, change also requires effective leadership, whether the change is transformational or incremental. This chapter considers contemporary leadership research, theory and practice that has illuminated the quest for leading change and transformation successfully. Some of the conceptual models, frameworks, tools and beliefs that affect the ability to successfully lead change are also examined. The chapter begins by exploring the difference between change management and change leadership. The leadership characteristics needed to motivate and lead people through change are highlighted. This is followed by a review of some of the challenges faced when leading change, as well as how to address them. The influence of power and politics on change is then discussed, including the impact on leaders. The chapter introduces the concept of people-centred leadership and how this can be effective during change and transformations. The chapter concludes by outlining the implications for leaders of the key issues discussed and recommends approaches to motivate and lead others to change. Key questions are addressed such as: what is the difference between managing and leading change? What is the role of leaders in the change process? What are the implications of different leadership styles for organizational change? What are the different leadership enablers of change? How can leaders engage people in transformations? What is the impact of power and politics on change? And what do leaders need to do to nurture people through transition once transformation is on its way?

LEARNING OUTCOMES

By the end of this chapter you will be able to:

- appreciate how the nature of leadership can help to achieve change and transformation in organizations;
- distinguish between leading and managing change;
- identify and address the challenges that leaders face in gaining commitment from people to change;
- consider how to use a people-centred leadership approach;
- apply techniques for leading people through transition and transformation.

Change management or change leadership

Management and leadership are both needed for organizational change, and although they have different roles to play they are also similar in many ways. Leadership involves influence, as does management. Leadership entails working with people, which management also involves. Leadership is concerned with the effective achievement of goals, as is management. But leadership is also different from management. Leadership produces change, transformation and disruption, while management produces order and consistency. Raymond Caldwell highlights the differences between the roles of leader and manager:

> Leaders... envision, initiate or sponsor strategic change of a far-reaching or transformational nature. In contrast, managers... carry forward and build support for change within business units and key functions. (2003: 291)

The difference in the roles is defined further by Anne Stoughton and James Ludema (2012) who say that leaders provide a framework for change by communicating their commitment to it, adopting reporting systems and prioritizing issues for attention, while managers adopt the new ways of thinking and behaving to translate the organization's vision for change into action. Afsaneh Nahavandi agrees with this distinction and emphasizes the difference in long- and short-term approaches of leaders and managers:

> Whereas leaders have long-term and future-orientated perspectives and provide a vision for followers that looks beyond their immediate surroundings, managers have short-term perspectives and focus on routine issues within their own immediate departments and groups. (2000: 13)

The assumption in such definitions is that leadership is about creating a vision for change, while management is about translating the vision into agendas and actions. Although there are differences between leadership and management, the two constructs do overlap. Both are needed to ensure that people are engaged and committed to change, in order to effectively embed it in an organization. Leadership, however, is needed in order to successfully introduce and sustain change. For while organizational change must be well managed, it must, first and foremost, also be well led.

Discussion questions

What are the differences between change leadership and change management?

What roles do leaders play in contrast to managers in the organization in which you work, or one you are familiar with?

What role do you play and why?

The transformation of leadership

What leadership means within the context of organizational change

Leadership has been defined and conceptualized in many different ways. Researchers tend to define it according to their individual perspectives and the aspect of leadership that is of most interest to them. This means that there is no universally agreed definition of leadership. Of the many definitions on offer Peter Northouse suggests the following, which is probably the most comprehensive and succinct within the context of organizational change: 'Leadership is a process whereby an individual influences a group of individuals to achieve a common goal' (2012: 9). This is similar to Gary Yukl's definition of leadership as 'the process of influencing others to understand and agree what needs to be done and how to do it, and the process of facilitating individual and collective efforts to accomplish shared objectives' (2006: 8). Such definitions suggest several components central to leadership, including: 1) leadership is a process; 2) leadership involves influencing others; 3) leadership happens within the context of a group or team; 4) leadership involves achieving goals; and 5) these goals are shared by leaders and individuals. The very act of defining leadership as a process suggests that leadership is not a characteristic or trait with which only a few certain people are endowed at birth, but instead something that can be developed. It is the process that translates into acts. It is in his or her acts of leadership that the leader exists.

Viewing leadership as a process stresses that it is a two-way, interactive event between leaders and individuals rather than a linear, one-way event in which the leader affects individuals only. It means that leaders affect and are affected by their employees either positively or negatively. More importantly, it means that leadership is not restricted to just one person in a team, department or organization who has positional power, usually the formally appointed leader. Instead it makes it available to people throughout the organization.

Theoretical perspectives on leadership

In the leadership literature there are several different perspectives and lenses from which leadership is viewed. Many textbooks offer a chronological account of the theory of leadership and how it has evolved since the 'Great Man' theory popularized by Thomas Carlyle in the 1840s. Traditionally leadership research is primarily based on classic bi-factorial models such as tasks and relationships. This focus has moved to paradigms such as charismatic leadership and visionary leadership. In the context of change, transformational leadership has always been a popular approach, espoused in the literature.

Transformational leadership concerns transforming the way that people feel about themselves and what is possible and raising their motivation to new highs, resulting in performance beyond previous expectations (Bass and Riggio, 2006). In the context of organizational change, transformational leaders personalize a vision and work closely with employees to make it a reality. This interpersonal bridge building allows employees to understand better the changes required in their work routines and practices, and it provides assurance that managers are likely to support changes as they are incorporated. In a *McKinsey Quarterly* article, Boaz and Fox (2014) describe the impact of the transformational style of Geoff McDonough, the CEO of Sobi – an emerging pioneer in the treatment of rare diseases. McDonough developed a vision for the clinical and business impact of Sobi's biological development programme in neonatology. He saw the possibility of improving the neurodevelopment of tiny, vulnerable newborn babies and therefore of giving them a real chance at a healthy life. McDonough built bridges between Sobi's siloed legacy companies. He focused on the people who mattered most to everyone – the patients – and promoted internal talent from both companies, demonstrating his belief that everyone could be part of the new 'one Sobi'. He also recruited key players from outside the organization to the management team, restructured the organization and created an entirely new business model. McDonough's leadership helped to successfully integrate two legacy companies and increase market capitalization from US $600 million in 2011 to $3.5 billion in 2015.

Despite the evident benefits of transformational leadership, such as that demonstrated by McDonough and others, it is not without its limitations. Joseph Nye Jr, a political scientist and former dean of the John F Kennedy School of Government at Harvard University, advises caution in extolling the virtues of transformational leadership. In his analysis of the leadership styles of US presidents in relation to transformational and incremental change, he says:

> Theoretical expectations that transformational leaders make all the difference and incremental/transactional leaders are simply routine managers greatly mis-states the roles of leaders. Exaggerating the importance of transformational leadership is not necessarily the best way to understand... leadership needs in the 21st century. (Nye, 2014: 124)

In support of this view Hendrik Hüttermann and Sabine Boerner (2011) advise against blind enthusiasm for transformational leadership. They argue that 'the role of transformational leadership in fostering the innovativeness of cross-functional (diverse) teams is ambiguous' (2011: 833). Hüttermann and Boerner suggest that although it may help to prevent relationship problems that impede innovation it may also encourage excessive dependency on the leader in resolving problems. Their sensible suggestion to deal with this is for people to be supported in basing their self-confidence and self-efficacy on their own skills and competencies rather than on those of their leader.

Leading change is complex and rather than depending on one style, such as transformational leadership, it needs to involve multiple forms of leadership engaged in different approaches, behaviours and activities, depending on the context of the organization.

Leadership philosophies

Depending on the type and scale of change, different styles of leadership may be appropriate. In my book on leadership co-authored with Brian Howieson, entitled *Public and Third Sector Leadership: Experience speaks* (Howieson and Hodges, 2014), we adopt the lens of the leadership philosophy. We identify the most prevalent leadership philosophies as: *adaptive, authentic, distributed, ethical, servant* and *shared* leadership. Each of these philosophies is briefly described below within the context of organizational change and transformation:

- *Adaptive*
  Adaptive leadership recognizes that there are basically two kinds of problems that people confuse when trying to find solutions. First, there are technical problems where an adequate response has been developed; there are one or more experts with general credibility and there is an established procedure to follow. The second kind of problems are adaptive problems where there are no set procedures, no recognized experts and no adequate responses developed. The definition of the problem is not clear cut and technical fixes are unavailable. This calls for adaptive leadership where the leader does not have the answers. Instead, the leader has to bring people together to find new solutions that will succeed (Heifetz and Laurie, 1997). Within the context of organizational change and transformation, adaptive leadership is an emergent process that occurs when people with different knowledge, beliefs and preferences interact in an attempt to address drivers for change and solve issues. The result of this emergent process is the production of creative ideas and an adaptive resolution to an external or internal threat or opportunity.

- *Authentic*
  Authentic leadership emphasizes the importance of consistency in a leader's words, actions and values. Gary Yukl (2006) suggests that authentic leaders have positive core values such as honesty, altruism, kindness, fairness, accountability and optimism. These core values motivate leaders during times of change to do what is right and fair for people, and to create a special type of relationship that includes high mutual trust and transparency, including open and honest communication and an emphasis on the welfare and development of individuals.

- *Distributed*
  Distributed leadership is based on the idea that the leadership of an organization should not rest with a single individual, but should be shared or 'distributed' among those with the relevant skills

(Gronn, 2000). A distributed leadership perspective recognizes that there are multiple leaders and that leadership activities are widely shared within and between organizations. It focuses upon the interactions, rather than the actions, of those in formal and informal leadership roles and is primarily concerned with leadership practice and how leadership influences organizational and instructional improvement (Spillane, 2006). Distributed leadership is about connecting people across the organization (Aitken, 2010). It acknowledges that change in organizations can be led from the top, the middle or the bottom and that it is the work of all individuals who contribute to leadership practice, whether or not they are formally designated or defined as leaders.

- *Ethical*
  The Centre for Ethical Leadership at the University of Texas in Austin (**www.utexas.edu/lbj/research/leadership**) defines ethical leadership as knowing your core values and having the courage to live them in all parts of your life in service of the common good. Peter Northouse (2012) offers five principles of ethical leadership – respect for others, service to others, the importance of fairness and justice, honesty, and the building of community in our practice – the origins of which can be traced back to Aristotle. Although not inclusive, these principles provide a foundation for the development of sound ethical leadership during times of change and transformation in organizations.

- *Servant*
  Servant leadership is leadership that reflects the desire to serve the needs and interests of individuals. Larry Spears (2002) identifies 10 characteristics that are central to the development of servant leadership: listening; empathy; healing; awareness; persuasion; conceptualization; foresight; stewardship; commitment to the growth of people; and building community. Servant leadership is unique when compared to other styles of leadership. The idea that a leader should serve others is a paradoxical concept that confuses many people. Even so, when trying to produce change, servant leadership is an effective way to motivate individuals. Its unique emphasis on the concern for people's well-being can help to create commitment to change.

- *Shared*
  Shared leadership is a process of influence that is built upon more than just downward influence on individuals by an appointed leader. Within the context of change and transformation, shared leadership is the sharing of power and influence among a group of individuals rather than centralizing it in the hands of a single person.

Such leadership philosophies focus on what kind of leadership should be offered and contain value-based ideas of how a leader should be and act, and the sources of a leader's power. A philosophy 'provides us with far more and deeper references to society, politics and civilization than models or styles' (Howieson and Hodges, 2014: 245). These philosophies seem extremely pertinent following decades of corporate scandals where the behaviour, role and impact of so-called transformational leaders have been severely questioned (Hodges, 2011). In its place must come more transparent, authentic and peer-based ways of leading. As Linda Gratton says in her book *The Key* (2014), we are truly in the midst of a transition from the old order to a new, emerging order. The old order was signalled by powerful leadership, supported by legions of PR-speak, and followed by employees prepared to engage in a parent–child relationship. What is coming is a new order where the hierarchies are becoming dismantled and followers are becoming more demanding.

This transition is by no means complete. We are in a time of debate and exploration where new leadership role models are emerging, which may be more pertinent to change than the traditional transformational leadership approach.

Activity

From your experience, identify one person you consider to be/or have been a leader of a successful change or transformation. How would you describe their leadership philosophy? How did this person's leadership influence the change effort?

Leadership enablers of change

The key to successful change is not only the right philosophy of leadership but also the right approach and attitude. Bad attitudes can hinder the leadership of change. John McGuire (2012) characterizes these as:

- *'Just let George do it'*: waiting for somebody else to do what needs to be done, to show the way, to make a decision.
- *'Yes, but...'*: agreeing to lead change but wanting to control it.
- *'Either/or'*: a lack of time to deal both with difficult people issues and with pressing operational matters at the same time.
- *'Are we there yet?'*: being impatient to complete the change.

Leading people effectively through change means having a positive approach and attitude, along with a sense of purpose, sense building, commitment, innovation, sponsorship, collaboration and energy. Each of these critical leadership enablers of change is discussed below.

Sense of purpose

Leaders must be able to inspire confidence in others. They must create a sense of purpose and embody the vision for change in order to help those around them to deliver the change. Leaders must define a sense of purpose that carries meaning for the organization and the people who contribute to its growth. This sense of purpose is like a guide who takes a group of people on an expedition across complex and difficult paths. It must be embodied by the leaders embarking on the trail and by the people who follow along with them. The expedition will succeed if the relationships that are built between members of the group are strong, trustworthy and focused on a shared goal, in spite of and thanks to the changes and differences embodied by each member.

The purpose is the shared direction that people are moving towards. It tells people why they should change. The need to co-create and articulate the purpose and a vision of change is a key enabler of change. Whenever possible the purpose of change should be co-created by not just one person but by a group of people who will be involved in driving the change forward. The chief executive of the UK's national grid, Steve Holliday, says that building a common purpose helps to shift the things you want to shift without any question and that: 'To move the whole organization in one direction, you go on and on communicating that message and enthusing people, and explaining why that's the right thing to do' (Prevett, 2013).

The elements that are required for a purpose to be successful include: clarity, connection, goals, stories and passion.

Clarity

Clarity is one aspect that all leaders must strive to attain in all areas of communication if they want to have any type of success. If the purpose is not clear then the people will not be clear. People need to understand what is being proposed and how it will affect them. Statements of the overall purpose also need to be short enough to be remembered. Sandvik Materials Technology, a Swedish producer of advanced alloys and ceramic materials, captured the purpose of its transformation as becoming 'the Toyota of the metals industry' (Isern and Pung, 2007).

Connection

Connection of the purpose refers to its ties to the past and the present. Although the purpose is primarily set in the future, how it is related to the history of an organization can validate those people who have worked hard and sacrificed to build what already exists.

Goals

The purpose of the change determines its *goals*. Establishing goals is a key ingredient to communicating a strong purpose. The goals should be SMART (specific, measurable, agreed, realistic and timebound). Communicating the purpose and goals of the change means being open about any challenges. One way that this can be done is through stories.

Stories

Stories are a helpful part of communicating the vision and purpose. Stories of those involved in the process of making the purpose happen, or stories of people who have accomplished similar tasks, makes the purpose seem real and achievable. It can make the purpose come to life and help gain the assistance of those still on the fence. When a leader's version of the transformation story is clear, success comes from taking it to employees, encouraging debate about it, reinforcing it and prompting people to infuse it with their own personal meaning. Leaders need to invest great effort in visibly and vocally presenting the transformation story. One of the most important and hardest parts of transformation is to convince people of the need for it. The CEO of the State Bank of India, Om Prakash Bhatt, emphasizes the importance of this. When the bank was floundering, he says that, 'no one ever told executives the real state of the company', so they did not see the need for change (Malone, 2009). By explaining the truth to them, Bhatt laid a foundation for a fundamental transformation.

The story's ultimate impact will depend on not just having compelling answers to questions but also the leader's willingness and ability to make things personal, to engage other people openly and to spotlight successes as they emerge. Leaders who take time to personalize the story of the transformation can unlock significantly more energy for it than those who dutifully present a set of PowerPoint slides that their working teams created for them. Personalizing the story forces CEOs to consider and share with others the answers to such questions as: why are we changing? How will we get there? What will be different? How does this relate to me? Leaders need to include experiences and anecdotes from their own lives in order to underline their determination and belief, and to demonstrate that obstacles can be overcome.

Once the story is out, the leader's role becomes one of constant reinforcement. As Procter & Gamble (P&G) CEO Alan G Lafley says, 'excruciating repetition and clarity are important, employees have so many things going on in the operation of their daily business that they don't always take the time to stop, think and internalize' (Aitken and Keller, 2007). Leaders have to help people to internalize the need for change and what it will mean. This needs to be done with passion.

Passion

Passion is the motor behind the vehicle of the purpose. The passion that leaders have and demonstrate for the purpose of the change can help to inspire and motivate individuals to trust and willingly engage in the change. Carolyn Aitken and Scott Keller (2007) describe how as part of his change story Klaus Zumwinkel, the chairman and CEO of Deutsche Post, talked about his passion for mountain climbing, linking the experience of that sport – and the effort it requires – to the company's transformation journey.

It is important for any potential change and transformation that leaders make sure that their passion matches their aspiration. This can be done by leaders asking themselves questions such as:

- How strongly do I feel about the need for this change?
- What convinces me that it can be accomplished?
- Can I convey enthusiasm about the change when I talk about it?
- How committed am I to lead this through to completion?
- What sacrifices am I willing to make to ensure that the change is implemented and sustained successfully?
- How will I continue to motivate people to make the relevant changes?

Passion displayed by leaders can be contagious and can spread throughout an entire organization.

In sum, a sense of purpose about the change needs to have clarity, connection, goals and passion. This can help to make and build sense of the change.

Sense building

Leading people through change means distinguishing between sense-making and sense-building activities. Sense making, as Karl Weick (1988: 2012) explains, is the process whereby people give meaning to experience. It is a retrospective process that uses evidence from past events to construct a storyline that makes sense in the present. Sense building, on the other hand, contains a notion of construction and looks to the future. Valerie Gauthier (2014) points out that the process of sense building involves setting a goal by connecting the sources of knowledge, including sensory data. Leaders need to build sense for people in times of change, as Gauthier says:

> Dealing with the uncertainty and complexity requires an ability to make sense of our environment retrospectively. When building sense for an organization, the complex interactions between different entities must be carefully addressed in a co-ordinated and collaborative setting. (2014: 50)

The challenge for leaders is to get a handle on the sheer complexity of change. Issues do not always present themselves with black-and-white solutions, nor are they always amenable to rational and overly logical thinking. Instead they come as complex, interrelated sets of factors in which action in one sphere is likely to lead to unintended consequences in another. Leaders must be able to make sense of the complexity of change in order to gain commitment to it.

Commitment

Although leaders envision and drive change, success is largely contingent on the commitment and engagement from people involved in the process.

Employees are the ones responsible for behaving in ways conducive to proposed change and often have to learn new ways of doing things. Commitment to change is therefore an important enabler of change. Irrespective of how brilliant the purpose may be, if employees do not buy into it then very little will change. One way to build commitment is to create an environment in which the people most affected by change have a role in shaping it. Such involvement was carried out by the Indian manufacturer Larsen & Toubro, which managed to include 7,000 employees in defining the purpose for a company-wide organizational change.

It is not only the people who will be affected by the change or transformation who need to be committed to it – leaders themselves also need to be committed to the change and retain their commitment until the change is embedded. The Moorhouse Consultancy (2014), in their Barometer on Change, found that almost half (47 per cent) of senior leaders are not committed at all or, at most, only partially committed to change initiatives. This can lead to the boomerang effect, where initial changes start to fade when leaders lose interest or stop paying attention to a change initiative. This is a worry, as commitment from leaders is critical to making change a success.

A lack of commitment from leaders can be shown by: their lack of acceptance of ownership and responsibility for the change initiative; a lack of eagerness to be involved; an unwillingness to invest in resources; a reluctance to take tough decisions when required; a lack of awareness of the impact of their own behaviour; inconsistent messages; and failing to hold regular reviews to discuss progress. Change efforts that lack commitment from leaders can result in a lack of dedicated effort, conflict and resistance to change from others in the organization.

Leaders need to stay engaged during the transformation. When leaders disengage from the process, withdraw their support or declare victory too early and refocus their attention on other priorities this can result in employees, at all levels, reverting back to old ways of working and behaving. Leaders need to ensure that the change takes root and the benefits are realized. Such commitment involves effective and tenacious sponsorship.

Sponsorship

Leaders need to provide active and visible sponsorship of transformational programmes. This needs to be done not only at the start of a transformation but throughout its implementation until it becomes a sustainable part of how the organization operates. Richard Smith (2015) suggests a number of key activities that make a sponsor effective, including:

- maintaining and articulating a clear and attractive vision for the change, showing how it links to the organization's strategy;
- gaining the commitment and involvement of senior and line management, using influence and interactions to advocate the project consistently;

- championing the change, building and maintaining a sense of urgency and priority for it;

- confronting those who are blocking the change and clearing a path for it to succeed;

- genuinely acting as a role model for new behaviours;

- communicating about the change consistently, using a variety of media;

- training, mentoring and coaching management and remaining accessible to them throughout;

- ensuring that resources are provided for the change, especially people and training;

- aligning the organization's infrastructure, environment and reward systems with the change initiative, especially the way that performance is measured and managed;

- engaging in ongoing alignment of the particular initiative with other organizational initiatives and with the organization's wider strategic goals.

Such activities are visible signs of ongoing sponsorship from leaders and can help to build collaboration for the change.

Collaboration

Collaboration is a key enabler of leading organizational transformations. Leaders need to actively build the collective capacity for change by establishing strong collaboration across the organization. Companies that do this include, for example, Morning Star and Infosys.

Morning Star is a California-based tomato-processing company. The company has developed a number of instruments and procedures for collaboration, including the Colleague Letter of Understanding (CLOU). Every Morning Star employee has to produce such CLOU, which outlines how they will achieve their performance objectives, as well as the personal mission statement that everyone is involved in writing (Hamel, 2011).

A collaborative process, such as CLOU, can be used to bring employees together to discuss and to make decisions about the collective future of the company. This kind of high-involvement collaborative process has been used by several other companies, including: Southern New England Telephone, to prepare for deregulation and the emergence of competition; Jackson Hole Ski Resort, to reconsider their strategic direction; and the Seaport Hotel and World Trade Center, when they opened under new management (Stoner, 2013).

Similarly, the Indian information technology company Infosys has created a global network that enables thousands of employees across 33 countries to have their voices heard, to exchange solutions to problems, and to have their own innovative ideas addressed. This 'wise crowd' has created a fast and continuous flow of information from around the world with rapid feedback loops. It has also created a collaborative network of change champions. The benefits of such collaboration are outlined by Nupur Singh, head of the HR function in Europe at the Tata Group's Consultancy Services:

> We encourage collaboration by encouraging a leadership style that is not about micromanaging. We want people to trust each other. So we encourage leaders to define the end results, the accountability and their responsibility. A leader defines the vision, sets the boundary but does not control the outcome phase, and creates freedom within the boundary. (cited in Gratton, 2014: 66)

Fostering such collaboration empowers individuals so that they can participate effectively in change and transformation. When people engage in a shared task, and know what they and others are responsible for, then the whole task runs more smoothly and builds a stronger degree of trust. So building collaboration is vital, even when people are working virtually and across geographical boundaries. Creating a network of positive, committed people provides a crucial foundation for change.

Energy

Encouraging and sustaining energy is a key enabler of change for leaders. As N R Narayana Murthy, chairman of the board and former chief executive of India's Infosys, says: 'The first responsibility of a leader is to create mental energy among people so that they enthusiastically embrace the transformation' (cited in Aitken and Keller, 2007). For transformational change, energy has to be maintained for an extended period of time. All too often, though, a transformational effort starts with a big bang of enthusiasm, only to see energy peter out. Although most leaders acknowledge the importance of energy in organizational change, many struggle to unleash it or keep it at high levels throughout a transformation. Senior executives, for example, typically get excited about a big idea and dive straight into initiatives and task forces, wrongly assuming that one speech from the CEO will get everyone on board. Many transformations generate excitement and hope in their early stages, but the executives driving them fail to harness that enthusiasm and channel it throughout the transition period. Unless employees receive clear direction and an understanding of how they themselves can contribute to the overall purpose, their energy may rapidly decline. Likewise, they may flounder if they face too many conflicting priorities. Negative energy, such as cynicism, must also be addressed, especially during the early stages of a transformation. Negative energy can, according to Josep Isern and Caroline Pung (2007), be dissipated in a variety of ways. For instance, by ensuring that visible successes emerge quickly, eliminating unnecessary bureaucracy, including low-priority, energy-sapping tasks, and emphasizing fair processes. Clearly, it is not enough to mobilize or unleash energy; it must also be channelled appropriately and sustained in order to maintain the engagement of individuals.

Sustaining change requires the enthusiasm and commitment of large numbers of people across an organization for an extended period of time. All too often, though, a change effort starts with a big bang of vision statements and detailed initiatives, only to see energy peter out. The opposite, when change escalates maniacally through a culture of relentless enthusiasm, is equally problematic. Either way, leaders will find it hard to sustain energy within the organization unless they systemically restore their own energy (physical, mental, emotional and spiritual), and serve as role models for others to do the same.

Activity

Identify what an organization can do to create and sustain the energy of individuals during a transformation.

In the following case study James Muir describes the role of leaders in a transformational change programme at the Northumbrian Water Group.

CASE STUDY   The 'Our Way' journey at Northumbrian Water Group

Written by James Muir, trainer and coach

Northumbrian Water Group (NWG) operates as Northumbrian Water, Essex and Suffolk Water, with some smaller commercial operations UK-wide. We ensure our customers have a constant supply of clean, clear water that tastes good and we effectively remove and treat waste water to meet the needs of current and future generations. We aim to deliver the best value for money and to be best prepared for the future. The UK water industry has five regulators, with business plans, performance and pricing regulated by Ofwat. Affordability of water is a major consideration for our customers and Ofwat, and we foster innovation to continuously improve our performance. The regulatory regime operates incentives and penalties, with customer service being a key metric, measured by the Service Incentive Mechanism, or SIM. Looking forward to 2017, the market for 'non-domestic' customers opens to retail competition, bringing 'once in a generation' change. We see our reputation for customer service as being a real differentiator in the new market.

The success of our teams has been widely recognized, including the Queens Award for Sustainability, North of England Excellence (Company of the Year; Leadership), Business in the Community (Platinum Plus; National Excellence – Engagement and Well-being), Utility Week (Company of the Year) and The Sunday Times Best Companies (One Star). However, our belief is that to be absolutely recognized as the leading water company we must consistently demonstrate the highest level of service for all our customers. Our 3,000 people share the vision to be the national leader in the provision of sustainable water and waste water services. Our values – *customer-focused, results-driven, creative, ethical and one team* – are well-embedded and provide a framework for our actions and decisions, supported by our highly customer-focused mindset called 'Our Way'.

In 2012 we initiated the 'Our Way' programme to make a step change in customer experience, employee engagement and efficiency. We had a solid foundation of flexible, enthusiastic and highly effective people and our customers rated our service at upper quartile. But we wanted to take it further. We identified a key partner, Mary Gober International (MGI), who has a proven track record of enhancing customer experience. The first step was critical – to engage the top executive team in the value that MGI could add – so after selecting key influencers to attend a taster session, a dedicated immersion session took place for the executive team, who pledged total support. A project leader was appointed, and a steering group was established. After a pilot NWG programme involving a diagonal slice of people company-wide, the steering group consulted with participants to tailor the 'Gober Method' into 'Our Way'. Working in partnership with MGI, we established an initial programme that saw over 3,000 people attend a one-day seminar in cross-functional groups, delivered in a dedicated building by a dedicated team of NWG staff. The delivery style was innovative, fun and inclusive, and customized so that people could see how the techniques would work for them at home as well as at work. People were strongly encouraged to attend, and over time Our Way gained its own momentum and everyone took part. The internal communications strategy and our top-level leadership strategy were aligned with 'Our Way' as we embedded the new mindset, language and style consistently across the business. 'Our Way' was woven in to recruitment, performance management, leadership development, health and safety, procurement and other key business processes, in addition to customer service and arrears collection We included everyone in the business regardless of their hierarchical position or role. A short-term focus on obvious customer-service givers would have only scratched the surface. We knew that to evolve our culture we must reach out to every team, so the ethos became authentic internally as well as externally. This holistic, inclusive, engaging approach was imperative, and building in-house capability was a fundamental building block to the success of the programme.

The core 'Our Way' day gave clear tools and techniques for how people could personally develop their behavioural approach to deliver a positive, can-do attitude by having a clear and focused mindset. To underpin this, all 470 people managers attended a two-day coaching module to develop confidence in role-modelling it, linking it to their areas of the business and leading their teams towards our behavioural expectations. The Our Way team ran focused events to tailor the approach to different types of work, such as written communication, Twitter, face-to-face customer operations and so on.

Although the first phase of Our Way saw improvements in customer experience, we were not consistently achieving the top SIM score. Feedback indicated that whilst most people bought into the Our Way principles, the language was not real to them and they needed more help to translate it into their working environments. Some leaders had slipped back to old ways due to the demands of their roles. The challenge was to ensure that all leaders understood the impact of their actions and, as strong influencers, the need to lead by example and coach their teams.

In 2014 the executive team reviewed the Our Way strategy and it was evolved to a simpler style (illustrated in Figure 4.1), which still honoured the Gober Method but felt more 'like us'. 'Our Way' became simply 'how we do things around here'.

FIGURE 4.1   'Our Way' strategy

All leaders have attended a refreshed 'Leading our Way' workshop to raise awareness of their personal role, and the impact of making tiny incremental gains. We have now achieved our highest SIM scores, and have a net promoter score of 46. The Our Way journey continues. It is clear to us that cultural change is a long-term investment. It is organic and for it to be successful it must be monitored, adapted and refreshed. Leaders must be engaged and understand their part – this takes time and support in order to get it right. Looking forward, our focus will continue to be on supporting our people 'in everything we think, feel, say and do', and as the demands on the business change so will the 'Our Way' programme.

Engagement of middle managers

An ability to engage with people and to engage them throughout the transformation journey is an important aspect of leading people through change. In change initiatives employees may often prefer to keep their heads down and let the change roll over them. Leading change has to be, therefore, an active process of engagement. Leaders starting a transformation need to put a priority on finding sufficient and scalable ways to engage managers. Although the support of senior managers is important to the success of any change programme it is unlikely to be sufficient; the senior team need to enrol middle management.

The engagement of middle management is important because middle managers are the recipients and purveyors of change. For example, structural changes might result in cost cutting and staff reductions, which may not only mean that middle managers are not only uncertain as to the future of their team and also their own future but also that they may have more work to do in the meantime. Downsizing and delayering often mean that middle management are asked to exercise greater spans of control and do more work, while at the same time they may be experiencing greater job anxiety. They may quickly become disillusioned or feel isolated and anxious about their future in the organization. And, as Paul Lawrence points out, there are many change initiatives that have 'crashed upon the rocks of middle management' (2014: 110). Robyn Thomas and Cynthia Hardy (2011) say that if the leadership team fail to engage the middle managers in change, then middle managers may exercise their power by co-operating to the minimum extent that they feel they can get away with, focusing instead on protecting themselves and their turf. This can result in what Lawrence (2014) calls the 'frozen middle'. If, on the other hand, middle management is engaged in the change and involved in discussions about it from its inception, then this layer of management has the potential to act as a crucial facilitator of change. Middle managers must be engaged if they are to be able to implement change, with commitment and enthusiasm.

In practice, engaging the support of middle management and the layers of management below may not be easy, and needs to be assessed regularly.

Measurements of engagement

One way of assessing the commitment of people is to use the ADKAR model (Hiatt, 2006). This is a set of five sequential building blocks, all of which are needed in order to engage people in change. The five building blocks are:

- awareness of the need to change;
- desire to participate and support the change;
- knowledge on how to change;
- ability to implement required skills and behaviours;
- reinforcement to sustain the change.

The following questions can be asked as part of these building blocks:

- Do you understand why the changes are taking place?
- What do you think about this change?
- How do you feel about this change?
- What do you see your role as in this change?
- What are your views on this change?
- What experience do you have of this type of change?
- How do you think your work will be affected by this change?
- What are your ideas about this change?
- What would you change about this change?
- Why do you think this change is needed (or not)?
- If you could tell the CEO one thing about this change, what would it be?
- What are you already doing in your day-to-day work that supports the change?
- What parts of the change do you think will be a challenge for you?
- What experience do you have of previous changes?
- How do you think this change will be of benefit to the organization/ to you/your team?
- What will hinder you most during this change?
- What will help you most during this change?

It is important to ask these questions and listen attentively and to check periodically that individuals are still committed to the change. Measures of engagement can include:

- Do people know what the change is and what it is trying to achieve?
- Are people generally supportive of what the change is trying to do?

- Are people prepared and informed about what the change means to them?
- Are people meeting agreed deadlines?
- Are there any capability gaps preventing commitment?

Commitment can be increased through asking questions and involving middle managers (and other stakeholders) in decisions about the change. This does take time and energy but it is much more powerful to ask questions than just to talk at people. Leaders need to be aware of who needs to be engaged around the purpose of change, as well as who is vital to making the change agenda happen, and focus their energy on them. A key way to gain commitment from people to change is through encouraging innovation.

Innovation

Innovation is the means, at all levels of the organization, to translate the purpose that the leader has articulated into tangible business outcomes. It becomes the vehicle that the leader uses to take their vision and ideas to market. According to Valerie Gauthier, to be innovative involves creating: 'a culture of resilience, agility and processes that enable the organization to navigate through unknown waters to a new destination' (2014: 40).

The word innovation is often associated with Apple – the multinational technology company. Apple's vision of innovation is embedded in Steve Job's simple words: 'connecting the dots'. Apple's capacity to make innovative products is the result of a vision and hard work. The vision for their products is perceptive and sensible. For example, the vision for the iPod was 'all my music in my pocket'. Being able to make such a vision come to life involves experimentation, trials and errors, sharing ideas, challenging proposals, making mistakes, and creating prototypes. Innovation, such as that at Apple, combines action and impact.

Developing an environment for innovation is a difficult task. In providing leadership tips for developing an innovative organization, David Horth and Jonathan Vehar (2012) suggest that leaders create a mandate for change, backed by a strategy that embraces innovation by gathering people around them who share their passion for innovation. Bryan Robertson (2014), former director of lean transformation at the Direct Line Group – a UK-based insurer – outlines how this works in practice and how he has observed some individuals leading innovation:

> When I see leaders consistently holding problem-solving sessions and welcoming problems as opportunities for improvement, I know that it is a great sign. Another good sign is when people begin to share ideas... when people start to show pride in telling others about their ideas – instead of keeping them to themselves – I know the change is meaningful.

An MIT Sloan Management Review article by Whelan and colleagues (2011) explores research that shows how companies need both 'idea scouts' and 'idea connectors' in order to generate innovation. The idea scouts seek out new technologies around the world and provide new ideas, but translating these ideas into effective innovation requires connectors, also called innovation brokers, who connect the ideas into coherent and relevant concepts. Marissa Mayer is an example of how idea connectors can play a crucial role in a company. Valerie Gauthier (2014) describes how Mayer, in her executive position at Google, played a central role in fast-tracking investment to new ideas by allowing all Google employees to pitch new ideas three times a week. Mayer selected the best ideas and then leveraged her position to influence decisions and processes to champion the ideas to Google founders Larry Page and Sergey Brin. Similar approaches are followed by other companies, for example: the DuPont fibre Kevlar – one of the most successful and profitable innovations of the chemical company DuPont – was created when a team explored ideas in 'free time' (the time that employees have to discuss ideas). Companies such as DuPont, Apple and Google have built their own innovation capability. This is also the route that P&G have taken. P&G have a wide portfolio of products embracing food products, such as Pringles, to hygiene products, such as Pampers nappies for babies. It is a product range that needs constant invigoration and innovation. P&G's mechanism for innovation is their connect and develop strategy. This works by tapping into the company's vast global network of technology entrepreneurs working out of six hubs around the world. An initial problem brief is defined and then sent out to the network, which is encouraged to give time to solve the problem. Ideas are generated by the network and are then assessed by a project team on the basis of their alignment with the goals of the business; they are then subjected to a battery of practical questions, before a decision is made as to whether or not the idea will be trialled.

Such approaches for generating and developing ideas are vital to establish in order to allow time and space for generating innovative ideas, as well as tolerance for failure.

Learning from failure

Companies such as DuPont and Google have found that 'free time' can increase the breadth of the intellectual rigour of ideas and amplify wisdom and insights. But these insights have little impact unless people feel empowered to act on them. So what can leaders do to encourage the risk taking that enables people to learn more – and for their intellect and wisdom to be amplified? Lynda Gratton (2014) describes how Ratan Tata, who led the Tata Group for several decades, encouraged innovation by creating the Tata Group Innovation Forum. The forum is a 12-member panel of senior Tata Group executives and CEOs from independently run companies. From all over the world employees submit entries to be reviewed by their peers and the forum for annual awards. There are three categories of award. The first two are found in most companies – the first is for the teams that have recently implemented a promising innovation and the second is for teams that have created leading-edge pilot projects. The third category is more unusual and is called 'Dare to Try' and recognizes attempts to create a major innovation that failed to get the desired results.

It is evident in this example from Tata that leading change entails creating opportunities for failure as well as innovation. As the film director and actor Woody Allen says, 'If you are not failing every now and again, it's a sign you're not doing anything very innovative' (cited in Judge, 2011: 105). Clearly not all new ideas will work out as hoped, so ideas that lead to dead ends are an inevitable part of the innovation process.

The enemy of innovation is the fear of failure in terms of the consequences of blame, punishment and shame. In a study by Joanna Barsch and colleagues (2008) only 38 per cent of senior executives said that they consciously took action to learn from their failures in innovation and encouraged others in their organization to do the same. Worse still, only 23 per cent of employees felt encouraged by their managers to learn from their failures. Failure should, however, be accepted and individuals encouraged to learn from the experience.

Learning from failure creates and reinforces learning. The former CEO of P&G, A G Lafley, speaks of failure as a gift. In an interview in the *Harvard Business Review* (Dillon, 2011) Lafley explains how he learned from failed acquisitions. He learnt by analysing the root causes of the failures and found that all of them were of a relational nature, such as slow or inadequate integration; synergies that did not materialize; cultures that were not compatible; and leadership that would not play together in the same sandbox. Lafley used the knowledge and experience he gained from failed acquisitions to implement a new approach when P&G acquired Gillette. For this acquisition he put in place a dedicated team and processes, and focused on value creation and integration. These new tactics led to revenue synergies and the success of the merger. Lafley also learnt from the merger with Gillette that some of the issues to do with people could have been done differently, particularly the failure to retain some key people and to make optimal use of others. It is important to take time to learn from failures and identify what can be done differently next time.

Discussion questions

How often do you think lessons are learnt from organizational change?

How do you know they are?

How often do you think lessons learnt are actually put into practice?

Why are they often not put into practice?

How can you ensure that lessons are put into practice?

Power and politics

To understand how to lead people effectively through change, leaders need to understand the power and politics within the organizations, as power and politics often sit at the heart of the change agenda. Power and politics are natural phenomena in any organization, yet they traditionally get a 'bad press'. How power is used can have an impact on transformations, either positively or negatively, while political behaviour has the potential to prevent change from being successfully implemented. The process of leading people through organizational change more often than not involves dealing with power and politics.

Transformations provide excellent opportunities for gaining, keeping or increasing leaders' power – or losing it. Ambitious leaders of change can be very power conscious. Marianne Mast and colleagues (2010: 460) call it 'power motivation'. Power is not, however, just a matter of an individual's formal position in the organization but also their personal characteristics and experience. People are more likely to enthusiastically accept and commit to an individual whom they admire or whose expertise they respect, rather than someone who solely relies on their position for power. Leaders who use their expertise, knowledge, skills and capabilities to influence people during transformations are therefore more likely to gain their commitment rather than a leader who wields their power to coerce and threaten people.

The one kind of power that is universal, held by every person in every role in every organization, is silent veto power. People can exercise this kind of power by doing nothing to support or implement a change. They can ignore change by denying that it requires that they do anything different from what they are already doing, or they can disclaim any responsibility for it. So unless people have a compelling reason to co-operate, they can slow down changes using the power of silent veto.

The successful implementation of change means overcoming not only powerful vested interests but also the powerlessness that people may feel, which can impede any initiatives. Leaders can do this by building in stability to ensure that some things remain the same, such as location and hours of work. Such sources of stability are anchors for people to hold on to during change. People need to know what will remain stable and what is likely to change. The power of leaders to influence the actions and reactions of others is critical in enabling them to cope with the politics of change. Leaders (and managers) need to identify and manage key stakeholders, especially those who can and will use their power to subvert any change (stakeholder management is discussed in Chapter 5).

Politics is power in action – people exercising their power in overt and covert ways that can be difficult to understand or navigate. Change can trigger and intensify political behaviour as it may threaten to push individuals out of their comfort zone, as well as jeopardize existing practices and routines, status hierarchies, information flows, resource allocation and power bases. Political behaviour can be triggered by a diversity of opinion, values, beliefs, interpretations and goals during organizational change. Individuals who believe that they will lose out in some way, or who feel that there are better ways to achieve the same result or better results, are likely to put up a fight. If their voices are not heard, and where the stakes are high and the issues are important, some people are likely to demonstrate their opposition through covert, political means. Such political behaviour is not only inevitable in the context of organizational change but also necessary in stimulating debate. Leaders need to generate energy and enthusiasm and to build a coalition of support that can help to manage the subversive political elements.

Challenges of leading change

Leading change in any organization has many challenges. The challenges are varied and can depend on factors such as the content, context and process of change. Specific challenges for leaders personally include: adaptability and alignment, changing the rules of the game, taking bold decisions and changing one's mind.

Adaptability and alignment

One of the greatest challenges for those leading change is building adaptability to a rapidly changing external environment. Leaders must deal increasingly with ambiguities, the unknown and the unpredictable. In contrast to the past, where changes were observed shortly after they occurred and where sufficient time was present to make adjustments, the increasing velocity of change does not always allow time for plans to make corrections. This means that leaders need to adapt as they see change occurring. For leaders, the leadership of change means developing a purpose and case for change, crafting strategies to bring the purpose into reality, ensuring that people are engaged and collaborating in the change, and that everyone involved in the change is mobilizing their energies towards the same goals. This is a process that Alan Hooper and John Potter (2000) call emotional alignment. The importance of alignment and adaptability is made in a report by the World Economic Forum:

> Alignment... galvanizes people around the aspirations and objectives of the company.
> People know what is to be done, and understand how they as individuals contribute to the whole. Adaptability enables the organization to change rapidly and effectively in response to external threats or opportunities.
>
> (2000: 5)

The report goes on to say that:

> Alignment without adaptability results in bureaucratic, sclerotic organizations that can't get out of their own way... Adaptability without alignment results in chaos and resources wasted on duplicate and conflicting efforts. (2000: 10)

One of the greatest challenges is therefore ensuring that people are aligned to and can adapt to change. This means that everyone knows the rules of organization and how change operates.

Changing the rules of the game

The rules of change are the unconscious rules of the organization. It is what everyone learns when they join an organization yet they are never explicitly taught. It is everything that operates behind the scenes and drives behaviour in the business. These are not the conscious mission statements, values and behaviours rewarded at annual appraisal time. Instead, they are what everyone understands to be the way that things really get done, or not, as illustrated in the following case study.

CASE STUDY Changing the rules of the game in a housing association

Written by Lindsey Agness

I worked as a consultant on a project some years ago in a government-owned organization, where attempts at changing engrained behaviours kept stalling. At its height, this was an organization with over 15,000 employees and sales of over £1 billion per year. Research was carried out by the consultancy team to uncover the real rules of the game (ROTG). It made interesting reading. The key rules were as follows:

- We say we want simplicity and clarity, but the way we act and what we really want creates complexity.

- We are uncomfortable with conflict, and prefer comfortable failure to uncomfortable success.

- We would rather focus on changing processes than dealing with the people issues.

These ROTG were undermining many of the change initiatives that were being implemented. Leaders were giving up too easily at the first point of resistance because they were not comfortable dealing with people issues and conflict, and were used to quietly sweeping failures under the organizational carpet. The consultancy team concluded that most of the key observations were not about deficiencies in the processes, but about the way that people led, communicated and discharged their responsibilities. None of the process improvements required would deliver success until these issues had been dealt with. This feedback came as a shock to the leadership team, who had no idea how endemic these issues had become. It served as a shock tactic to get them to start thinking differently about the challenges ahead. Sadly, the leaders were not able to turn the organization around in time and it ended up being decommissioned. In this case the leaders failed to make bold decisions.

Taking bold decisions

Change can often involve making tough decisions, which is not something that all leaders are comfortable with. Simon Walker, chief executive of the British Private Equity & Venture Capital Association (BVCA), says that the hardest decisions are having to make changes that lead to people leaving the company, especially people who have served for a long time. Walker refers to it as a grim and difficult business (Lynch, 2013). Yet taking bold decisions is often necessary: especially for transformational change. Tom Glocer at Reuters drove through, at times, very unpopular change but saved the company; while Bob Ayling at British Airways (BA) was much criticized about the bold decisions he took – that ended up saving the airline. So taking bold decisions can be challenging but ultimately may help to save a company.

Activity

Think of a change initiative in your organization, or an organization known personally to you, define and evaluate its rationale for change and consider whether or not it was a bold decision. This activity may be carried out by you alone or by all members of a group, who should then share their conclusions and identify what these have in common, which are unique and why.

Changing one's mind

Another challenge of change for leaders is recognizing that it is okay to change your mind. Leaders, especially in the field of politics, are often very reluctant to change their minds and do a U-turn. Changing one's mind is felt to be almost a crime, a terror that brings shame on a leader. Adrian Furnham (2012) says that, 'it is not that difficult to say, "Yes, I was wrong; I have changed my mind" ... I too am fallible, but now I believe we are on the right path.'

Role-modelling desired behaviour

A key challenge for leaders is knowing what to change at a personal level in how they role-model desired behaviours. For whether leaders realize it or not, they seem to be in front of the cameras when they speak or act. Joseph M Tucci, CEO of EMC, the US-based information storage business, says: 'Every move you make, everything you say, is visible to all. Therefore the best approach is to lead by example' (Aitken and Keller, 2007). Yet research by McKinsey suggests that half of all efforts to transform organizational performance fail because leaders do not act as role models for change (Boaz and Fox, 2014). In other words, despite the stated change vision, purpose and goals, leaders tend to behave as they did before.

To build commitment and energy for change, leaders need to take actions that role-model the desired change. Difficulties arise when leaders believe, often mistakenly, that they already are the change. They commit themselves to personally role-modelling the desired behaviours. Then, in practice, nothing significant changes. The reason for this, according to Carolyn Aitken and Scott Keller (2009) is that most leaders do not count themselves among the ones who need to change. The challenge for leaders is knowing what to change at a personal level. This will only occur when leaders recognize that they themselves must change. For instance, when the founder of Infosys, N R Narayan Murthy, decided to take on the role of chief mentor at the company it meant that he had to reinvent himself, because it involved moving from his CEO position. As he explains, 'You have to sacrifice yourself first for a big cause before you can ask others to do the same... A good leader knows how to retreat into the background gracefully while encouraging his successor to become more and more successful in the job' (cited in Aitken and Keller, 2007).

Leaders can develop role-model behaviours through activities such as: 360-degree feedback on their behaviour specific to the change initiative's goals and objectives; a commitment to personal development objectives; and professional coaching to help achieve these objectives. The approach taken by Kevin Sharer, CEO of Amgen – the multinational biopharmaceutical company – was to ask each of his top 75 managers, 'What should I do differently?' and then share his development needs and commitment publicly with them. Another option to consider is called 'the circle of fire'. This involves every participant receiving feedback directly from his or her colleagues in relation to the change, such as 'What makes you great?' and 'What holds you back?' (Aitken and Keller, 2009).

Leaders need to ensure that they support and practise any required new types of behaviour and, in order to inspire others to change, they need to actually demonstrate Ghandi's famous aphorism, 'Be the change you want to see in the world'.

Discussion questions

Identify any other challenges in leading change, for leaders personally, that have not been discussed in this section. How could they be handled?

Or:

Share with colleagues the challenges that you have faced in an organizational change initiative. Discuss how you handled them, what the outcomes were, and what you learned from the experience.

Change and people-centred leadership

Inspiring others to change

During change initiatives the focus is frequently more on the process (technical) than the people aspects of change. Patricia McLagan (2002) says that taking a purely rational and technical approach to change – by making sure that it is technically sound and offers economic advantage to the organization – tends to lead to the false assumption that people will naturally absorb the change. To avoid making such an assumption a people-centred approach to leadership is a vital aspect of change. To achieve this John Kotter (2012) suggests removing structural barriers, providing training, aligning systems and confronting individuals who are undermining authority. While these suggestions are strong ones, leading people effectively through change is so much more than simply setting up the company in a more efficient manner.

For change to be successful, it is critical that leaders drive and sponsor it, fostering a sense of purpose and confidence in their employees and providing the motivation to change. Yet it would appear that this is something that many leaders lack the ability to do. Research by the Moorhouse Consultancy (2014) shows that more work needs to be done by leaders in order to build confidence amongst people in the ability of leaders to deliver successful change. The research found that although board members are positive about their own ability and the ability of their peers, only 52 per cent of those reporting to the board state that they feel leaders have sufficient experience and under-standing to successfully lead the change agenda. To inspire people to go further and initiate collective change, leaders need to be able to motivate others to change, whether it involves changing how they work or how they behave.

Individuals and/or teams need to know how their work will change, what is expected of them during and after the transformation, how they will be measured, and what success or failure will mean for them and those around them. Leaders should be as honest and transparent as possible.

Most leaders contemplating change know that people matter. It is, however, all too easy to focus on the plans and processes that do not react emotionally, rather than connecting to the more difficult people issues.

Connect with the disconnected

Change can be hard for people, especially if it is transformational and disrupts established ways of getting things done. Julie Battilana and Tiziana Casciaro (2013), in a study of the UK's National Health Service (NHS), highlight how leaders can succeed through their personal networks. These authors say that the type of network that is better for implementing change varies depending on the situation. It depends on how much the change causes the organization to diverge from its institutional norms or traditional ways of getting work done, and how much resistance it generates as a result. Consider, for instance, an attempt by a hospital to transfer some responsibility for the discharge of patients from doctors to nurses. Battilana and Casciaro call this a 'divergent change', which violates the deeply entrenched role division that gives doctors full authority over such decisions. In the legal profession, a divergent change might be having to use a measure other than billable hours to determine compensation. In academia, it might involve the elimination of tenure. Such changes require dramatic shifts in values and practices that have been taken for granted. A 'non-divergent change' builds on, rather than disrupts, existing norms and practices. Many of the NHS initiatives that Battilana and Casciaro (2013) studied were non-divergent in that they aimed to give even more power to doctors, for example, by putting them in charge of new quality-control systems. So whether the change is divergent or non-divergent influences the type of network to use.

A bridging network helps to drive divergent change, whereas a cohesive network is preferable for non-divergent change. Cohesive networks are made up of people with similar interests and experiences and are the best kind of networks for delivering small-scale incremental change. For trans-formational change, bridging networks that connect disparate individuals and teams that were previously disconnected are better. Bridging networks are the most effective mechanisms for transformations because they create the opportunity for fresh thinking about learning – and novel experiences. Networks are therefore key to connecting people during change and for developing emotional ties.

Activity

Think about the kinds of networks you have. How might they match different types of change?

Identify ways that you could connect people who are disconnected from a change imitative.

Emotional ties

Inspiring individuals to invest time and energy in change is an important aspect of leading people through change. This does, however, depend on the emotional ties between leaders and individuals. Leaders have strong ties when they interact with 'people like them', such as people with the same life experiences, beliefs and values. Research by Brian Carolan and Guy Natriello (2005) shows that people are more likely to be influenced to adopt new behaviours or ways of working by those with whom they have strong ties and who they like and trust. There are, however, drawbacks to using strong ties to spread change as they can reinforce silos and groupthink and restrict the ability of a leader to spread the change beyond their own professional group or peers. As a result, the amount of knowledge that gets circulated around the system may be severely restricted and limit the likelihood of innovation.

Alternatively, when leaders build weak ties they reach out to people who are not like them and this helps to build bridges between disparate teams and individuals. This approach creates the potential to mobilize all the resources relevant in the organization that can potentially contribute to implementing and sustaining the change. This is the basis on which many of the great social movements were able to deliver widespread changes. For instance, the reason why Martin Luther King Jr was able to inspire a multitude of followers was that he cultivated a large number of weak ties. As a result, people felt that they trusted him, even though they barely knew him. Today, the mass adoption of social media and virtual social networking systems creates the potential for a greater number and much wider range of weak-tie relationships.

During change there is a tendency for people to revert to strong-tie relationships, to stick to what and who is known and who can be trusted. The information flows of leaders are therefore often based on strong ties. Yet weak ties should not be ignored, as they are more important than strong ties when it comes to searching out resources and innovative thinking in times of change.

Summary

Leading change and managing change are different but mutual processes. Each is necessary but neither is sufficient alone. Leading change is one of the most challenging activities and requirements that leaders face in organizations. It is a very public activity as leaders are being watched from all angles, and what they do and how they do it is an important element in successfully bringing about change. Although transformational leadership research and theory have much to offer leaders, particularly with respect to the engagement of themselves, managers and employees, other leadership philosophies – such as authentic, shared, service, ethical and distributed – may be more appropriate depending on the context of the change and the culture of the organization.

Leaders need to create a sense of purpose about the change in order to help people to understand it before committing to it. Without a sense of purpose, particularly at the start, major changes can stall or fail to gain traction. A sense of purpose also helps people to sustain their energy through the transition. It gives them the resolve to continue moving forward, rather than go back to the status quo. The more that people share and understand the purpose early in the initial development of the change initiative, the better. Leaders need to share it, believe in it and, ideally, get other individuals involved in creating it.

The leadership of change depends on the attitudes, values and actions of leaders, as leading people through change is about showing the way and helping people in order to engage them in the transformation. It means working out how to involve people most effectively in the change from the beginning, once the need for change is identified. It also entails being aware of organizational politics and watching for the influence of power in the way that people relate to each other. As a process change also requires energy, there is no substitute for a leader directing his or her personal energy and commitment throughout a transformation and, in turn, energizing those around them.

Implications for leaders for leading change

From this chapter there are some key practical implications for leaders of leading people through change:

- *Do not underestimate the level of input*
  Where transformational change is occurring, be involved and visible, champion the change, and demonstrate the values and behaviours that others need to foster.

- *Encourage innovation*
  Be willing to enable a culture that fosters and celebrates innovation, in order to make the organization and the people within it more engaged and open to change. Innovation is often seen as the preserve of the executive team or the research and development (R&D) function. This will fail to engage the creativity throughout the organization. Leaders should consider the words of the actor Robert Redford who comments on the great success of the Sundance Film Festival: 'If you create an atmosphere of freedom, where people aren't afraid someone will steal their ideas, they will engage with each other, they will help one another and they will do some amazingly creative things together' (Zades, 2003).

  Identify what organizational factors create barriers to innovation. Once you have identified them, remove them in order to create the freedom for innovation.

- *Learn from failure*
  Learn from experience by testing as many ideas as possible. Tests are most reliable when many roughly similar pilots can be observed, some containing the new idea and some not.

  Appreciate that change brings with it a risk of errors, mistakes or failure. These bring with them something positive, namely the opportunity for both leaders and their staff to learn, improve and develop. Celebrate and learn from failure and share mistakes (see Chapter 9 for further discussion on learning).

- *Support managers*
  Ensure there is a good system of cascading and support for all managers – enable less experienced managers to seek further support rather than find them avoiding having the team conversations because they just do not know how to approach it. Support managers to be able to have the right conversations with their teams – ensure managers are given the information they need to be informed – do not let them find out the latest updates at the same time as staff; ensure they have a window in which to process information for themselves and then be in a position to support staff.

- *Connect the changes*
  Try to avoid a plethora of change programmes going on at the same time, or, if there are, then ensure that they are connected and make sense.

- *Change yourself first then others will follow*
  Leading change means changing yourself, what you do and how you do it, as well as changing others. Nothing kills a change initiative faster than leaders who espouse certain behaviours and attitudes, but demonstrate different ones. For instance, if a leader announces the importance of controlling costs more carefully, but then arranges for an extravagant team away day for their senior management team, the rest of the organization will notice. Hence show care in the behaviours you exhibit.

References

Aitken, C and Keller, S (2007) [accessed 16 October 2015] The CEO's Role in Leading Transformation, *McKinsey Quarterly*, February [Online] http://www.mckinsey.com/insights/organization/the_ceos_role_in_leading_transformation

Aitken, C and Keller, S (2009) [accessed 16 October 2015] The Irrational Side of Change Management, *McKinsey Quarterly*, April [Online] http://www.mckinsey.com/insights/organization/the_irrational_side_of_change_management

Barsch, J, Capozzi, M M and Davidson, J (2008) [accessed 16 October 2015] Leadership and Innovation, *McKinsey Quarterly*, January [Online] http://www.mckinsey.com/insights/innovation/leadership_and_innovation

Bass, B and Riggio, R (2006) *Transformational Leadership*, 2nd edn, Erlbaum, New Jersey

Battilana, J and Casciaro, T (2013) The network secrets of great change agents, *Harvard Business Review*, **91** (7) pp 62–68

Boaz, N and Fox, E A (2014) [accessed 16 October 2015] Change Leader, Change Thyself, *McKinsey Quarterly*, March [Online] http://www.mckinsey.com/ insights/leading_in_the_21st_century/change_leader_change_thyself

Caldwell, R (2003) Change leaders and change managers: different or complementary?, *Leadership & Organization Development Journal*, **24** (5) pp 285–93

Carolan, B and Natriello, G (2005) [accessed 16 October 2015] Strong Ties, Weak Ties: Relational Dimensions of Learning Settings, *Annual Meeting of the American Educational Research Association, Montreal* [Online] http://citeseerx. ist.psu.edu/viewdoc/download?doi=10.1.1.138.7033&rep=rep1&type=pdf

Dillon, K (2011) 'I think of my failures as a gift': interview with A G Lafley, *Harvard Business Review*, **89**, pp 86–89

Furnham, A (2012) Be proud of U-turns if they take you in right direction, *The Sunday Times*, 25 November, p 2

Gauthier, V (2014) *Leading with Sense: The intuitive power of savoir-relier*, Stanford University Press, Stanford

Gratton, L (2014) *The Key*, McGraw-Hill, London

Gronn, P (2000) Distributed properties: a new architecture for leadership, *Educational Management Administration & Leadership*, **28**, pp 317–38

Hackett, R (2014) [accessed 16 October 2015] The 25 Best Global Companies to Work For, *Fortune Magazine* [Online] http://fortune.com/2014/10/23/ global-best-companies/

Hamel, G (2011) First, let's fire all the managers, *Harvard Business Review*, **89** (12), pp 48–60

Heifetz, R A and Laurie, D L (1997) The work of leadership, *Harvard Business Review*, January–February, **75** (1) pp 124–34

Hiatt, J M (2006) *ADKAR: A model for change in business, government and our community*, Prosci Learning Centre Publications, Colorado

Hodges, J (2011) The role of the CEO and leadership branding: credibility not celebrity, in *Corporate Reputation*, ed R Burke, G Martin and C Cooper, Gower, London

Hooper, A and Potter, J (2000) *Intelligent Leadership*, Random House, London

Horth, D M and Vehar, J (2012) *Becoming a Leader Who Fosters Innovation*, Centre for Creative Leadership, North Carolina

Howieson, B and Hodges, J (2014) *Public and Private Sector Leadership: Experience speaks*, Emerald, London

Hüttermann, H and Boerner, S (2011) Fostering innovation in functionally diverse teams: the two faces of transformational leadership, *European Journal of Work and Organizational Psychology*, **20** (6) pp 833–54

Isern, J and Pung, C (2007) [accessed 16 October 2015] Driving Radical Change, *McKinsey Quarterly*, November [Online] http://www.mckinsey.com/insights/ organization/driving_radical_change

Judge, W (2011) *Building Organizational Capacity for Change: The strategic leader's new mandate*, Business Expert Press, New York

Kotter, J P (2012) *Leading Change*, Harvard Business Review, Massachusetts

Lawrence, P (2014) *Leading Change: How successful leaders approach change management*, Kogan Page, London

Lynch, A (2013) [accessed 16 October 2015] Leading Edge: Simon Walker – Winners Never Lose Touch With Reality, Says the Head of the Institute of Directors, *Sunday Times*, 2 June [Online] http://www.thesundaytimes.co.uk/sto/public/Appointments/article1267193.ece

Malone, R (2009) [accessed 16 October 2015] Remaking a Government-Owned Giant: An Interview with the Chairman of the State Bank of India, *McKinsey Quarterly*, April [Online] http://www.mckinsey.com/insights/financial_services/remaking_a_government-owned_giant_an_interview_with_the_chairman_of_the_state_bank_of_india

Mast, M S, Hall, J A and Schmidt, P C (2010) Wanting to be boss and wanting to be subordinate: effects on performance motivation, *Journal of Applied Social Psychology*, **40** (2), pp 458–72

McGuire, J (2012) [accessed 16 October 2015] 4 Bad Attitudes That Hinder Change Leadership, *Leading Effectively* [Online] http://www.leadingeffectively.com/4-bad-attitudes-that-hinder-change-leadership/

McLagan, P (2002) Change leadership today, *Training & Development*, November, **56** (11), pp 26–31

Moorhouse Consultancy (2014) [accessed 16 October 2015] Barometer on Change, *Moorhouse: London* [Online] http://www.moorhouseconsulting.com/insights-publications/publications/2014/barometer-on-change-2014/

Nahavandi, A (2000) *The Art and Science of Leadership*, Prentice Hall, New Jersey

Northouse, P G (2012) *Leadership: Theory and Practice*, Sage, London

Nye, J (2008) *The Powers to Lead*, Oxford University Press, New York

Nye Jr, Joseph S (2014) Transformational and transactional presidents, *Leadership*, **10** (1), February, pp 118–24

Prevett, H (2013) Culture wasn't built in a day, *The Sunday Times*, 24 February

Robertson, Bryan (2014) [accessed 16 October 2015] Interview with Bryan Robertson, Former Director of Lean Transformation, *Direct Line Group* [Online] http://www.mckinsey.com/client_service/operations/latest_thinking/bryan_robertson

Smith, R (2015) A change management perspective, in *The Effective Change Manager's Handbook: Essential guidance to the change management body of knowledge*, ed R Smith, D King, R Sidhu and D Skelsey, pp 1–77, Kogan Page, London

Spears, L C (2002) Tracing the past, present, and future of servant leadership, in *Focus on Leadership: Servant leadership for the 21st Century*, ed L C Spears and M Lawrence, pp 11–24, Palgrave Macmillan, New York

Spillane, J P (2006) *Distributed Leadership*, Jossey-Bass, San Francisco

Stoner, J L (2013) [accessed 16 October 2015] Try Collaborative Change for a Change, *Seapoint Center* [Online] http://seapointcenter.com/collaborative-change/

Stoughton, A and Ludema, J (2012) The driving forces of sustainability, *Journal of Organizational Change Management*, **25** (4), pp 501–17

Thomas, R, and Hardy, C (2011) Reframing resistance to organizational change, *Scandinavian Journal of Management*, **27** (3), pp 322–31

Weick, K E (1988) Enacted sensemaking in crisis situations [1], *Journal of Management Studies*, **25** (4), pp 305–17

Weick, K E (2012) *Making Sense of the Organization: The impermanent organization*, vol 2, John Wiley & Sons, London

Whelan, E, Parise, S, De Valk, J and Aalbers, R (2011) Creating employee networks that deliver open innovation, *MIT Sloan Management Review*, **53** (1), pp 37–44

World Economic Forum (2000) *Creating the Organizational Capacity for Renewal*, Booz Allen & Hamilton, New York

Yukl, G (2006) *Leadership in Organization*, 6th edn, Pearson/Prentice Hall, London

Zades, S (2003) [accessed 16 October 2015] Creativity regained, *Inc Magazine*, [Online] http://www.inc.com/magazine/20030901/sundance.html

Further reading

Archer, D and Cameron, A (2009) *Collaborative Leadership: How to succeed in an interconnected world*, Routledge, London

Bryman, A, Collinson, D, Jackson, B, Uhl-Bien, M and Grint, K (2011) *The SAGE Handbook of Leadership*, SAGE Publications, London

Coetsee, J and Flood, P C (2013) *Change Lessons from the CEO: Real people, real change*, John Wiley, Chichester

Greenfield, A (2008) *The 5 Forces of Change: A blueprint for leading successful change*, Management Books, Cirencester

05
Fostering commitment and ownership

KEY POINTS

- Managing change is complementary to the leadership of change and, together with leadership, necessary for effectively managing people through change.
- Managers play a crucial role in the implementation of change. They are the people who translate the vision or purpose into reality through strategies, action plans, accountabilities, objectives, key performance measures, tasks, action and outputs, and are directly responsible for the teams of people who have to adapt their ways of working in order to embed the change.
- For change to be successful, managers need to know who is involved. Any individual or groups with an interest or involvement in the change and its outcomes is known as a stakeholder. Being able to identify and categorize stakeholders is crucial for prioritizing and identifying different influencing strategies.
- Managing people through change can be achieved either through commitment, where people actively want to change, or through compliance, where they will change because they are instructed to do so.

Introduction

The literature on organizational change is often positioned from the point of view of people who come to decide on a new vision, strategy or structure, or to merge, acquire or downsize. The perspective of those who are directly affected by the decision to change and have to manage and implement it is often ignored. Those are the people who must take on new tasks, develop new skills, be transferred, regarded, retrained and manage others though the change. Although leading change is vital, it is not alone a sufficient condition for successful change. Change must also be managed – it must be planned, organized, directed, controlled and measured. Change management is important to the success of organizational change. It is complementary to the leadership of change and, together with leadership, necessary for engaging people in change and transformation. However, its perceived importance is not matched by its actual success, often because of poor management.

This chapter explores how to manage people through the change process. It begins by defining what managing change means. In particular, the chapter discusses how to foster engagement and ownership. Within this context the role of managers in the change process is examined, as well as what managers need to do to manage people through change. Specific approaches are considered of how to gain commitment from individuals collaboratively throughout the transition journey, such as involvement in the decision-making process, creating a sense of shared ownership and enabling individuals to actively contribute to the shaping of the change intervention. The chapter also examines key factors for managing people through change, such as identifying the readiness for change, stakeholder engagement and managing conflict. Since transformation can be a long-term process, those managing change must be able to sustain the momentum for change. So how to analyse the impact of change on people and ways to maintain momentum throughout a change process are also considered. Several questions are addressed in the chapter, including: what are some of the key principles underpinning the way that change is managed? How can individuals and teams be supported through change? What can be done to build ownership of change? How can managers identify whether or not people are ready for change? How should stakeholders be identified and managed? How can the impact of change on people be identified?

LEARNING OUTCOMES

By the end of this chapter you will be able to:

- explain why change initiatives so often fail or fall short because of poor management;
- appreciate what is involved in managing people during change;
- assess the readiness of individuals to change;
- conduct an impact analysis of change on individuals;
- identify key stakeholders and ways of influencing them to support the change;
- apply the information and ideas in this chapter to manage people through organizational change effectively.

Change management

Definition

Management can be thought of as a function that is part of an organization's formal structure. This is aptly outlined in Laurie Mullins's (2010) characterization of management as: taking place within a structured organizational setting and with prescribed roles; directed towards the attainment of aims and objectives; achieved through the efforts of other people; and using systems and procedures. Management is about ensuring that processes and people are working efficiently and effectively, which concerns not only maintaining the status quo but also changing it.

Management and change are synonymous. As Robert Paton and James McCalman point out, management and change are synonymous:

> It is impossible to undertake a journey, for in many respects that is what change is, without first addressing the purpose of the trip, the route you wish to travel and with whom. Managing change is about handling the complexities of travel. It is about evaluating, planning and implementing operational, tactical and strategic journeys. (2008: 3)

So change must be managed – it must be defined, communicated, planned, organized, directed, implemented, monitored, controlled and measured. Good management of change is vital for change to happen. While leadership of change is about showing the way and enabling it to happen, management of change is about making it happen.

How change is mismanaged

Change management is important to the success of the organizations. However, its perceived importance is not always matched by its actual success. Indeed, 'plus ça change, plus c'est la même chose' – 'the more things change, the more they stay the same' – an unfortunately suitable epigram for change management.

Trying to change is fraught with difficulties. Take, for example, the banking and finance sector. Following one of the most turbulent periods in its history, which began with the financial crisis of 2007–08, the sector has been facing more complex and dramatic change than ever before. Global regulatory requirements have been forcing banks and finance organizations not only to change their structures, processes and procedures but also to change the way they operate. Yet it appears that the sector is struggling with managing such changes. This is evident in the findings from Moorhouse Consulting's Financial Services Survey (2012) which reveals that nearly half of the organizations in the sector are not coping with the volume of regulatory change, which comprise 40 per cent of all change projects. This lack of success of organizational change is further evident in Moorhouse's (2014)

Barometer on Change survey of 200 UK boardroom directors. This survey found that only 38 per cent of respondents could claim that over 80 per cent of their transformation programmes were successful. Reasons cited for the lack of success include: projects running off at tangents; changes in objectives; a lack of ownership from stakeholders; an inability to manage costs; and a lack of defined milestones – all of which relate to change being mismanaged.

Change efforts can be mismanaged in a number of ways. There may be inadequate day-to-day management skills such as poor planning, monitoring and control; a focus more on the tasks than on the people involved; a lack of milestones along the way or failing to monitor progress and take corrective action; or a lack of the necessary resources such as budget, systems, time and information, and the necessary expertise, such as knowledge and skills.

Change is all too often regarded and conducted as a 'quick-fix'. This usually fails to address sufficiently the real requirements of change and their implications for the organization as a whole and therefore causes unforeseen and unacceptable disruption. Related to this, change initiatives are frequently the result of the naive adoption of management fads. Such fads tend to deal with only one aspect of an organization without regard for the impact on the people in the organization. Change initiatives may also fail because of the use of incomplete change models and a lack of capability to implement and sustain the benefits.

Another way that change is mismanaged is impatience. The Centre for Creative Leadership (2012) says that the challenge of transition is often underrated:

> A change that takes 12 weeks to plan and implement typically takes 100 to 120 weeks to integrate. Poorly planned, it may take 200 weeks. Yet managers and consultants rarely allow more than 26 weeks! Without providing time and attention to transition, organizations fail to see desired benefits of change efforts.

The perception that the time and money required for change is wasteful can result in the management of change being largely ignored in many organizations until problems crop up and then managers have to invoke change – and then they have to do so too quickly.

Change may be mismanaged when corporate policies and practices remain the same and become inconsistent with the purpose of the change. For example, the performance criteria used in appraisal and reward policies may not support and reinforce the change to a desired performance-driven, teamwork-oriented culture, and such inconsistencies can result in a disincentive or lack of incentive to change behaviour. Managers may also fail to make mutually supportive changes in terms of changes in roles, responsibilities and governance structure, thus resulting in an inconsistency among the changes desired, the changes achieved and their knock-on effects.

Change can be mismanaged when the impact of previous changes are ignored, as the history of change in an organization shapes employees' attitudes towards future change and how they behave towards it. Managing change entails addressing and resolving this issue before proceeding with new change initiatives in order to avoid a strong likelihood of derailment later. As Prashant Bordia and colleagues say:

> As when driving a car, changing the direction of an organization should involve a 'rear view' inspection of the change management history. (2011: 25)

Managers need to pay attention to employee change beliefs arising from the history of change in the organization, otherwise the ghosts of changes past will return to haunt them.

Change can also be mismanaged when mangers ignore the pace – how fast or slow the change needs to be implemented; the sequence, such as the time order of key elements in the change process; and the linearity – the orientation, continuance and resolution in the change process. If the process of change is mismanaged this can affect its success. So managers need to be aware of how change can be mismanaged and the impact that this can have on the success and sustainability of the change. The starting point to prevent change being mismanaged is to be clear on the role of managers.

Activity

Share with colleagues (or other students) your experience of how change has been mismanaged in your organization or in an organization known to you personally. What similarities and differences are there in your accounts?

Discussion questions

What do you think is the most serious way in which change is mismanaged? Why?

How can this be prevented?

How can managers prevent the 'ghosts' of changes past returning to haunt them?

What impact on employee trust and receptivity to change can the 'ghosts of change' have?

The role of managers

Managers play a crucial role in managing people through change. They are the people who translate the vision or purpose into action and are directly responsible for the teams of people who have to adapt their ways of working in order to make the change initiative a success. This cannot, however, be done in isolation – managers need to link in with leaders. The interaction between leaders and managers is important for creating strategic alignment within an organization. While leaders define the purpose and set the direction for change, managers must translate the purpose of organizational change into something that is more tangible and personal for individuals – and address the issues that might prevent or inhibit individuals from taking ownership of the change. The role of managers is therefore critical in connecting the work done at the organizational level to the reality that people have to change at the local level, such as departmental and/or team, in order for the initiative to be sustained. Managers are often brought in to work on change initiatives once the business case has been approved and implementation is about to start, or when it has already started. In order to ensure participation and build support, the involvement of managers should commence well before the start of any change initiative. This can be done by involving managers in developing the business case for the change, so that they can provide their views on which ideas will work in practice, and how acceptable different approaches will be in their own areas. If this is not possible, then at the very least, managers should be informed about the work that is being done on the change and what they will need to do.

Managers have to ensure that the directives for the change are implemented and they also have to deal with the emotional reactions of individuals to the change. This must all be done whilst maintaining performance standards and business-as-usual activities. If individuals are relatively new to management then they may not have experience or knowledge of what managing change involves, or managing others through change. Therefore it is important that managers get the support they need to effectively navigate change.

Navigating change

According to David Dinwoodie and colleagues (2015) from the Centre for Creative Leadership, the role of managers involves navigating change at three levels: self, others and organization. For each level, managers need to ask the following key questions:

1 *Self*
How do I cope with change? What do I find challenging about change? What do I need to do differently? What is my default management style when faced with managing transformational change? How does my behaviour impact on those around me? How do I ensure we have the capability for change throughout the organization?

2 *Others*
How can I help people through change? How should I acknowledge and respond to the different feelings and reactions that people have to change? How do I build relationships and persuade supporters,

detractors and fence-sitters to support the changes I am managing? How can the change be sustained through people?

3 *Organization*
How do I manage change in the context of the power and politics of the organizational culture? How do I influence leaders with my ideas and thoughts about change? How do I manage internal and external stakeholders?

Managers need to be able to navigate each of these three levels effectively. This is particularly important so that the health and well-being of staff are not affected by change.

Activity

Think of the changes in an organization in which you are familiar, or have recently been personally involved in managing. These may or may not have been successfully implemented. In your experience, what are the things that helped and hindered these changes? On reflection, how many of these could be classified as technical issues and how many are really people issues?

How much time did you spend focusing on people issues as opposed to technical ones?

Managing people's health and well-being

Many changes fail, even though brilliantly orchestrated, because people still have concerns such as will they be negatively impacted financially or will positive work relationships become fractured? Managers need to identify these concerns and, where possible, work to eradicate or lessen them. Failure to pay constant attention to managing personal issues, before the change is fully anchored in the workplace, can result in lost momentum or erosion of the change. If the personal issues of committed individuals are ignored and their commitment is lost, the negative impact of individuals withdrawing their support either openly or covertly can be highly damaging to the implementation effort. The ability to develop individuals who are committed and willing to take ownership of the change will depend on a manager's ability to adopt a supportive approach throughout the transformation. When positive performance towards the change is observed it must not be taken for granted that it will be maintained. Managers need to identify behaviour that indicates a lack of commitment or resistance to the change, discuss these behaviours with the individual/s concerned and address issues that may be concerning individuals such as job security, financial impact, work relationships, levels of responsibility, and learning and development needs. Managers need to respond effectively and in a timely manner to the personal concerns and reactions of people to the change, in order to maintain their sustained personal support. In particular, managers need to be cognizant and responsive to signs of change fatigue.

Change fatigue

As outlined in Chapter 2, change can be a difficult emotional experience for some employees. A study carried out by Moorhouse Consulting (2012) into financial services organizations entitled 'Too Much Change?' found that there was concern among managers about the ability of staff to cope with the volume and complexity of change being implemented. Nearly half (48 per cent) of respondents felt that front-line staff were not coping well with change. The survey concluded that workers in the financial sector were struggling with change overload. Similar signs of change fatigue are evident in the pharmaceutical industry. After decades of cost cutting, restructuring, transformations and turnarounds, the organizational health of the industry is suffering. A survey of pharma companies conducted by Gayane Gyurjyan and colleagues (2014) indicates that many employees feel that they are suffering from a lack of clear direction and an overemphasis on short-term delivery. The quotes below are indicative of the comments from the study:

> 'We have been through three reorganizations in the last two years. We no longer fully understand who does what, and honestly, we don't really try; it might change again soon.' *Head of Sales*

> 'We are supposed to do more work always with fewer people. With all these pressures and changes, we are not really thinking about our customers and their needs, but about our survival.' *Country head of primary care*

> 'I moved my family across three countries for this company. Now I have no idea where it's going or even if it will be here in two years' time.' *Regional CFO*

The disaffection shown in these comments illustrates how change fatigue can creep in. Managers need to be mindful of the impact of too much change or mismanaged change in order to prevent change fatigue leading to stress.

Stress

Change can affect employees' mental health, physical health and well-being at work. It can create anxiety and stress in people, even for those managing and leading change. Stress is defined as a particular relationship between the person and the environment that is appraised by the person as taxing or exceeding his or her resources and endangering his or her well-being. Individuals use their cognitive appraisal (see Chapter 1 for a definition) to determine if the source of pressure is a challenge, threat or non-threat and to evaluate the course of action for coping with the stressor. The appraisal process depends on an individual's perceptions, expectations, interpretations and coping responses. When applied to organizational change it is the degree to which employees appraise a change as threatening and how they cope with it. Change has the potential to produce a number of stressors for individuals.

Sources of stress during change

One source of stress for individuals during change is uncertainty. Uncertainty, or lack of knowledge or predictability of one's circumstances, can lead to feelings of a lack of control, which in turn can lead to stress. During change there can be uncertainty about various issues such as job security, workload demands or uncertainty about functions and reporting structures (uncertainty is discussed in Chapter 3).

The challenge for managers is to convince employees that the change will have benefits for them and their team. While leaders will have the big picture in mind and think of the overall organizational context, employees are more focused on the relevance and impact of change on their personal circumstances, such as whether it will affect their job role, responsibilities or rewards. People need to have information about the change in order to appreciate and understand the relevance of it. Timely and accurate information, as well as participation in change-related decision making can help to reduce uncertainty and enhance employees' sense of control over their work circumstances.

Another source of stress during organizational change is the threat of loss of tangible or intangible resources. At a tangible level, organizational change can lead to the loss of jobs, work roles, status and rewards, and an increase in undesirable aspects such as skills obsolescence or an increase in workload. At an intangible level, change can drain psychological resources as it can result in feelings of unworthiness, stemming from the need for individuals to acknowledge their lack of experience, knowledge or capabilities to cope with the change.

Those who want the change to be successful often find themselves working long hours, dealing with problems, trying to overcome the doubts of others and doing everything needed to implement the change. This can result in another source of stress – role strain. This can be caused by not being involved in decisions, inadequate managerial support, having to maintain standards of performance when trying to implement a change, and having responsibility for people who are uncooperative or have concerns about change.

Such stressors can affect managers (and leaders). For managers who do not naturally see the change as an opportunity this can be stressful. Managers need to become aware of what triggers their stress – and learn coping mechanisms. Once they have mastered this they can help others to learn how to cope with the stress that change can cause. Managers should also use the support from HR (as discussed in Chapter 8) to help themselves and their staff to cope with stress.

Commitment or compliance

In any transformation managers have to decide whether they will achieve changes through compliance or commitment. Commitment is where people actively want to change, whereas compliance is where they will change because they are instructed to do so. If the change initiative involves introducing a new system, work procedure or changes to legislation then compliance may be all that is needed. But if the initiative depends on changing attitudes, for example, improved customer service or cross-functional co-operation, then the aim must be to get commitment. Without it, individuals might quickly revert to their old ways of working as soon as the change is implemented and the spotlight is off them. Figure 5.1 shows the routes that can be taken for achieving change through commitment or compliance. The starting point is when individuals are made aware of the change. At this point, they need to understand what will happen and why. They will either engage with the change and see its implications for themselves, or have a negative perception of it. If they engage with the change they will see it as an opportunity, move on to testing the proposed change, implement it, and then be committed to embedding and sustaining it. If individuals choose instead to avoid the change, then managers may be forced to get them to comply with it. Both routes require investment. The compliance route requires investment in processes to administer, monitor and, if necessary, enforce compliance. Approaches for gaining commitment include managing stakeholders, engaging in dialogue, team building, recognizing the emotional responses to change and addressing them, and building capability for change. Commitment

FIGURE 5.1   Compliance and commitment to change

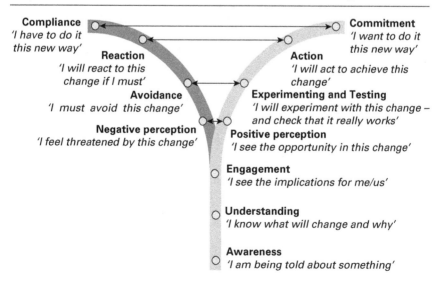

needs investment in winning hearts and minds, and in communicating with and responding to employees' feedback. Building commitment takes time and effort, so efforts need to be targeted so that they concentrate on the right people at the right time.

Managers must select the right route for the change in their organizations. The route chosen depends on: 1) the kind of change; and 2) the level of commitment required for the change to be successful. Both incur costs but at different stages. With compliance, heavy costs can occur later on in the transition, especially if old habits return and the change is not sustained. With commitment, costs occur early on through taking the time to involve people and to enable them to feel a sense of ownership for the change.

Ownership of change

Managers need to ensure that employees, as well as themselves, feel a strong sense of personal ownership for change. That way, they will put far more effort into making it a success. Building ownership calls for action on two fronts: 1) tightening managers' formal accountabilities; and 2) mobilizing self-directed change in the organization. Mary Meaney and colleagues (2010) liken the first to a military campaign and the second to a marketing campaign. The military campaign drives delivery of the transformation through a clear governance structure with well-defined roles and objectives. Leaders are held accountable for outcomes at four levels: an executive steering committee has overall responsibility for the initiative; a programme management office (PMO) is charged with co-ordinating the programme; executive sponsors provide leadership and guidance; and managers and project teams are responsible for achieving individual targets and milestones. In contrast, the marketing campaign aims to enlist the active involvement of staff at every level by tapping into the informal networks that play a powerful role in communication and motivation.

The employee ownership that begins with collectively developing initiatives is amplified when management devote sufficient and appropriately skilled resources to a transformation, defining clear roles and responsibilities so that individuals feel accountable for results and enabled to take initiative. Indeed, having clear roles and responsibilities and ensuring that the best talent is working on a transformation are key tactics for managing change.

People often say that they do not know how they fit into the change because they have not been involved in the planning process. The response from managers tends to be: 'Here's the change; this is why we have to change, here is how it will change – now own the change.' This does not work. What does work is ownership. Robert Tannenbaum and Warren Schmidt (1973) provide a useful framework for considering the levels of control that different stakeholders have during a change initiative, and what can be done to maximize control and so increase the probability that change will be accepted and sustained. They highlight four levels of control: tell, discuss, involve and empower.

- *Tell* (one-way communication). This is the bare minimum of control. At best it can generate understanding but very little ownership. It can lead to criticism and produce unsolicited advice about the proposed change.
- *Discuss* (two-way communication). This gives people a voice and allows them to question what is going to happen and why. It can lead to constructive feedback and buy-in to the change.
- *Involve.* This involves people directly in bringing about the change and can harness energy and support for the change. The joint problem-solving approach can result in strong commitment to the change, as people see it as their solution that is being implemented. This can help to create the likelihood of success.
- *Empower.* People with direct responsibility or accountability for defining and implementing change will be committed to the change and see it as their project and responsibility to sell it to others. They will want to ensure that it is implemented successfully.

Ownership of change needs to be built and maintained by managers. People need to own the change, that is, to take personal responsibility for those aspects of the change that they can control or influence. Ownership is often best created by involving people in identifying problems and crafting solutions. It is reinforced by incentives and rewards. These can be tangible (for example, financial compensation) or psychological (such as camaraderie and a sense of shared achievement).

Powerful processes to create ownership provide ways for people to connect with the change effectively. It is critical that there are processes that help people to build the commitment and capability to own the change. If this does not happen, it is very probable that the change will be either ignored by the people impacted or there will be minimal compliance. The latter is where people do the minimum necessary to avoid censure but rarely engage with the intent or spirit of the change. There are several ways of managing change so that this is prevented and so that people take ownership of change, including:

- ensuring readiness for change;
- involving people at every level;
- engaging teams;
- defining activities.

Ensuring readiness for change

To prepare for change, managers need to assess the readiness of people to transition to the new ways of working. Readiness for change refers to organizational members' beliefs, attitudes and intentions regarding the extent to which changes are needed, the extent to which employees have positive views about the need for change and believe that these changes have positive implications for themselves and the wider organization, as well as the organization's capacity to successfully make those changes (Armenakis, Harris and Mossholder, 1993). In others words, readiness for change denotes employees' beliefs that the organization can initiate a change and also engage in the practices that lead to it being successfully implemented.

An individual who is ready to change is one who exhibits a proactive and positive attitude towards change, which can be translated into willingness to support and own the change. An individual's readiness depends on whether they perceive the benefits of change as outweighing the anticipated risks. Each person perceives the significance of change differently. As a result, the readiness level may vary on the basis of what employees perceive as the balance between the costs and benefits of the status quo and the costs and benefits of change. Research suggests that people's acceptance or support for change is partially a function of the degree to which the change impacts them personally and is also dependent on their self-efficacy. Alannah Rafferty and colleagues (2013) propose that an individual's self-perceived readiness for change is a function of the individual's belief that change is needed, that they have the capacity to undertake change successfully and that the change will have positive outcomes for their job and/or role. So employees who are confident about their abilities and are able to cope with stressful events, such as change, tend to perceive change as positive and, as a result, they experience high levels of readiness to change.

The state of an individual's readiness can range from being excited about and open to the change, to being fearful of, or anxious about it and opposed to giving up their current ways of working. Imran Hameed and colleagues (2013) show empirically that the identification employees have with the organization – that, is the psychological bonding between an individual and his or her organization – has a significant positive effect on readiness for change. Yet during change many managers fail to deal with uncertainty, impose decisions on employees and fail to reassure employees of their worth to the organization. This can lead to a decrease in an individual's identification with the organization and, consequently, can decrease their readiness for change. In turn, this may cause employees to oppose change at a time when the organization really needs their support. The likelihood of a manager being able to implement and manage change successfully without people being change ready is arguably like a toddler trying to walk before they are able to crawl, which is possible for some but impossible for most. In other words, if an organization is not change ready then failure may be perceived as the only predictable outcome of a change initiative.

Assessing an organization's change readiness can help managers in identifying the key issues that they need to address in planning and implement change. It allows activities to be targeted where they are most needed, and resources and time to be allocated and managed effectively. There are several approaches to readiness assessment that managers can use singly, in concert, or in multiple combinations. We will briefly outline three of these approaches. The first approach to assessing readiness involves observing employees' reactions to proposed change. Such observation is intended to be relatively unobtrusive. It can involve being attentive to rumours, increases in absence or turnover, or any unusual behaviour that can be associated with denial or resistance to change. A second approach to readiness assessment involves directly soliciting reactions from employees in one-to-one or small group interviews, with managers interviewing their employees about their views and feelings about the change. A third, more formal approach, is to conduct an organizational survey. Such a survey can help to provide feedback anonymously about concerns, issues, ideas and suggestions. A suggested checklist of questions to use for a change readiness assessment survey can be found in Appendix 5.1 (at the end of this chapter).

It is important that feedback is gathered from various levels. Not conducting a change readiness assessment increases the risk of change not being achieved and benefits not being realized. In sum, readiness encompasses the extent to which employees are optimistic about the need for change, and believe that the change has positive implications for themselves and the wider organization. Managers need to be able to diagnose, assess and create individual readiness change by involving the appropriate people – at every level – who will be affected by the change.

The following case study about an international oil and gas company, written by Richard Turner, illustrates the importance of ensuring that employees are ready for change.

CASE STUDY Implementing lean and Six Sigma in the oil and gas industry

Written by Richard Turner, chief operations officer, JDR Cable Systems

This case outlines the challenges faced by an offshore oil and gas (O&G) company – DUCO Ltd – to implement a continuous improvement methodology called lean, which was originally developed by Toyota to reduce waste in the car industry.

Upstream in the O&G industry, away from the extraction and refining processes, there is an extensive supply chain of product manufacturers. One of the key products used in almost any subsea supply chain operation is an 'umbilical'. The umbilical provides a connection to key pieces of equipment on the seabed and connects the subsea architecture back up to the surface; it provides electrical power, hydraulics, gas and data. Historically the umbilical's market was fairly uncompetitive, with high market concentration and typical oligopolistic forces. In that environment there was little stimulus for change or improvement. In the last 10 years two things have really changed the dynamics in the market. First, the market has become more competitive through a combination of an increase in the number of companies competing for work and also cost-reduction pressures from customers. Second, after a number of high-profile disasters such as Macondo in the Gulf of Mexico, there has been a quality revolution in the industry whereby customary practices and the status quo have become unable to deliver what is required. Faced with these external factors many companies have looked outside of the O&G industry and attempted to draw from established practices and principles from the automotive and semi-conductor industries such as lean.

A couple of years ago DUCO Ltd, an umbilical manufacturer, followed this industry trend and engaged with a government-led organization called Manufacturing Advisory Service (MAS), whose consultancy was designed to support the implementation of lean and Six Sigma practices whilst reducing the cost of implementation through government subsidy. The programme appeared to be a win–win for the company, with free consultancy to help improve quality whilst reducing cost and improving on-time delivery. MAS agreed to run a pilot in the stores area of the company. This area was badly in need of reform and had regularly been highlighted as an area of weakness in customer audits. A team was assembled to be trained in the basics of lean and that team would then implement these practices into their area through a blitz-style workshop designed to provide rapid and visible results. However, the project was quickly and dramatically derailed. The problems started on day one of the workshop when the facilitator from MAS began to present generic 'car plant' material to participants. This was immediately met with an 'it won't work here as we don't make widgets' attitude from the team, which festered into an all-out row by the middle of the day. This resulted in the facilitator being physically removed from the building by a member of the company's senior management team, who had been completely unconvinced and in fact offended by the notion that they could – and that they needed – to learn from others using such a methodology. Everyone knew about this incident, everyone knew it was about lean and everyone knew then that lean would not work in umbilical manufacturing.

The lean programme was dropped until a year later, when the management team was restructured and new leaders were brought in, including those with expertise in lean. The barriers to implement lean were now even higher, as not only was it attempting to implement lean in a different type of environment but also the company still had a strong memory of the MAS incident.

The second attempt to implement lean involved a totally different approach. Initially a great deal of time and effort was spent doing nothing and focusing heavily on communication, mostly face to face. Over a period of a month every person in the business attended a presentation on the 'Business Excellence Programme'. The content of the presentation was carefully crafted to take the key ideas, tools and philosophies from lean but at the same time internalizing them in order to make them relevant to the business and to the people who would be using it. This internalization process included the use of specific examples from within the business but also comprised the use of imagery that was industry relevant such as taking a textbook entitled *Lean Temple* and displaying it as a lean oil rig.

The communication was extremely well received and although it did not change the attitudes about lean overnight it did succeed in opening the ears and minds of the employees. It allowed them to understand first of all the need for change but, also, that by pragmatically applying tools and techniques from other industries in a way that was meaningful, relevant and effective for the organization there would be an improvement that would make their jobs easier.

Following on from the initial communications an extensive value stream mapping (VSM) process was conducted. This involved taking a cross section of people from across the company and allowing them to map the current business processes, and also go out and talk to people in all departments in order to collect and collate ideas for improvement. These suggestions were then 'baked' into the 'future state map' that became the road map for the future. In a similar way to the communication session, the VSM had a profound effect on the organization and helped to contribute to creating a state of readiness for change. At the start of the mapping exercise the team dynamic was a little awkward, and everyone thought they knew the answers. As they went through the different steps of their end-to-end business processes many, if not all, people involved were surprised, if not totally shocked, by what they saw and what they learned. The VSM process is often referred to as 'learning to see', which was definitely evident in this case. The process really opened the participants' eyes to the fact that they had the need and, importantly, the possibility to make significant changes for the better.

Following on from the VSM a number of projects were launched across the business, which delivered significant and measurable results. The tools used were the same lean tools that were intended to be used a few years earlier; the difference was in the approach. By identifying the stimulus for change, by showing the vision for the future, by internalizing the content, and by allowing people to actively participate and contribute to the planned activities the status quo was unlocked, resistance all but eliminated and readiness for change was achieved. Ultimately, the change was successfully delivered.

Why did the initial attempt to introduce lean fail? What could have been done differently?

Was the company ready for change?

What might individuals do that would lead you to think that they are ready for change?

What might individuals do that would lead you to think that they are *not* ready for change?

Involve people at every level

Managers often fail to take into account the extent to which people can make or break a change initiative. The path of rolling out change is immeasurably smoother if people are asked early in the change process for input on issues that will affect their jobs. Front-line people tend to be rich repositories of knowledge about where potential glitches may occur, what technical and logistical issues need to be addressed and how customers may react to changes. In addition, their engagement can smooth the way for complex change initiatives, whereas their resistance will make implementation an ongoing challenge. Managers who resist early engagement with employees at multiple levels of the organizational hierarchy often do so because they believe that the process will be more efficient and quicker if fewer people are involved in planning. This is short-sighted, as involving as many people as possible can help enable them to take ownership of the change. This was evident at IBM, where after the leadership team had defined values for the organization they declared a 'values jam', which was a website where anyone in the company could post comments, responses, suggestions and concerns. Based on the feedback received, changes were made to the company values. Although such an approach may take longer in the beginning, ensuring broad involvement saves untold headaches later on. Not only does more information surface, but people are also more committed when they are involved and engaged in developing a plan for change.

Engaging teams

When managing a change initiative it is important to consider the variety of teams and team structures that exist within the organization. Those structures can be harnessed to provide energy and direction for the change, or they can become obstacles. During any change initiative there is a need to bring teams of people together, to share information, exchange ideas and generate solutions to challenging issues. Too many managers make the mistake of imposing solutions developed by a small, exclusive team – often from corporate headquarters. A better approach for transformational change is to establish a core team that includes hand-picked employees and/or volunteers from across the organization. A larger, cross-functional team may add complexity at the start of a transformation, and achieving alignment may initially take longer, but an inclusive team can generate more co-created solutions and organization-wide buy-in. Such a team can also make better-informed decisions and develop specific and realistic solutions.

Any team works better with a certain level of clarity about individual and shared responsibilities for engagement and collaboration within a change initiative. Clarity about roles, responsibilities, accountabilities and operating processes helps to reduce confusion. A RACI chart is a simple way to provide such clarity; RACI stands for:

- *Responsible*: the individuals who have responsibility for making decisions and/or doing the work.

- *Accountable*: individuals who are accountable for the completion of the work. This is often the project manager or project sponsor. This is the role that individuals responsible for doing the work are accountable to.

- *Consulted*: these are the people who provide information for the project. This is usually several people, often subject-matter experts.

- *Informed*: these are stakeholders who are affected by the outcome of the project and who need to be kept informed about progress. When there are clearly defined roles and responsibilities it is easier for people to know what is expected of them, and for them to complete their work on time, within budget and to the required standard. A RACI matrix (see Table 5.1) can be used to outline, agree and communicate roles and responsibilities.

TABLE 5.1   RACI matrix

Phase	R	A	C	I
Identify need	Manager	Sponsor	HR; subject experts	Team
Plan	Manager, team	Manager	HR; subject experts	Stakeholders
Implement	Manager, team	Sponsor	HR; subject experts	Stakeholders
Reviews	Manager	Sponsor	HR; project team	Stakeholders

Implementing change with impact

Implementation is a crucial stage of any change or transformation effort. There is significant value to be gained from getting implementation right. Good ideas for change are only part of the equation, and managers need to think about their implementation approach from the beginning to ensure that these ideas result in real, sustainable change and positive impact. The challenges of change implementation vary depending on geography, industry and an organization's strategy, which means there is no one-size-fits-all approach to achieving success. When considering transformational change, managers must first understand the current situation, what needs to change and how, and plan their approach to implementation accordingly. To ensure that you consider the key aspects of implementation you may wish to use the checklist in Appendix 5.2 (at the end of this chapter) in order to validate an existing change plan.

Activity

Use the checklist in Appendix 5.2 to carry out an audit on a specific change that you are currently involved in managing, or one you are familiar with. Identify the areas for development.

Managing conflict

During change, managers are frequently faced with conflict situations that need resolving in order to avoid delaying the change initiative. Stephen Robbins (2005) defines conflict as a process that begins when one party perceives that another party has negatively affected, or is about to negatively affect, something that the first party cares about. If conflict is not dealt with or is handled badly it can leave fractured relationships and reduce the potential for a successful outcome of change. An effective skill for managers to use to address conflict is negotiation.

Negotiation

Negotiation is the art of finding solutions to problems that are acceptable to all parties. The solutions may not be those that the parties involved had hoped or planned for at the outset of the negotiations, but are acceptable so that all parties leave the discussion feeling reasonably satisfied with the eventual outcome. Good negotiation is a planned activity, not an impromptu one. Often, however, managers are called with almost no notice to negotiate, and it is therefore important to develop strong negotiation skills to cope with all circumstances during transformations.

In simplest terms, negotiation is a discussion between two or more people who are trying to work out a solution to a problem. This interpersonal or intergroup process can occur at a personal level, as well as an organizational level. When people negotiate, they usually expect give and take. While they have interlocking goals that they cannot accomplish independently, they usually do not want or need exactly the same thing. The disputants will either attempt to force the other side to comply with their demands, to modify the opposing position and move towards compromise, or to invent a solution that meets the objectives of all sides. The nature of their interdependence will have a major impact on the nature of their relationship, the way negotiations are conducted, the outcomes of these negotiations and, ultimately, on the success of the change.

Outcomes of negotiation

There are three different outcomes that can come out of negotiations. They are often expressed as win–win, win–lose and lose–lose. Unfortunately, these terms suggest that there is a battle between each side of the negotiation. In a win–win situation, both parties are satisfied with the outcome, whether or not it was exactly what they had set out to achieve. In a win–lose situation, one side is the winner, and so by default, the other party is the loser. This is largely based on the attitudes of those entering into the negotiation – that it was somehow competitive and thus someone had to win. Entering into negotiations with the aim of solving a problem will help you to avoid this situation. In a lose–lose situation, both parties leave the negotiation feeling that they have not achieved their intended outcome. Again, it is based on the erroneous premise that negotiation is competition, rather than a problem-solving activity.

All three labels – win–win, win–lose and lose–lose – are applied both to the approach that the negotiators have taken to the negotiations and to the outcome of those negotiations. Just as you get what you measure, so in negotiating your approach this determines your outcome.

A win–win can be achieved when all parties approach the negotiations as problem-solving through discussion and debate. There are several steps you can take to ensure that this happens:

- *Distinguish between the personalities involved and the problem*
  It does not matter what you think of the person with whom you are negotiating. Imagine that the other person is someone you like, regardless of your true feelings. Realize that the issue here is the solution to a problem and not your relationship with the other negotiator.

- *Accept that there may be more than one solution*
  If your focus is solely on a narrow solution, your entire negotiating stance will be built around your attempts to achieve that solution and you will shut your mind to other possibilities. Think broader and accept that a number of solutions may be possible.

- *Look for solutions, not for fights*
  From the outset, work towards finding a solution. Negotiation is not a battle. If you treat it as a battle, either you or the other people

will lose. If you treat it as a way of solving a problem, there are no winners or losers – just solutions.

● *Establish the negotiation as something constructive*
From the outset, discuss the issue in positive terms. Preface the negotiations with a positive summary of the situation. Involve the other people in the process of solving the problem and show, with sincerity, your ability and willingness to accept the other party's viewpoint.

Everyone should walk away from a negotiation feeling comfortable about the result. A boastful or arrogant attitude towards the negotiation can only cause hostility. Allow the other party to feel good about the negotiation, but be careful not to patronize them as you do so.

Conflict resolution

A comprehensive and practical approach to conflict resolution is the one devised by Kenneth Thomas and Ralph Kilman (1974), which identifies the following five styles or modes of handling conflict: competing; collaborating; avoiding; accommodating; compromising. Figure 5.2 illustrates an adaptation of these different styles, which a colleague and I used in a leadership development programme for women in the Middle East. Table 5.2 describes the different styles, the behaviours for each style and when it is appropriate to use each style.

FIGURE 5.2   Individual styles of handling conflict

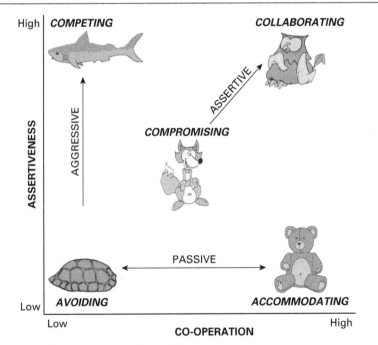

SOURCE: Adapted from Thomas and Kilman (1974)

TABLE 5.2 Conflict styles and behaviours

Strategy	Behaviour	When Used
Avoiding 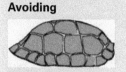 ***The Turtle*** *Turtles withdraw into their shells to avoid conflicts. They stay away from the issues over which the conflict is taking place and from the people they are in conflict with. Turtles believe it is hopeless to try to resolve conflicts. They feel helpless. They believe it is easier to withdraw (physically and psychologically) from a conflict than to face it.*	• Ignoring conflicts and hoping that they'll go away • Putting problems under consideration or on hold • Invoking slow procedures to stifle the conflict • Use of secrecy to avoid confrontation • Appeal to bureaucratic rules as a source of conflict resolution	• When an issue is trivial or more important issues are pressing • When you perceive no chance of satisfying your concerns • When potential disruption outweighs the benefits of resolution • To let people cool down and regain perspective • When gathering information supersedes immediate decision • When others can resolve the conflict more effectively • When issues seem tangential or symptomatic of other issues
Accommodating  ***The Teddy Bear*** *Teddy Bears want to be accepted and liked by other people. They think that conflict should be avoided in favour of harmony. They believe that conflicts cannot be discussed without damaging relationship, and if conflict continues, someone will get hurt. They prefer to give up their goals to preserve the relationship.*	• Giving way • Submission and compliance	• When you find you are wrong – to allow a better position to be heard, to learn, and to show your reasonableness • When issues are more important to others than to yourself – to satisfy others and maintain co-operation • To build social credits for later issues • To minimize loss when you are outmatched and losing • When harmony and stability are especially important • To allow subordinates to develop by learning from mistakes

TABLE 5.2   *continued*

Strategy	Behaviour	When Used
Competing **The Shark** *Sharks try to overpower opponents by forcing them to accept their solution to the conflict. They seek to achieve their goals at all costs, relationships are of minor importance. They do not care if other people like or accept them. Sharks assume that conflicts are solved by one person winning and the other losing. Winning gives them a sense of pride and achievement; losing a sense of weakness and failure.*	• Creation of win–lose situations • Use of rivalry • Use of power play to get one's own way • Forcing submission	• When quick, decisive action is vital – eg emergencies • On important issues when unpopular actions need implementing – eg cost cutting, enforcing unpopular rules, discipline • On issues vital to company welfare when you know you are re right. • Against people who take advantage of non-competitive behaviour
Compromising **The Fox** *Foxes are moderately concerned about their goals and relationships. They seek a compromise. They give up part of their goals and persuade the other party to give up part of theirs. They seek the middle ground where both parties can find some common ground and get something.*	• Bargaining • Looking for deals and trade-offs • Finding satisfactory or acceptable solution	• When goals are important, but not worth the effort or potential disruption of more assertive modes • When opponents with equal power are committed to mutually exclusive goals • To achieve temporary settlements to complex issues • To arrive at expedient solutions under time pressure • As a back-up when collaboration or competition is unsuccessful

TABLE 5.2 *continued*

Strategy	Behaviour	When Used
Collaborating *The Owl* Conversations might be challenging but the outcome is a better outcome for both parties, because of the nature of the conversation	• Always keep win–win in mind • Push harder than any of the other styles to get the best solution • Seek out new and innovative solutions	• Really important to get the absolute best outcome for both parties • When you have time to focus on getting the best out of a situation • When longevity is important • When you need to set a good precedent for the future

Managers (and leaders) should not assume that one approach for handling conflict will always be the best. Instead there is a need to select the most appropriate style for the situation. Like leadership style (see Chapter 4), conflict-handling style is situational in its skilful application and its effectiveness. Consider the following guidelines in order to identify the most appropriate style to use:

- Use *competing* when quick, decisive action is vital on important issues or where unpopular changes need to be implemented, such as cost cutting or downsizing.

- Use *collaborating* to find an integrative solution when concerns from all individuals are too important to be compromised, when the objective is to learn, to merge insights from people with different perspectives, to gain commitment to change, or to work through feelings about the change.

- Use *avoiding* when an issue is trivial or when more important issues are pressing, when potential disruption outweighs the benefits of resolution, to let people cool down and regain perspective, when gathering information supersedes immediate decision, or when others can resolve conflict more effectively.

- Use *accommodating* to allow a better position to be heard, to learn and to show reasonableness, to satisfy others and maintain co-operation, when harmony and stability are important, or to allow employees to develop by learning from mistakes.

- Use *compromising* when opponents with equal power are committed to mutually exclusive goals, to achieve temporary settlements to complex issues, or to arrive at expedient decisions under time pressure and as a backup when collaboration or competition is unsuccessful.

To manage conflict effectively, managers (and leaders) need to know who their stakeholders are and their attitude to the change. In the next section we discuss stakeholder management.

Stakeholder analysis

For change to be successful, managers need to know who is affected by the change and who needs to be involved with it. Any individual or group with an interest or involvement in the change and its outcomes is known as a stakeholder. Being able to categorize a stakeholder is crucial for prioritizing and identifying appropriate influencing strategies. The benefits of using a stakeholder-based approach are:

- Managers can use the opinions of the most powerful stakeholders to shape projects at an early stage. Not only does this make it more likely that stakeholders will support the change, but also their input can improve the quality of the process.

- Gaining support from powerful stakeholders can help to win more resources. This makes it more likely that change projects will be successful.

- By communicating with stakeholders early and frequently, managers can ensure that they fully understand what is happening and understand the benefits of the change. This means that they can actively support the change when necessary.

- Managers can anticipate what people's reaction to the change may be, and build into their plan the actions that will influence and win people's support.

Steps in stakeholder analysis

To carry out a stakeholder analysis the following three steps are proposed:

1 *Identify key stakeholders*
  This first step in stakeholder analysis is to identify who are the key stakeholders. This is best done as a group exercise. Get together with a few people who have knowledge about the different parts of the business, and ask:
  - Who will be affected by this change?
  - Who will be responsible for making it happen?
  - Who will be accountable for it?
  - Who will benefit from the change?
  - Who can influence the change?

2 *Analysing stakeholders*

Once all the key stakeholders have been identified you then need to assess how they will impact the change. To do this consider the following:

- How much influence do they have to make the change happen, or to prevent it from happening?
- How supportive are they of the change? Do their actions match their words?
- How much change will they experience themselves? How easy or difficult will it be for them?
- What is their interest in the change?
- How much power do they have? Is their power positional or relational?

Since analysing stakeholders is inevitably a subject exercise you should involve others in the analysis.

3 *Manage stakeholders*

The final step of the stakeholder analysis is to develop an understanding of the most important stakeholders and identify how they are likely to respond, so that you can work out how to win their support. For this you can use the template for a stakeholder plan in Appendix 5.3 (at the end of this chapter). This exercise of analysing and managing stakeholders will give you a guide to where you need to devote your time and effort. Stakeholders who are not committed to the change and who can influence the project represent a potential risk. Unless they are proactively managed, project costs could escalate, time-scales slip and benefits may not be fully realized. The stakeholders who are optimistic and supportive of the change need to be engaged in it.

Identifying and analysing stakeholders is a continuous activity, as new stakeholders may emerge during a change process and old ones may leave the organization or move to another job where they are no longer involved or impacted by the change. As change progresses, its scope may alter and some stakeholders will become less relevant, or they may lose interest. The management of stakeholders is therefore an ongoing and dynamic activity.

Activity

In the example below, Table 5.3, what would you consider to be the problem areas? How much effort do you think should be devoted to each of the stakeholders or stakeholder groups?

TABLE 5.3 Stakeholder analysis

Individual or Team (including job title)	Role in the Change (ie leader, influencer, participant)	Level of impact (ie how the change will affect them)	Degree of supportive (high/ medium/ low)	Level of influence (high/ medium/ low)	Issues/ reasons/ consequences
Managing Director	Leader (sponsor)	Low	Medium	High	Has a lot of competing priorities – may not have time to fully support the project.
Team leaders	Participants	High	Medium	Medium	Have key role in implementing change and supporting teams. May need training/support to develop skills.
Team members	Participants	High	Low/medium	Low	See reasons for the change but if not well managed then job performance and morale will be affected.
IT Director	Influencer	Low	Low	High	Needs to authorize resources for the project. Does not currently see it as a priority.

Defining activities

Once managers have considered the stakeholders they also need to consider the specific change management tasks. The range of possible activities is broad. It is a question of working out what will best help to meet the change initiative, as defined in the scope and objectives, and how to work with key stakeholders. The essence of this is to identify the tasks that are necessary to give the change the greatest chance of success. The key activities involved in managing change include (but are not limited to):

- ensuring there is a clear expression and understanding of the reasons for the change, and helping the sponsor to communicate this;
- identifying people who need to be involved in specific change activities, such as design, testing and problem solving, and who can then act as ambassadors for change;
- assessing all the stakeholders and defining the nature of sponsorship, involvement and communication that will be required;
- planning the involvement and project activities of the sponsor;
- planning how and when the changes will be communicated, and organizing and/or delivering the communications messages;
- assessing the impact of the change on people;
- planning activities needed to address the impact of the change on the team/department/organization;
- ensuring that people involved and affected by the change understand the process;
- making sure those involved or affected have help and support during times of uncertainty and upheaval;
- identifying training needs driven by the change, and planning when and how they will be addressed;
- identifying and agreeing the success indicators for change, and ensuring that they are regularly monitored, measured and reported on.

Remember, these are just some typical change management activities. Others may be required in specific situations. Equally, some of the above may not be within only one manager's remit, so planning has to be done carefully, and co-ordinated with the other managers involved.

The following case study describes how Nissan used a project approach to manage change activities across its Russian and European sites.

CASE STUDY   Changing processes at Nissan

Written by Yulia Johnson and Audrey Polyakov, programme managers at Nissan

In August 2013, a fundamental business change in how parts were ordered and assembled was introduced in the Nissan Russian plant, located in St Petersburg. The plant employed 1,000 people prior to the change and 1,500 after the change. Before the change the plant used to assemble vehicles by batches of 12 following the 'complete knock down' (CKD) method. The CKD process involves the manufacturing of vehicle assembly parts all over the world several months prior to the product completion in the Russian plant. Such a process meant that there was a lack of flexibility when any specification changes were required. The CKD process had three main disadvantages. First, Nissan industrial operations in the country could not be synchronized with customers' requirements. Second, the method imposed constraints on the optimization of the supply chain. Third, it prevented acceleration and effectiveness of the production.

The new process that was being implemented – individual parts ordering (IPO) – meant that the method of managing the assembly business shifted Nissan operations in Russia to a different level. The new process provided the business with the required flexibility by allowing a car to be manufactured in any specification, quantity and sequence. Individual ordering and delivery of the components would also make a significant contribution to the optimization of the logistics costs. Once it was agreed by the company's executives that the benefits of the new process would outweigh the cost of its implementation, a strategic change programme was kicked-off to implement the process. It meant introducing changes not only in the Russian plant but also in the European headquarters and other regional plants.

The change consisted of a complete redesign of processes across the organization and affected every employee, despite the common assumption that it was a straightforward software implementation project. The new process would enable the Russian plant to influence vehicle design decisions and provide the plant with more flexibility and independence. It would also enable the plant to construct a production plan synchronized with customer demand, and to mix an assembly of simple and complex specifications on one production line.

These fundamental modifications produced changes in all downstream processes. One of the major elements introduced in the downstream areas was the management of production sequence on the shop floor. This was a newly introduced regional system that had not been used in Nissan before. To ensure efficient synchronization between the material handling and the production, another piece of software was implemented. To synchronize the needs of the plant with suppliers and external warehouses a copied regional system was implemented. This had impact on the finance and customs departments due to changes in the different types and structure of information that was received about components delivery and manufacturing. As a result, the finance system required a complete redesign to ensure it was connected to the new processes.

The scope of the change included three main phases. First, the framework was created to clarify how programme elements should work together, including the planning and development of the systems. Second, procedures and staff training were developed. Third, system testing and cutover had to be planned as a separate activity. To implement the programme 27 elements of software had to be changed or replaced, more than 3,000 new skills had to be procured, and 100 people had to be 100 per cent dedicated (during 18 months) to the project from local and regional functions.

The scale of the initiative involved a high level of complexity in terms of changing processes. There were a number of challenges. The most significant complications were associated with the variety of individuals involved in the change, in terms of culture, experience, age, gender and language. The staff involved felt that it was a complex initiative because they could not appreciate and understand the whole scope. They tried to stay away from the training events about the new processes because they did not understand how to deal with them. To address this the programme manager, with the assistance of the project management office (PMO) function, sliced and diced the scope into digestible pieces. This helped people to understand and appreciate the scope better.

Another key challenge was the difference in cultures and positions. On one side were the process owners – the Russians – demanding and high-maintenance individuals, who kept asking for more without giving a proper evaluation of the impact on the overall programme. On the other side were the staff from the UK plant, which was perceived as Big Brother. The UK team were responsible for overseeing the Russian plant and making sure everything went according to the plan. Therefore, the Russian programme staff had to follow various restrictions and constraints imposed by the UK team, which according to the perceptions of the Russians could not grasp the whole complexity and differences of processes in Russia.

The Nissan project management methodology, based on Project Management Institute (PMI) principles and called PMWay, was applied to the IPO and modified to fit the programme due to the scale and complexity of the change. The structure of the work streams, and projects within it, were developed and built into a framework to control the performance of programme elements. The framework was called a responsibility matrix. It was an Excel spread sheet with assigned project roles of staff working on the programme in Russia and Europe. The project leaders appreciated a simple file and the fact they knew how their activities fitted into the overall picture and how they should interact with each other. It is important to highlight that local project managers were nominated to lead almost all elements. Project leaders got engaged with the change and engaged the rest of the organization. In the past, the project managers for local projects were always people from Europe who, according to the Russian team, simply wanted to deliver their objectives and did not worry about the views and feelings of the local people involved. It was also important that the local team had formal responsibility for the change. They had to report their status, risks and issues in their non-native language in front of the steering committee. It was a tough task but they realized it was a big statement of their status as well. Ultimately, those employees who were not formally a part of the programme felt left out and isolated. The programme was a tough challenge but it became a rewarding exercise for those involved in it.

A communication plan was introduced, which felt more like a formality rather than a value-added activity. As the change programme progressed, the communications were appreciated by the team, since it kept them informed of developments. An online collaboration space for people was implemented. Within the collaboration space, the most important framework was a risk and issue log. It was not easy to engage people in using the log. However, when they got engaged in it and started to speak the language of risks and issues, they learnt to focus on their actual problems rather than on the things they interpreted as risks and issues simply because they were not easy tasks to achieve. This taught the project leaders to verbalize and visualize their problems, engage other people in their issues and work together instead of trying to blame each other. The project leaders learnt to decide for themselves what they could solve within the programme and what they needed to report to the steering committee. The programme manager succeeded in building a direct relationship between the steering committee and the programme team members. He made sure that the project team realized their level of responsibility but was also able to interact directly with top management, whom they would never face in their day-to-day functional role.

Everyone involved in the programme learnt many good things and things they would avoid doing in the future. Amongst the good lessons learnt it is worth mentioning the overall project management approach. IPO served as a good example for Nissan Europe of how a change management approach should be engaged for non-new vehicle launches. The Nissan employees, who arrived from Russia to perform the change, had been in the company an average of 20 years. They knew the business very well and had a lot of experience and technical knowledge. However, they did not have experience in managing change in a proper way. In fact only after the implementation of IPO was it formally recognized that the organization was lacking in change management expertise. For the new programmes that are in progress now, consultancies are engaged to specifically perform the change management.

A major lesson learnt is that anticipating unexpected issues and having a positive attitude is always required even if the planning progresses smoothly. There is a direct link from this lesson learnt to the next one, which is about the engagement of the executive sponsor. There needs to be ongoing sponsorship for change from the top of the organization, which is one of the factors that helped to make the programme a success.

The overall approach to the IPO change seemed to have been fairly successful. It is important not to simply deliver the results, especially as in Nissan it is a given that results will be achieved. Everyone has to deliver and perform. The challenge is to keep enjoying the rollercoaster ride. The majority of local programme members have clear views about this change. After the programme had ended one could clearly sense a feeling of boredom when talking to them. They said that they now would like a repetition of 'IPO'. What better indicator of a good change management than positive feedback from the people affected?

Impact analysis of change on people

An impact analysis is a technique designed to unearth the unexpected negative effects of a change on an organization. It provides a structured approach for looking at a proposed change, so that managers can identify as many of the negative impacts or consequences of the change as possible. First, this makes it an important tool for evaluating whether the change should go ahead. Second, once the decision to go ahead has been made, it helps to prepare for and manage any serious issues that may arise. All too often organizations do not undertake an impact analysis. This is one reason that so many changes end in failure, as unforeseen consequences can wreak havoc.

The challenge of impact analysis

The challenge in conducting an impact analysis is to capture and structure all the likely consequences of a decision; and then, importantly, to ensure that these are managed appropriately. For smaller decisions, it can be conducted as a desk exercise. For transformations that will affect the whole organization, it is best conducted with an experienced team, ideally with people from different functional backgrounds from across the organization. With a team like this, it is much more likely that all of the consequences of a decision will be identified rather than if the analysis is conducted by one person.

How to use an impact analysis

To conduct an effective impact analysis, use the following steps:

1 *Prepare for impact analysis*
   The first step is to gather a good team, with access to the right information sources. Make sure that the change proposed is clearly

defined, and that everyone involved in the assessment is briefed about what is proposed and the issues/challenges that it is intended to address.

2 *Identify the major areas affected*
Now identify the major areas affected by the proposed change and think about whom or what it might affect. Managers need to involve the people most likely to be affected by the change, as they will have more insight into the consequences of the change. For each of the major areas identified, brainstorm all of the different elements that could be affected. For example, if looking at departments, list all of the departments in the organization. If looking at processes, map out the business processes. For instance, starting with the process the customer experiences, then moving on to the business processes that support this. The extent to which this can be done depends on the scale of the change and the time available.

3 *Evaluate impacts*
Having listed all of the groups of people and everything that will be affected in an appropriate level of detail, the next step is to work through these lists identifying and listing the possible negative and positive impacts of the change, and making an estimate of the size of the impact and the consequences of the decision.

4 *Manage the consequences*
If the impact analysis is being used as part of the decision-making process, it will need to be considered whether it is worth going ahead with the change given the negative consequences on the people it will cause and given the cost of managing those negative consequences. If the analysis is for a change that has already been given the go-ahead, the following will need to be considered:

- the actions required to manage or mitigate these consequences;
- how to prepare the people affected so that they will understand and ideally support change rather than fighting against it;
- the contingency strategy needed to manage people should negative consequences arise.

Few changes happen in isolation. The effects they cause can be diminished or amplified by other things that are going on. When thinking about the impact on people, managers need to think about the context they are operating in, and also think about how people might react to the change and work with it or against it.

Activity

Make a list of the actions that you will now do on a change project that you are working on, as shown in Figure 5.3.

FIGURE 5.3 Action list for a change project

Action	By When	Who Needs to be Involved

Activity

Based on the information you have from this chapter on managing change and your experience of change, create a synthesized set of criteria for assessing and developing the characteristics needed for a manager to be able to manage change effectively.

Summary

Managers need to identify the most appropriate approach for managing people through change. According to Rue By (2007) there are only two approaches to organizational change management: the conscious and the unconscious. Both may involve the application of any of the conventional approaches. The conscious approach can be suggested to be continuous, proactive and driven by awareness, choice and decision. Such an approach should not merely concern one individual manager's approach to change management, but rather form the foundation of the organization's change management approach. Alternatively, the unconscious approach can be perceived as discontinuous, reactive and driven by organizational crisis, fear and chance. For instance, people may argue that 'A lot of the change efforts we see have a feeling of despair'. The initiators of unconscious change management often know it is not going to work and that it is too late, but are trying to do something about the situation. Owing to the nature of these two different approaches, it may be suggested that the former approach provides a greater probability of successful change management because employees are psychologically ready for change, while the latter provides greater probability of failure, as by the time change is initiated it is already too late. The former approach acknowledges continuous change readiness as a critical success factor. Organizations need to be ready to absorb and implement change as and when required. Consequently, readiness is fundamental to the successful management of any change within any organization.

The management of a change initiative is also dependent on individuals having the necessary ownership to make a transition from old to new ways of working. To encourage ownership involves managers being cognizant of people's concerns. If managers respond well to employees' personal concerns, the change will be more effective than if employees' concerns, especially their anxieties, are ignored.

Change is not a single, continuous process, but rather is broken down into a number of different activities. The significance of this is that managers will need to consider what strategies are appropriate for the different activities, rather than decide on a single approach that can be applied throughout the process and, at the same time, remain flexible and reactive to changes as they happen. This, of course, will require more effort and preparation time, but the reward is likely to be that change happens more smoothly and efficiently.

With regard to organizational change, leadership and management are complementary processes. Without managing change effectively, change initiatives and efforts will fail or disappoint, however good the leadership might be. So managers of change need to make sure that they understand and support the organization's vision, purpose and strategies for change, and also the underlying values that will inform it.

Implications for managers in the change process

From this chapter there are some key practical implications for managers in how to manage people through change:

- *Actively seek to gain commitment to change*
  Change management is an activity that involves engaging and gaining commitment from individuals. Identify in advance those individuals

who are likely to react positively to change and ask their advice and assistance in planning and implementing the change.

● *Provide the relevant support to individuals*
To manage employees' transition from resistance to commitment people require lots of information, training, support, involvement and appropriate rewards in order to feel valued, more in control of their destiny and committed enough to commit fully to the change.

● *Recognize and reward people's contribution to change*
Too many changes can be distracting, confusing and/or exhausting. Try to minimize the number of changes happening simultaneously and avoid change for the sake of change. Acknowledge the hard work of change by allowing some people to focus exclusively on the change as part of a core team – and ensure that their efforts are recognized and appropriately rewarded.

● *Assess the readiness for change*
Assess employees' readiness to change. Assessing the dispositional aspects of individual readiness to change contributes to the selection of employees for positions or assignments that inherently entail changes, or of employees who will become responsible for change implementation. The implication of overlooking the importance of individual readiness to change may result in the expected benefits not being produced, or even in failure to implement the change simply because people are not ready to change.

● *Identify and manage stakeholders*
Conduct a stakeholder analysis to identify key supporters and blockers of the change as early as possible. Use the opinions of the most powerful stakeholders to shape projects at an early stage. Not only does this make it more likely that stakeholders will support the change – their input can also improve the quality of the project. Communicate with stakeholders to ensure that they fully understand what is happening and understand the benefits of the change, so that they can actively support the change when necessary.

● *Anticipate reactions to change*
Anticipate what people's reaction to the change may be, and build into the plans the actions that will influence and win people's support.

● *Analyse the impact of the change*
Use an impact analysis to help think through the full impacts of a proposed change. This should be an essential part of the evaluation process for change decisions. It provides the ability to spot problems before they arise, so that contingency plans can be developed. This can make the difference between well-controlled and seemingly effortless change management – and an implementation that is seen as a shambles.

References

Armenakis, A, Harris, S and Mossholder, K (1993) Creating readiness for organizational change, *Human Relations*, **46** (6), pp 681–703

Bordia, P, Restubog, D, Jimmieson, N L and Irmer, B E (2011) Haunted by the past – effects of poor change management history on employee attitudes and turnover, *Group & Organization Management*, **36** (2) pp 191–222

By, R T (2007) Ready or not..., *Journal of Change Management*, 7 (1), pp 3–11

Centre for Creative Leadership (2012) *Leading Effectively e-Newsletter*, Center for Creative Leadership, December

Dinwoodie, D, Pasmore, W, Quinn, L and Rabin, R (2015) Navigating Change: A Leader's Role, White Paper US: Center for Creative Leadership

Gyurjyan, G, Parsons, I and Thaker, S (2014) *A Health Check for Pharma: Overcoming change fatigue in the pharmaceutical industry*, McKinsey & Company, London

Hameed, I, Roques, O and Arain, G A (2013) Nonlinear moderating effect of tenure on organizational identification (OID) and the subsequent role of OID in fostering readiness for change, *Group & Organization Management*, January, pp 1–27

Meaney, M, Pung, C and Wilson, S (2010) *Voices on Transformation: Insights from business leaders on creating lasting change*, McKinsey & Company, London

Moorhouse Consulting (2012) *Too Much Change? Financial Services Survey 2012: The results*, Moorhouse, London (October)

Moorhouse Consultancy (2014) [accessed 16 October 2015] Barometer on Change, *Moorhouse: London* [Online] http://www.moorhouseconsulting.com/insights-publications/publications/2014/barometer-on-change-2014/

Mullins, L J (2010) *Management & Organizational Behaviour*, 9th edn, Pearson Education, Harlow

Paton, R and McCalman, J (2008), *Change Management: A guide to effective implementation*, 3rd edn, SAGE, London

Rafferty, A E, Jimmieson, N L and Armenakis, A A (2013) Change readiness: a multilevel review, *Journal of Management*, **39** (1), pp 110–35

Robbins, S P (2005) *Organizational Behaviour*, FT/Prentice Hall, Harlow

Tannenbaum, R and Schmidt, W H (1973) How to choose a leadership pattern, *Harvard Business Review*, May–June, pp 3–12

Thomas, K W and Kilmann, R H (1974) *Thomas-Kilmann Conflict Mode Instrument*, Xicom, Inc, New York

Further reading

Conway, E and Monks, K (2011) Change from below: the role of middle managers in mediating paradoxical change, *Human Resource Management Journal*, **21** (2), pp 190–203

Dea, W (2013) Change management fails for three reasons, *Huffington Post*, 18 July

Dike, D (2014) [accessed 16 October 2015] Why change? Why not?, *Management Issues*, 27 August [Online] http://www.management-issues.com/opinion/6442/why-change-why-not/

Witzel, M (2014) *Managing for Success*, Bloomsbury, London

Appendix 5.1 – Change readiness assessment template

	Information Source	Status Red/ Amber/Green	Actions
Track record			
Have past changes met with opposition?			
Were past changes poorly understood?			
Have recently introduced changes had limited or little success?			
Willingness to change			
Do leaders share a common change vision?			
Is the vision clearly defined and communicated?			
Do people understand the benefits of the change?			
Are people frustrated or dissatisfied with current ways of working?			
Do managers demonstrate strong support for the change?			

	Information Source	Status Red/ Amber/Green	Actions
Have people operating the processes/systems to be changed been involved in the new designs?			
Do people feel that there has been too much change recently?			
Is the track record of this type of change one of success or failure?			
Do people believe that the change will be successfully delivered?			
Do different people hold different ideas about the change?			
Do people know what to expect?			
Are objectives clearly defined?			
Change Resources			
Does senior management support the change?			
Does the proposed change place greater demands on people?			
Have the right resources been made available to the change team?			

	Information Source	Status Red/ Amber/Green	Actions
Have all critical stakeholders been identified?			
Has a stakeholder management plan for each stakeholder been developed?			
Are key stakeholders supportive of the change?			
Ability to change			
Do managers have the capability to manage the change?			
Do leaders act as role models?			
Is the past track record of this type of change one of success or failure?			
Is change usually imposed or is commitment to change usually the approach taken?			
Have lessons been learnt from past changes?			
Do leaders champion the removal of barriers to change?			

	Information Source	Status Red/ Amber/Green	Actions
Allowed to change			
Do change plans exist with clear objectives and milestones?			
Are responsibilities clear and understood?			
Is new knowledge passed around the organization effectively?			
What barriers get in the way of change?			
Do people usually need permission from senior managers before they change anything?			
Do people feel able to raise issues with their manager, even if it means disagreeing with them?			
Are people encouraged to learn when things go wrong?			
Is information freely shared?			
Is two-way dialogue encouraged?			
Do managers obtain and act on feedback and concerns about change?			

Appendix 5.2 – Managing people through change: a checklist for managers

At the definition and start-up phase

- Change purpose:
  - Can you say what the compelling reason for the change is? If not, who do you need to speak to for clarification?
  - Can you describe what the business will look like when the change has been implemented?
  - Is there more you can do to develop the vision? Who would need to be involved?
  - How will the vision be achieved?
  - Does the plan identify clear phases and deadlines?
  - Is the timetable realistic?
  - Is responsibility for change clear?
  - Have you planned how the purpose will be communicated to people affected by the change? Is this reflected in your communications plan?
  - On how wide a scale will the change be introduced?
  - Are the people involved supportive, informed and prepared?
- Managing stakeholders:
  - Do you have the full picture of everyone who will be affected by the changes?
  - How will people be affected by the changes? How are they likely to react?
  - Who are the key players who will need to be involved for the change to succeed?
  - What do they know about the change? Where are the potential showstoppers?
  - Have you identified how you will manage stakeholders and documented this in a stakeholder management plan?
  - Do you have a communications plan that ensures regular communications to all key stakeholders?
- Measuring benefits of change management:
  - Have you identified the changes in skills, attitudes and behaviours that will be necessary for the project to succeed?
  - Have you discussed and agreed these with your sponsor and other key stakeholders?
  - Have you identified the measures that can be used to track those changes?

During project implementation

- Change purpose:
  - Do you now have more detail about what the organization will look like?
  - How clear are the steps towards achieving the vision?
  - How is the detailed picture of the future being communicated to people affected by the change?
  - How well understood is the purpose by people affected by the change?
  - How positive do people feel? Does the vision need to be made more compelling?
- Managing stakeholders:
  - Are the actions identified in your stakeholder management plan being implemented? How effective have they been?
  - Do you need to make any revisions/additions to your plan as the change progresses?
  - Have any stakeholders changed?
  - How committed are those stakeholders whose commitment is crucial to the project?
  - How certain are you that they really are supporting it?
  - How are you ensuring that the people most affected by the change are actively engaged in the implementation?
  - Is your communications plan giving people as much relevant information as early as possible?
  - How are you measuring the effectiveness of communications?
- Ownership:
  - Does the change impose controls on people?
  - Does the change reduce the discretion or initiative of managers or others?
  - Are those people who are affected being consulted?
  - Are there incentives and benefits?
- Training and development:
  - Are people being provided with specific training and development?
  - Is the training flexible and geared to people's needs?
  - Are you targeting the right people for the training and development?
  - How are you measuring the impact of the training and development?

- Managing stress and anxiety:
  - Are people stressed?
  - Is performance declining because of stress levels?
  - Is there a higher incidence of people issues, such as volatile behaviour between teams and/or individuals?
- Measuring benefits of change management:
  - Are change management problems (such as stakeholder resistance) being logged as risks?
  - Are you able to make a link between change management issues and the likelihood of the benefits being realized?
  - What measures are you putting in place to evaluate the effectiveness of skills development?
  - Are benefits clear and direct for the people involved?

Post-implementation

- Change purpose:
  - How does the organization look now compared to the original purpose?
  - Can you explain the reasons for any differences?
  - Are there any lessons to be learnt for the way the purpose is defined and communicated in future projects?
- Managing stakeholders:
  - Have you ensured that your sponsor understands his/her role in monitoring and measuring the benefits post-implementation?
  - Are there people in place to ensure that commitment is sustained after implementation, so that people do not revert to old behaviours or retreat into comfort zones?
  - What lessons can be learnt for future change initiatives about building and maintaining stakeholder commitment?
- Measuring benefits of change management:
  - Have non-financial measures (such as customer satisfaction, staff turnover rates) been built into the benefits tracking process?
- Embedding change in the organization:
  - How will the change become a natural part of everyday life?
  - How well have you addressed the problem you set out to solve?
  - What will you do to recognize and reward achievements?
  - What remains to be done?
  - What are your next steps?
- Reviewing the change:
  - How will you review the sustainability of the change?
  - How can you learn from any lessons learnt?

Appendix 5.3 – Stakeholder management plan

Stakeholder	Stakeholder Role	Action	Action Category	Action Owner	Timing	Performance Measures	Feedback
Stakeholder 1							
Stakeholder 2							
Stakeholder 3							
Stakeholder 4							

06
Engaging people through dialogue

KEY POINTS

- Communications about change should be tailored and scaled to the needs and concerns of the specific stakeholders affected.
- At the heart of communicating about change is dialogue. Creating change using dialogue is about changing the conversations that shape everyday thinking and behaviour. It is about creating organizational conversations that lead to understanding and action.
- A lack of communication can encourage rumours that can demoralize people and result in distrust and a lack of commitment to the change.
- Gaining commitment to change means that managers and leaders need, at times, to get into the 'zone of uncomfortable debate' (ZOUD) with other people. The ZOUD focuses on conversations about complex or hard-to-resolve change issues, whether they involve a department, a team or an individual.

Introduction

The role of communication during organizational change is well established. Indeed, the management of communication processes that deliver key messages at the appropriate time to stakeholders is considered in the literature on change management as a vital component of all successful change initiatives. Yet it is often ignored, especially at the start of a change initiative, or in many cases done badly and therefore fails to address the concerns raised by people. The first question employees often ask as they face significant change is 'How will this change affect me?' To appreciate why this is a key concern, put yourself in the shoes of Shirley Woods. Shirley is an account executive for B&C Inc. She manages relationships with a handful of partner organizations that deliver high-quality services to the customer. In a casual conversation with a co-worker Shirley learns that the company may be acquired. Her first thought is that her job may be in jeopardy or that she will not get the promotion she expects this year. That night she and her partner discuss the situation. Job security is particularly important for them as the couple have two young children. Shirley's fears escalate. The next day the company's CEO sends a brief but enthusiastic e-mail to all employees announcing the acquisition. Shirley approaches her manager and asks, 'How will it affect me?' Her manager is equally shocked and concerned. This story illustrates how what appears to be a positive change to the leadership team of an organization can create anxiety in employees if they do not receive adequate information about how it will affect them.

The challenge is that communication, although viewed as an important part of the change process, is often ignored and dealt with in a cursory manner. Some managers are far too fond of sending a presentation by e-mail, which either goes unopened and is deleted or, at best, is skim read. Few people take the time to read an e-mailed presentation and are even less motivated to make changes as a result of it. At best, such e-mails are seen as a necessary evil. Their overuse springs from a mindset that if the case for change is presented as logically as possible then people, being rational, will buy into it and take the appropriate set of actions. E-mailing important news about change is also used as a corporate 'get out of jail free' card. Those involved with change can remain in their respective offices with their doors firmly closed, safe in the knowledge that when asked they can say, 'Well, it's not my fault; I told everyone what was going on.' In fact, they did not tell everyone – they sent them an e-mail presentation. That is not communication; it is hiding behind technology.

The aim of this chapter is to explore the importance of communication during change. Specifically, it focuses on dialogue, which is used even less frequently during change yet it plays a crucial role in leading and managing people successfully through change. Attention is given to how dialogue enables leaders, managers and other employees to discuss issues and potential changes, make better sense of the change and, therefore, enables greater commitment to, and ownership of change. The chapter focuses on promoting dialogue with employees through traditional mediums, such as town hall meetings, forums for staff representations, focus groups, and so on, as well as contemporary channels such as social media. In particular, it focuses on how to engage employees in conversations about change. The importance of dialogue and other forms of communication in eradicating uncertainty, gaining commitment and building trust among individuals and teams in an organization is explored. The chapter concludes by introducing an approach called the 'zone of uncomfortable debate' (or ZOUD), which helps to facilitate conversations about complex or hard-to-resolve issues to do with organizational change. Several key questions are addressed, including: what are the most appropriate communication strategies and tools to use? How can managers and leaders create effective dialogue during times of uncertainty? What affects the quality of dialogue? How should difficult conversations be managed? How should rumours be addressed?

LEARNING OUTCOMES

By the end of this chapter you will be able to:

- identify the challenges of communicating about change;
- craft communications about change for specific audiences;
- select and use social media and collaboration tools to improve communication during times of change;
- develop a plan for managing stakeholder communication;
- effectively prevent rumours occurring, through the use of effective communications and dialogue;
- engage in dialogue in order to appreciate how others are making sense of the change and to appreciate their perspectives;
- enter the ZOUD in order to focus on conversations about complex or hard-to-resolve change issues.

Communicating change

Change too often fails simply because of a lack of proper or sufficient communication. An article in the *Guardian* newspaper about redundancies at Microsoft illustrates how communication can vary. The article describes how in 2014 Microsoft's CEO Satya Nadella announced that he would realign the company's workforce by laying off approximately 18,000 employees, more than 14 per cent of its workforce. As part of the job reductions, the company expected to eliminate 12,500 positions in its Nokia Devices and Services division. In an e-mail to staff, Nadella outlined that the company would be offering severance to all impacted employees as well as help with job transition, wherever possible. Nadella ended the e-mail with the promise that 'We will go through this process in the most thoughtful and transparent way possible.' In contrast, Stephen Elop, vice-president for devices at Microsoft, sent a lengthy letter to staff about the redundancies, which began with 'Hello there' and was peppered with management jargon such as 'ramp down', 'right-size' and outlined a desire to 'help people do more'. It was only in the final paragraphs that Elop acknowledged that 12,500 professional and factory roles would be axed from Nokia's devices and services division. He concluded, 'These decisions are difficult for the team, and we plan to support departing team members with severance benefits' (*Guardian*, 17 July 2014). These announcements vary in their content and language but both lack confidence in communicating the purpose and impact of the change.

The way in which an organization expresses change and the words and images it chooses to represent transformations is important. What is said about change is one thing, how it is said is another, but just as important. Effective communication requires close attention to language and commitment to work with words that are well defined and associated in ways that are specific to the company. Communication about change has to be characterized by sincerity and honesty. This does not mean that the communication needs to be spontaneous and improvised. Instead, well-orchestrated communication that is prepared with care and attention as to how it is translated to different audiences can be very effective. Steve Jobs's keynote addresses for Apple, for example, are renowned as examples of carefully orchestrated moments of communication.

So leaders and managers must craft their communication with care and consider how their words will affect their audience. Achieving the right impact with communications comes with understanding what is most relevant at any given time for various people.

Impact of communications

Quality communications can have a significant impact on the outcomes of change. Empirical research has consistently demonstrated that effectively managed communication during change is related to a range of positive employee outcomes. For example, research shows a direct association between high-quality change communication and reduced anxiety (Rafferty and Restubog, 2010) and uncertainty for employees (Allen *et al*, 2007), as well as enhanced self-efficacy to cope with impending changes (Parker, Jimmieson and Johnson, 2013). Furthermore, communication can help to shape employees' reactions to change. A study carried out by Nerina Jimmieson and Katherine White (2011) into a hotel undergoing a rebranding exercise showed that high-quality communication helped employees to support and adjust to the change.

In order to engage people in change, time and energy must be invested in communications so that fears, concerns and doubts are addressed. Communication about change therefore needs to be accurate, useful, adequately address employee concerns, and be presented in a timely and appropriate way. Deborah Barrett (2002) identifies five specific goals for communications about change. It must: 1) ensure clear and consistent messages to educate employees in the company vision, strategic goals and what the change means to them; 2) motivate employee support for the company's new direction; 3) encourage higher performance and discretionary effort; 4) limit misunderstandings and rumours that may damage productivity; and 5) align employees behind the company's strategic and overall performance improvement goals. This framework emphasizes the need to convince employees that the proposed change is necessary in order to improve the viability of the organization. In addition, it advocates tailoring the communication to ensure that employees can see the relevance of the change to their jobs. Such advice on how to communicate organizational change is helpful but is very general and tends to assume a one-way communication process rather than a multiple approach. For communication about change to be effective it must go up, down and across an organization's hierarchy and be of a high quality.

The importance of communication as a change practice

Managers are often reluctant to provide employees with all the information needed to make sense of difficult managerial decisions. However, crafting and providing a change message that is high in quality is essential for reducing uncertainty and stress reactions, and increasing engagement. The importance of quality communications is highlighted by Adobe – the multinational computer software company – during a series of acquisitions it carried out. The CEO, Shantanu Narayen, describes the importance of communication during this time:

> What it required, honestly, was an incredible amount of travel. People would joke about how often they heard me, and others in the management team, constantly reiterating what was going on. In the end, though, there was no substitute for the power of repetition – or of wearing out the shoe leather.
> (Waters, 2014)

As Narayen says, it is important to repeat key messages so that they are listened to and understood. Managers must cater for the different needs of their employees when designing and implementing communications. Although people clamour to hear the view of leaders, this does not mean that they will be prepared to accept whatever message is delivered. The message needs to make sense in order to encourage engagement and energy for the change. As Paul Lawrence says: 'for a message to make sense it must resonate with the recipient's perspective on the change, be experienced as open and transparent and be delivered with authenticity and sincerity' (2015: 49).

It is important to communicate from the start of a change or transformation. Often management are reluctant to communicate at the early stages, due to too many unknowns and a risk that people will become concerned about potential issues before any answers or reassurances can be given.

The following case study, written by Tom Stern, illustrates the impact that a lack of communication has on people.

CASE STUDY   Communicating through change

Written by Tom Stern, cardiovascular marketing-product director, Janssen Pharmaceutical Companies of Johnson & Johnson

During my first role as a middle manager, the company I was working with made the decision to conduct a restructure in preparation for new product launches. As a result of the restructure a number of staff roles were to be made redundant. I was notified that I needed to inform 90 per cent of my team that they were going to be displaced. Myself and other managers were asked to delay delivering the unfortunate news until December (after being told about it in September) because the senior leadership team wanted the staff to remain focused on their work for the remainder of the year and continue to improve business performance. This meant that for three months 200 middle managers were asked to remain silent about the redundancies. However, the news was the worst-kept secret. Throughout the organization, everyone anticipated that change was coming and not all of the managers remained silent.

Once the announcements had been made in September to the managers, the senior leaders remained silent. There was no access to the leadership nor did they check-in with managers. At the middle-management and non-leadership level, speculation began about what the impact of the change would be, with questions such as: 'Am I going to lose my job?' and 'As I had a better evaluation than my colleague does that mean that I won't lose my job?' Information started to slowly leak out. I began to receive phone calls from my team asking me about their job status, as they had heard from their peers who had already unofficially received notification that their jobs were secure.

After the announcement in September, I had met with my team and informed them that change was coming in December and that I was unable at that time to share more details with them. In my mind, I knew I had to be accessible to my team. I was not even sure if my own job was safe but knew I could not abandon my staff. We eventually made it to December and I communicated to 90 per cent of my team that they were to be laid off. Emotions varied but I was fortunate to help all of them to find employment within or outside of the organization. However, the leadership team remained invisible throughout the restructuring process and as a result there was a lack of support and commitment for the change.

If the senior leadership team had communicated a vision of where the organization was going in three to five years, they probably would have had greater support. If they had been visible and accessible, it could have helped people to embrace the change and acknowledge that the leadership was supportive of what we were going to encounter. Instead, neither happened and no one embraced the change nor believed in the direction in which the organization was going. As a result, we lost an additional 15 per cent of the retained employees the following year.

A year later the individuals on the senior leadership team changed and the organization continued to restructure in preparation for new product launches. However, our new senior leadership was vocal and shared a vision that was based on internal employee insights. Throughout the year, the senior leadership implemented a quarterly road show. They targeted different areas of the country to learn about the morale of the organization. They segmented the employee insights and developed task forces for each common theme. The task forces were responsible for developing solutions for issues identified. These were then introduced and the feedback was extremely positive. The annual internal survey results reflected a shift in internal morale based on the leadership team listening, being present, transparent and demonstrating forward thinking. Though the company continued to reduce staff, the organization was much more receptive, based on the commitment of the leadership team and their ability to communicate throughout change rather than avoid it.

When formal communication channels are not effective, as is evident in the above case study, then people will fill in the gaps with rumour and conjecture, which can be more damaging and very hard to dispel in the later stages of the change process.

Addressing rumours

Rumours play a role in most, if not all, aspects of organizational change. Rumours are 'information statements that circulate among people and are instrumentally relevant and unverified' (DiFonzo and Bordia, 2007: 16). The central defining feature of rumours is that they are unverified – they are not secure evidence that would signify veracity. This does not mean that all rumours are false; they may indeed be true but still lack the accompanying substantiation or imprimatur demonstrating authenticity. Lack of communication or inconsistent messages – and the resulting misunderstanding of the aims and process of change – encourage rumours that may demoralize people and cause a lack of commitment to change.

Rumours are difficult to control once they have begun to spread. They may create negative opinions or cynicism about change. Prashant Bordia and colleagues (2006) surveyed employees of a large public hospital in Australia that was undergoing major changes to its structure and operational procedures, as well as relocating to a new building. The study found that nearly half the rumours reported were about the impact of the change on jobs, including rumours predicting job losses, negative consequences for career advancement, negative changes to the type of work, and a loss of job facilities. The second largest type of rumour was about the true or real nature of the change. The third most frequent set of rumours alleged poor and incompetent change management: including wastage, misplaced priorities and cynicism about reasons for the change and the consultation process. Such rumours can pose a risk to change because they distract employees from their roles and responsibilities to support and drive the change forward.

Managers and leaders have a choice to either address or ignore rumours. It is recommended, however, that managers address rumours. Rumours cannot be abolished or hidden away or even stopped. Trying to do so can only lead to the further spreading of rumours, leading to a negative impact on change. Recommendations for addressing rumours in the workplace include the following:

1 Establish an open dialogue (see the section below on dialogue) with employees.

2 Address immediately any rumours that have the potential to damage the transition and transformation.

3 Act quickly to address rumours in order to avoid their spreading further.

4 Establish procedures for addressing rumours and a rumours training programme that coincides with the organization's ethics training programme or a similar type of training programme.

5 Hold 'town hall' meetings to address issues about organizational change initiatives and provide the latest information to employees.

6 Identify and talk with people who are creating a negative work environment by spreading false rumours.

7 Attempt to understand how individuals who are spreading rumours are interpreting the change.

The human dimension of communication

An individual's interpretation of change is unique and is affected by the way in which they process information about it. The brain can only absorb a limited amount of detail through the senses in any one moment. To avoid becoming overwhelmed, the brain filters information, in effect taking mental shortcuts to process information. However, shortcut processing can easily lead to misunderstandings, incorrect assumptions and biased thinking. Ranji Sidhu (2015) lists four biases (confirmation, status quo, availability and bandwagon effect) related to communication that can occur during change:

- *Confirmation bias*: this is a tendency for people to pay attention only to information that confirms their beliefs and ignore evidence that indicates otherwise. This leads people to argue against the need for change. To address this bias, leaders and managers need to ensure that they repeatedly communicate the vision and purpose of the change – and that the reasons for the change are communicated with objective evidence shown to back it up, including the losses and problems that will be avoided by changing. People should also be engaged in discussions so that they have an opportunity to develop new insights about the situation.

- *Status quo bias*: this is a preference to keep things the way they are and to avoid change. People with this bias will not agree that the change is needed, or they may say that they agree but show inertia and will take little action to make change happen. To address this bias, leaders and managers need to: ensure communication messages include what will continue and remain the same, as well as what will be changing; indicate practical next steps; and continue to communicate the purpose of the change.

- *Availability bias*: this is a tendency to perceive the more memorable or easily available information as the most significant. For example, instances of something not going so well, such as aspects of a new system not working, can lead to people complaining and being negative about changes. To address this bias, leaders and managers need to communicate when and how specific issues raised are being dealt with, and frequently highlight and share success stories.

- *Bandwagon effect*: the more that people come to believe something, the more others want to hop on the bandwagon. For instance, teams who are resistant to change start to influence others and resistance spreads. It can, of course, work the other way – as momentum builds, people actively start to adopt the changes. To help overcome this bias, leaders and managers need to start to communicate success stories early, such as how successful a pilot project was, and continue throughout the change process and get others involved in communicating these messages.

To accommodate the needs of diverse groups, different types of communication should be considered. People have different preferences for the way they receive and process information, so the same messages need to be conveyed using different formats and styles. It is also important to make an emotional connection with people when communicating with them, in order to achieve engagement with the change.

Impact of communications on emotions

Engaging people emotionally in change cannot happen without effective communication. Ken Blanchard and Scott Blanchard (2013) describe a US Department of Education study by Gene Hall and colleagues at the University of Texas, which identified the most important needs concerning communication that employees have when they are asked to co-operate in a change initiative, as follows:

- Not so much questioning why change is happening and why it will be good for the organization as having clear and complete factual information so they can understand what is wrong with the way things are, what the change is, why it is needed and how quickly.

- Questioning what impact the change will have on them personally and how the change will be implemented.

- As change starts to be implemented, questioning what are the expected benefits, relevance and payoff of the change and evidence of its positive impact.

- Questions about employee involvement, co-ordination and co-operation.
- Questions about refining the change effort as it approaches full adoption.

Effective communication involves providing the right type of information with the right channel for the purpose of different audiences. The choice of language, tone, structure and content must be appropriate to the context and audience. Successful communication needs to appeal to people's emotions. This emotional engagement is necessary in order to achieve fuller engagement. Three ways in which this can be done are through the use of: actions and symbolism; analogies and metaphors; and compelling stories.

Actions and symbolism

As Rosabeth Kanter says: 'Leaders must wake people out of their inertia' (2003: 5). Kanter goes on to say that leaders must get people excited about the change. The purpose of the change is not just a picture of what could be, but a call to become something more. The aspiration must be so compelling that it is worth the extra time and effort to achieve it. Kanter says that inspiring visions need to provide a picture of the future, drawing on the following elements:

- *Destination*: where are we heading?
- *Difference*: what will be different because of the change? What will people be saying and doing differently?
- *Outcome*: what positive outcomes will be obtained? What will be the benefits? What will people gain?
- *Target*: what key performance measures/objectives will make the outcome/s concrete?
- *Message*: what memorable image, slogan or headline conveys the essence of the goal?
- *Actions*: what tangible actions can be taken to make the goal a reality?

These elements are important because sometimes people do not understand what the leader is talking about when they first announce a transformational change. They may nod at the words, but do not understand or appreciate the meaning. Symbolic actions are therefore important as well as words. How the vision/purpose is conveyed matters. A leader's personal enthusiasm, reflected in their passion for the change, matters as much as the words they use.

To be perceived as credible and trustworthy, a leader has also got to recognize the importance of non-verbal communication, as it is especially crucial for leaders to communicate congruently, that is, to align what they are saying with their body language. When non-verbal messages conflict with verbal messages, people become confused. Mixed verbal and non-verbal signals can also have a negative effect on perceptions of trust. Symbolic actions are therefore as crucial in terms of not only verbal but also non-verbal communication, both of which need to be in sync.

Analogies and metaphors

Analogies and metaphors are useful in framing communications about change in order to gain legitimacy and understanding of it among stakeholders. Joep Cornelissen and colleagues (2011), in exploring the conditions and uses of analogies and metaphors in gaining support for transformational change, conclude that analogies are more effective in the context of additive changes – where changes can be framed in relation to past, established practices that are familiar to stakeholders; while metaphors are more appropriate for substitutive changes – when a proposed change is a break from the past and therefore avoids the constraints of past commitments, and yields the opportunity for comparisons beyond the organization or industry that resonate with the values and social identities of stakeholders. Relational analogies and metaphors that convey a system of connected counterparts and underlying causal relationships, rather than common attributes, are more likely to be judged as relevant and insightful of a particular change and are also more likely to be granted with legitimacy. The effectiveness of analogies and metaphors in framing and communicating change is dependent on the extent to which they are culturally familiar to stakeholders and to which they relate to their motivations. Analogies and metaphors can be used effectively in storytelling.

Creating compelling stories

Creating compelling stories helps managers and leaders to connect emotionally with people. Andrea Jung, the former CEO of Avon Products, has described how storytelling became important when the cosmetic company restructured in response to a decline in sales. Jung rejected the more efficient approach of delegating to managers the responsibility for communicating with employees about the restructure and of sharing information only on a need-to-know basis. Instead, she travelled the world to share her vision for growth and to discuss the difficult decisions that would be required in order to secure the company's future. The result was, according to Joanna Barsh and colleagues (2010), that employees felt that Jung was open and honest and made the harsh reality of job reductions easier to accept – by telling a compelling story about how she saw the future of the company. So stories can be effective in emotionally engaging people in transformations.

The art of dialogue

At the heart of communicating is dialogue. Creating change using dialogue is about changing the conversations that shape everyday thinking and actions.

This approach is about creating organizational conversations that lead to understanding and action. Dialogue allows more people to contribute to decisions about proposed change and to generate not only wisdom and a wealth of ideas but also immeasurable commitment. This means bringing together the right people to offer meaningful input and support. In the context of organizational change, dialogue is about people engaging in discussions about the why, how, what and when of change.

Listening and voicing

Dialogue has two components: listening and voicing. To listen most effectively leaders and managers need to enter into a dialogue curious as to what others are thinking, and the basis of their perceptions. Leaders and managers must be willing to put aside their own perspectives and listen attentively to the point of view of others. Listening is one of the most valuable leadership skills. The physicist Daniel Bohm, in his book *On Dialogue* – a treatise on how thought is generated and sustained on a collective level – writes that:

> Communication can only lead to the creation of something new if people are able to freely listen to each other, without prejudice, and without trying to influence each other. Each has to be interested primarily in truth and coherence. (2013: 3)

Bohm has observed group conversations that are like a game of ping-pong, where people are batting ideas back and forward and the object of the game is to win or to take points for themselves rather than listen to each other. Bohm believes that what is crucial is to create a dialogue where there is more of a common participation, in which people are not playing a game against each other, but *with* each other. Linda Gratton in her book *The Key* describes how she has experienced dialogue at Royal Dutch Shell, where the conversation within a group unfolds and is recursive rather than linear and directed. This gives participants time to reflect on the subtle implications of their assumptions and creates a context that is relaxed, non-judgemental and curious. Gratton says: 'I have experienced that what this creates is an increasing sensitivity within the group of similarities and differences and we listen more carefully to each other' (2014: 202).

A leader who listens is one step down the road to inspiring, influencing and engaging the members of their organization. Leaders who do not listen can quickly find themselves surrounded by people who are alienated or demotivated. Leaders need to learn to be quiet and listen. Often people in the organization, if they are asked questions and listened to, will have the answers to how to address challenges and what type of change is required. When NetApp – the data storage and cloud-computing company – wanted to share its updated corporate strategy with employees, instead of sending a company-wide e-mail the CEO Tom Georgens and 20 other senior executives embarked on a Strategy Roadshow, visiting 24 cities around the globe, listening to employees in person and getting their feedback about the strategy and what needed to change.

A good listener will listen not only to what is being said, but also to what is left unsaid or only partially said. Effective listening is difficult when a leader or manager listens from a different agenda. This can result in jumping too quickly to conclusions or it can lead to labelling the other person as resistant to change, which can often mean resistant to other people's agendas. When listening it is therefore important to set aside personal agendas and listen to the perspectives of others.

There is a fundamental difference between listening with an agenda and listening without an agenda. Listening without an agenda is hard. It entails recognizing the nature of personal agendas, including assumptions and beliefs that underlie that agenda, and putting aside the concerns that others may not see things the same way as managers and leaders. Without listening there is no dialogue, and therefore no perspective sharing, no process through which to consider a shared purpose, and no opportunity to understand some of the personal and emotional issues that can show up as so-called resistance to change.

Leaders and managers who listen well are most likely to find that others will respond well to voicing. Voicing is about bringing new and diverse voices into the change conversation. The aim is to encourage new thinking and actions in the people who are affected by the change. It is about creating new perspectives, stories, narratives and other socially constructed realities that impact on how people think and make sense of things that, in turn, impact on how they act.

Barriers to engaging in dialogue

Dialogue is challenging and requires effort from leaders and managers. Engaging in dialogue may be hard if a leader or manager believes in the sanctity of positional power. For someone who believes that people should do as they are told, engaging in dialogue may seem like a waste of time and raise questions such as: why encourage people to explore possibilities when it has already been decided what needs to happen next? What is the point in encouraging people to come up with ideas that they will only have to be dissuaded from?

Dialogue may also be difficult when a leader or manager fears being asked difficult questions or does not listen well. It may also be especially difficult if employees are based in different countries. In order to overcome such barriers Infosys – the Indian information technology company – has created a network to enable dialogue with its employees across the globe. For Nandita Gurjar, global head of HR at Infosys, the momentum has been extraordinary and captured the wisdom of the crowds:

> For the young at Infosys, communication was a big issue. They felt it is
> a very top-down approach. As a result they came up with the technology to
> make communication two-sided and more fluid. This comprised Infi TV and

Infi radio to be broadcasted on the intranet. They also came up with something like Facebook, which we call Infi bubble and that gets 100,000 hits a day.

(cited in Gratton, 2014: 26)

The need for constant communication that Infosys finds so crucial is also key to how the US software company Cisco encourages dialogue and co-operation among its employees. In order to connect its thousands of project teams, Cisco has built an intranet that enables employees and contracts to connect and communicate across the world. This is crucial because most Cisco employees spend as much as half their time working from home, whereas more than 40 per cent are located in a different city from their manager. Cisco offices have also been redesigned to include conferencing facilities to allow multiple participant meetings. Building this communication network has been an advantage for the company. There has been a number of occasions when the executive team have been able to deal speedily with a crisis because they have had the ability to hold emergency discussions at very short notice with participants around the world (Gratton, 2014). So creating effective dialogue has real advantages for companies.

Creating effective dialogue

People value dialogue and conversation. It takes much longer than e-mail but is infinitely more effective. To create effective dialogue try to avoid going to all meetings with detailed and well-prepared presentations as this can inhibit dialogue. Instead initiate a conversation with people. When I was working on the outsourcing and turnaround of a utilities company in the late 1990s we used an old concept called 'brown bag lunches' to start conversations about the changes. Basically it meant that you could invite anyone you wanted from any level in the organization to come and join you for a sandwich. Participants could talk for no more than 5–10 minutes about the changes, and then invite other people to talk, share ideas and raise concerns. This approach was always so much more powerful than doing presentations. People felt they had a voice and an opportunity to express their views. It was not a panacea but it was certainly an early part of building acceptance for the changes.

In summary, dialogue is not a one-off event that precedes effective change, nor is it something that should be ignored. As Paul Lawrence says:

An absence of dialogue means that the leadership of the organization are unlikely to be aware of what the rest of the organization is thinking and feeling... The leader's message may be logical and articulate but if it does not address what matters, it is likely to be heard as being irrelevant and/or implausible. (2015: 99)

By participating in dialogue individuals can become more informed about other people's perspectives, concerns and ideas. It is through dialogue, as opposed to monologue, that leaders and managers can understand what people are thinking and feeling about change, so that they gain their commitment to it and address their concerns.

Planning dialogue

The components of successful dialogue include devising a strategy for dialogue and including feedback as part of the dialogue. Each of these is briefly described:

- *Strategy*
  A strategy outlines what is to be achieved through dialogue and the overall approach. The strategy should consider:
  - What are the overall objectives and desired outcomes of the dialogue?
  - Who are the specific audiences?
  - What are the key issues that need to be discussed?
  - What are the methods and channels for dialogue (eg social media sites)?
  - When should it take place?
  - How will the impact be monitored and feedback obtained?
  - What are the performance measures to measure the effectiveness of the dialogue?

- *Feedback*
  Feedback is a crucial part of dialogue. It is required in order to measure the reach of and response to dialogue. This can be tracked by how employees react and respond to it; how motivated and engaged people are with it; and whether it has stopped rumours.

  Feedback should be regularly sought and, where possible, actioned. A global business software company, which I lead a research project for, implemented a transformational programme to change leadership behaviours across its international sites. The programme was to be cascaded to different countries by senior managers. The managers in each country were asked to engage in dialogues with their employees about the programme. The group HR director then contacted a sample of workers in each country to ask them what they knew about the change and where it had not been communicated. This survey provided a wealth of information on where countries had successfully communicated the change. The managers in the countries where dialogue had not taken place were asked to do so and were given coaching to help them to be more effective.

  Feedback, as part of dialogue, enhances confidence and trust that people's voices are being listened to and respected. There is a wide range of methods for capturing feedback during change from individuals. The most common include: pulse surveys; one-off surveys; focus groups; and individual interviews:

- *Pulse surveys*
  Pulse surveys are a way of checking in with people who may be affected by a change in order to learn their perceptions about it. A pulse survey, for example, can be used when a change has been

announced in order to capture early impressions, and also during implementation to check how well the change is working and what, if anything, needs to be altered or improved with the process.

● *One-off surveys*
One-off surveys are useful for taking a snapshot of opinions and feelings from a large group of people. They can be repeated during the change process in order to see if people's readiness, acceptance and engagement are altering in anyway.

● *Focus groups*
Focus groups can provide rich data on why something is happening. They can, for instance, be used to probe into the results from a survey.

● *Individual interviews*
Individual interviews can be used to explore sensitive subjects that people may not be keen to discuss in public. The data from interviews can be rich and personal to the individual. Although, it may not reflect the thoughts of the organization as a whole, it can be useful to understand what is driving an individual's behaviour.

In sum, the experience of giving and receiving feedback in a constructive and honest way develops both resilience and humility. It should form part of any dialogue process and is a great exercise to be practised over and over during change.

The case study below, written by Travis Callaway, an analyst for private equity venture capital at Strategic Group, Alberto, Canada, illustrates how feedback is key to gaining commitment to change and creating a willingness to change.

CASE STUDY   The fear of change in a Canadian advertising company

Written by Travis Callaway, director of operations and research

A small Canadian advertising company, after nearly 15 years in operation, was saddled with a brand and image that were, at best, stale and, at worst, entirely inappropriate for the calibre of clients that the organization was pursuing. To address this issue, the organization's president brought in an external consulting and marketing firm to facilitate a complete rebrand, with the intention of positioning it as a more sophisticated, upscale and blue-chip organization. After six months of market research the external consultants produced a reimagined vision for the organization, with a new name, logo, mission statement and target markets. The organization's president eagerly accepted the new vision and made plans for the gradual change from the old to the new brand. This meant breaking away from the established culture and pushing forward in an entirely new direction with the same team of employees – which is much easier said than done.

As a junior manager in the organization at the time of the transition I was directly responsible for a team of three. I had no input into the rebranding exercise during its planning stages and was informed of the new direction only when it was presented by the president and vice-president to the entire organization. This placed me in the unique and uncomfortable position of simultaneously being led *and* leading others through a period of organizational change. Having had no formal management education or training at the time, and being entirely unaware of change management theory or practice, I found it necessary to make it up as I went along. It was through this trial-and-error process that I learned some of the dos and don'ts of leading people through change.

One major don't was assuming that the entire team would share enthusiasm for the change. Along with myself there were two members of my team who were entirely convinced that the rebrand was necessary and thus enthusiastically bought in. There was, however, one team member who did not share our enthusiasm. During team meetings to review new policies and communication methods this individual would uncharacteristically challenge everything I said and roll her eyes at teammates' suggestions, often questioning the value of teammates' offerings but rarely providing suggestions herself. This individual obviously wanted nothing to do with the rebrand and was not shy about making her feelings known. After several weeks of disruptive behaviour from the team member I was forced to confront her about her atypically negative attitudes. During our conversation it became evident that her negative sentiment was borne of fear about what the organization's rebrand meant for the future of the team and her role within the team and the organization. She disclosed that she had a friend who had worked for a firm that had gone through a similar rebranding exercise several months before, which had resulted in her friend's contract being terminated as the firm's rebranding strategy ultimately resulted in layoffs. Consequently, the member of my team viewed the change process from an understandably tainted angle, which was generated by the experience of someone close to her. Along with my superiors I had erroneously taken as given that the rebrand would excite the team, without acknowledging the reality that for many people change is a very scary thing. Thus, assuming that change generates even remotely similar feelings within all those affected is something I have learnt is both erroneous and naive. I informed the organization's president of the team member's fears, which prompted the president to send a companywide memo offering assurance that the new vision for the firm included the entire existing team.

Conversely, a significant 'do' from my experience is the importance of soliciting and encouraging the feedback and opinions of those who will be affected by change. I regularly asked my team for suggestions on what they would do if directing the change and for feedback on the various stages of the change process. Similarly, the organization's president and vice-president regularly sought my opinion and, when appropriate, would put forth the suggestions to the external consulting and marketing firm for inclusion in the change plan. Some significant alterations to the firm's relaunched website resulted from feedback given by both the writer and other members of the team. Although the majority of feedback was not incorporated into the planned change programme, the solicitation of the feedback was still highly beneficial for accelerating the ultimate success of the process.

I observed how those whom the change is being forced upon were given an opportunity to help guide that change and saw both how significantly it reduced feelings of anxiety and also how it brought to light legitimately useful insights. Encouraging feedback from the entire team not only allowed the managers to identify and address both real and perceived issues but it also created a participative change environment.

Nearly six years later the company is thriving and growing rapidly. Although I have now left the organization I still maintain strong ties to it and I am immensely proud of what has been accomplished since the change process commenced. The organization successfully repositioned itself both in the marketplace and in the eyes of its existing clients, many having significantly increased their commitments to the organization in the years since the rebrand. Feedback from these long-term clients and from members of the organization's value chain confirms their improved perception of and trust in the company. It is the success of the change process behind the rebrand that ultimately deserves the credit for the organization's improved fortunes and its standing in the eyes of its clients and partners. This change process was certainly not flawless, as evidenced by the negative attitude of one member of my team, but management's commitment to soliciting the feedback of the entire organization throughout the process undoubtedly contributed to its ultimate success.

Discussion questions

What can be done to prevent individuals making false assumptions about how change will impact on them?

What benefits are there to feedback? Identify how feedback can be built into a change process.

Using social media to communicate

Social media is becoming the new communication channel for many organizations. The traditional 'water cooler' chat is being replaced by the use of social media – the virtual water cooler. Using Facebook, Twitter, YouTube, instant messaging, video conferencing and web meetings can help organizations to communicate successfully about change. The ways in which social media technologies can support dialogue include:

- *Building collaboration.* Social networking and collaboration applications can bring employees together to discuss and share experiences, both the successes and the setbacks. People with common interests or related roles can form online communities to learn from and support one another.

- *Establishing more effective dialogue.* Social media tools provide an effective and fast channel for dialogue. In addition, by monitoring and participating in online discussions, managers can more readily see where any misunderstandings or concerns exist across the organization and take steps to address them. Mohsin Ghafoor and Trinity Martin (2012) describe how one global resources company established a presence on Yammer, a social network that enables co-workers to communicate and share information with one another. According to Ghafoor and Martin, 70 per cent of the company's employees signed up for Yammer after its initial launch and 25 groups were created to discuss work-related issues, with over 2,000 messages posted each month. Such social media-based collaboration platforms can be used by employees not only to voice ideas and concerns but also to get responses and information about transformations.

- *Generating ideas.* Social media can be effective in generating ideas related to a change initiative. Organizations can use online collaboration platforms such as video casts, webinars and live web meetings in a variety of ways to encourage people to connect and share ideas.

- *Sharing current practices through a knowledge network.* Knowledge networks such as Twitter, Yammer and Facebook can help employees to get information, share innovative practices and receive answers in timely ways.

- *Improving employee involvement and engagement.* One of the critical success factors for managing transformational change programmes is engaging employees in the change (as discussed in Chapters 4 and 5), helping them to feel ownership and tapping into their energy for change. Social media and collaboration solutions allow information to flow in multiple directions rather than just from the top down. For example, by using wikis and micro blogs – applications for sharing short bursts of information in Twitter-like fashion – organizations can crowdsource ideas and involve employees more directly in the ideas about new initiatives.

According to a study carried out by Accenture (Ghafoor and Martin, 2012) social media tools can reduce the time an organization needs to navigate transformational change and deliver a better change experience from the employee's perspective; this, in turn, builds a foundation of capabilities for change. Social media is therefore an important addition to traditional communication channels

ZOUD – the zone of uncomfortable debate

Gaining engagement and commitment to change at times means that managers (and leaders) need to get into a 'zone of uncomfortable debate' (ZOUD) with other people. The ZOUD focuses on conversations and communication about complex or hard-to-resolve change issues, whether they involve a team, a business unit or an individual. Often, when leaders and managers have to do this the stakes may be high, emotions raised and personal opinions may differ. The quality and manner in which leaders and managers can deal with such issues determine how well and how fast progress is made on the difficult things to do with change and whether priorities get dealt with first or are avoided in favour of easier tasks. Entering the ZOUD is not about seeking confrontation or being aggressive. Rather, it is an approach for bringing difficult issues into the open in a structured and mature manner.

How to enter the ZOUD

To enter the ZOUD you need to:

1 First, review the situation. Why is it important that the issue is dealt with now? What needs to be achieved, and what are the desired outcomes? Where are the difficulties in the discussion, and why? What is the best time and place to start the debate, and how will you do justice to the issue? This first step clarifies your own thinking, planning, objectives and motives.

2 Identify your own wants and needs and, if possible, those of others involved. Needs are must-haves; wants are 'nice-to-haves'. Needs are the minimum requirement for success in a particular discussion or debate. For example, you need to get from a group discussion a clear commitment to a proposed change. You may also want to explore specific motivations as to why individuals are concerned about the change.

3 Be objective. Deal in facts, not gossip or assumptions. Basing a discussion on tenuous assumptions can lead to the wrong approach or focusing on the wrong outcomes. Look for the value and truth in

opposing views and facts from others by keeping an open mind. Describe the issue precisely.

4 Retain flexibility of thinking and approach in a ZOUD rather than starting out with a rigid mindset. The focus is on the deliverables. You may have to adapt and change to get what is required or alter your timescales and perspective as you discover more about an issue. Remember that there might be a better outcome than you first envisaged as a result of entering into the ZOUD.

5 Understand what triggers your own emotions and whether these 'buttons' are being pushed, intentionally or otherwise. Balance the need for a calm and rational approach with your passion for success and results.

6 Consider the input and views of others. Where are others in this ZOUD? Is it new to them, or were they expecting a discussion? If it is new, they may be starting from a position very different from yours, and they may need time to reach an understanding of a particular situation or to see your viewpoint. Actively listen rather than marshalling the next part of your argument. Discussions on tough issues are a journey towards resolution and progress. If you are chairing a debate or leading a discussion, seek to steer the conversation by reading the ebb and flow of the arguments between individuals, ensuring that it is a useful investment of people's time to be in this process. A ZOUD is not a spectator sport, and you should never seek to sideline people who have a contribution to make. Likewise, make it your responsibility to bring in those people who may appear less at ease with the process, whether you are the chairperson or not.

7 Be authentic and honest. Compassion, empathy and a measured approach can be a great way of opening up a debate. However, nothing confuses people more than finding someone adopting a false or contrived position. A lack of authenticity can only serve to undermine a discussion and diminish the respect of individuals by others.

8 Be prepared to accept your personal ownership of why a particular debate or discussion is uncomfortable. Has an employee's concerns been left unattended? Mistakes happen, and a ZOUD is not a one-way street. Accept responsibility and let other people know that you have done so.

9 It is not just one person who enters a ZOUD. There will be times when others need to raise difficult issues with you and take you into the ZOUD. When this happens, be aware that it could be difficult for them. When you are heading into a ZOUD be mindful to encourage behaviours and attitudes that are effective.

Summary

The days when communication during change was merely an afterthought are long gone. Today we live and do business in a world where communication is pervasive. Information is sent and received across the globe in seconds. Opinions, attitudes and perceptions are formed equally as fast. A lack of understanding, a casual rumour, too much information, or not enough information, can influence the success or failure of engaging people in change. Creating change using dialogue is about changing the conversations that shape everyday thinking and behaviours. It is about creating organizational conversations that lead to understanding and action. Three factors drive successful dialogue during organizational change. The first is that an organization must encourage dialogue early, frequently and consistently. There must be an ongoing strategic approach to dialogue before, during and after any organizational transformation. Dialogue is, and must be, a constant. The second is that the greater the value an organization has for its dialogue, the greater the likelihood for success. The third is that leaders and managers need to encourage dialogue with care. Dialogue with care means choosing the channels for dialogue strategically, tailoring the approach to the aims of the change initiative, authentically engaging in conversation and being sensitive to the pace and timing of dialogue. This means bringing together the right people to offer meaningful input and support. So dialogue allows more people to contribute, generating not only wisdom and a wealth of ideas but also commitment and engagement to change.

Implications

From this chapter there are some practical implications for leaders and managers in how to communicate and foster dialogue with people during transformations:

- *Communicate consistently*
  Be clear what the change is for and why it needs to happen – and communicate consistently with all staff.

- *Use stories, metaphors and analogies*
  Effective communication connects the hearts and minds of the people in an organization. Stories, metaphors and analogies are powerful ways to communicate complex information in compelling ways. Stories are narratives with plots, characters and twists that are full of meaning. Telling stories can often be the catalyst for momentum behind a change initiative. Metaphors and analogies are inferential techniques to transfer the meaning of something that is known to another thing that is unknown. Since organizational change requires people to try something new or move into the unknown, then communication that relies on stories, metaphors and analogies can make the unknown more attractive and understandable.

- *Address rumours*
Everyone understands that there has to be some closed-door
conversations – but be as open as you can about the need for change
and its parameters, and don't allow the negative gossip to take hold.
Rumours need to be addressed. Policies and procedures for dealing
with rumours should be established alongside a comprehensive
ethics training programme to address how to report or deal with the
workplace rumour mill, from the perspectives of both the employer
and the employees.

- *Engage in dialogue as an ongoing activity*
Engaging in dialogue is an ongoing change activity. Listening to how
others are making sense of the change and sharing their perspectives
is vital. Attempting to drive through change without dialogue may
meet with opposition, even if the message has been clearly thought
through and articulated.

- *Develop and implement a stakeholder communications plan*
Know your stakeholders and where the positive influencers are
and use them effectively as part of the communication team.
A stakeholder analysis (as discussed in Chapter 5) will show who
needs to be kept informed about the 'what', 'when' and 'how' of the
change. Communication should be concentrated on key stakeholders
who have the most impact on the change. An example of a template
for a stakeholder communications plan can be found in
Appendix 6.1 (at the end of this chapter).

- *Enter the ZOUD*
Do not be afraid to have the difficult conversations. In every
organization there are uncomfortable issues. An uncomfortable
issue is a taboo subject, something that people in an open forum will
not talk about in order to avoid an emotionally charged discussion.
These issues are often uncomfortable because people are concerned
about releasing emotions that may jeopardize working relationships.
These are often the issues that are described as 'the elephant in
the room'. In addition to uncomfortable issues there are often
inconsistencies, which if not addressed or given the opportunity
to be discussed can call into question the credibility of the change.
Avoiding discussion of such issues will only hold back progress, but
using ZOUD can help to shine a light on the 'elephant in the room'.

References

Allen, J, Jimmieson, N L, Bordia, P and Irmer, B E (2007) Uncertainty during
organizational change: managing perceptions through communication,
Journal of Change Management, 7 (2), pp 187–210
Barsh, J, Mogelof, J and Webb, C (2010) How centered leaders achieve
extraordinary results, *McKinsey Quarterly*, October

Barrett, D J (2002) Change communication: using strategic employee communication to facilitate major change, *Corporate Communications: An International Journal*, 7 (4), pp 219–31

Blanchard, K and Blanchard, S (2013), 6 steps for successfully bringing change to your company, *Fast Company*, 1 August

Bohm, D (2013) *On Dialogue*, Routledge, London

Bordia, P, Jones, E, Gallois, C, Callan, V J and DiFonzo, N (2006) Management are aliens! Rumors and stress during organizational change, *Group & Organization Management*, 31 (5), pp 601–21

Cornelissen, J P, Holt, R and Zundel, M (2011) The role of analogy and metaphor in the framing and legitimization of strategic change, *Organization Studies*, 32 (2), pp 1701–16

DiFonzo, N and Bordia, P (2007) *Rumor Psychology: Social and organizational approaches*, American Psychological Association, Washington DC

Ghafoor, M and Martin, T (2012) [accessed 3 January 2015] Six ways social media technologies can accelerate large-scale change, *Accenture* [Online] http://www.accenture.com/SiteCollectionDocuments/PDF/Accenture-Outlook-Six-Ways-Social-Media-Technologies-Accelerate-Large-Scale-Change.pdf

Gratton, L (2014) *The Key*, McGraw-Hill, New York

Kanter, R M (2003) *Leadership for Change: Enduring skills for change masters*, Harvard Business School, Massachusetts

Jimmieson, N L and White, K M (2011) Predicting employee intentions to support organizational change: an examination of identification processes during a re – brand, *British Journal of Social Psychology*, 50 (2), pp 331–41

Lawrence, P (2015) *Leading Change: How successful leaders approach change management*, Kogan Page, London

Parker, S L, Jimmieson, N L and Johnson, K M (2013) General self-efficacy influences affective task reactions during a work simulation: the temporal effects of changes in workload at different levels of control, *Anxiety, Stress & Coping*, 26 (2), pp 217–39

Rafferty, A E and Restubog, S (2010) The impact of change process and context on change reactions and turnover during a merger, *Journal of Management*, 36 (5), pp 1309–38

Sidhu, R (2015) Communication and engagement, in *The Effective Change Manager's Handbook*, ed R Smith, D King, R Sidhu and D Skelsey, pp 210–57, Kogan Page, London

Waters, R (2014) [accessed 16 October 2015] Monday Interview: Shantanu Narayen, Adobe CEO, *Financial Times* [Online] http://www.ft.com/cms/s/0/4178b02c-b758-11e4-981d-00144feab7de.html#axzz3V8cbfEyV

Further reading

Patterson, K, Grenny, J and McMillan, R (2011) *Crucial Conversations: Tools for talking when stakes are high*, 2nd edn, McGraw-Hill, London

Appendix 6.1 – Template for a stakeholder communication plan

Stakeholder (Individual or group)	Objectives (What level of commitment do you need? Do you need active support or do people just need to be kept informed?)	Key Messages (What will the stakeholders want/need to know and do?)	Type of Activity /Media (eg presentation, workshop, one-to-one meeting, newsletter, etc)	Frequency/Timing (timings should anticipate key milestones – make sure people have adequate warning of major changes)	Responsibility/ Sign-off (Who should carry out the activity? Who is responsible for ensuring that it is done?)

07
Understanding and carrying out culture change

KEY POINTS

- While there is universal agreement that culture exists in an organization and that it plays a crucial role in shaping behaviour in organizations, there is little consensus on what organizational culture actually is. The most popular definition is the one by Edgar Schein (1997) that describes organizational culture as consisting of artefacts, espoused values, beliefs and basic assumptions.

- To understand a culture, leaders and managers need to be aware of the tangible and non-tangible aspects of what constitutes an organization's culture. Leaders and managers need to be aware of this before even considering changes to the culture.

- The functionalist school of thought proposes that culture can be managed or manipulated, while on the other hand, the 'purer' school of thought refutes such claims. According to the purest view, organizations do not have cultures, they *are* cultures, and this is why cultures are so difficult to change.

- Attempting to change a culture is fraught with inherent difficulties as it takes time to change the deep roots of a culture within an organization.

- The culture web can be used to analyse the culture of an organization as it is now, what an organization wants its culture to be, and then the differences between the two.

- Culture will only start to change as people work, relate and behave differently. Thus, to change an organization's culture is to change the attitudes and behaviours of people in the organization.

Introduction

There is no common consensus about what culture is and how it can be changed. In a general sense, culture describes the way that people behave together, what they value and what they celebrate. The shape and form of organizations contributes to their culture. For instance, family-owned enterprises are the clearest examples of organizations with an inbuilt cultural strength. Partnerships, such as those in the professional services, are also, historically, fierce guardians of strong cultures, which is one reason why mergers between them are rare. Such deals often founder on differences or never reach completion, as was evident when Roland Berger, the German management consultancy, decided not to ally with the consulting arm of Deloitte Touche Tohmatsu. Companies, particularly those seeking to compete with smaller, faster-growing rivals, may try to encourage a fresh culture by carving out new divisions in new locations. The Spanish telecoms group Telefónica, for instance, preferred to establish a digital arm of the company in London's Soho, home to innovative media groups, rather than on its campus in unglamorous Slough. Changing an existing culture is, however, notoriously difficult, as is evident in this quote from Paul Bate:

> Changing the culture? It's like trying to kill a dinosaur. You know, you can shoot it in its tiny brain, but the legs keep thrashing for a very long time afterwards. (2000: 498)

Art Kleiner (2001) in the Booz and Co online publication *Strategy+Business* goes as far as saying that:

> Most blanket attempts to change the culture of a whole company are wasted efforts. No matter what the change message is, large companies are so diverse that an influential minority will be predisposed to hate it.

The aim of this chapter is to explore whether an organization can change its culture and, if so, how? The chapter begins by discussing the different definitions and perspectives of culture and then outlines a classic framework for diagnosing the culture of an organization. Examples of organizations that have attempted to change their culture are provided and the factors that have helped or hindered sustaining a culture change are discussed. The final part of the chapter examines how organizations can embrace and sustain change by transforming their culture and considers approaches for doing this through people.

LEARNING OUTCOMES

By the end of the chapter you will be able to:

- define what is meant by the culture in an organization;
- appreciate the different perspectives on organizational culture;

- use the culture web as a tool to analyse the current culture of an organization; what an organization wants its culture to be; and then the differences between the two;
- identify how culture can be managed;
- decide whether or not cultural change is feasible and achievable in your organization;
- identify ways of managing culture in an organization.

Organizational culture

What is organizational culture?

If you want to provoke a vigorous debate, start a conversation on organizational culture. While there is universal agreement that, 1) it exists, and 2) that it plays a crucial role in shaping behaviour in organizations, there is little consensus on what organizational culture actually is, never mind how it influences people's behaviour and whether it is something that can be changed. This is a problem, because without a reasonable definition (or definitions) of culture we cannot hope to understand its connections to other key elements of an organization, especially the people who work in it. Nor can we develop good approaches to analysing, preserving and transforming cultures. So if we can define what organizational culture *is* it will give us a handle on how to diagnose issues, and perhaps even to design and develop better cultures, if we wish to do so. The most popular definition that many researchers, as well as practitioners, have adopted is Edgar Schein's model. Schein (1997) provides a three-dimensional view of organizational culture, consisting of artefacts, espoused values and beliefs, and basic assumptions:

- *Artefacts*: these are the visible language, behaviour and material symbols that exist in an organization. They include the architecture (such as offices or open-plan seating); technology and equipment (for instance, does everyone have laptops/iPads?); dress codes; rituals and ceremonies (such as development events, award ceremonies and away days); and courses (eg induction). A company that has evident artefacts and works hard to portray its corporate culture is Starbucks. The culture of the company is rooted in the entrepreneurial values of Howard Schultz who, when he took over the company, attempted to captivate the essence of Italian coffee bars. From the beginning, Schultz set out to create a different kind of company – one that not only celebrated coffee and its rich tradition but, as part of its culture, also brought a feeling of connection to its customers. The Starbucks mermaid logo is a key artefact that is visible to all. The similarity of Starbuck's coffee shops around the world, from design to food, is also part of their cultural blueprint and helps the company to relay their culture at the most basic level.

- *Espoused beliefs and values*: these are the shared principles and rules that govern the attitudes and behaviours of employees, making some modes of conduct more socially and personally acceptable than others. Values are often evident through stories, myths and rituals. For Starbucks, one such story that is frequently told is how in 1981 Howard Schultz walked into a Starbucks store and, from his first cup of Sumatra coffee, was drawn into Starbucks. He joined the company a year later and then travelled to Italy and became captivated with Italian coffee bars and the romance of the coffee experience, taking it back to the United States.

- *Basic assumptions*: these are the taken-for-granted beliefs about the organizational environment that reside deep below the surface. Basic assumptions help to formulate organizational values and these become shared assumptions that serve to guide how organizational members interact with one another. For example, connection to customers is a basic assumption of Starbucks – staff are expected to connect with all customers through the service they provide.

As Schein's model points out, in order to understand an organization's culture we need to be aware of the tangible and non-tangible aspects of what constitutes it. Culture is, however, like an iceberg. Only part of it is visible, which makes it difficult to see all the elements of it, and hence to identify and define them. The artefacts are above the waterline and are tangible for everyone to see, while espoused beliefs and basic assumptions are below the waterline and invisible. This is what makes culture so hard to define and change, because much of it is intangible and invisible to people inside and outside an organization.

Discussion questions

Using Schein's model, describe the culture of your organization, or an organization you are familiar with. Give examples of the artefacts, beliefs, values and assumptions.

Or, alternatively:

Describe the culture of your university. Identify some of the formal and informal rules that exist. How do you see these enacted?

Cultural perspectives

The position that one takes with regard to defining and understanding culture will have considerable impact on questions of whether culture can be managed, to what extent it may be managed and how it may be managed. Constantine Andriopoulos and Patrick Dawson (2009) identify three dominant characteristics of culture:

- Culture is a *shared phenomenon*. Culture is viewed as a kind of social or normative binding that is shared by a given group and holds together potentially diverse members. In a corporate setting, the group may be the whole organization or one of a number of groups within it. Multiple-group cultures may be associated with functional or geographical groups within the organization. Thus subcultures exist in and across organizations.

- Culture *exists at two levels*: the surface (visible) level and deeper (less visible or invisible) level. The surface level includes elements such as audible and visible patterns of behaviour exhibited by the group, and physical artefacts such as the design of the buildings or decor. The deeper level of culture relates to the values that the group shares and the norms that establish the kind of behaviours that organizational members should expect from one another. These values may be shared across the organization, such as explicitly stated in the company's mission statement, but which are usually termed 'espoused values'. Espoused values are the desired corporate values put forward by leaders that are often out of line with the values in use, that is, the values that are actually enacted by employees through formal practices and other, more indirect processes such as jargon, humour, organizational stories, ceremonies and rituals. Researchers argue that the degree to which the values in use reflect the espoused values often determines the strength of the culture in organizations (Martin, 2002). Once values have been established within the group, norms then allow members to understand the types of behaviours that are expected of them in different situations.

- Culture is *learned*. New members in an organization learn about the culture that prevails in an organization through formal and informal, explicit and implicit, cultural socialization processes. The process whereby an individual is introduced to a culture is referred to as *socialization*. Although socialization is often most evident when a person joins an organization, it is an ongoing process through which individual behaviours, values, attitudes and motives are influenced to conform to those seen as desirable in the organization. In this sense, culture deals with the ways in which individuals try to make sense of their environment, and is learnt through interaction between group members. Culture therefore serves as the glue that binds people together in providing a sense of identity and belonging.

Activity

Using the internet, find three companies in different countries and categorize them according to their different cultural perspectives.

The management of organizational culture

There is an ongoing debate as to whether culture can actually be managed and therefore changed. There are two main schools of thought on this. The first is what has been described as the *functionalist school*. Members of this school (such as Kotter and Heskett, 1992; Schein, 1997) believe that competitive advantage can be attained by manipulating or managing the organizational culture. There is no shortage of examples of organizations claiming to manage or manipulate their culture. For example, Yum! Brands, Inc, based in Louisville, Kentucky has nearly 38,000 restaurants in more than 120 countries. Its restaurant brands include KFC, Pizza Hut and Taco Bell. The company has developed and implemented a people-first culture of fun, and recognition driven by its 'How We Win Together' principles. Yum's entire global people-first culture is built around reward and recognition in order to drive results.

In contrast, a 'purer' school of thought refutes claims that culture may be managed or manipulated in the way that Yum has done. Researchers (such as Ogbanna and Harris, 2002) adopting this view frequently contend that culture is an integral part of an organization and not something that can be changed subject to the whims of top management. They argue that there is very little point in trying to control a phenomenon that is embedded in the very roots of an organization's existence. According to this view, organizations do not have cultures, they *are* cultures, and corporate culture simply cannot be managed because it exists within the subconscious assumptions and values that guide people's behaviour. From this perspective, a deep-rooted, permanent change of culture would require changing the deeper beliefs and basic underlying assumptions that, without people's awareness, guide their behaviour – a task that the purists say is extremely difficult, if not impossible, to complete.

In recognizing the difficulty in attempting to manage culture, Andrew Pettigrew (1990) has identified seven reasons why culture is hard to change:

1 *Levels*: culture exists at a series of levels, from beliefs and assumptions to cultural artefacts.

2 *Pervasiveness*: culture is not only deep; it is broad and embraces all organizational activity.

3 *Implicitness*: much of culture is taken for granted; therefore it is difficult to change, as it is part of people's thinking and behaviour.

4 *Imprinting*: culture has deep historical roots.

5 *Power*: culture has connections with power distribution in an organization; certain power groups may have a vested interest in the prevailing beliefs and cultural behaviours remaining as they are.

6 *Plurality*: organizations often have a heterogeneous culture, that is, a set of subcultures with different norms and behaviours.

7 *Interdependence*: culture is closely connected with the politics of the organization, as well as with its structure, systems, people and priorities.

Such factors are among the reasons why an established culture has a tendency to fight to preserve itself and its members and to remain the same – unchanged. For example, across the globe, sectors such as health, banking, education and governments have all fought to keep the status quo rather than change their cultures. This is evident in the findings from the study of a large-scale change programme within a hospital, which was conducted by Paul Bate (2000). A cultural transformation was needed to transform the hospital from a rigid, divided hierarchy into a more flexible and collaborative networked community. The study found that the readiness of the hospital to embrace innovation and change of any kind was extremely weak. The challenge was how to create commitment and engagement for the transformation when the employees were not willing to change, and when loyalty and trust between employees had broken down. It eventually proved too difficult to implement the changes, because the culture was too strong. So if an organization has a strong culture, as was the case with the hospital, it can be very difficult and, in some instances, impossible to change.

In sum, the audience that the functionalist school of thought appeals to is attracted to the simple, almost heroic, representation of the corporate leader as a cultural warrior, as typified by Jack Welch of General Electric or Carly

Fiorina of Hewlett Packard, leading the organization to a new cultural dawn. The purists, on the other hand, warn of the complexity of culture in relation to it being crafted as a source of competitive advantage. While the view that organizations can easily change their cultures may be considered by some as optimistic, the contrary view – that organizational culture cannot be changed – may equally represent an incomplete account of the complexity and dynamism of culture change. So can culture be changed and, if so, how might this be done? This requires an understanding of the reasons why an organization might want to change its culture, how to diagnose an organizational culture, and whether to change or not change the culture. Each of these issues will be examined in turn.

Discussion questions

How is culture defined in the organization in which you work?

Which of the culture perspectives discussed above do you agree with and why?

Do you think culture can be planned and changed? What might be some of the challenges that an organization thinking of changing its culture might encounter and what might they do to prevent problems before they start the change?

Why would an organization want to change its culture?

Most leaders have a yearning at some time to change the culture of their organization. The drivers for this might include the need to develop a customer-focused culture, a team-based culture, an entrepreneurial culture, a learning culture, a cost-conscious culture or an ethical culture in order to improve the performance and productivity of the organization. According to Gareth Morgan (2006), culture is the challenge of transforming the mindsets, vision and beliefs that sustain existing business realities, effectively creating a new way of life for those working in the organization. In practical terms this means that culture change is not simply about the larger, obvious changes to strategy, structure and processes but is about changing the behaviours of people. So culture starts to change as people work, relate and behave differently. To change an organization's culture is therefore to change the attitudes and behaviours of people in the organization. This is what Marissa Mayer attempted to do when she took over as chief executive at Yahoo. In her first year as CEO, Mayer made some transformational changes, launched dozens of apps, and purchased 16 start-up companies. However, her most infamous change was requesting that everyone work on-site rather than at home. Mayer's reasons for changing the culture at Yahoo, and her attempt to do so, are outlined in the following case study.

CASE STUDY   Culture change at Yahoo

When Marissa Mayer moved from Google to take over as chief executive at Yahoo, she found a Silicon Valley campus that was very different from the one she had left at Google. There were empty car parks and entire floors of offices that were nearly empty, as many employees were working elsewhere or at home. Although employees were paid Yahoo salaries, some did little work for the company and a few had even begun their own start-ups on the side. These were among the factors that led Mayer to announce that she was abolishing Yahoo's work-from-home policy, saying that to create a new culture of innovation and collaboration at the company, employees had to report to work. According to an article by Claire Miller and Nicole Perlroth (2013) in the *New York Times*, entitled, 'Yahoo Says New Policy is Meant to Raise Morale', former employees said that Mayer made the decision not as a referendum on working remotely, but to address problems particular to Yahoo. They painted a picture of a company where employees were aimless and morale was low, and a bloated bureaucracy that had taken Yahoo out of competition with its more nimble rivals. Many of Yahoo's problems were also visible to people outside the company. It had missed the two biggest trends on the internet – social networking and mobile. Its home page and e-mail services had become relics used by people who had never bothered to change their habits. It had ceded its crown as the biggest seller of display ads to Facebook and Google, and its stock price was plummeting. Miller and Perlroth (2013) say that inside Yahoo there was a mixed reaction to the change to the working-from-home policy. Some employees were angry because they said that they were able to be highly productive by working remotely, and that it helped them to concentrate on work instead of the chaos inside Yahoo. Others were worried as they occasionally stayed home to care for a sick child or receive a delivery.

Inside the company, though, there were deeper cultural issues that were invisible from the outside. Yahoo had withstood many changes over the years, starting with a turnover of six chief executives in five years, each with his or her own deputies and missions for the company. This led to confusion among the workforce about the company's goals, and frustration that projects would be pulled midstream by a new chief executive. The company had hired many managers to oversee new technology products, but the extra levels of management slowed down product development. Miller and Perlroth highlighted how Mayer has attempted to address such issues:

> Employees said that unlike previous chief executives, who focused outside
> Yahoo, Mayer prioritized fixing the company internally and motivating

*employees. She introduced free food in the cafeterias, swapped employees'
BlackBerrys for iPhones and Android phones and started a Friday all-
employee meeting where executives take questions and speak candidly.*

However, when it came to changing the work-at-home policy, Mayer had neglected
to first establish a sense of urgency throughout the company for the need to
change the way of working.

Discussion questions

How would you define the culture of Yahoo?

How appropriate was Mayer's decision to stop home-working in
attempting to address the cultural issues in Yahoo?

What should Mayer have done to establish a sense of urgency for
the change?

Activity

Based on your experience, identify possible approaches for changing the
culture in an organization with which you are familiar. What barriers might
get in the way of the approaches you have identified?

Diagnosing organizational culture

Cultural web

To help describe and understand the culture of an organization Gerry
Johnson and colleagues (2008) devised the cultural web, which offers a
framework for understanding the interrelated elements that make up the
culture. The cultural web can be used to look at the culture of an organization as it is now; what an organization wants its culture to be; and then
the differences between the two. The elements of the culture web are stories
and myths, rituals and routines, control systems, organizational structure,
power structures and symbols:

- *Stories and myths* are told by members of the organization to one
  another, to outsiders and to new recruits. Stories and myths embed

the present culture in its organizational history and flag up important events and personalities.

- *Rituals and routines* are ways that members of the organization behave towards one another and signal what is important and valued. They include training and development programmes, and promotion and assessment processes.

- *Control systems* are the ways that the organization is controlled and measured, including financial systems, performance management systems, and reward and recognition processes. They emphasize what it is important to monitor in an organization, and what it is important to focus attention and activity on.

- *Organizational structure* includes both the formal structure defined by the organizational chart and the informal lines of power and influence that indicate whose contributions are most valued.

- *Power structures* involve key stakeholders who have the greatest influence on decisions, operations and the strategic direction of the organization. Such structures include the positional and relational power held by individuals.

- *Symbols* include visual representations of the company such as logos, the layout and size of offices, dress codes, titles, and the type of language and terminology commonly used.

These elements together influence the cultural *paradigm*, which is the set of assumptions about the organization that are taken for granted and the way in which things work in the organization.

Activity

Use each element of the culture web to analyse either the culture of the team or the organization in which you work or one you are familiar with:

1   Use the findings from your analysis to: 1) describe the culture; 2) identify the factors that are evident throughout the culture.

2   Now that you have identified the current culture, use the elements of the culture web to identify the desired culture that the team or organization needs.

3   Compare the current culture and the desired culture and identify the differences between the two.

4   With your colleagues, identify the factors that need to change. Prioritize these changes and draw up an action plan with your team and other key stakeholders.

To change or not to change the culture

To change an organization's culture is complex. Many would say that it is better to avoid doing this if possible. It is often assumed that, because organizational culture is a largely invisible or intangible organization property, it has a life of its own and is almost impossible to change. According to John Salaman and David Asch (2003) organizational culture is more useful as an explanation of organizational behaviour than as a prescription on how to change an organization. Salaman and Asch criticize what they term the excessive marketing of cultural change prescriptions and the myth, often pervaded by consultants, that a culture can be changed. Salaman and Asch warn of the inherent difficulties and the time that it takes to change culture.

Yet many experts (including consultants) disagree with these arguments and suggest that organizational cultures can be managed by various approaches. One such approach is 'symbolic management', where managers attempt to influence the deep cultural norms and values of an organization by shaping the surface cultural elements such as symbols, stories and ceremonies that people use to express and communicate cultural understanding. This shaping can be done in several ways. For example, leaders can issue public statements about their vision for the future of the company. They can recount stories about themselves and the company. They can use and enrich the shared company language. In this way, they not only communicate the company's central norms and key values but also devise new ways of expressing them.

I witnessed this some years ago while working as an HR consultant for an international bank. I was involved in a change programme with the credit-card business of the bank. The aim of the culture change was to move from a process-driven culture to a customer-focused culture. At the start of the programme the CEO of the credit-card business gathered together his managers, all 50 of them, into a conference hall to launch the cultural change programme. The CEO stated with conviction and gravitas: 'I want you all to be working with me to deliver our change agenda. I hope that you will all support me with regard to changing what does not work for us at present and what we think will work for us well in the future. Your views and ideas are very important to me.'

The CEO then held similar meetings in different locations. This kind of symbolism asserts commitment for the change agenda. The value of such commitment cannot be underestimated; nor can the cost of failure related to its absence.

Leaders and managers who practise symbolic management realize that everything they do broadcasts a message to employees about the organization's norms and values. They consciously choose to do specific things that symbolize and strengthen a desired culture. Managers at companies ranging from Disney to DuPont agree than managing symbols and the culture they support is critical to organizational success. For example, the three-point star logo of Mercedes cars is synonymous with quality in most people's minds – and even very young children recognize that the two golden arches symbolize McDonald's. So symbolic management involves the manipulation of symbols, telling stories, performing ceremonies and anointing heroes, which are all part of managing culture. The following case study illustrates the impact of attempting to change the culture within a contact centre.

CASE STUDY   Changing the culture of a call centre

I worked, at one time, as an internal consultant for an outsourcing company. The company outsourced processes in call centres, where employees had to wrestle with a deadline on the amount of time available to make and close a call, and the amount of calls they had to make in a specified time. The company won the contract for outsourcing a Scottish-based call centre and I was part of the team responsible for the transition of the culture from the previous US owners. The existing culture was one in which the staff were forced to put up their hands to request a drink of water or permission to go to the toilet. The physical environment of the centre was dull, with worn carpets and old furniture. Statistics of shame (name and shame lists) were published each week with the names of staff who had not answered calls quick enough or had taken too long with a caller. Staff were demoralized, dissatisfied and on the verge of leaving.

When the company took over the call centre at the stroke of midnight, the transition team entered the centre and began changing the appearance of the physical working environment. Old notice boards with tattered notices warning staff what they could and could not do were removed and replaced with posters outlining company values. The name and shame lists of who had not answered calls on time, or who had talked too long to a customer, were removed. On every desk was placed a cup and a computer mat with the company logo on them. When the staff returned to work the next day they were greeted by the changes. Over the next six months, old stained carpets were replaced; new chairs (in the corporate colours) replaced the old ones; staff no longer had to ask to go to the toilet or to take a coffee break. All employees attended an induction programme, received daily bulletins about what was changing and why. Focus groups were set up to encourage staff to suggest their own ideas about what needed to change and to get them involved in project teams to make the change happen; managers were visible and 'walked the floors'. But in the early months of the transition the staff rebelled – strikes were held – and hit the news. Staff had grown accustomed to the status quo, despite it resembling the environment of the scientific management school of management – yes Taylorism was still alive and well in the 21st century. It took a lot of time and involvement of staff, managers and union members to persuade the employees that the change was for the better. There were months of cynicism, opposition and rebellion. Managers and the transition team had to constantly communicate what was happening through different media, but importantly they had to model the behaviour that reflected the values of the company. They had to demonstrate trust, integrity and honesty.

Gradually the physical environment gained colour, the staff acquired the skills needed to perform their jobs and the threats of leaving to go to other call centres began to decrease. HR issues began to be addressed such as performance management. Individuals were organized into teams (with wacky names that they suggested themselves) and team targets were set, in collaboration with team members. Individual employee and team-of-the-month awards were introduced. Over 12 months there was a gradual shift in employee morale and motivation. The cynicism that had been rife in the early months began to disappear. The level of fun was raised with themed Fridays (Mexican, French, Italian and so on). Staff were encouraged to suggest improvements and then to help implement them. Employees began to feel valued and empowered to deliver great service. Only then did the staff at the call centre begin to change their attitudes to their job, customers and managers, but it took over two years for this to happen.

Discussion questions

What were the main challenges faced in attempting to change the culture at the call centre?

Critically evaluate the approaches that were taken to change the culture of the call centre. What else might have helped to change the culture?

Has the culture of your organization, or an organization that you are familiar, changed over the last few years? If yes, how did this change happen? Was it intentionally managed? What was the effect of this change?

Challenges of culture change

Cultural interventions, such as the one described in the case of the call centre above, are difficult, but they can be successful. Leaders need to clearly define their vision, purpose and goals and have a plan for how to achieve them. They also need the willingness and ability to discard any preconceptions and adjust their plan when reality does not line up with their expectations. Leaders are likely to encounter resistance at first (as the chef Jamie Oliver did: see the case study below) if they approach changing the organization's culture in a heavy-handed, top-down way. But when they approach culture more thoughtfully, taking a holistic view of how the organization works in practice, they can make a real difference, even in parts of the culture that seem intractable.

CASE STUDY Changing the way we eat

When British chef Jamie Oliver arrived in Huntington, West Virginia in the United States, his aim was to change people's eating habits – in the way he had done with a similar project that had proved successful in the UK. Oliver chose Huntington because it had been dubbed the unhealthiest city in the United States by the US Centre for Disease Control and Prevention, due to the high rates of heart disease and diabetes among its population. Half of the town's adults were considered obese. As food in any community is closely tied to culture, Oliver's attempt to change the town's eating habits provides an example of how difficult it can be to change cultural behaviours.

Oliver went to Huntington with confidence that his goals and his charisma would be enough to make the change happen. However, he immediately faced opposition. First from the local disc jockey Rod Willis, who criticized Oliver and proclaimed that: 'We don't want to eat lettuce all day.' The disc jockey reduced Oliver to tears, questioning his ability to effect change and his motives for attempting to do so. The second opposition came from the head cook at the Central City Elementary School, Alice Gue. Oliver had assumed that Gue would naturally share his attitude towards the unhealthy food she had been serving. But Gue was antagonistic – she was proud of her existing menu and resistant to making any changes to it.

Oliver had expected the people of Huntington to respond more positively to his proposed changes; he completely underestimated the cumulative power of inertia and collective attitudes. Once he realized that the resistance came from a culture, rather than from individuals, he set out to learn about the culture of the community instead of trying to defeat it. Oliver began by holding listening sessions with locals and he began to immerse himself in the community. He opened a store called Jamie's Kitchen in Huntington, where he offered free advice on nutrition and cooking lessons. As Oliver got to know the residents of Huntington, he realized that he faced a formidable information and education barrier. Examples include one class of first-grade children who could not identify a tomato – they insisted that it was a potato – and one family refusing to change their eating habits. Oliver talked with the family at length about nutrition. He went food shopping with them, buying them fresh ingredients. But when he returned later to their house, he found that many of the fresh ingredients had not been eaten. Oliver realized that providing information was not enough. Oliver had to lead the change by addressing people's behaviour first. So he turned his focus from *how* they ate to *what* they ate. He began with peas.

Oliver was determined that the Central City schoolchildren should eat peas for lunch. To accomplish this, he dressed up in a green costume and raced around the school grounds trying to get the kids to engage with him as a pea. He used rewards and recognition, handing out stickers after lunch that said 'I've Tried Something New'. Not every child co-operated, but many peas were eaten and Oliver had begun to lay the foundations for further and deeper changes. For the children who participated, peas became a bit of evidence, drawn from direct experience, of the possibility and value of change. Oliver had demonstrated that children could eat healthy food enthusiastically, that they could support one another without ridicule, and that all of this might actually be good for them.

The more time that Oliver spent in Huntington, the more success he enjoyed. Essential to this turnaround was his cultivation of allies within the community. For example, he sought out the most influential teachers, who already had the trust of the schoolchildren. Once they saw that better health was possible, the teachers warmed to the idea of encouraging and even prodding the children to make smarter choices for their lunch. Oliver's persistent but respectful approach eventually earned the confidence of Alice Gue and Rod Willis. Many people in the town began to internalize the value of change. It was no longer simply good for Oliver but also good for their community.

Oliver moved on to change the eating habits of the children at Huntington High School. However, here he changed his approach and, not coincidentally, his demeanour, donning a leather jacket and toning down his children's-talk-show-host speaking style. He explicitly recruited 'ambassadors of change' – a group of students who met with him and signed on to promote his ideas.

After several months in Huntington, Oliver managed to catalyse change among many groups of people at the elementary school, the high school and in the community at large. Oliver's success in Huntington came partly from his ability to energize and motivate the citizens, build informal networks, and help individuals to experiment with new healthy-eating behaviours. But Oliver also deployed formal mechanisms similar to the ones that leaders and managers often turn to when embarking on a transformation in a corporate setting, such as redesigning reporting structures, setting goals and communicating priorities to the whole organization. These activities are commonly seen as primary levers for aligning the organization in the same direction. For Oliver, these formal mechanisms included finding food suppliers for the school kitchens that could provide healthy food within the budget, working with the state school inspector to modify policies concerning what counted as serving a healthy meal, and training the kitchen staff in cooking healthy food from scratch.

The impact of the culture change is summed up by Steve Willis, pastor of Huntington's First Baptist Church, 'This isn't going to change lives. This is going to save lives.'

Adapted from Jamie's Food Revolution [Online] **https://www.youtube.com/watch?v=oLgmk323H6k**; and R *von Post* (2011) Eat Your Peas: A Recipe for Culture Change, *Strategy + Business* [Online] **http://www.strategy-business.com**: **http://www.strategy-business.com/article/11205?pg=all**.

Discussion questions

Review Oliver's approach to changing the culture – what might he have done differently?

What are the key lessons you can learn from Oliver's experience?

How might you apply these lessons in your organization, or an organization that you are familiar with?

Patterns breaks

The concept of the 'pattern break' is a useful one for culture change. A pattern break is a series of abrupt interruptions that permanently break a habit or state. In the context of change this can be translated to mean that something has to happen in order to shatter the status quo and let people know, especially supporters of the existing culture, that there is a need for change. Examples of pattern breaks include: revamping the reward and recognition systems; reducing the levels of hierarchy in an organization's structures; outsourcing non-vital functions; exiting staff from the organization who are not performing; abolishing designated car-parking spaces for senior staff; and adopting flexible working methods such as desk sharing. A pattern break does not have to be major in size: for instance, abolishing designated parking spaces will have as much impact as many other items on the list. A pattern break does, however, need to align with the changes that are to be achieved. For example, outsourcing non-vital functions or adopting flexible working methods may be aligned with major budget cuts. Pattern breaks are required when the current culture has a very strong immune system. In the following case study Lindsey Agness describes how pattern breaks have been used in a housing association.

CASE STUDY   Pattern breaks

Written by Lindsey Agness, MD, The Change Corporation

As part of a consultancy team I was asked to review the performance management systems within a housing association that managed housing and related services to over 11,500 homes. This was a business where a smaller organization had merged with a much larger one. The smaller organization was not delivering to its key performance indicators and my consultancy team was asked by the Association Board to find out why. After carrying out an initial diagnosis of the culture, the consultancy team shocked staff when we described the climate as more like a 'country club' than a profitable business. The senior management team blamed this on the quality of the business data as opposed to weak management. In fact, there were far bigger critical people-management issues at stake. The consultancy team found that most staff were not working to annual objectives and did not have a personal development plan. Though some staff had one-to-one performance reviews with their managers, the ongoing paperwork was very poor, with few staff using the correct forms and many review sessions were not written up. Most important was the fact that the majority of one-to-one sessions were informal and reactive, and the quality of the conversations and degree of challenge in them was questionable.

My consultancy team needed to demonstrate to staff quickly that the 'country club' culture was no longer acceptable. To do this they did three things to introduce a pattern break into the business. First, an audit of the one-to-one sessions was carried out, with little notice, to assess the quality of the paperwork and conversations that were going on. Second, all senior managers received the feedback that the culture was like a 'country club'. Third, a new performance management system was put into place across the business with a follow-up evaluation after six months. This demonstrated to managers that the leadership team were serious about the change process and that it would be followed through. All managers also received training in how to set objectives for staff and engage their staff in quality conversations. Within 12 months the financial turnover of the association had increased by 17 per cent. Staff turnover, sickness levels and rent arrears had outperformed the target performance measures and the tenants' (customers) levels of satisfaction had remained stable.

Creating a culture for change

For organizations, trying to move from one culture to another can be challenging. One such company is the Japanese pharma company Takeda. In order to become more global, the company began by changing its internal culture and buying in external staff such as Yasuchika Hasegawa, its president. An international advisory board was also created, bringing in Karen Katen of Pfizer and Sidney Taurel from Eli Lilly, as well as Tachi Yamada, a Japanese-born executive who had spent his adult life based in the United States. The working language at senior levels was switched from Japanese to English, both for board meetings and the global leadership committee, aided by simultaneous translation. At more junior levels, a requirement for high levels of English proficiency among recruits was introduced, and the company aggressively recruited non-Japanese staff who were encouraged to work for extended periods in Japan. Non-Japanese leaders were also recruited to run the company's international divisions. Such outsiders did, however, face challenges. The linguistic challenges were nothing compared with the challenges to make decisions. For instance, while the Japanese staff focused on making decisions by consensus, the staff from Western cultures were used to debate, including strong dissent, before making decisions. The experiences of Takeda hint at some of the issues that may be encountered by companies facing a cultural shift.

A strong culture, such as that of Takeda, can oppose any attempts to change it. A strong culture can also be dangerous if it leads to groupthink, or mutually reinforcing bad behaviour.

Encouraging and sustaining an organizational-wide culture that promotes the generation and implementation of new ideas among organizational members is central to nurturing cultures of change and developing creative and innovative work settings. Organizations such as Amazon – the online retailer – have creative cultures and pride themselves on sustaining intra-organizational value and behavioural norm systems that enable the perpetual development and introduction of original products. For instance, Amazon has changed online shopping models across the globe. To achieve this, leaders at Amazon nudged – or even possibly shoved – the transformation, as outlined in the following case study.

CASE STUDY   Amazon

Amazon.com was founded in 1994 and launched in 1995 as a new way, or model, of selling books. The company leaders took the approach of identifying customer needs and working backwards to find new ways to distribute goods and services. Their philosophy was a balance of two opposing lines of thinking. The first was that not listening to customers would lead to failure; the second was that *only* listening to customers would lead to failure. Amazon's leaders mixed these two philosophies to give customers something they needed, but did not know they needed. With this approach, Amazon has changed the way that retail operations work. Amazon now distributes anything from books, computers and food through multiple partners via the internet. Under this new operating model, potential competitors have became partners, helping Amazon to grow its customer base through expanded product lines. Changing to this collaborative model was an easier task because Amazon's organizational culture is receptive to change. The culture encourages idea generation in many innovative venues, such as eco-friendly packaging, waste reduction, energy initiatives and facility logistics. The entire Amazon model of online shopping is revolutionary, and is generated by the innovative culture that was originally built by the company's founders from the very beginning.

Not all organizations are like Amazon, and those that take too long to adjust may over time disappear into the background, while replacement organizations with forward thinking and change-receptive leaders will take over. So how can organizations embrace change by transforming their cultures? One approach for doing this is to stimulate an innovative culture.

Stimulating a culture of innovation

Creativity and innovation are the basis for sustainable change. Creativity is the generation of new and original ideas, associations, methods, approaches and solutions in relation to a problem or need – while innovation is changing something, making it better or doing something new, by implementing or applying the outputs of creativity. Innovation is therefore the application of a new idea to initiate or improve a product, process or service. How can an organization become more innovative? An excellent model is W L Gore, best known as the maker of Gore-Tex fabric. Gore has developed a reputation as one of the world's most innovative companies by developing a stream of diverse products, including guitar strings, dental floss, medical devices and fuel cells. What is the secret of Gore's success? What can other organizations do to develop a track record for innovation? For instance, Procter and Gamble (P&G) is a company that uses a new growth factory, which is a network of novel structures and capabilities to rapidly shepherd new products and business models from inception to market. The resulting innovations range from a 33-cent razor for customers in emerging economies to Tide Dry Cleaners establishments with drive-through windows and 24-hour drop-off and pick-up. The success of P&G suggests that collective innovation needs to be managed and embedded across an organization to achieve significant success.

In order to build and sustain a culture that promotes the generation and implementation of new ideas Constantine Andriopoulos and Manto Gotsi (2002), in their study of Lunar Design – a product development consultancy in Silicon Valley – identify four principles that promote innovative cultures:

1 *Start with a collaborative approach to management.* This is an approach whereby employees are constantly aware of the company's actions and are able to voice their views and opinions in numerous formal and informal occasions. It is a key principle for fostering a creative culture.

2 *Create a 'no fear' climate.* Creating a culture that supports perpetual experimentation is essential in mobilizing innovation-enhancing behaviours. Regarding ideas as the company's most valuable assets, initiating 'blue sky' internally driven projects, and creating a mentoring system that supports individuals in their creative endeavours are some of the things that Lunar Design does to foster a 'no fear' culture.

3 *Encourage stretching beyond the comfort zone.* An ability to stretch beyond a person's comfort zone is essential when it comes to engaging staff with challenging projects. This involves asking employees to work on projects that do not necessarily reflect the nature or level of their expertise. This not only brings fresh perspectives to the creative process but also enhances the learning experience of employees.

4 *Celebrate individuality and encourage uncertainty.* Creative employees need to have autonomy over their work and be able to express themselves and their passions in the working environment. Diversity in the workplace is essential, which is why companies such as Lunar Design strive to recruit people from different countries, educational backgrounds and work experience.

This list of principles for creating innovative cultures has been extended by Karen Ann Zien and Sheldon Buckler (2004) who propose the following seven principles:

1 *Sustain faith and treasure identity as an innovative company.* The crafting of an innovative culture requires creating an environment of faith and trust that good ideas have a likely chance to become great products. In good times and bad, truly innovative companies maintain creativity and innovation as key corporate priority.

2 *Be truly experimental in all functions, especially at the front end.* Experimentation is a critical part of the creative process. It is essential to encourage employees to go wild in their creative endeavours and then to encourage them to take sensible risks.

3 *Structure real relationships between marketing and technical people.* Promoting close and meaningful relationships between the technical innovators and the market-driven business minds is another essential principle for promoting a culture of creativity and change.

4 *Generate customer intimacy.* Creativity and innovation in corporate settings are not about fulfilling the needs of artistic individuals. The commercial reality requires creative organizations to anticipate and meet market-driven requirements. Innovative organizations achieve customer intimacy by observing potential users, interviewing key stakeholders, and studying customer lifestyles and product decisions.

5 *Engage the whole organization.* Visionary leaders engage the whole organization in generating and implementing novel solutions. This happens through formal and informal communication such as meetings, e-mails, social media sites and impromptu discussions.

6 *Never forget the individual.* Innovative organizations should not forget the individual. Acknowledging and celebrating individual idiosyncrasies, providing ample opportunities for personal expression, and encouraging employees to follow their passions and work on challenging projects are all important in mobilizing cultures of change, creativity and innovation.

7 *Tell and embody powerful and purposeful stories.* The role of hero/heroine stories and the efforts in keeping the company's innovative vision and history alive help to reinforce creative processes. Keeping these stories alive is critical in sustaining creative cultures.

Such principles as those outlined above can be incorporated by leaders into the way that innovation is conducted and becomes part of the culture. Two further activities that leaders should consider for encouraging creativity and innovation are to do with effective leadership, and relate to a strong supportive corporate culture. One is to make better use of existing talent for creativity and innovation by enabling and encouraging formal and informal networking, as connections and networks enable people to share and discuss potential innovations. The other is to foster a culture of creativity and innovation based on mutual trust, by empowering employees to experiment and fail – once, twice, or as many times as it takes. Acknowledging and celebrating individual idiosyncrasies, providing ample opportunities for personal expression and encouraging employees to follow their passions and work on challenging projects are all important in mobilizing cultures of change, creativity and innovation. Innovative organizations, such as P&G and Lunar Design, tend to have similar cultures. They encourage experimentation. They reward both successes and failures. Unfortunately, in too many organizations people are punished for failures. Such cultures dampen risk taking and innovation, as people will only be willing to try new ideas when they feel they will not be penalized. Managers in innovative organizations recognize that failures are a natural outcome of new ventures.

The key to success in encouraging creativity, and thereby enabling innovation, is learning from failure and then putting the lessons into practice (as discussed in Chapter 9). The enemies of creativity and sustainable innovation are 'short-termism' – the pernicious consequence of a need or desire for quick rewards and gratification – and fear of failure in terms of the pernicious consequences of blame, punishment and shame. In research carried out by McKinsey consultants Joanna Barsh and colleagues (2008), there is shown to be a large gap between the aspirations of executives to innovate and their ability to do so. The research found that only 38 per cent of senior executives said that they consciously took action to learn from their failures in innovation and encouraged others in their organization to do the same. Worse still, only 23 per cent of employees felt encouraged by their managers to learn from their failures.

A strong culture of creativity and innovation can be developed through effective leadership. There needs to be a vision of creativity and innovation reflected in the organization's mission statement or purpose, core values and strategies that operationalize them. Leading change successfully entails role-modelling creativity and innovation and using the skills of networking, coaching and facilitation for creativity and innovation. Innovation needs to be done properly and profitably through engaging people.

Leading and managing people through change entails creating opportunities for experimentation and failure and, as a result, early successes in applying their learning from those failures. In turn this creates and reinforces the desire and capability for innovation and change through empowerment and engagement of managers and employees alike. Leaders need to create a culture of creativity and innovation from which sustainable change follows.

Delivering sustainable culture change

If you decide that there are valid drivers and an urgent need to change the culture or your organization then consider the strategy for culture

FIGURE 7.1   Strategy for culture change

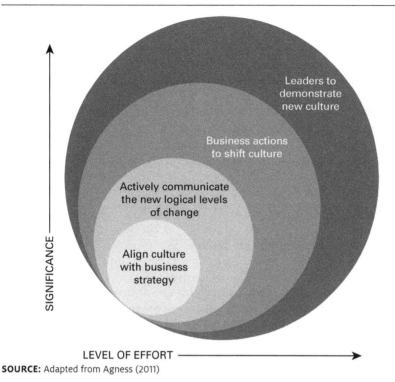

SIGNIFICANCE

Leaders to
demonstrate
new culture

Business actions
to shift culture

Actively communicate
the new logical levels
of change

Align culture
with business
strategy

LEVEL OF EFFORT ⟶

SOURCE: Adapted from Agness (2011)

change (below). This has been developed after many years of working with organizations to deliver a sustainable culture change initiative that delivers long-term change. The diagram in Figure 7.1 illustrates a strategy for culture change. The horizontal axis represents the level of effort required and the vertical axis is the significance or the impact on the culture of each activity. The key activities shown in the diagram are: align the culture with the business strategy; actively communicate the new logical levels of change; business actions to shift the culture; and leaders to demonstrate the new culture.

Align the culture with the business strategy

Whilst this is a relatively passive step in the strategy it is still important to define the desired outcome. In any culture, change leaders need to set out the vision, purpose, values, beliefs, capabilities and behaviours that align and reinforce the strategic direction of the business. In terms of the level of effort and impact, this activity takes approximately 10 per cent of the effort of the culture change initiative and has little impact on its own. Yet, it sets a firm foundation for change.

Actively communicate the new logical levels of change

Active dialogue is an essential component of any culture change programme (dialogue is discussed in Chapter 6). This involves defining and actively managing stakeholder groups, and developing a strategy and planning for dialogue. In terms of the level of effort and impact, this activity probably takes approximately 20 per cent of the effort of the culture change initiative and begins to have an impact on the business as staff are engaged in dialogue about the rationale for the change and what it will mean for them. However, these initial two activities will not in themselves deliver a strategy for long-term change, because there is still no real incentive for staff to do anything differently and commit to the change process.

Take business actions to shift the culture

This is all about how to reinforce change at an organizational level. Key examples include changing HR policies and procedures to align to the culture changes, such as: performance management, reward and recognition, recruitment and promotion. This will ensure that changes are embedded within the business. Too many culture change initiatives miss out this vital activity. They define the new world and they communicate it. Yet, they continue to reward and promote against the old values and behaviours, which destroy everything that has been achieved.

Leaders demonstrate the new culture

Achieving cultural change is a difficult and lengthy process and requires leadership resolve. Leadership is by far the strongest lever of cultural change, accounting for approximately 40 per cent of the impact of change. Leaders need to demonstrate the values, beliefs, capabilities and behaviours they want their staff to demonstrate. Often leaders adopt a 'do as I say' way of behaving rather than 'do as I do'. Some even seem to believe that it is okay for them to carry on as before whilst everyone else in their organization changes – for example, leaders still receiving large pay increases whilst staff salaries are frozen. Nothing sabotages the success of culture change more than leaders not demonstrating the required changes in behaviours and ways of working.

Putting it all together

Culture change requires clarity about what should change, as well as focus, determination, courage and resilience. To achieve this, leaders should choose methods that create the *pattern break* effect (as described earlier in this chapter) – that is, those that stand out in stark contrast to how it is done now. From the outset, leaders and managers need to take the initiative and keep going, or the old culture will begin to dictate the terms and conditions regarding how the change will be carried out, especially as embedded beliefs, values and patterns of behaviour wield tremendous voltage.

Summary

So, can culture be changed? Culture change is most likely to occur where there is a dramatic shock that calls into question the relevance of the current culture. Even then it will not happen overnight but will be gradual. Fundamentally, cultures are not changed by new thoughts or words, they are changed by new behaviours that reinforce desired cultural attributes. Possible approaches are structural reform, regulatory intervention and a change of executive leaders. For example, General Motors (GM) car plant in Fremont, California, transformed its culture by adopting the lean manufacturing behaviours advocated by its venture partner, Toyota Motors. Nothing was as transformative at this particular plant as the simple act of empowering front-line employees to stop the productive line at any time due to quality concerns. This policy had a dramatic impact on the revitalization of the unionized plant.

To achieve such changes in culture takes time and the message needs to be constantly reiterated, in person, by leaders and managers. It is about changing behaviours in order to get the culture that the organization wants. Most changes to culture happen without the bells and whistles of grand culture-change programmes but through incremental and transformational change that has a cumulative impact on the culture of an organization.

Implications for managers and leaders

Several practical implications for leaders and managers attempting to change an organization's culture can be drawn from the areas discussed in this chapter:

- *Think carefully before embarking on a culture change*
  On the one hand, the functionalist school of thought proposes that culture can be managed or manipulated, while on the other hand, the 'purer' school of thought refutes such claims. According to the purest view, organizations do not have cultures, they *are* cultures, and this is why cultures are so difficult to change. Although the functionalist school believes that cultural interventions are difficult, they believe that they can be successful. To follow the functionalist approach there needs to be a clearly defined purpose, goals and a plan for how to reach them. There also needs to be the willingness and ability to discard any preconceptions and adjust the plan when reality does not line up with expectations. Approach culture thoughtfully, taking a holistic view of how the organization works in practice.

- *Know the current culture*
  Before culture change is contemplated conduct an analysis of the present culture and the desired future culture as well as the triggers

for the change (see Chapter 1 for a discussion on the triggers and drivers for change). To understand a culture means being aware of the tangible and non-tangible aspects of what constitutes it, before even considering changes to the culture. An essential rule for any culture change should be 'know your own culture, then change it if necessary'. Use a tool, such as the culture web, to carry out an analysis of the culture.

● *Practice symbolic management*
Symbolic management involves influencing the deep cultural norms and values by shaping the surface cultural elements – such as symbols, stories and ceremonies – that people use to express and communicate cultural understanding. Consciously choose to do specific things that symbolize and strengthen a desirable culture. Telling stories, performing ceremonies and anointing heroes might seem a waste of time but, in reality, playing down the importance of such symbolic management can have disastrous consequences.

● *Create a culture of innovation*
Encouraging and sustaining an organizational-wide culture that promotes the generation and implementation of new ideas among organizational members is central to nurturing a culture of change in developing creative and innovative work settings.

● *Engage people in the culture change*
To change a culture requires commitment and ownership with what is happening. This can be done, in part, by engaging in dialogue with employees (see Chapter 6 for further discussion on dialogue), as well as giving employees the opportunity to provide feedback that is listened to and taken seriously.

The case study below by Tony Wilson, general manager at Parker Hannifin, describes the importance of engaging people during a culture change in a manufacturing division.

CASE STUDY   Culture change in a manufacturing division

Written by Tony Wilson

A couple of years ago, I was asked to lead one of three business units in a manufacturing division with the aim of making it profitable. The key focus of the division was designing manufacturing and selling equipment within the oil and gas markets. The business unit, which I took over, was a mature business unit with US $30 million turnover, which was making a loss of 5 per cent return on sales

(ROS). The target was to achieve a minimum of 15 per cent ROS. Two other business units within the division were profitable, although not achieving the 15 per cent target. All three business units were renowned for their autocratic leadership.

After taking on the role, in order to understand the challenges I began by interviewing a number of people, including production operators, staff, suppliers of components and services (both internal and external to the division) and customers. The key focus of these interviews was to address the following questions:

- What were the issues?

- Who were the customer base and did they feel part of a team or have any affiliation to the organization?

- What were the leadership styles and the impact of these styles?

The feedback from these interviews ranged from the production operators and staff stating that they were not aware that they belonged to a business unit as 'no one communicates with us', suppliers stating that they were not aware of a business unit as they just delivered to the factory, to customers complaining that the business did not talk to them. It was clear from the feedback that there were a number of areas that needed to be improved, including: all functions and the vast majority of individuals wanted to have an input into the running of the business; everyone pointed out that communication on how the business was performing was vital and that support or input into planned actions to improve performance was fundamental; and the leadership style needed to be a more open consultative approach with two-way feedback.

A number of drivers for change were evident. First, it was clear that improved financial performance was required. Second, from employees at all levels there was a desire for greater communication and engagement. They wanted to know more about: the goals and objectives of the business unit and how we were performing against those targets; how the employees could support improvement plans; and, more importantly, what the values were that the business unit would hold to that would set them apart from the other two business units. Third, suppliers were looking for a set of key contacts whom they could question and build up relationships with, whilst customers were looking for a partner that shared their strategic vision and with whom they could grow, or at least rely upon to support and sustain their profitable growth. Overall, the issues identified that needed to be changed were: leadership, values, communication and teamwork.

There was a need for a different style of leadership from the autocratic approach that currently existed. The vision had to be supported through values that were not merely wallpaper but shared by all. And a robust communication plan and team structure were also needed. To achieve change in these areas would require input and engagement throughout the business unit, as well as training and development.

There were many challenges to the change process from inside and outside the business unit. Employees were sceptical of the change. Comments included: 'yes we have heard all of this before' and 'it is just the flavour of the month'. From within the division, especially from the leadership within the business units, there was apprehension of the impact that this change would have on individuals. The challenge from a customer and supplier perspective was to avoid extra bureaucracy that would slow down – or even increase the cost of – an already poor service.

Following the feedback from the interviews I decided to hold a 'What Does Good Look Like' (WDGLL) event. The major challenge was who to involve in the event. I canvassed a number of employees from each department and asked for volunteers to form a project team. To my surprise 27 employees volunteered. At this stage only internal employees were invited to take part, as the event would involve developing the vision for the business unit. A date was set and some pre-work was sent to all the volunteers to complete regarding a vision for the unit, as well as asking the volunteers to canvass views from their peers.

The first action during the event was to agree a vision for the business unit. We began by reviewing the visions of key competitors in the markets that our business unit operated in. The team were then tasked to create a vision statement that would be understood by all employees within the business unit. The agreed vision statement was: *To be the number 1 supplier of gas generation systems and solutions within our chosen market.*

The second stage was to create a draft set of ground rules for the team. A simple brainstorming exercise was performed to produce a list of relevant statements and/or words. This list was refined to create a set of eight ground rules that were later expanded to become our values. Once this was complete, the team were tasked with creating a 'current state model' and then a 'desired future state' for the business unit. Once this was complete the two models were compared and rated through a simple rating process, for example: *Rating key: 0–3 = Poor; 4–6 = Average; 7–10 = Good.*

Next the team created a force field analysis (as shown in Figure 7.2) in order to identify the driving and restraining forces for moving to the desired new state. The data from the force field analysis enabled the team to develop action plans for each driving and restraining force. These action plans included: a full presentation to all employees in the business unit of the findings and actions; regular business updates to all employees; the introduction of an appraisal system; and the implementation of a learning and development process.

FIGURE 7.2 Force field analysis

| | | | | | | | | | Driving Forces | | | | | | Restraining Forces | | | | |

Driving Forces

Good Value Stream Maps

On Time Delivery

Trained and Motivated teams

Supportive Management

Good data available

F = 4 × 10 = 40

F = 5 × 4 = 20

F = 4 × 8 = 32

F = 3 × 7 = 21

F = 5 × 10 = 50

Current State

Restraining Forces

No VS Owner

Shipping Times

Poor quality of parts from suppliers

F = 4 × 10 = 40

F = 5 × 4 = 20

F = 4 × 8 = 32

Desired State

| +5 | +4 | +3 | +2 | +1 | 0 | -1 | -2 | -3 | -4 | -5 |

score 1 to 5 for impact to business

score 1 to 10 for control/influence

Following the WDGLL event a review took place of what went well and areas for improvement. The main areas of what went well were the inclusiveness and teamwork approach, while the areas for improvement consisted of ensuring that the actions would be rolled out and monitored.

The vision became the main focus for the business unit and the ground rules were expanded by the team to become the business unit values. High-performance teams were trained and established to deal with problems and build-up relationships with suppliers and customers. Meetings were set up with customers to share the vision and to identify joint profitable growth objectives.

Overall the business unit witnessed not only profitable growth over the next few years but it also won many awards for engagement, in terms of high-performance team accomplishments from both the corporation and external bodies.

The key lessons from this change initiative focus on the power of employee engagement and the part that leadership plays in affecting the outcome. The employees highlighted in their interviews at the very beginning of this process that they would like to be more involved in decisions about the business. Through the change programme a culture was created that allowed all employees the opportunity to get involved in the running of the business through regular communication events; and setting personal goals that were achievable, meaningful and aligned to the vision – and then measured regularly against performance. Allowing all employees the opportunity to develop themselves through training events, and also celebrating their learning successes with them through both formal and informal recognition techniques, again had a positive impact on the improvements that the business unit witnessed. There were also changes in the performance management process, with an emphasis on how important it was to have regular reviews of progress, supported by a robust training and development process.

The power of dealing with poor performance through developing, teaching and coaching – rather than the autocratic approach of telling people what to do – was also a success. To support this approach a simple 'Skills versus Desire' chart was utilized, as shown in Figure 7.3. This tool enabled conversations to take place that, in some cases, allowed employees to make a decision about their future. One case in particular comes to mind where an employee of more than 10 years' service voluntarily left the organization to work in a charity. Other cases have occurred were employees who were seen as 'problem children' became 'superstars' through being helped to identify the barriers to their performance and/or by being allowed to be more involved in the business. To conclude, employee engagement was crucial to making the change a success and to sustaining it.

FIGURE 7.3 'Skills versus Desire' matrix

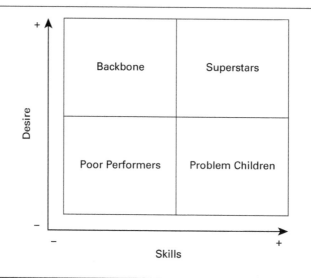

References

Agness, L (2011) Changing the rules of the game, *Strategic HR Review*, **10** (5), pp 11–16

Andriopoulos, C and Dawson, P (2009) *Managing Change and Creativity*, SAGE, London

Andriopoulos, C and Gotsi, M (2002) Creativity requires a culture of trust: lessons from Lunar Design Inc, *Design Management Journal*, Spring, pp 57–63

Bate, P (2000) Changing the culture of a hospital: from hierarchy to networked community, *Public Administration*, 78 (3), pp 485–12

Bate, S P (2012) *Strategies for Cultural Change*, Routledge, London

Barsh, J, Capozzi, M and Davidson, J (2008) [accessed 15 October 2015] Leadership and Innovation, *The McKinsey Quarterly*, January [Online] http://www.mckinsey.com/insights/innovation/leadership_and_innovation

Johnson, G, Scholes, K and Whittington, R (2008) *Exploring Corporate Strategy: Text and cases*, Pearson Education, London

Kleiner, A (2001) [accessed 16 October 2015] The Cult of Three Cultures, *Strategy+Business* [Online] www.strategy-business.com/article/19868?pg=all

Kotter, J P and Heskett, J L (1992) *Corporate Culture and Performance*, Free Press, New York

Martin, J (2002) *Organizational Culture: Mapping the terrain*, SAGE, California

Miller, C C and Perlroth, N (2013) [accessed 16 October 2015] Yahoo Says New Policy is Meant to Raise Morale, *New York Times*, 5 March [Online] http://www.nytimes.com/2013/03/06/technology/yahoos-in-office-policy-aims-to-bolster-morale.html?_r=0

Morgan, G (2006) *Images of Organization*, SAGE, London

Ogbanna, E and Harris, L C (2002) Organizational culture: a ten year, two-phase study of change in the UK food retailing sector, *Journal of Management Studies*, **39** (5), pp 673–706

Pettigrew, A M (1990) Longitudinal field research on change: theory and practice, *Organization science*, **1** (3), pp 267–92

Salaman, G and Asch, D (2003) *Strategy and Capability: Sustaining organizational change*, Blackwell, Oxford

Schein, E (1997) *Organizational Culture and Leadership*, 3rd edn, Jossey-Bass, San Francisco

Zien, K A and Buckler, S (2004) Dreams to market: crafting a culture of innovation, in *The Human Side of Managing Technological Innovation*, ed R Katz, pp 478–96, Oxford University Press, New York

Further reading

It is worth looking at the following:

The documentary 'Jamie Oliver's Food Revolution' shows how a UK chef attempts to plant a seed of change in the culture of eating in West Virginia and the barriers he faces [Online] **http://www.youtube.com/watch?v=ValbvmcpSEk**

James Martin has more luck when he attempts to change the food served in hospitals in the UK. Watch how James copes with changing the culture of hospital kitchens. 'Operation Hospital Food' with James Martin [Online] **http://www.youtube.com/watch?v=oouafoD2ijk**

PART FOUR
Building capabilities

08
The role of HR in transitioning people through change

KEY POINTS

- HR professionals have a significant role to play in any change or transformation at a strategic or operational level.
- HR should be involved from the start of the process and clearly established as a mutually supportive partner working with leaders and managers. They can act as facilitators, strategists, pastors and/or consultants.
- HR can support the diagnosis, preparation, implementation, monitoring and sustainability of change.
- Where change initiatives cross national boundaries it is possible that leaders and managers will have to handle people differently in different jurisdictions, according to local customs, practices and legal requirements. It cannot be assumed that what works well in one country will also work well in another. It is therefore important that HR is involved in change across international boundaries.
- By focusing exclusively on high fliers, organizations often overlook those performers who are critical for the success of any transformation effort but may not be seen as high potential.
- Changes to structures, reporting lines, processes and culture cannot be made in isolation. These elements are interrelated and will impact on the culture of the organization. Success in ensuring that the impact of change is considered across functions/departments and across international boundaries requires strong management supported by HR expertise.

- Synergy and mutual benefit can be achieved when internal and external HR consultants work in partnership on transformations, and when the contract with external consultants includes the transfer of skills and knowledge to internal HR consultants.

Introduction

Managing and leading change is at the heart of HR's role in organizations. The nature of HR's participation and the context in which it operates may have altered in recent decades, but supporting organizational change and transformation remain a key component of its role. The aim of this chapter is to discuss that role.

HR, or human resources management (HRM), can be defined as 'how an organization effectively harnesses and maximizes the value of its people to achieve its strategic goals' (Cole *et al*, 2015: 536). HRM translates transformation strategies into people requirements that link transformation with specific HR issues. The role of HRM during transformations has evolved from providing purely personnel administration to providing strategic support. This shift is due to a number of factors. First, changes in the environment in which organizations now operate and their need for HR to support them in responding and adapting to ever-changing environmental pressures. Second, the complexity, speed, depth and the global reach of change. HR staff may be working for managers that operate transnationally and are based in a different location, or even country. Third, the nature of the change will affect the contribution expected from HR. It might be that their professional HR knowledge and skills are required, such as for a new bonus scheme for sales and marketing staff; or designing and implementing a competency matrix for senior management. So the role of HR is affected by factors related to the change. The overall purpose of the HR function during change is to support managers and leaders, as well the other people affected by the change, and to help them through transitions.

In this chapter the role of HR professionals in organizational change is examined. The chapter begins by discussing the importance of HR during the transition that people go through during transformations. Attention is given to HR's strategic and operational role in the diagnosis, planning, implementation, monitoring and sustaining of the benefits of change through people. The chapter also discusses the importance of performance management in helping to embed changes to work activities and behaviours. Examples are provided about HR's approach to change, as well as the challenges they face and how they address them. In particular, the role of HR during restructuring is examined. The chapter concludes by discussing the consultancy role that HR can play, as well as considering the benefits of employing external and internal HR consultants. Key questions are addressed such as: what role can and should HR play in organizational change? How can the proposed benefits of change and their measures be integrated into performance management systems? How should HR support restructuring? How can key employees be retained during transformation? What are the benefits of using internal versus external HR consultants?

LEARNING OUTCOMES

By the end of this chapter you will be able to:

- appreciate the important role of HR during change and transformation;
- implement a strategy for involving HR in change initiatives;
- integrate the proposed benefits of change and their measures into performance management systems;
- work with HR professionals to understand the factors in a new organization design that needs to be balanced when restructuring;
- identify and retain staff who are critical to the organization;
- recognize when to use internal and external HR consultants.

The importance of HR during change

HR is important to both the transition that people go through during transformations and to the long-term sustainability of change initiatives. HR can support change at an operational and also a strategic level, as HR understands the people elements of the organization and how changes to one part of the organization can have repercussions for people and other areas across the organization. In particular, HR understands how the organization should engage, incentivize, develop and manage its people through change. Crucially it may also have the management information required to understand the totality of the workforce, its demographics and change capabilities, as well as the current baseline and the future projections of the composition of the workforce. HR can therefore help to support managers and leaders with the people dimension of transformations.

Most change initiatives focus on the technical aspects of change but fail to focus on the people factors that are needed to create a sustainable and engaging transition. As discussed in Chapter 2, people go through many emotions during transitions. Yet too often the people dimension is considered after the transformation process has started and, in many cases, towards the end of the process. This is too little, too late and does not create the desired change in working practices, skills, knowledge or behaviour at all levels in order to deliver business benefits. In an article entitled 'The irrational side of change management' McKinsey consultants Carolyn Aitken and Scott Keller (2009) outline the results of a survey of executives from around the world. The survey shows that only one in three change projects succeeded. The high rate of failure is attributed to a lack of attention to the 'people factor'. This is not a surprising finding since it is a factor that is frequently ignored during change, despite the fact that people need to be committed to a change initiative – to engage with it and to embed it. And critically, they need to be included in the process from the start. To create successful change, people must feel that they are instrumental in influencing the direction of change and included in the decision-making process as well as the implementation. HR can play a vital role in enabling this to happen.

HR can support managers to adopt facilitative, inclusive ways of working with people prior to, during and after a change initiative in order to ensure it is embedded and ultimately sustained. HR can also help to identify the capabilities (see Chapter 9 for a discussion on capabilities) required for transformation. HR can take the lead in ensuring that the capabilities, as well as the commitment of people, are optimized for change. By doing so, HR can play a significant role in easing people through transitions. This is illustrated in an article in *HR Magazine* entitled, 'Managing change is at the heart of the HR role', by Fiona Morgan, the HR and change director at the pharmacy group Lloyds. Morgan discusses the role of HR within the company during a change programme that was launched in response to radical changes in the external marketplace in which the company operates. The changing structure and nature of the health-care sector as a whole presented an exciting new opportunity for the company to offer a wide range of new health-care services to customers, such as diabetes testing, medicine usage reviews and cholesterol screening. It also meant up-skilling pharmacists. HR's role was to help employees understand why the change was happening and how the new skills and services they were being asked to deliver would ultimately mean a greater role for pharmacists in health-care provision, alongside GPs and hospitals. Morgan describes how HR provided the tools to make the change happen. She describes how, during the change process, teams were required to work together who had not done so before and how HR supported them to achieve the change goals.

HR practices and policies can have a major impact on how change is carried out. It is important to ensure that actions taken during change comply with agreed policies and procedures in order to prevent costly official complaints, appeals and industrial action. For instance, if the change involves redundancy, HR can advise on the procedures to be followed. If there is likely to be an impact from the change on employment, contracts and/or terms and conditions of staff, HR needs to be consulted. Failure to follow HR policies can lead to disputes and, in some cases, being escalated to external bodies such as trade unions and work councils in order to achieve a resolution. A lack of engagement with people can also lead to prolonged and costly industrial action. HR can help to facilitate employee relations between management and employees. Time must therefore be included in the planning of change for consultation and negotiation with HR.

HR can also help prevent people from reverting back to their old ways of working, by advising where existing policies and procedures can be used to reinforce desired new working practices. HR policies and procedures can act as powerful levers to bring about change, since they can have a visible impact on the working practices and behaviours of employees. Importantly, HR can advise where changing policies and procedures will avoid reinforcing old and unwanted behaviours. So HR has an important operational role to play during change.

The strategic role of HR

HR leaders have a significant strategic role to play in any transformation process. For HR to succeed with change it has to have HR leaders who are active not passive and able to identify solutions to help business leaders and managers. In particular, HR leaders need to be able to diagnose issues and identify the need for change – and not just react to dictates from leaders. At a strategic level HR also needs to support the development of a culture of learning, innovation and change, and identify ways to measure the impact of each of these. HR also needs to be able to manage the power and politics of the organization (see Chapter 4 for further discussion on power and politics).

The roles that HR should play in an organization have been much debated in the literature (for example, see Ulrich and Brockbank, 2005). Gwen Wileman (2007), for example, proposes that the role of HR when related to change should be one of a facilitator in order to develop plans that turn strategy into action, and maximize the capability and readiness of the department in order to achieve this proposed change. Raymond Caldwell (2001) suggests a typology of four roles for HR during change and transformation – champions, adapters, consultants and synergists:

- Change champions are those professionals or executives at the head of an organization who can envisage and lead HR policy changes with far-reaching effects across the organization. This role integrates business strategy with HR strategies of change at the highest level of the organization.

- A change adapter is a middle-level HR generalist who is capable of providing support for the change within business units and other key areas. Adapters translate the vision of the change into actual tangible actions, and sustain the change process.

- Change consultants are specialist HR professionals who implement key stages of the change initiative.

- Change synergists are senior HR managers who are able to strategically integrate and deliver large-scale and multiple change projects across the whole organization. Within this role, synergists will concurrently co-ordinate a number of change projects within an organization, each with its own unique structure and set of limitations.

Specifically, HR leadership needs to focus on ensuring that the following are aligned with the transformation strategy: the HR strategy; HR policies and practices; the training and development strategy; performance and talent management systems; resource management; norms, values and behaviours. The specific activities involved in such strategic activities are expanded on by Charlotte Edgley-Pyshorn and Jeroen Huisman (2011) in their study of the role of the HR department in organizational change in a British university. The study identifies a set of activities that HR leaders should pay attention to when a transformation is being considered, including:

- ensuring that individuals have a clear understanding of the need for and aim of the change;
- ensuring that people are kept motivated and informed so that they continue to commit to the change and that it does not die out through a lack of awareness and priority;
- identifying and providing necessary training and development for all relevant staff;
- constant re-evaluation of the transformation as it progresses in order to identify any new or amended needs that are required.

Whatever the nature of the change, HR should be involved at a strategic level from the start of a transformation. As Jeanne LaMarsh (2004) says, the most important action is for HR to proclaim itself a strategic partner of change in order to be fully viable in the process. When HR is not clearly established as a mutually supportive partner, leaders and managers may well struggle to support individuals through the transition. The most significant risk is to involve HR in the transformation process only after decisions about the people implications have been made, even ones that may seem positive. Involving HR early in discussions about prospective transformations that affect people enables potential legal and regulatory implications to be identified and planned for. So early engagement with HR can help to provide a strategic view of the impact that the transformation will have on people practices. You may find it useful to use the template in Appendix 8.1 in order to help structure initial discussions with HR about proposed changes.

Key HR activities

The key activities that HR can contribute to during change are:

- diagnosis;
- preparation;
- implementation and monitoring;
- sustainability.

Diagnosis

Early engagement with HR enables a timely diagnosis of the people factors to be conducted and solutions identified that are most likely to succeed. This can make the difference between successful and less successful change initiatives.

Diagnosis is key in identifying potential people issues, some of which will help to drive the change forward and others that may block its successful journey. HR needs to understand the challenges and issues that employees impacted by the change may have during and once the change is embedded. Jeanne LaMarsh (2004) describes this as the 'delta', the dip that occurs post-introduction of a change and ends after the change is adopted. This can result in a variety of emotional responses (as outlined in Chapter 2). HR needs to be able to work with managers to identify the reasons for various reactions and what type of support people will need.

HR should address the following questions as part of diagnosis:

- What are the key people drivers for change; what is the need for change?
- Do leaders and managers support the change?
- Will the change affect a specific group of employees/teams/ departments/functions or the entire organization on a regional, national or international basis?
- How will it affect work/shift patterns, reward and remuneration, benefits, location?
- Will it change the numbers or the demographics of employees?
- How might people react to the proposed change/s?

Preparation

The preparation stage involves sharing the need for change, starting to engage people in the process, and encouraging dialogue and listening. Most employees inherently will not feel that change is needed, especially if the status quo appears to be working and the business is doing well. HR can work with managers to highlight the need for change. They can do this by painting a picture of the issues with the current situation and the rationale for the change. By focusing on the challenges faced, HR can help employees to understand and appreciate more clearly that change is needed and beneficial. Perry McIntosh and Richard Luecke define this as reframing situations so that people can look at them in a new way: 'Framing is a mental window through which we see reality' (2011: 34). By reframing the situation, employees can take a step back and understand the need and/or benefit of the change.

In preparation for starting a transformation, a project or programme team must be established to plan and co-ordinate it. This team will need to include experienced members who can address the demands inherent in a transformation. HR can work with senior management to identify team members and help define their roles and objectives, as well as any incentives they will receive as part of the team, such as overtime pay or bonuses. HR can *facilitate* sessions that identify how the team will work together and identify the ground rules they will play by. HR can also provide *pastoral care* to the team, through coaching, and support them during times of pressure and stress.

HR can also encourage employee commitment, which relies on employees having a sense of being treated with fairness and having trust in the organization. Mismanaged change can lead to a lack of commitment. HR can provide support to managers to ensure that commitment is effective. In addition, HR has the expertise to advise on those aspects of the change that will need to be negotiated with employee representatives such as work councils and trade unions. In such ways, HR can help to *facilitate* the effective and ethical transition of people to new employment arrangements.

Timing is a critical focus for HR during this preparation stage. Change will inherently require more time from employees as they are asked to accomplish daily tasks while implementing the change. HR needs to identify any concurrent changes that could apply pressure on people and assess whether individuals have the capability and capacity for additional changes, or alternatively if the timing of the change should be adjusted.

As well as timing, HR needs to consider the impact of the pace at which the change will be implemented. For example, due to an increasing competitive online marketplace, a company may have to set up an online site as quickly as possible to stop a haemorrhaging of sales to other online suppliers. On the other hand, a company implementing a change in its supply chain across its global operation may need more time to incorporate such changes. If change needs to be implemented quickly, the number of people involved in the transformation process may have to be limited, as the more people are involved, the slower the process might be. If the number of people involved is limited then there is an increased likelihood that employees may feel ignored and oppose the process. Conversely, when pace is not an issue, there should be time for wider employee involvement, which will help to foster employee ownership and commitment.

As part of the preparation stage, HR should also encourage the leadership team to develop a culture of dialogue across the organization. One of the worst things that can happen when preparing for change is an inconsistency in understanding. Managers and HR need to ensure that employees understand the rationale for the change and how it will impact on them.

The best way to find out if change is working is to ask the people involved in it. The challenge, however, is getting enough people within an organization to open up and provide an accurate cross-section of views. Observation, focus groups and one-to-one interviews are useful, as well as floor walks in which HR visits individuals to see how they are adapting to the change and to address any concerns.

Another effective approach that can provide a more nuanced view is what Steven Sakson and George Whitmore (2013) call a 'listening team'. A listening team can include up to 12 managers from all levels and parts of the organization and with different ranks and tenures, but all must have a reputation as someone whom people trust. Each listening-team member makes listening to people a core responsibility, through everyday conversations, huddles and one-to-one interviews. Sakson and Whitmore suggest that every two weeks or so the team should meet to compare notes and address questions such as:

- Does there seem to be ownership and commitment to the change?
- Are any individuals/teams struggling to let go of old ways of working?
- Are any policies, practices or structures impeding the transformation?
- What additional information, skills or assistance do people need?

As well as listening to employees' issues and concerns, the team should also listen to and identify what ideas can be realized. Listening to employees views demonstrates that they are valued – and can create a greater sense of fairness for employees throughout the change process. Leaders and managers will also need to know whether the change is working and effective. HR can add value in *facilitating* the feedback process.

A key element in listening is the power of silence. Managers and leaders need to be aware that if someone does not answer a question immediately, they should avoid rushing in to fill the silence. People should be given time to think and time to talk about issues that may be difficult or sensitive. The existence of the listening team should be well known across the organization and everyone should be invited to speak with team members. This way, people will understand that HR and other leaders respect and want to hear their views. The listening team should summarize their findings and then provide recommendations to the leadership team, who must take action to address the issues and ideas identified and inform staff of the actions taken.

Implementation and monitoring

Most of the vital steps in the diagnosis and preparation stages must be repeated in the implementation phase. HR must continue to listen to people's views and encourage managers and leaders to do the same. HR must also build employee confidence in the change. One way to do this is to ensure that employees have the skills, knowledge and capabilities to contribute to the change process and to any prescribed new ways of working and behaving. This is vital as change requires learning new things and unlearning old habits. Yet according to the SHRM 2007 Change Management Survey Report, 44 per cent of respondents listed insufficient time devoted to training and development as a major challenge of change. Ensuring that employees have the relevant capabilities for change is critical, and HR can help managers in identifying the required training and development gaps and then the necessary interventions to address the gaps (this is discussed further in Chapter 9). Specific questions that HR need to ask include:

- Do we have the required capabilities to enable success?
- What capabilities would enhance success?
- What are the time and resources needed to make this training and development happen?

With this information HR, along with organizational development (OD) specialists, can develop training and development interventions to address the gaps. HR needs to ensure that a training and development strategy is developed to support change. HR specialists can also identify and provide specialized training and support for those individuals who may have a harder time managing and adapting to the change (such as coaching or stress management workshops). In some cases, timely and appropriate training and development can substantially reduce or even help individuals to avoid the stress and anxiety often associated with change. This can help to ensure that individuals are able to embed and sustain the change.

Sustainability

When a change initiative is successful and realizes benefits, the question then is how to sustain that change. HR can help employees to see the change as a norm, part of business as usual, and not just a fad, so that old habits are broken and employees transition through the transformation. There is, however, evidence to show that this is a stage that HR tends not to be involved in. According to research by Mark Crail (2007) only 10.4 per cent of HR managers are involved in the change process during the later stages. Yet HR can help to embed and sustain the change by supporting people through it, including leaders and managers. In its *pastoral* role, HR can provide help by offering coaching, counselling, or often just the opportunity for managers to share their concerns and challenges. It is critical that managers (as well as other employees) can be open and honest with HR about the support they need without reproach or retribution. Creating a support system is akin to reinforcing the foundation of a house that is holding everything else in place. When people are supported it helps them to achieve benefits from the change.

Sustaining change also involves consistently reviewing change initiatives and continually asking the questions:

- Is this change still offering us a competitive advantage?
- Are the intended benefits being realized?
- Does the transformation have the support and sponsorship it needs?

To address such questions, HR must pay attention to what is happening with a transformation. They must keep in mind the intended aims and objectives of the change and monitor that the people benefits are being achieved. Furthermore, HR must ask if these expected benefits still align with organizational strategy. If the change is no longer effective or no longer in alignment then it needs to be reviewed, revamped or discontinued. Not every change is appropriate to sustain, but change is always happening.

In the following case study, Or Kaynar describes how he supported an organizational transformation when he was head of HR for an international online gaming group.

CASE STUDY   Winning hearts and minds – the role of HR in organizational transformation

Written by Or Kaynar, HR and Operations director at AppsFlyer

In my experience one of the 'chicken and egg' questions of change relates to what should proceed and what should precede in order to create a success – is it actions or attitudes? Some managers believe that a successful change should start with a thorough explanation of the reasons or rationale for the change, in order to modify attitudes and create a favourable atmosphere in which change would be easier to accomplish and sustain. Others believe that a successful change must start by determined actions that will demonstrate as quickly as possible the value of the change and, in turn, this will shape the opinions and attitudes of the people involved in the change, making them more receptive to it. In this case study I describe an organizational change in which, to some extent, both approaches were tried.

A couple of years ago I was head of the Human Resources function in an international online gaming group. The company consisted of two big divisions – an online marketing division dealing with promoting the group brands, and a research and development (R&D) division, which provided development and platform maintenance services for the whole group. The R&D division was divided into professional teams, according to the software environments that they were developing.

The company was facing some difficult challenges. On the one hand, the company, operating in a very competitive industry, was reliant on its ability to constantly develop new games and new features to existing games. Such developments required substantial effort and time in terms of planning and development. On the other hand, the growing inventory of online operating software (also known as 'software in production'), required large amounts of ongoing maintenance and incremental enhancements. The latter developments were very tempting for R&D engineers to focus their time on, as they were both urgent and crucial for the regular operation of the group's websites, and quite easy and short to implement in the case of the enhancements. However, by spending their time on these activities R&D was drifting, in a semi-conscious manner, towards a situation in which big innovative projects of new games and software were being delayed indefinitely. Furthermore, the people who took the decisions on what and where to focus priorities were the team managers who were not always knowledgeable enough about the business priorities. It became clear to the group CEO and to the CTO (chief technology officer), in charge of all R&D and IT that a change was desperately needed.

Following the best practice set out by other organizations our CEO, a very charismatic and dominant character, decided that R&D should split into two parallel development lines – one line would be called 'Projects' and deal only with long-term development projects, such as new games or substantial software. This line would continue to be led by the current two team managers and have a strategic importance in the further development of the group. The other line was to be called 'Service delivery', and would be in charge of maintenance and small, quick software implementations and features. This team would be headed by new managers, and due to its critical role in the ongoing operation of the business would consist of the most experienced engineers, the ones with the broadest knowledge of the company software inventory and platform. The CEO was very clear that this change was crucial and urgent. For him there was no time to lose in carrying out the restructure.

There were several lessons learnt from this change. The first lesson was that it is not enough that the CEO feels the urgency for the change, it also has to be appreciated and understood by the people about to go through the change. In these early stages of implementation the two team managers about to become project team managers had very little to gain from the change – they were about to lose some of the best of their team members to the service delivery team, as well as some of the high-profile maintenance work, which they had been doing. Although these team managers were being pushed hard by the CTO (pushed himself by the CEO) to implement the change, it was clear that they were dragging their feet in moving to the new structure and supporting it in front of their teams. There was a real risk of this change slowly vanishing, or a high-volume collision between the CEO and these managers – a collision that would not end without casualties. At this point there was a clear need for HR's help in communicating the need for change, and creating a coalition of managers to ensure consistency in the words and actions. To achieve these goals we had to go back and consult with the managers, not only on how to implement the change but also on why the change was needed. This required a lot of debate and slowed down the change implementation significantly, but after the discussions were complete we had not only gained a deeper understanding of the challenges that the change was facing but also strong support for the change from the managers who had originally opposed it so strongly.

This brings us to a second lesson learnt – the success of change depends not only on a strong strategy, but also on implementation based on deep understanding of the organization about to change. Following inputs from managers and HR several changes were made in staffing the teams and in the communication plan, which proved to be extremely valuable in the implementation of the change. These discussions helped us to understand particular difficulties that team members were having due to the change and helped us to prepare for them in advance, the importance of which could not be exaggerated. We learnt that one of the keys to starting a change plan is ensuring that every team member affected by the change feels that he/she has been considered during the design stage of the change. Even if the end outcome is not ideal for each individual, the feeling that they are consulted, or at least thought of, provides a sense of fairness that is vital for willing participation and co-operation in the change implementation.

Ultimately, the change process described was successful and, as with most change processes in hi-tech companies, achieved within limited time. The service delivery team was established and ultimately included most of the talented developers in the R&D division, and later on it became the best school for developers due to the wide and fast exposure that the work of this team required. The boundaries between this team and the projects teams were eventually well defined. The key lessons that I learnt from this change include: the importance of meticulous and well-consulted design; the need to create a sense of urgency; the need to create a coalition supporting the change; and the importance of making sure that all stakeholders are considered during the design of the change.

Discussion questions

What role was played by HR in this case?

How might HR have helped in the initial stages of planning for the change?

What worked well and what could have been done differently to involve the stakeholders in the change?

Managing performance

To help sustain change it is important that new working practices and behaviours are rewarded. One way to do this is through a performance management system. The performance of individuals and teams should be in line with the required changes. This involves the monitoring of performance against the objectives for the transformation in order to ensure that people take ownership of the actions required to embed the change. If there are measurable objectives, then individuals will be able to see how the change is progressing and how they contribute to it. Specific, measurable, achievable, relevant and timebound (SMART) objectives should be identified for each individual and team involved or affected by the change. The proposed benefits of change and their measures should be integrated into performance management systems in order to ensure consistency in what is required in how people behave and work. This involves aligning responsibilities for implementing the change and for benefit management with individual's performance objectives, so that there is clarity about what people are responsible and accountable for. Performance objectives should also be aligned with the reward and recognition processes.

Recognition helps to motivate people to change. The IT company Cisco has launched a recognition programme across the enterprise called 'Connected Recognition', which identifies and celebrates outstanding employee work immediately. The programme seeks to eliminate the bureaucratic lag between employees' achievement and recognition. Anyone can nominate a colleague for an award. Cisco's CEO John Chambers says, 'Today's technology markets are moving at such a fast pace that it requires companies like us to be in a constant state of preparing, supporting and enabling our employees so they adapt, develop and grow to meet these new challenges' (cited by Hackett, 2014). Recognition is important not only for its motivational pat on the back but also for its publicity value; it means that a team/department or organization is aware of what is possible, who has done it, and the capability that there is in the organization.

Rewards, whether financial or non-financial, need to be relevant, fair and cost-effective. In most organizations, reward and remunerations may need a radical overhaul depending on the transformation being implemented. For instance, it may mean moving to a reward system that emphasizes the performance of the team rather than the individual. HR needs to ensure that reward and remuneration cover how individuals are compensated, including non-financial.

In sum, the day-to-day operations in HR will always be important and it is critical that they are done well. HR needs to support people through the change process. To do this, HR needs to be effective at assessing individuals' readiness for change, setting the groundwork for the change to happen, supporting people through the change, monitoring the progress of people during the transition, helping to sustain momentum, and ensuring that change is sustained through people. As this happens, HR professionals will themselves continue to develop the capabilities to lead and manage change, as well as developing and encouraging a working environment that supports people through transition. HR's role should therefore involve the diagnosis, preparation, implementation, monitoring and sustainability of transformation. In many organizations this will involve HR working across global borders.

Discussion questions

What are the benefits and problems in using performance management to manage change initiatives? What is your overall conclusion about its usefulness?

Working across global borders

As many organizations now operate in global markets it is an imperative to engage with workers at not just a local and national level but also at a wider global level. Where transformation initiatives cross international boundaries, leaders and managers will have to handle people differently in different jurisdictions. They will need to understand the customs, practices and legal requirements relevant to the different countries in which they operate. Such differences must be recognized in order to engage appropriately with employees. It cannot therefore be assumed that what works well in one country will also work well in another. Changes in work patterns, numbers employed and consultation processes about changes may have a legal and a regulatory impact. For instance, adopting work–life balance measures may involve different changes in Denmark compared to China. In some countries, there may be no trade unions or work councils to face or convince of the need for change. While in others there may be formal employee consultation procedures. The employee relations challenge of operating across boundaries has a variety of dimensions including legal, cultural, organizational and economic. The first source of advice on these issues should be HR. Once the changes are implemented, HR's ongoing responsibility will be to revise and realign country-specific factors continually, as the transformed organization's priorities evolve. The HR function, as the shaper and custodian of people practices, will be instrumental in sustaining any required change in working practices and behaviours across borders for the benefit of the organization, its people and its customers.

The role of HR during restructuring

HR can play a key role in the transitions that take place during restructuring. In simple terms, the structure is the way that the organization divides tasks and establishes reporting lines to make up a chain of command, so that individuals are accountable at various stages of a process. Structure defines reporting lines, span of control and levels of accountability, as in whether authority is centralized or devolved. The structure is the framework used for co-ordinating different activities and resources to ensure each part of an organization works towards a sub-goal that contributes to the overall goal of the organization.

Changes to the structure or restructuring is common practice in many organizations. It can range from minor changes in the physical layout of a team to introducing or decreasing a layer of management, through to downsizing the workforce, rearranging departments, breaking the organization into smaller work teams or, in the case of Zappo, completely changing the structure. An article on the online blog Quartz (**http://qz.com/161210/zappos-is-going-holacratic-no-job-titles-no-managers-no-hierarchy/**) describes how the online retailer Zappo has replaced its traditional organizational structure with a holacracy – a radical operating system where there are no job titles and no managers. The aim of a holacracy is that authority is distributed and decision making and problem solving are more effective as everyone becomes a leader of their own roles. Traditional hierarchies are replaced by self-governing teams know as circles, in an effort to make the company more agile and innovative. It is a structure in which people have flexibility to pursue what they are passionate about. One of the early adopters of this type of structure was Twitter. A less radical restructure was carried out by Time Inc., whose brands include magazines such as *PEOPLE*, *Entertainment Weekly* and *InStyle*. The company was forced to restructure in order to grow beyond print, embrace new technologies, new products, new markets and new customers. The restructure involved dissolving the company's complex matrix organization and removing multiple structural layers. In an article in the *New York Post*, entitled 'Time Inc. CEO: Layoffs, big organizational changes coming today', Andrew Beaujon (2014) describes how the aim of the restructuring was to consolidate the US brands of the company into a single portfolio, streamline decision making across the entire organization and complete the integration of American Express Publishing. According to Beaujon, the new structure would give the company more operational flexibility, speed-up decision making and encourage the development of new cross-brand products and revenue streams to help stabilize and grow top-line revenues. The restructure involved hundreds of redundancies, as well as the launch of new projects to drive greater operational efficiencies. Restructures, such as the ones carried out by Zappo and Time Inc, are complex to introduce because of their impact on the interconnectedness of the organization.

Changes to structures cannot be made in isolation, since the structure is interrelated to reporting lines, systems, processes, people and strategies, and if these are not taken into account then the restructuring may not be successful. This is evident in the case of Avon – the beauty company, known for products such as Skin-So-Soft and ANEW skincare. In an article entitled 'Avon: the rise and fall of a beauty icon' **Beth Kowitt** (2012) describes how Avon has restructured several times due to the rise in sales of low-priced beauty products at supermarket chains, the obsolescence of its direct-selling model for beauty items, and ill-advised forays into fashion, jewellery and more expensive skincare products that have alienated many customers. All this has resulted in a decline in sales. Kowitt describes how the CEO has instituted restructures in an attempt to return the company to profitability. There is, however, according to Kowitt, a growing sense that these restructures might be too little, too late, especially as Avon's previous restructuring attempts have all failed. Kowitt concludes by quoting Ali Dibadj, an analyst with Sanford C Bernstein and Co, as saying: 'The world around Avon has changed – they can't just do things the way they used to.'

Success with restructuring requires strong management supported by HR expertise. The HR department can work with senior management to identify all of the factors that need to be taken into account, such as the number and type of roles required, reward and remuneration systems, and diversity and equal opportunity issues. For instance, before the start of restructuring, basic HR steps such as reducing recruiting efforts, stopping contracts for temporary staff and improving transparency about vacant positions can reinforce the organization's commitment to its employees. Employees who are concerned about the impact that a restructure will have on their role can create anxiety not just for themselves but also for their colleagues, so HR must address any concerns quickly. HR can take actions such as finding new opportunities for employees whose roles are being made redundant, especially if they are people who the organization is keen to retain. HR can also set up outplacement support for staff exiting the organization. HR's experience and support is therefore valuable during restructuring.

Mergers and acquisitions

More extreme and more difficult to manage is a restructure that involves a merger or acquisition where different systems are not aligned. This can create some real problems, particularly if one company perceives it is the victim of a takeover and the relationship between the companies is strained. This was the case when US food company Kraft Foods launched a hostile bid for Cadbury, the UK chocolate maker. Cadbury was the final acquisition necessary to allow Kraft to be split into two companies: a grocery business and a global snacks business. **Kraft** needed Cadbury to provide scale for the snack business, especially in emerging markets such as India. In an article in the *Financial Times*, Scott Moeller (2012) says that the challenge for Kraft was how to buy Cadbury when it was not for sale. Not only was Cadbury not for sale, but it also actively resisted the Kraft takeover. Eventually a deal was struck between the chairmen of the two companies. Such a merger or acquisition (whether hostile or friendly) can benefit from the involvement of HR.

HR can play a specific role during mergers and acquisitions in a number of ways including:

- *Due diligence*
  Prior to the merger or acquisition, HR can play a key part in the people due diligence. This involves identifying what data is required and then analysing it so that there is an overview of the people issues, especially any deal breakers, before the deal goes ahead. Richard Schuler and Susan Jackson (2001: 249) highlight that this can involve: gaining knowledge of the make-up and motivation of the companies' workforces; conducting an analysis of the organizational structures; comparing benefits, compensation policies and the contracts of both companies; and assessing the cultural match between the two companies.

- *Organizational design*
  Once the deal is signed there will be a need to review the structure of the organizations. The redesign of the structures will need to include the integration of HR processes and procedures; transition of employees onto new terms and conditions; and support for staff whose roles have been made redundant either through redeployment or outplacement schemes.

- *Managing the learning and development strategy*
  This will involve building learning and development into the formal agreements between the companies; identifying and addressing development needs of staff; designing and delivering induction programmes; and ensuring that development activities are followed up and individuals are given opportunities to apply their learning in practice.

- *Co-ordination and adaptation of performance and talent management systems*
  This will include: the assignment of individuals to key positions; transfer of people to equivalent levels (grades) in the new company; the integration of career management and professional development processes; retention of key employees in the short and long terms; and a merger of reward and remuneration systems.

- *Transformation of corporate cultures*
  Mergers and acquisitions often involve companies with very different cultures coming together. HR can carry out a diagnosis of the different company cultures; support employees during integration into a new culture; ensure ethical standards are maintained before, in the process of, and after integration; and help with identifying and managing key stakeholders across the companies.

Retaining staff

HR and managers need to work together during times of organizational change, especially during mergers and acquisitions in order to identify people whose retention is critical. Too many companies approach the retention of key employees by throwing financial incentives at senior executives or high performers. By focusing exclusively on high fliers, organizations often overlook those performers who are critical for the success of any transformation effort but may not be seen as high potential. According to Sabine Cosack and colleagues (2010) these hidden gems might be found anywhere in the company. For example, such hidden gems may be the product-development manager in an acquired company's R&D function who is nearing retirement age and no longer on the company's list of high potentials, yet who is crucial to ensuring a healthy product pipeline, or the key financial accountant responsible for consolidating the acquired company's next financial report. Even if the employee's performance and career potential are unexceptional, their institutional knowledge, direct relationships and/or technical expertise can make their retention critical. An effective approach for employee retention is to start with identifying all key players, but targeting only those who are most critical and most at risk of leaving. Once HR and managers have generated a list of key players, they can begin to prioritize groups and individuals for targeted retention measures. The key is to view each employee through two lenses: first, the impact that the individual's exit would have on the organization, given the focus of their role in it; and second, the probability that the individual will leave. Suitable retention packages then need to be identified for each individual.

One-size-fits-all retention packages are usually unsuccessful in persuading a diverse group of key employees to stay. Instead, HR should tailor retention packages to specific employees. Although financial incentives play an important role in retention, money alone cannot persuade an individual to stay. Non-financial incentives are often more effective than cash and may include flexible work arrangements, assistance in finding schools and nurseries for employees' children, increased holiday allowance and so on. It is important to design incentives appropriately and use them in a targeted way. This is highlighted in a *McKinsey Quarterly* report, entitled 'Retaining key employees in times of change', by Sabin Cosack and colleagues, who say that:

> Targeting retention measures at the right people using a tailored mix of financial and non-financial incentives is crucial for managing organizational transitions that achieve long-term business success. (2010: 5)

Employee retention must not be viewed as a one-off exercise in which it is sufficient to get the incentives packages right. Incentives should be reviewed periodically, as individuals' preferences may change.

Employee assistance programmes (EAPs)

To support people through transition HR can provide employee assistance programmes and outplacement programmes, such as psychological and career counselling and help with updating their curricula vitae (CV), conducting job searches and enhancing their interview skills. To set up an employee assistance programme (EAP) HR needs to receive early notification from management about any proposed changes. The aim of the EAP is to assist employees on a one-to-one and/or team basis:

- One-to-one: employees need to be able to contact EAP at any time during transition for assistance with a broad range of issues, including feelings of loss, stress and anxiety as well as career issues. The EAP should be offered to people who indicate that they are having problems in specific areas and/or experiencing deteriorating work performance.

- Team: employees whose roles are being made redundant and/or those remaining in the organization – so-called survivors – will benefit from team-briefing sessions that provide them with facts about how the change will affect their jobs (including any redundancies, as well as redeployment options), and provide opportunities to discuss their emotions as they transition through the change. Such sessions should focus on how they are affected as a team, and help them to identify coping strategies for the team.

An EAP will help to find out how individuals and teams are responding and reacting to the impact of the change, as well as providing employees with the opportunity to express their feelings. There should also be a process for following up with employees in order to provide ongoing support.

Internal and external HR consultants

An organization needs to respond to what is happening in its environment and may have a limited choice in how it does this, because of situational factors and the competing demands of different stakeholders. However, its choice of response is influenced by its internal capability. In many situations, the organization can manage the challenges it faces; however, there are times when it may need assistance from HR consultants.

Consultancy – expert and process

Consultation is a two-way interaction – a process of giving and receiving help. Consulting is aimed at helping a person, team or organization in mobilizing internal and external resources to deal with change efforts. HR consultancy can be provided in a number of ways during change; the two most common approaches are *expert* and *process*. The *expert* HR consultant tells the managers what the right answer is – they solve the manager's problem for them. The expert HR consultant will make decisions on what needs to happen within the organization, such as when an organization faces an increase in staff turnover and attempts are being made to stop the loss of key staff.

At the other end of the spectrum, HR consultants can facilitate and provide support and guidance to the organization. For example, the *process* HR consultant helps managers to understand the management and people processes at work in a way that enables the managers to deal with the problem themselves. For example, the process HR consultant focuses on how to change – and this is more effective in engendering long-term transformation because it engages employees in the process. Typically, the process HR consultant will leave the managers more skilled or more able to solve their problems, and with greater ownership than before the HR consultant started on the change initiative. This is less common with an expert HR consultant.

Another way of considering consultancy is to examine whether the consultant is taking the lead, that is, suggesting to the managers that a particular situation should be examined or if they are following the manager's lead. Figure 8.1 illustrates the different HR consultancy positions.

FIGURE 8.1 HR consultancy positions

PROACTIVE

Initiating discussion with managers about a possible problem or opportunity and its solution, for example: 'We need to replace the sales performance management system.'	Initiating discussion with managers by raising his/her awareness of, or concern about, an issue or opportunity, for example, 'I notice that new sales performance data is wrong again. I wonder…'
Responding to managers' requests for the right answers or for the problem to be removed and fixed, for example a project manager.	Responding to managers' requests to help sort out an issue or opportunity.

REACTIVE

EXPERT ←——————————————→ PROCESS

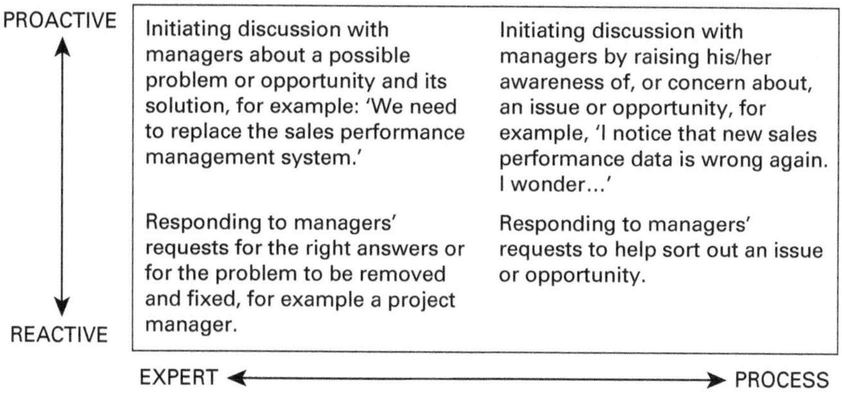

Activity

Using the HR consultancy framework ask yourself:

- Where do I find it most comfortable to be?
- Where do I find it least comfortable to be?
- Where does the organization want me to be?
- Do I need to change my consulting approach to support change in the organization?

External consultants

The need to deliver what is best for the organization is one of the reasons that many organizations engage HR consultants to help with diagnosing and guiding the change. The advantages of external HR consultants are that they provide additional resources and expertise that the organization needs, as they are not caught up in the internal power and politics. External HR consultants do, however, need to be aware of the political behaviour, power plays and the culture and subcultures of the organization, so that they can manage around them, as well as remain outside of them and not get caught up in them. If hiring HR consultants to help with a transformation is a feasible option, then it is important to clarify the expectations of both the organization and the HR consultants and to establish clear ground rules for the consultancy engagement.

Internal consultants

In exploring the nature of internal HR consultancy it is useful to compare the approach with external HR consultancy as this helps to highlight critical aspects of the role. In examining differences between the two it is not intended to set one group against another but to simply recognize that there are key differences and that they can influence selection decisions concerning which route to take.

Performing an internal HR consultancy role can be difficult. External consultants can walk away, while internal consultants have to stay and maintain relationships with their colleagues. However, great synergy and mutual benefit can be achieved when internal and external HR consultants work in partnership and when the contract with external HR consultants includes the transfer of skills and knowledge to internal HR consultants.

The difference between internal and external HR consultants

In exploring the nature of HR consultancy it is useful to compare the approach between internal and external HR consultancy as this helps to highlight critical aspects of the role. Questions for managers to consider when deciding whether or not to use internal HR consultants include:

- Does the internal HR consultant understand this business? How do they demonstrate that understanding?
- Do I sense I can trust them to respect confidences? How would they deal with an issue of competing loyalties?
- Do they have the relevant experience of this kind of transformation?
- Do they have the right tools for managing change and the knowledge to use them effectively? What experience do they have?

- What change capabilities do they have? How do these relate to this transformation?

The following list highlights some of the differences between using internal and external HR consultants. You will see from the following list that some of the differences can be used to promote a case for using internal HR consultants as opposed to external HR consultants. Internal HR consultants are usually:

- Likely to understand the overall drivers for change in the organization better than external HR consultants.
- Able to potentially generate more internal commitment to a change initiative.
- Often a lower cost option.
- In a position that they may have developed an approach or methodology for transitioning people through change that is ahead of any HR external consultancy group and more appropriate for organizational context.
- Aware of the language and the culture of the organization. They know how things work and how to get things done.
- Able to identify with the organization and the need for change.
- Able to spread their knowledge and experience throughout the organization and, in this way, enhance the organization's capability for change.
- Potentially lacking the apparent credibility of some external HR consultants.
- Prone to being too emotionally involved in the organization, which will perhaps influence their ability to be truly objective about a transformation.
- Required to live with the consequences of their advice, as they will still be around long after the external HR consultants have left.

External HR consultants are usually:

- Employed for a fixed period to work on a specific transformation.
- Presented as experts as they tend to have specialist expertise and experience of change that is not present in the organization. This is often combined with an extensive knowledge of specific industries.
- People who display high levels of energy, motivation and commitment (all needed to sustain change through people).
- Not always conversant with the business context.
- A flexible resource as the organization is not burdened with their long-term costs – when the change is implemented the consultants will leave.
- Able to transfer into the organization the knowledge and expertise from the different businesses in which they have worked.

- Not emotionally involved in organizational issues and can therefore be more objective and critical in reviewing the proposed approach for change.
- Often invested heavily in new approaches and methodologies for organizational transformation, so they have something new to offer.
- Not always required to live with the consequences of their work.
- Not always entirely honest when they say, 'we have done this before'. What they often mean is that 'we haven't but we have really great people and expertise and we are really confident we will find a solution'.
- Capable of developing a sense of dependency from managers, in that managers think, 'we cannot function without you now'.

To help decide whether or not there are benefits for your organization in using an external HR consultant use the checklist in Appendix 2. Check which reasons you think apply in your case and, if possible, get a colleague to validate your view.

The capability of HR for transformations

Depending on the type of role that an HR professional is taking on – whether it is that of facilitator, strategist, pastor or consultant – they need to have the capabilities not only to adapt to change but also to identify when it is needed and how to successfully support people through transition. According to the SHRM (2007) Change Management Survey Report, only 23 per cent of companies have HR staff devoted full-time to change management programmes. This means that 77 per cent of HR professionals who encounter change management initiatives will be dealing with change on an ad hoc or inconsistent basis. This does not bode well for HR developing the right capabilities to support people through change if they are only infrequently involved in it. Yet there is a belief that the lack of the right skills has been and will continue to be the principal reason for HR's lack of involvement in transformations. As Peter Reilly and Tony Williams say, 'Where HR falls down is in the area of high-level impact' (2006: 173). This comment is supported by the findings of a Kaisen consulting survey, which found that HR lacked power and confidence. The survey concluded that the function's greatest needs were in self-belief, assertiveness and openness to others. HR could do management's bidding but it was less able to influence a change (Pickard, 2004). In support of this, Mark Birchenhough (2004) says that there have been complaints about HR's change management skills in the UK's National Health Service. Such findings raise the issue not only about HR's support for change but also about having the capability. It would therefore appear that HR lacks sufficient capabilities for change. In addition, HR structures have failed to keep pace with the rate of change that the broader organization demands. In the introduction to the report of a survey by the CEB entitled *Key Imperatives for HR in 2015*, Michael Griffin, executive director of CEB says:

> Despite focus and investment aimed at improving HR capabilities, the function's impact has remained largely flat in the eyes of the business. In fact, less than one-fifth of line managers rate the HR function as effective or very effective. (CEB, 2015: iii)

To address such concerns the CEB survey found that 81 per cent of heads of HR are looking to make changes to their operating model in order to adapt.

For HR to be considered a valid player in the support of transformations they must first prove that they can develop change capabilities and be seen as credible partners for leaders and managers in supporting people through transitions. To ensure that they have the change capabilities HR need to ask themselves:

- Do we know how to be strategic?
- Do we know when to make the right interventions?
- Do we have the necessary diagnostic skills to identify challenges and solutions?
- Do we have the necessary skills to be effective?
- Can we influence the rationale for change and the business plan?
- Can we ensure that the people issues are taking priority?
- Can we support the sustainability of the change through people?

To address such questions it is vital that capabilities for change are built within HR for effectively supporting people through change.

Summary

Change is about people, as all change affects someone. As HR's purpose is to focus on the people in an organization, they should be involved from the start of a change initiative, especially if it is transformational. The most significant risk is to involve HR in the transformation process only after decisions about the people implications have been made, even ones that may seem positive. HR's involvement in various aspects of change can make the difference between successful and less successful initiatives by, for example, their involvement at the initial stage in setting up the transformation team; advising leaders on the availability of expertise within the organization, such as identifying any capability gaps; training and development needs; as well as the design of restructures, new roles and new working practices. HR also need to play a role in assessing the impact of change on the individuals and supporting them. This involves understanding stakeholder concerns and the appropriate methods of dialogue to reach various stakeholder groups; identifying ways to maintain and improve performance and motivation;

encouraging employee commitment; and ensuring performance management is used effectively to monitor objectives and behaviours.

Supporting people through the transition should be at the heart of HR's role, especially as it is their responsibility to balance the desired business outcomes and management expectations with an understanding of the people issues. In order to plan and manage change effectively it is important for HR to understand who will be impacted by it and when, where, how and why they will be affected. By taking the lead on this, HR has a vital role to play in creating an environment for success.

In sum, there are a number of roles that HR can play during change and transformation. First is the role of *facilitator* in terms of helping people to understand about the change, and how they can adapt their behaviour and working practices to implement it. HR can be both a facilitator of change – helping people to transition through the change with adequate support and dialogue – and also an expert on legal matters, such as employment laws in different countries. HR can also be facilitative in assisting with the design of new structures, systems and policies to meet the demands of the organization and to embed the change. This may involve developing a mentoring programme for leaders, designing a flexible working policy or introducing a new incentive scheme to retain employees. Second, is the role of *strategist*. HR can and should play a primary role in identifying the need for and implementing a change initiative. This means that the HR department should be considered an interventionist with a strategic agenda. Third, HR plays a *pastoral* role focusing on interventions that nurture the staff and develop them to ensure commitment and engagement, and ensure that employees are treated in an ethical way. Fourth, HR's role is one of a change *consultant*. So, if HR has the right capabilities it can play a strategic, facilitative, pastoral and/or consultative role, as part of organizational transformations.

Implications for HR

There are a number of practical implications for HR that can be identified from the key issues discussed in this chapter:

- *Ensure HR is active in any change process*
  Ensure there is a very active and knowledgeable HR team who can support in terms of understanding policy and legalities, and who themselves know the answers without referral. An effective HR team can make all the difference to a manager or staff member feeling supported rather than disillusioned.

- *Engage early in the transformation process*
  HR needs to ensure that they are engaged early in any transformation or change initiative. It is a significant risk if HR is only engaged in the transformation process after decisions about the people implications have been made, even decisions that may seem positive.

- *Clarifying the role that is needed*
  HR can add significant value during change and transformation in a number of ways, including: diagnosis; planning; implementation; monitoring and ensuring that change is sustained through people.

- *Develop capabilities for change*
  Training and development for HR staff is crucial so that they can lead and manage change. Providing HR with adequate training and development will give them both the capabilities and credibility necessary to support people through change.

References

Aitken, C and Keller, S (2009) The irrational side of change management, *McKinsey Quarterly*, 2, pp 100–09

Beaujon, A (2014) Time Inc. CEO: layoffs, big organizational changes coming today, *New York Post*, 4 February

Birchenhough, M (2004) A Change is as good as a rest, *People Management*, 20 May

Caldwell, R (2001) Champions, adapters, consultants and synergists: the new change agents in HRM, *Human Resource Management Journal*, 11 (3), pp 39–52

CEB (2015) *Key Imperatives for HR in 2015*, CEB, London

Cole, T, Lunn, M, McGarvie, U and Rouhof, E (2015) Organizational considerations, in Smith, R, King, D, Sidhu, R and Skelsey, D *The Effective Change Manager's Handbook: Essential guidance to the change management body of knowledge*, ed R Smith, D King, R Sidhu and D Skelsey, Kogan Page, London

Cosack, S, Guthridge, M and Lawson, E (2010) Retaining key employees in times of change, *McKinsey Quarterly*, 3, August, pp 135–39

Crail, M (2007) HR's role in managing organisational change, *IRS Employment Review*, p 885

Edgley-Pyshorn, C and Huisman, J (2011) The role of the HR department in organisational change in a British university, *Journal of Organizational Change Management*, 24 (5), pp 610–25

Hackett, R (2014) [accessed 16 October 2015] The 25 Best Global Companies to Work For, *Fortune* [Online] http://fortune.com/2014/10/23/global-best-companies/

Kowitt, B (2012) [accessed 16 October 2015] Avon: the rise and fall of a beauty icon, *Fortune* [Online] Fortune.com. http://fortune.com/2012/04/11/avon-the-rise-and-fall-of-a-beauty-icon/

LaMarsh, J (2004) Building a strategic partnership and HR's role of change manager, *Employment Relations Today*, 31 (3), pp 17–27

Luecke, R and McIntosh, P (2011) *Increase Your Influence at Work*, Amacom, New York

McIntosh, P and Luecke, R (2011) *Increase Your Influence at Work*, Amacom, New York

Moeller, S (2012) [accessed 16 October 2015] Case study: Kraft's takeover of Cadbury, *Financial Times*, 9 January [Online] http://www.ft.com/cms/s/0/1cb06d30-332f-11e1-a51e-00144feabdc0.html#axzz3asKLNQq2

Morgan, F (2009) [accessed 16 October 2015] Managing change is at the heart of the HR role, *HR Magazine*, August [Online] http://www.hrmagazine.co.uk/hro/opinion/1015629/managing-change-heart-hr-role

Pickard, J (2004) One step beyond, *People Management*, **10** (13), 30 June, pp 26–31

Reilly, P and Williams, T (2006) *Strategic HR: Building capability to deliver*, Gower, London

Sakson, S and Whitmore, G (2013) Communications strategy: a vital (but overlooked) element in lean-management transformations, McKinsey Operations Extranet

Schuler, R and Jackson, S (2001) HR issues and activities in mergers and acquisitions, *European Management Journal*, **19** (3), pp 239–53

SHRM (2007) *2007 Change Management Survey Report*, SHRM Research Department, Alexandria

Ulrich, D and Brockbank, W (2005) *The HR Value Proposition*, Harvard Business Press, Boston

Wileman, G (2007) The challenge of strategic leadership: leading cultural change, in *Strategic Leadership of Change in Higher Education*, ed S Marshall, pp 174–87, Routledge, Abingdon

Further reading

Cheung-Judge, M-Y and Holbeche, L (2015) *Organization Development: A practitioner's guide for OD and HR*, Kogan Page, London

CIPD (2005) *HR's Role in Organising: Shaping change*, CIPD, London

Wright, P, Boudreau, J, Pace, D, Sartain, L, McKinnon, P and Antoine, R (eds) (2011) *The Chief HR Officer: Defining the new role of human resource leaders*, Wiley, London

Appendix 8.1 – Framework for initial discussions with HR about change

This is a framework that helps to get initial meetings started between managers and HR. You might already have areas of interest or concerns in mind that you want to explore, or you can start with a blank sheet of paper. An A4 version of this will allow you to take notes on it.

Areas of interest or concern	What is happening now?	What specifically would 'better' look like?	What would we have to change to get better?	What obstacles might there be?	What would help us to change?	What would the benefits be?

Appendix 8.2 – Using external HR consultants

The reasons why people use consultants will usually fall into one or more of the categories below. It is important for the consultant to understand which ones apply in any assignment if it is to be successful. Check which reasons you think apply in your case and, if possible, get a colleague to validate your view:

- To gain an independent point of view.
- To obtain an impartial decision.
- To validate a change initiative already planned.
- To confirm that the change initiative already taken was right.
- To add credibility to a favoured or planned change process.
- To acquire additional resources to undertake work required to implement the change.
- To have someone safe to share secrets with.
- To solve the apparently insoluble.
- To provide a scapegoat.
- To gather information to assist decision making.
- To gain reassurance that opportunities are being effectively identified and taken.
- To minimize the risk of the unexpected.
- To demonstrate that a problem is being addressed.

Once you have reviewed this, consider the following questions:

- What are the implications for you of this result?
- What should you do, and not do?
- What 'rules of engagement' will you wish to agree?

09
Building capabilities for change

KEY POINTS

- Learning is the process of acquiring knowledge through experience, which leads to an enduring change. To learn from experience it is necessary to make the time to reflect on that experience.
- Learning to reflect on learning is a fundamental part of any change process. Reflecting on learning helps to identify what went wrong, how to fix it and what to do differently.
- Organizations that engage in learning enable staff at all levels to learn collaboratively and continuously and to put this learning to use in sustaining change in their organization.
- Capabilities are competencies that comprise individual and collective knowledge, skills and attitudes as well as structural, cultural and contextual factors.
- Change capabilities are the ability to plan, design and implement all types of change and transformations effectively and efficiently, causing minimal negative impacts on people and operations, so that business benefits are achieved and embedded into operations.
- Building capability is about maximizing the contribution of people for the benefit of the organization and the individuals within the organization in a planned and managed way.
- Resilience is a critical capability for coping with change. Resilience helps people to make sense of change more quickly, so that they understand the impact of it. It also helps individuals to maintain higher performance levels and improves their sense of well-being.
- To meet the challenges of change, transition and transformation, leaders require multiple intelligences including: contextual, cognitive, emotional, social, cultural, moral, spiritual, behavioural and political intelligences.

Introduction

Rarely is there just one change happening in any organization; often there are multiple changes happening simultaneously across an organization. In order to cope with this, organizations need to learn from previous changes and build the capability to lead and manage people through change effectively.

This chapter will enable managers and leaders to appreciate what is meant by learning, in the context of sustainable change, and to identify the necessary capabilities that are needed to manage different change initiatives. The chapter is split into two parts. The first part focuses on organizational learning – what it is and why it is important. In particular, the concept of learning from change is examined, including how it can be developed. In the second part of the chapter specific capabilities are identified not just for managers and leaders but also for other people affected by change. One key capability required by everyone involved in change is resilience, and the importance of this is discussed. Attention is also given to the multiple intelligences required to effectively lead people through change. The chapter concludes by considering how to build capabilities for change. Some key questions are addressed such as: how can organizations learn from the failure as well as the success of change and transformation? How can organizations harness and apply the knowledge and lessons learnt from change interventions? What are the key capabilities for change? How can an organization build capabilities? What capabilities should leaders and manager develop to effectively lead and manage people through change?

LEARNING OUTCOMES

By the end of this chapter you will be able to:

- reflect on the learning from change initiatives and share learning across teams and the organization;
- identify the capabilities required to lead and manage people through change effectively;
- appreciate the multiple intelligences required to lead people through change and how to develop such intelligences;
- build capabilities for change among individuals, within a team and across the organization.

Learning and reflection

Learning from the success and failure of change

Learning is described as 'the process of acquiring knowledge through experience which leads to an enduring change in behaviour' (Huczynski and

Buchanan, 2010: 732). A learning organization is concerned with continuous improvement. It is also involved in an ongoing process of organizational development. Consequently, a learning organization is an organization that has the capability to change and adapt. Learning in organizations can be enhanced by the implementation of a process for reflecting and reviewing learning and lessons learnt. This will enable learning from success as well as failure to be shared throughout the organization, and increase the chances of creating sustainable change through people.

As change is about doing something new or in a new way, it is less predictable and more risky than merely maintaining the status quo. Therefore errors, mistakes and failure are more likely. The interesting thing about errors, mistakes and failure is that they are potentially a great source of learning – although this will only work in a culture that responds positively and constructively to mistakes and failures, and considers them opportunities to learn and improve.

Leadership plays an important role in the development of learning in an organization. Peter Senge (1990) says that the role of a leader in a learning organization is that of an architect – a teacher and a steward for the express purpose of clarifying the mission, vision and values; specifying strategies, structures and politics; and creating efficient learning processes. Similarly, William Hitt (1995) says that leaders are needed to empower all members of an organization to learn by developing a shared vision, providing resources, delegating authority, celebrating successes and, most importantly, by being a learning architect.

Leaders have an influential role to play in creating a culture favourable to continuous learning. Leaders (and managers) need to enable and engage people to enhance their commitment to learning and encourage them to learn from their experience of change and share it with others. So, it is important that leaders and managers recognize the value of learning as a continuous individual and collective process and that time is given for people to reflect on their learning from change.

Reflection

To learn from experience it is necessary to make the time to review that experience, as we tend to get more learning from an experience when we reflect on it. Reflection is a fundamental part of any change process, both during and after transition.

There is much that can be learnt about change if time is taken to reflect on what went well and what could be done differently in the future. James Evans (2012) describes how reflective learning formed part of an organization-wide change programme to improve communication and collaboration in a US art college. A learning and development (L&D) advisory board was set up in the college to provide support and direction to the change programme. Evans highlights the key lessons that were learnt by the L&D advisory board as:

- Maintaining a high level of engagement with the change process can be difficult for executives as they balance their primary job responsibilities with the demands of a change.

- Regular meetings are required in order to stay connected, and a flexible approach from all involved is needed to maintain momentum.

- Documenting activities and sharing progress towards the change initiative's goals motivates members and builds grass-roots support.

- Maintaining patience is paramount. Organizational change is difficult and it takes time, and this needs to be kept in mind in order to help people to stay focused and positive when things get tough.

The lessons from Evans's study provide some useful points to consider. They also show that it is important to recognize the value of learning as a continuous collective process.

So organizations that engage in learning and reflection enable staff at all levels to learn collaboratively and continuously and to build on their capabilities for change.

Capabilities for change

Capabilities for change are competencies that comprise individual and collective knowledge, skills, attitudes and experience as well as structural, cultural and contextual factors. For leaders, change capability includes the potential to develop competencies, beyond what is immediately required for satisfactory performance, to enable effective and sustainable change. It is the ability of an organization to plan, design and implement all types of change efficiently with key stakeholders, causing minimal negative impacts on people and operations, so that benefits can be achieved and embedded into daily operations. Capabilities for change are therefore the mix of resources, competence, information and experience needed to achieve change.

Leading and managing people through change is not simply a matter of having the right knowledge. The best tennis players do not win Wimbledon or a medal in the Olympics by simply reading books or watching tennis matches: they practise. That is how they get better at their game. The same is true for great artists, musicians and writers. Malcolm Gladwell's (2008) book *Outliers* discusses the work of Anders Ericsson, who found that most people who gain mastery in any field have practised it 'for at least 10,000 hours'. For example, the pop group The Beatles played 1,200 live shows in Hamburg before breaking into the Hit Parade, and Bill Gates of Microsoft was already writing software when he was 13 years old. Managers need to differentiate between knowledge and skill. This means that not only do people need to be taught about change concepts, but they also need time to practise their skills.

In a survey of over 50 organizations, the Changefirst consultancy company asked more than 2,000 managers what they believed was the most effective way to help their organization implement change. The vast majority of participants (86 per cent) said that internal capability was the best way to implement change. This supports the findings of numerous surveys and reports, including a study carried out by McKinsey consultants Jennifer LaClair and Ravi Rao (2002). The study demonstrates a direct linear relationship between an organization's change management capabilities and the value it captures from projects. LaClair and Rao found cases where organizations with high change management capabilities had collected, on average, 143 per cent of the value they originally expected from their projects. Such findings are relevant to companies such as AstraZeneca, which has transformed from a pharmaceutical company by adding biotechnology to its portfolio in order to become a biopharmaceutical business. The company website (**http://www.astrazeneca.com/Research/capabilities**) outlines how, by growing their R&D capabilities, the company has enhanced their ability to develop differentiated treatments drawing on cutting-edge approaches, standardized best practice and increased capacity. The company's investment in R&D includes scientific collaborations; development of existing staff; recruitment of new talent; and a new infrastructure, including an informatics platform. In this way the company are building their capability to change.

In contrast, a lack of capability can impact negatively on the success of change. This is evident in a survey conducted by the Katzenbach Centre (Aguirre and Alpern, 2014). The survey found that the biggest obstacle to change is a lack of capabilities needed to make change last. Similarly, the Barometer on Change survey carried out by Moorhouse Consultancy (2014) shows that accessing the skills, experience and capabilities needed to deliver change is a growing concern amongst business leaders. The survey found that from 2013–14 the proportion of leaders doubled who said that they needed new skills and capabilities to deliver change. Conversely, over the same period the percentage of leaders who were confident that they would be able to access these skills dropped from almost half (47 per cent) to around one-third (35 per cent). The lack of capabilities is therefore a significant threat to the success of change initiatives.

Key leadership capabilities for change

'To lead is to live dangerously', say Ronald Heifetz and Marty Linsky (2002: 2). These authors go on to say that steering an organization through change upsets the status quo and leaves some people with a sense of loss, disadvantage or dashed expectations. And it is no surprise that enemies may be made who want to see the leader of such change eliminated. Surviving in this situation, Heifetz and Linsky suggest, entails managing the hostile environment and managing one's vulnerabilities. Managing the environment means operating not just in the fray but above it too, maintaining perspective, courting the uncommitted, making other people confront issues but reducing the heat with humour, interludes and visions of a brighter future, and mobilizing others to help resolve conflicts. In other words, leading people through change requires leaders with capabilities as well as established competencies.

Competencies for leading change are those that comprise individual and collective knowledge, skills and attitudes (KSAs). There are numerous lists of desirable competencies. For example, Ann Gilley and colleagues (2009) suggest three broad leadership competencies that are associated with the successful implementation of change. In order of significance these are the ability to motivate employees, the ability to communicate effectively, and team building. Using a case study in a German tourism company undergoing a major transformation Stefan Krummaker and Bernd Vogel (2013) investigated the change-related competencies of leaders and produced a model reflecting the following findings:

- Distinct characteristics of leaders' change competency along the two dimensions of readiness for change and ability to change. The former comprises: a desire to challenge the status quo; disengagement from routines; change-goal orientation; intention to act in change; purposefulness; and willingness to change. The latter comprises: transformational leadership skills; assertiveness; political skill; and timing and shaping of change tasks.

- Antecedents to change competency comprising contextual factors (such as appropriateness of change, and support for the change), leaders' competency potential (proactivity, hardiness, empathy and knowledge), and attitudes towards change (empowerment for change and change-related emotions).

- Beneficial effects of leaders' change competency (efficiency of change leader, employees' extra effort and satisfaction).

In a study of the public sector Susan Richards (2002) identifies the competencies, or what she prefers to term the 'habits', of successful change leaders, emphasizing the role of external relationships as well as internal management:

- Focusing on strategic purpose so that people know why they are asked to work in new ways.

- Listening carefully to staff so that the real issues inhibiting change are addressed.

- Listening to community stakeholders, working across organizational boundaries and engaging people in working together for change.

- Giving the highest priority to professional development – because leadership in bringing about change in professional settings must have legitimacy in the professional culture if it is to be effective.

- Working well with leaders of local services – because forward-looking organizations are building partnerships with others to establish seamless services across their boundaries.

- Giving priority to achieving results by sticking to their purpose rather than capitalizing on achievement in order to further their own careers.

- Telling the story of change creatively and frequently to help staff make sense of the complex and multiple reality of what is happening.

In comparison, managers must develop solid competence in planning, designing and implementing change. They must also learn how to facilitate change in their operational areas, including how to engage employees to build commitment and ownership of the changes.

The competencies required by leaders and managers are a mix of people-orientated and task-orientated behaviour. Julie Battilana and colleagues (2010) found significant but different relationships between effectiveness in task-orientated and people-orientated leadership behaviours and three activities inherent in the implementation of change – communicating, mobilizing and evaluating. In particular, they found that leaders who have better task-orientated competencies are more likely to focus on mobilizing and evaluating activities, and those who have better people-orientated competencies are more likely to focus on communication activities. The main practical implication of this study is that change implementation teams should comprise individuals who have complementary leadership competencies associated with task and people orientations.

Other studies look specifically at capabilities. For example, Paul Aitken and Malcolm Higgs (2010: 131–55) identify several specific capabilities that leaders need:

- being mindful and open to question and challenge;
- accessing the 'broadband' capability of organizational leadership – the diversity of individual differences in views of the world;
- creating a learning environment;
- sense-making about the future and strategic thinking;
- developing 'total' leadership – 'walking the talk' to model the desirable behaviour;
- transcultural competence;
- one-to-one relational skills, such as coaching;
- one-to-many dialogue skills;
- action learning;
- facilitation and process-consulting skills;
- emotional intelligence;
- ability to develop a dialogue and culture of challenge to performance throughout the organization.

In a McKinsey paper entitled 'How do I build leadership capabilities to drive business performance', Boris Ewenstein and colleagues (2010) identify a set of capabilities that they refer to as centred leadership. These capabilities comprise:

- *Meaning*: finding and communicating personal meaning in work, and in turn enabling others to tap into their own sources of motivation and purpose.

- *Framing*: seeing opportunity in adversity, framing even the most difficult issues in a way that leads to constructive, creative solutions.
- *Connecting*: proactively building a web of internal and external relationships.
- *Engaging*: generating the confidence to step up and act, engaging themselves and others in the face of risk and uncertainty.
- *Energizing*: investing systematically in their energy levels – physically, mentally and emotionally – and creating the institutional norms and practices needed to energize others.

Raymond Caldwell (2003) identified 67 potentially relevant capabilities from the extant literature on change and leadership, and recruitment advertisements relating to change, with the help of an expert panel who then took part in a Delphi-style decision-making process assessing the relevance and the degree of importance of the attributes to leading and managing change, on a scale of 1 (low) to 10 (high). This process produced two lists, showing both differences and commonality of key capabilities for leaders and managers, as shown in Table 9.1.

In my book *Sustaining Change in Organizations* (Hodges and Gill, 2015) I provide data from a group of executive MBA students who were asked what they thought were, from their experience, the key capabilities for change. The results are shown in Table 9.2.

Such lists as those shown in Tables 9.1 and 9.2 are useful and cover similar capabilities. To provide organization-specific capabilities for change HR needs to be engaged to work with managers to identify the most appropriate capabilities (see Chapter 8 for a discussion of the role of HR).

A helpful approach for doing this is to group them under the four headings suggested by Mark Wilcox and Mark Jenkins (2015) of exploration, envisioning, engagement, and execution:

- *Exploration*: this involves carrying out a diagnosis of the internal and external environment. Wilcox and Jenkins call it 'deep environmental scanning'.
- *Envisioning*: this is about creating a new, or modifying an existing, strategy in response to the opportunities and threats identified during the exploration phase.
- *Engagement*: this is how people are engaged and their commitment gained to the change.
- *Execution*: this is the actual delivery of the change.

Capabilities for change can be acquired, developed and embedded in an organization through the integration and socialization of individual capabilities – that is, the knowledge, skills, attitudes and experience of each individual.

TABLE 9.1 Key capabilities of leaders and managers for change*

Attribute	Leaders	Managers
Inspiring vision	92	–
Empowering others	88	88
Entrepreneurship	87	–
Integrity and honesty	76	–
Learning from others	72	79
Openness to new ideas	66	64
Risk taking	56	–
Adaptability and flexibility	49	69
Creativity	42	–
Experimentation	38	–
Using power	29	–
Team building		82
Managing resistance		58
Conflict resolution		53
Networking		52
Knowledge of the business		37
Problem solving		29

* Based on Delphi-style panel members' ratings of importance from 1 to 10, resulting in a maximum potential score of 100.

TABLE 9.2   Capabilities required for leading and managing change

Capabilities Required to Lead Change	Capabilities Required to Manage Change	Capabilities Required to Lead and Manage
Strategic management and vision • Creation and articulation of a vision • Setting of objectives • Choice of measurement tools	Coaching of others through change	Communication to different audiences using different media
Business knowledge • Knowing the competitive landscape • Delegation to the right people • Alignment of politics and competing interests	Project management	Emotional intelligence
Ability to influence and persuade	Listening	Flexibility and adaptability
Translation of the change vision into clear performance expectations	Empathy	Credibility
Behaving in a way that causes others to trust you	Providing feedback	Reflection and learning
	Focusing on outcomes with a 'big-picture' view	Celebration of success
	Anticipation and surfacing of conflicts	

SOURCE: Adapted from Hodges and Gill (2015)

Discussion questions

What capabilities do you think are important for leading and managing
people through change?

What are they, and why are they important?

Resilience

Resilience is a critical capability for coping with change and is required by
all people in all organizations. Consider, for example, the global financial
crisis that began in 2008–09 and created an environment of uncertainty and
anxiety. It put the future of companies and whole industries under question,
with only the most financially resilient surviving. Consider also the events of
9/11 in New York and the financial crisis in Greece in 2015, which can be
used to illustrate the need for resilience in corporate infrastructures. In a
Harvard Business Review article entitled 'How resilience works' Diane
Coutu (2002) points to examples such as Morgan Stanley's rapid response
to the 2008–09 financial crisis; and the actions of UPS to deliver parcels
successfully just one day after the devastating hurricane in Florida in 1992.
For many organizations resilience has a natural association with these kinds
of scenarios – how to keep processes, systems, networks and infrastructure
going when things go wrong. Resilience is, however, about much more than
just business continuity and disaster recovery. According to Ray Wicks
(2015) resilience requires: practising an ability to think positively; maintaining
perspective; developing a strong network of supportive relationships; and
an ability to cope by taking care of one's mind and body. Wicks says that:

> Managers with resilience have the ability to adapt and bounce back when
> change does not go as planned. Resilient managers do not dwell on failures;
> they acknowledge the problem and focus on what is needed to get change back
> on track, while learning from the experience. (2015: 511)

Resilience helps people to gain control much more quickly during times of
change. It can help them to maintain higher performance levels, improve
their sense of well-being and cope with fluctuating emotions. Resilience also
helps people to make sense of change more quickly, so that they understand
the impact on themselves and others. At the same time, resilience can help
people to deal with multiple changes without being overwhelmed.

Resilient people are not, however, immune to change; they experience the
effects just as anyone would, but they will move through the transition
faster and respond more positively. They may come to terms with the change
quickly, and experience much less turbulence throughout the transformation.
In an article entitled 'Increase your resilience to change' Audra Proctor (2014),

director and head of learning at Changefirst Limited, identifies the characteristics of resilient people as: optimism, self-assuredness, focus, open to ideas, willing to ask for support, structured and proactive. Each of these characteristics can be defined as follows:

- Optimism: resilient people believe that change will have a positive outcome. They are able to analyse change in a positive way that gives them hope for the future.

- Self-assuredness: resilient people have a strong but realistic belief in their own capabilities. As a result they tend to control change, rather than the change controlling them.

- Focus: resilient people have the focus needed to be able to prioritize activities effectively. They can pursue goals successfully, even in the face of adversity.

- Open to ideas: resilient people are open to new ideas. They look for opportunities to be innovative and to take risks.

- Ask for support: resilient people actively ask for support from others during times of change. They look for opportunities to learn from the experience of others as well as their own.

- Structured: resilient people are able to analyse the situation and create an effective plan to implement and sustain change, with enough flexibility built in to cope with any internal or external environmental changes.

- Proactive: resilient people are prepared to step out into the unknown and take the action necessary to make change happen.

These components of resilience all play a vital role in enabling people to cope with change. They can help people to manage the stressors of change in a more proactive, adaptive and positive way. Resilient people are able to draw on these qualities at the right time and understand when, for example, being proactive is more important than seeking support. Leaders can become more resilient by building the organizational capability to anticipate, prepare for, cope with and survive the effects of transformations. Developing resilience takes work and time, but there is clear evidence, according to Judith Proudfoot and colleagues (2009), that resilience training can boost individual and organizational confidence.

Discussion question

What are the key capabilities that employees need to possess to effectively manage change in your organization, or an organization that you are familiar with?

Intelligences for leading people through change

To meet the challenges of leading people through change, leaders require multiple intelligences. The qualities of serenity, courage and wisdom have long been suggested as desirable in leaders contemplating change:

God grant me the serenity to accept the things I cannot change;

Courage to change the things I can;

And the wisdom to know the difference.[1]

Leadership research has pointed towards exploring the multidimensional facets of intelligence (Hoffman and Frost, 2006). Stephen Zaccaro (2002), for instance, suggests that those who establish themselves as successful leaders consistently across different situations possess key social, emotional, behavioural and cognitive intelligences. Individuals with these capabilities are successful at interpreting diverse situational cues, dealing emotionally with the diversity of cues, calling upon an extensive behavioural repertoire, and selecting and enacting the appropriate behavioural responses.

It should be noted that a multidimensional approach to intelligence is somewhat controversial. Some psychologists argue that there is only one form of intelligence, which is cognitive, and that the emotional, social, cultural, moral, spiritual and behavioural or practical domains – and indeed any others – are subordinate to cognitive intelligence. The concept of multiple intelligences is, however, useful in understanding the human aspects of organizational change, particularly in relation to what leaders require in order to lead people through change effectively. To do this leaders require the following intelligences: cognitive, contextual, emotional, social, cultural, moral, spiritual, behavioural, relational and political.

Cognitive intelligence

Cognitive intelligence – thinking – includes aptitudes such as dealing with abstract concepts and complex problem solving, visionary capacity, mental ability and the ability to cope with complexity, and to express ideas clearly. Effective leadership during change requires the cognitive abilities to scan, diagnose, understand and recognize relevant information, reason with it, imagine possibilities, use intuition, learn, solve problems and make correct and effective judgements and decisions. Cognitive intelligence underlies the formulation of the vision and purpose of the change, as well as strategies for achieving the vision and purpose that will gain commitment from people.

For a leader to encourage problem solving, creativity and innovation in their staff, they need to possess cognitive intelligence. Without strong cognitive skills, it would be difficult for them to challenge and stimulate the cognitive capabilities of others. Cognitive intelligence can be assessed through both traditional IQ tests and problem-solving tasks.

Contextual intelligence

Effective leadership during change requires the skill of contextual intelligence, that is, interpretation that is an intuitive diagnostic skill that helps a leader to understand change, interpret the outside world, set objectives, and align strategies and tactics with objectives. Contextual intelligence implies an ability to discern trends in the face of complexity, as well as adaptability while trying to shape events. In particular, contextual intelligence requires an understanding of team and organizational cultures, individuals' needs and demands, and information flows and timing. Contextual intelligence allows leaders to adjust to internal and external situations. An example of this is the ability to identify emerging threats and opportunities in the external environment and respond to them quickly and appropriately through innovation and improvisation, and also being able to handle uncertainty during change. As Joseph Nye says, 'like surfers, leaders with contextual intelligence have the ability to judge and adjust to new waves and then ride them to success' (2014: 121).

Emotional intelligence

There are a number of definitions for emotional intelligence, such as that of Daniel Goleman (1998), but the most widely accepted definition is the one proposed by Mayer and Salovey (1997), who first coined the term. They define emotional intelligence as:

> The ability to perceive accurately, appraise and express emotions; the ability to access and/or generate feelings when they facilitate thought; the ability to understand emotions and emotional knowledge; and the ability to regulate emotions to promote emotional and intellectual growth. (1997: 10)

Emotional intelligence is about feelings and includes the abilities to perceive emotions in oneself and in others, to use emotions to facilitate actions, to understand the meaning of emotional cues, and to manage the emotions of others. Besides the ability-based competencies, it also includes traits such as empathy, conscientiousness, sensitivity and awareness of others' needs. Self-awareness is a crucial feature of emotional intelligence. It comprises awareness of one's own strengths, limitations, interests, likes, dislikes, motivational drivers, values, beliefs and attitudes. It also includes an awareness of how these characteristics affect how an individual perceives and responds to other people.

Emotional intelligence, in addition to cognitive intelligence, is central to identifying and promoting the shared values that support the vision, purpose and goals for change and to engaging and motivating people to support them. Emotionally intelligent leaders 'win people's hearts'.

The practical implication of this is that the better leaders understand themselves and the feelings of the people they work with, the more effective they will be in appreciating the impact of change on others and how they will react to it. Leaders need to use emotional intelligence to foster a positive climate as much as possible during organizational change. Ways of doing this, which are suggested by Myeong-Gu Seo and colleagues (2012), are:

- providing a compelling vision [and purpose] for change;
- reminding employees of favourable outcomes of any previous change initiatives;
- reducing uncertainty, fear and anxiety through timely, frequent and accurate communication;
- providing education and training to ensure employees' ability and confidence to do what needs to be done differently as a result of change;
- including employees in decisions about change in order to increase their sense of control and fairness during the change process;
- showing support and appreciation for employees;
- providing the opportunity for people to air their grievances or negative feelings.

The emotional intelligence of leaders can have an impact on how individuals respond to change. Roy Smollan and Ken Parry (2011) found that individuals reacted better to change when they perceived that their leaders understood people's emotional responses and were able to express and regulate their own emotions appropriately. This is important, as during change a leader is the person that people will look to for clues as to how to respond when they are uncertain. The leader is a key influence and sets the tone and climate of a team, or sometimes the whole organization. In practical terms, this means that the way individuals feel is influenced by the emotions of other people around them, including that of the leader. When someone smiles at us, for example, the part of our brain associated with smiling 'lights up' and we tend to smile in return. One of the great leadership skills, therefore, is the ability to accurately 'read', 'see', 'feel' and understand the emotional climate of the organization and to communicate and act in ways that are appropriate or consistent with and within that context.

So leaders need to be sufficiently high in emotional intelligence to be able to engage people in the change process and to motivate them to meet its challenges. For those who do not have a natural ability to demonstrate emotional intelligence, training is a potentially useful intervention – although any training in emotional intelligence must be rigorously designed, implemented and tracked to ensure that it is achieving its learning outcomes and that participants are comfortable in demonstrating emotional intelligence. Coaching can also be used to enhance an individual's emotional intelligence.

Social intelligence

Social intelligence, according to Stephen Zaccaro (2002), is the ability to read and adapt to diverse social situations. As Daniel Goleman (2006) says, social intelligence extends the notion of emotional intelligence to social situations, encompassing social awareness and social competency. Social awareness is the ability to instantaneously sense and understand others' feelings and thoughts as well as the states of social situations. Social competency is made up of social awareness and relationship management skills, and the ability to understand other people's moods, behaviour and motives in order to improve the quality of relationships.

Socially intelligent leaders possess the characteristics to detect the necessary skills for the task, attune themselves to intricate social cues, and manage their behaviours appropriately to influence the pertinent perceptions of other organizational members. Bernard Bass (2001) says that the characteristics of individuals with strong social intelligence include good oral communication skills, self-confidence, sociability, tolerance for stress and an understanding of the social dynamics of organizational problem solving.

Social intelligence is an important characteristic for leading change. It tends to be developed from experience and interactions with people, and learnt from successes and failures in social settings.

Cultural intelligence

Cultural intelligence is the capability to connect and interact with people in different cultures and to cope effectively with cultural diversity. This is important for leading people through change in cross-cultural and multicultural settings. Contextual intelligence, discussed earlier in this section, is associated with cultural intelligence.

According to David Livermore (2009) cultural intelligence consists of four components – drive, knowledge, action and strategy:

- *Drive* is an individual's interest and confidence to adapt to multicultural situations.
- *Knowledge* is an understanding about how cultures are similar and different.
- *Action* is the ability to adapt when relating and working interculturally.
- *Strategy* is the ability to plan for multicultural interactions.

Cultural intelligence concerns not only national, regional and ethnic cultures but also the subcultures within all of these groups. Soon Ang and colleagues (2007) found that high levels of cultural intelligence are associated with: flexibility and appropriate behaviour and actions when interacting with people from different cultures; a desire to learn how to behave in different cultural situations; an awareness of cultural norms; and an ability to adjust mental models accordingly. Low levels of cultural intelligence, according to Ang and colleagues (2007) are associated with: difficulty in interacting with people from different cultural backgrounds; a low tolerance for the cultural norms of others; and a lack of desire to learn about different cultures and behave accordingly.

Cultural intelligence is a malleable capability that can be enhanced by multicultural experiences, training and self-awareness programmes, as well as travel abroad. It focuses specifically on capabilities in multicultural contexts. As organizations are increasingly operating in countries across the globe, cultural intelligence is therefore an asset for leading people through change effectively.

Moral/ethical intelligence

Moral intelligence, described by Doug Lennick and Fred Kiel (2011) in their book of the same name, has more to do with values and behaviours than what we would think of as intelligence. Moral or ethical intelligence is newer and less studied than the more established cognitive, emotional and social intelligences, but has great potential to improve our understanding of learning and behaviour. Michele Borba (2001) defines moral intelligence as the capacity to understand right from wrong, to have strong ethical convictions and to act on them to behave in the right and honourable way. In the simplest terms, moral intelligence is the ability to differentiate right from wrong as defined by universal principles, which include empathy, responsibility, reciprocity, respect for others and caring for others. Moral intelligence, according to Lennick and Kiel, is 'the mental capacity to determine how universal human principles should be applied to our values, goals, and actions' (2011: 21). Lennick and Kiel (2011) consider moral intelligence to have four constituents:

- *Integrity*: acting consistently with principles, values and beliefs.
- *Responsibility*: a willingness to accept accountability for the consequences of actions and choices, and admit mistakes and failures.
- *Compassion*: actively caring about others.
- *Forgiveness*: forgiving mistakes.

Moral intelligence has taken on greater importance as a result of the increased focus on business ethics and of the moral questioning of the way in which business is done and how changes are initiated, led and managed. Lennick and Kiel (2011) say that truly great business leaders never sacrifice moral integrity for financial goals, and that doing the right thing produces the best companies, the best results and helps to lead people through change.

Spiritual intelligence

The spiritual dimension of leadership concerns the quest for meaning and a sense of worth or value in what leaders seek and do. Spiritual intelligence can be linked to other intelligences, such as contextual intelligence. As Joseph Nye (2014) points out, leaders with contextual intelligence are skilled at providing meaning or a road map by defining the problem that a team or group confronts. Spiritual intelligence is also linked to emotional intelligence. Danah Zohar and Ian Marshall contrast both intelligences, with reference to change:

> My emotional intelligence allows me to judge what situation I am in and then to behave appropriately within it... But my spiritual intelligence allows me to ask if I want to be in this particular situation in the first place. Would I rather change the situation, creating a better one? (2012: 5)

According to Zohar and Marshal (2012) spiritually intelligent leadership can be fostered by applying 12 principles:

1 Self-awareness: knowing what you believe in and value, and what deeply motivates you.

2 Spontaneity: living in and being responsive to the moment.

3 Being vision and value led: acting from principles and deep beliefs, and living accordingly.

4 Holism: seeing larger patterns, relationships and connections; having a sense of belonging.

5 Compassion: having the quality of feeling and empathy.

6 Celebration of diversity: valuing other people for their differences, not despite them.

7 Field independence: standing against the crowd and having one's own convictions.

8 Humility: having the sense of being a player in a larger drama, a sense of one's true place in the world.

9 Tendency to ask fundamental 'Why?' questions: needing to understand things and get to the bottom of them.

10 Ability to reframe: standing back from a situation or problem and seeing the bigger picture; seeing problems in a wider context.

11 Positive use of adversity: learning and growing from mistakes, setbacks and suffering.

12 Sense of vocation: feeling called upon to serve, to give something back.

Spiritual intelligence is therefore critical for personal growth and authentic leadership. Leaders need to recognize this and cultivate the skills of spiritual intelligence in themselves and their organizations.

Behavioural intelligence

Behavioural intelligence, which is how an individual physically behaves, consists of the skills of both using and responding to emotion. This is shown, for example, through non-verbal communication such as body language, and communicating in other ways through writing, reading, speaking and listening, using personal power, and physical actions. Behavioural intelligence is also evident in the skilful and flexible use of different leadership philosophies (see Chapter 4 for a discussion on leadership philosophies). Behavioural intelligence also underlies what Gerry Randell and John Tolpis (2014) call the 'micro-skills' of leadership, that is, the ways that leaders structure their interactions with followers and others, such as the physical acts of questioning, active listening, paraphrasing meaning and reflecting feelings, as well as the use of body language. Being able physically to act or behave in appropriate ways is essential to leading change. Behavioural intelligence can be developed through training and development initiatives such as coaching, or skills-based workshops.

Relational intelligence

Relational intelligence, or *savoir-relier*, as Valerie Gauthier (2014) calls it, is the ability to understand and collaborate with others and facilitate the development of relationships between individuals, cultures and ideas. It is an act, a capacity, a mindset and a process that enables leaders to build strong relationships. Gauthier describes the attributes of savoir-relier as being genuine, generous and generative. She profiles three Europe-based leaders who each demonstrate one of these attributes. The first is Clara Gaymard, the CEO of General Electric in France, who demonstrates the importance of being genuine, that is, growing your own self-confidence first and then helping others to grow. The second is the CEO of Apple's Europe, Middle East, India and Asia operations, Pascal Cagni, who demonstrates the importance of being generous. This means not expecting a quid pro quo. 'If you know when you are generous, then you are not really generous, because your generosity then has a purpose, an objective with an expected reward', writes Gauthier: 'Generosity does not expect return' (2014: 30–31). The third, Apollonia Poilâne – CEO of France's famous bakery – demonstrates the importance of being generative, which, Gauthier explains: 'means being capable of production and reproduction, able to foster innovation and influence... The generative leader must do more than simply act; he or she must act with sense and passion, to drive progress, to innovate' (2014: 40). Such attributes of relational intelligence can be developed and grown with practice and determination.

Political intelligence

Political intelligence, according to Joyce Hogan and colleagues (2010), is the ability to effectively understand others at work and to use such knowledge to influence others to act in ways that enhance one's personal and/or organizational objectives. It is having an understanding of the positions and strengths of various stakeholders, particularly the distribution of power sources. Gerry Reffo and Valerie Wark (2014) highlight that political intelligence has five facets: futurity, power, empathy with purpose, trust and versatility:

- Futurity: this means shaping the vision for change; setting the strategic direction; registering changing opportunities and risks; balancing different ways of thinking; and bringing focus and clarity to complex decision making.

- Power: this involves understanding where the power and influence reside in the organization; taking opportunities to influence and advance the vision for change; acting courageously; influencing stakeholders; and understanding complexity and explaining it simply and memorably.

- Empathy with purpose: this is seeing and feeling the perspectives of others; relating to the wider society; building shared empathy; inspiring passion and commitment; being empathetic towards humanity and acting to make the world a better place.

- Trust: this means behaving with integrity and honesty; acting ethically, transparently and inclusively; valuing projects and relationships that deliver long-term societal benefits; managing competing interests; and establishing a track record for delivering results.

- Versatility: this comprises of changing tack to fit the new demands, ranging from crisis to evolution; exercising self-command to calibrate responses and pace change to fit circumstances; maintaining focus and strength of purpose; exuding confidence; and recognizing political reality and working with the politics to achieve reality.

Political intelligence comes from the ability to use all of these five facets in harmony to enable leaders to build networks. Watkins and Bazerman, in their advice to avoid Enron-type disasters, say that: 'executives need to build good networks – both informal advice networks and formal coalitions for influencing political decisions' (2003: 80). Political intelligence is therefore the ability to influence people and situations, in an ethical manner. It can therefore be acquired through practice and role modelling.

The interaction between multiple intelligences

The multiple intelligences set out above interplay with one another in influencing how people are led through change. For example, contextual, cognitive, social, emotional and political intelligence are suggested by Kimberley Boal and Robert Hooijberg (2001) to have a positive impact on people's willingness to change. It is a leader's responsibility to use the right intelligences at the right time in order to engage each person in change initiatives, to respect them as individuals, to place trust and confidence in their ability to work effectively, and to listen to what they have to say. The interaction of the intelligences provides a useful framework for practitioners to identify the capabilities associated with leading change.

To ensure that individuals have the appropriate intelligences it is important to identify gaps and interventions to bridge them. Assessment centres are a useful tool for identifying an individual's level of ability for each of the intelligences. A study by Brian Hoffman and Brian Frost (2006) provides evidence to support the use of such centres for assessing the multiple forms of intelligence and identifying areas for development. Development gaps should then be addressed with appropriate interventions such as coaching, mentoring, workshops and practice.

Activity

- Identify what would improve your capability in each of the intelligences outlined above.

- Identify what development activities will help you to make improvements in your capabilities in each of the intelligences.

- Draw up a development plan outlining specific actions.

Building capabilities

Building capabilities for change is important because they give people the skills and abilities to engage more confidently in change. They also help to motivate people to make the required behavioural changes that are necessary to achieve objectives and successfully implement and sustain change. In a survey conducted by Richard Benson-Armer and colleagues (2015), which investigated the attitudes and experiences of executives in all of the main regions of the world, half of the respondents say that they see organizational capability building as one of their top strategic priorities, but they also emphasize that their companies need to improve how they build capabilities. Only one-quarter of the respondents describe their organization's capability-building programmes as very effective, with slightly over half saying that they are somewhat effective. There is therefore evidently a need to focus on building capabilities.

The value of building capabilities for change can be broken down into several benefits, including:

- An increase in competitive advantage for an organization.
- An improvement in the ability of an organization to execute a greater number of changes more effectively.
- A reduction in the costs of change. Even fully loaded with training costs, employment costs and so on, an organization will still save money by having the capability to plan and implement change themselves.
- An increase in the ability and motivation of people to sustain change.

These are some of the benefits of the case for building change capabilities. Such capabilities can be used in different environments or situations, and not just on the current change initiative but also on future ones. To effectively build such capabilities involves first identifying the capability gaps.

Identifying capability gaps

Change is resisted when it makes people question if they have the right skills and capability to do it. They might, for example, express scepticism about whether the new version of software will work or whether the introduction of digital marketing is really an improvement – when what they are really worried about is whether their current skills will be obsolete or that they lack the ability to adapt to or effectively work the new systems, or understand the new process and so on. To overcome this, organizations need to identify and address capability gaps.

The gaps in the capabilities for change need to be identified not just for managers and leaders but also for staff across the organization. A capability gap is where the change requires people to work in a way that they do not currently have the ability to do. To identify and address gaps involves: diagnosing the gaps; identifying development needs; designing and delivering appropriate interventions; and sustaining and monitoring how the learning is being applied.

Diagnosing the gaps

The first step is to analyse current skills and identify gaps. A gap analysis should begin by addressing the following questions:

- What are the current capabilities?
- What capabilities are required?
- Who needs to learn?
- What will they learn?
- Where will they learn?
- When will learning occur?
- How will they apply their learning?
- How will the application of the learning be monitored and measured?

Data can be gathered in a variety of ways such as through interviews, surveys, focus groups and assessment tools. Whatever approach is used to identify the gaps, the diagnostic should also determine the strengths and the development needs of individuals and also who should participate in specific interventions. Starting with leaders is usually a good idea, as it establishes a set of role models for the change. But beyond that, the approach should be to move through the organization in a way that best supports the business needs. That might mean focusing on people in specific roles or key positions that are affected by the change.

Assessment tools

A wide range of assessment tools is available to identify individual strengths and development needs. For example, psychometric tests provide scores and classifications that identify where an individual is on a specific scale and allow comparisons to be made between individuals. In simple terms, a psychometric test is a standardized activity or questionnaire that helps individuals to understand themselves better. In a team this is a good way to identify strengths, working styles and development needs. For instance, a feedback questionnaire might identify that Jill is innovative, influential and works best in teams, while Tim is focused, logical and prefers to work on his own. Used appropriately, psychometrics tests can be beneficial in improving the knowledge about individuals including motivations, strengths, areas for development, preferred thinking and working styles, and also strengths and preferred styles for communications, learning, management, being managed, and team working. There is a multitude of psychometric tests that measure a variety of characteristics, many of which are underpinned by established theories of the characteristics they purport to measure, such as the Myers Briggs Type Indicator (MBTI), which is based on Carl Jung's personality type theory. Other instruments include TMS (Team Management System), developed by Charles Margerison and Dick McCann. TMS focuses on building balanced, high-performing teams and creating energy and resilience for success. TMS provides a starting point for consideration and discussion of how individuals approach their work and their interactions with others in teams. The TMS profile does not, however, measure skill or experience: for example, an individual may have strong abilities and expertise in areas of work where others have less experience.

Many of the assessment tools are based on wider theories that seek to explain specific attributes such as learning styles (Kolb's model), social interaction styles (Transactional Analysis) or working preferences (Insights Inventory). Such assessment tools are usually completed online, using self-administered multiple-choice questions. Once the responses are analysed, the participant is told the type or profile that they fit, which depending on the tool used may be categorized according to letters, descriptors or colours. Feedback using the results of such tools should always be provided by an accredited facilitator. If used correctly the feedback can help to identify capability gaps for individuals and teams.

It is, however, important to issue a word of caution about the usefulness of such tests and profiles, as they do have limitations. Their statistical validity is open to question, the terminology used is often vague and general so as to allow any kind of behaviour to fit any personality type, and they tend to put people into boxes. Like all similar tools, the accuracy of the results from such questionnaires depends on honest self-reporting by participants. The feedback and categorization delivered as a result of answering multiple-choice questionnaires can be dangerous when it is not followed up with thoughtful feedback. People are too complex to be measured purely by psychometric tools. Yet despite criticisms these tools continue to be a popular way to identify individuals' preferences and capabilities.

Identifying development needs

Capability matrix

Once the specific change capabilities that an organization wants to develop have been identified, a capability matrix is a useful approach to use for assessing the individuals' strengths and areas for development against each capability. The case study of Aegon Asset Management, below, describes how a colleague and I, when working for a global consultancy firm, worked with the HR director of the company to design and implement an organization-wide capability matrix.

CASE STUDY   Aegon Asset Management

This case study focuses on Aegon Asset Management, part of the Aegon Group, one of the world's largest life insurance and pensions companies. Aegon owns pensions, life insurance, asset management and adviser businesses. Aegon Asset Management had historically been successful, but compared to its competitors it was not well known in the market. It had developed good products and services and had a good reputation. However, it was not as well recognized in areas other than pensions. When the CEO retired, his successor took the decision to review the company's brand. It was an opportunity to consider what the company stood for; what they wanted to be known for in the market; and what capabilities they required in order to achieve this.

The key drivers for change were to provide more customer focus, create a more distinct presence within the marketplace and to develop the relevant skills needed within the business to help it change. This involved refreshing the company brand in a way that made it more distinctive from its competitors and more attractive to customers. The HR director recognized the need to develop a capability framework to support the brand values and to influence how people at all levels within the organization should work and make decisions. My colleague and I used a critical incident technique to identify the key capabilities required by all levels of employees. The capabilities that were identified focused on a number of skills, including: customer focus; embracing change; encouraging excellence; acting with integrity; decisive action; team working; learning; and communication. To help embed the capabilities, a series of workshops were run for staff across the organization, outlining the new capabilities and enabling staff to identify for themselves how they would demonstrate them.

Activity

What capabilities are relevant for the organization in which you work, or an organization you are familiar with? What approach should be used to embed and sustain capabilities in an organization?

Designing an intervention

Once there is clarity on what capabilities need to be developed and by whom, the next step is to design the specific intervention to close the gap and that will best support the development need. This involves careful consideration of the design of the intervention, especially as people have different learning styles such as visual, auditory, reading/writing or kinaesthetic. It also means making choices about the type of intervention, especially as adults learn best when they go through alternating periods of action and reflection. This means that time is needed to apply what they learn and to be able to see the personal relevance of it. So, to create an effective learning intervention, there is a need to use a number of different development interventions.

The case study below of BankCo – a leading financial services group – outlines changes that the organization is faced with. Your task is to identify the capabilities for change required and the appropriate development interventions.

CASE STUDY BankCo

BankCo is one of Europe's leading financial services groups. In addition to providing a wide range of banking services, the BankCo Group includes other organizations that are well known in the financial and insurance services sector and that have been acquired within the last five years. BankCo is number one in

Europe for small-business customers, private banking and asset finance. In addition to Europe, the group has offices in the United States and Asia and employs nearly 100,000 staff.

BankCo invests heavily in the development of their employees. Everyone is encouraged to take responsibility for his or her own development. Personal development planning is an important element of their performance management system.

In the past few months BankCo has begun to change its hierarchical structure to one that resembles more of a networked organization held together by a number of familiar brands. Management has invested heavily in technology, including an intranet site in order to manage all parts of its network effectively and to ensure communication links across the group. A number of other changes have also recently been introduced, including a corporate mission 'to become the number one bank for customer satisfaction', along with revised strategic priorities that include:

- Delivering superior sustainable value by running the business with integrity and openness, delivering optimum financial results within clearly defined business principles.

- Financial inclusion and capability.

- Protecting customers and shareholders against crime and fraud.

- Managing our people to a global benchmark.

- Investing heavily in the communities in which we serve around the world through our charitable engagement and through supporting the causes that our staff care about.

These priorities have been well publicized throughout the organization, using a variety of methods including road shows, workshops and cascaded team briefings.

New HR policies and procedures to support the strategic priorities have been communicated in similar ways. Senior management is committed to ensuring that at every stage of every transformation there is full consultation and that appropriate relations, reward and resourcing policies are put in place, as well as development and training for staff.

The group has recently opened its own corporate university at its headquarters and is developing links to business schools to provide leadership development programmes. The group has also, in the past six months, opened a number of high-street 'Café Banks' in a joint venture with a chain of coffee shops, while the credit-card side of the operations and its customer relations are now managed in a joint venture by an international credit-card organization.

During the next three months further changes will be introduced on a pilot basis. The most important of these are: one-third of the company's branches will become pilot franchises, in which local managers can purchase a 25 per cent stake in the branch; and all operators in the customer call centres will be required to take more responsibility. Their role will change from one where they take an enquiry and pass it on to someone with the expert knowledge to reply to it, to one where they will have to answer the enquiry themselves.

To ensure that the group has the capabilities to implement and sustain the changes the group HR director has been asked to produce a development strategy. To help achieve this, consider the following questions:

1　How should BankCo facilitate learning and knowledge transfer within its organization?

2　What skills, knowledge and attitudes will the following need in order to cope with the proposed changes: a) local managers; b) call-centre operators?

3　How should BankCo ensure that local managers and contact-centre operators have the required skills and knowledge? What types of training and development interventions are required?

4　How should BankCo ensure that the changes are sustained?

Interventions for closing the capability gap

Training and development interventions are important contributors to building capabilities. Providing employees with adequate training and development can give them the knowledge, abilities and the skills necessary to adapt to new ways of working and to reinforce the required behaviour that will help them to move more confidently through transition. To identify the most relevant development intervention, you can use the template in Appendix 9.1 – High-level training and development audit: training needs analysis template. This provides a format for identifying the training and development implications of change initiatives.

The type of development intervention will depend on the individuals' development needs. Interventions can include formal training and development programmes delivered in a workshop or online. Formal training programmes are not, however, enough to generate change capability. A more practical and innovative intervention is one that Boris Ewenstein and colleagues (2010) call 'forum and field'. In the forum, participants learn new tools and techniques in group settings and work with each other to practise and prepare to apply them in their everyday work. Forums are designed carefully to ensure that participants experience the kind of 'moments of truth' that make learning really stick, such as rehearsing a challenging conversation and getting feedback from observers. This provides a safe and supportive environment for participants to enhance their capabilities. Participants need to leave the forum with a personal action plan, which they will have shared with the wider group. The action plan should identify how the individual will apply their insights in real-life situations in the workplace, which is where the bulk of the learning takes place. Action plans might include having a difficult conversation with a line manager or member of staff, or working on a challenging project in which there is an opportunity to enhance specific skills.

Interventions also need personal follow-up in order to track progress. This may include review meetings with an individual and their manager to discuss development objectives, or one-to-one coaching or mentoring. People will need time to apply their learning in practice and to receive feedback on what they are doing well and what they need to improve on.

In the following case study Russell Borland describes how a coaching programme was effectively introduced to change behaviours when he worked for the investment consulting practice Hymans Robertson LLP.

CASE STUDY   Growing a business through others

Written by Russell Borland, partner and executive coach, Leading Figures

My journey into management and leadership was not planned in advance. I graduated with a mathematics degree, a subject where most questions had an answer, with little room for ambiguity, and in the first few years of my career I applied that rigour in the field of quantitative investments. I then joined the investment consulting practice of Hymans Robertson LLP, a partnership of consulting actuaries and investment consultants. My thinking gradually changed through the discipline of providing advice to clients (principally advice to trustees on the investment arrangements of corporate pension schemes) while navigating the needs of various stakeholders. Client solutions were not driven solely by number crunching, but by commercial and emotional drivers that could not always be quantified such as: how do trustees balance the needs of the sponsoring employer with their obligations to scheme members? How confident do they feel in making important decisions that affect people's finances? How do they ensure fairness in the provision of pensions to the different generations in the workforce?

I was drawn into management partly through curiosity and partly by a desire to put some order into an expanding business. In addition, when I considered my strengths as objectively as possible, I felt I could make the biggest contribution by helping to develop the infrastructure, processes and culture of the business rather than focusing solely on winning and servicing clients, although the latter was part of my job. The management roles I held included Investment Practice Manager and firm-wide Managing Partner. In both roles my approach was to provide leadership in a competitive market by: seeking to deliver the highest level of advice and service to our clients; developing a brand and experience that clients and staff were proud of; and generating a suitable level of profit.

My fellow partners were in broad agreement with these objectives, but the challenge was deciding how we could achieve them. The solution, in my view, was relatively straightforward: invest in and develop people who could help us to achieve these objectives. It was here that we met some challenges. The first was in terms of investing in business professionals in those areas that do not generate immediate income, such as Marketing, HR and IT. The concerns about the non-profit-generating departments included: can we afford such overheads in the short term? What evidence do we have that such investment in these functions will pay off in the long term?

Some of these concerns were addressed by the recruitment of a full-time finance director who had experience in the professional services arena and who understood and mastered the art of influencing, a critical skill in a partnership environment. In other words, it was helpful to employ business professionals who had an understanding of the change process. But we also had a critical mass of partners who supported the initiative; this was key in carrying out the changes we wished to push through.

The partners in the firm were creative self-starters and valued their independence of thought and actions. Changing accepted business customs and introducing new procedures, such as those promoted by the business professionals, met with some resistance. We had a few false starts, particularly with issues relating to clients; the culture of the business was such that partners developed strong personal relationships with their clients and naturally guarded such relationships. For example, rolling out a new client contract without involving the partners in its creation, then expecting them to discuss it with their clients, was not particularly effective. So we changed course, consulted more and included partners in the rollout, collecting feedback on how clients reacted to the contract and making modifications where appropriate. Clearly there has to be balance, as being overly collaborative on all aspects of running the business would slow decision making. By reconsidering when and how we should have consultations, and with whom, this allowed progress to be made in a constructive manner. A few successes under our belt created a sense of momentum, and new procedures – provided they were well thought through and clearly explained in advance – became easier to introduce over time.

Raising the quality standards was also encouraged in the client-facing practices. Leaders were challenged to recruit client-facing consultants who could help to drive the business forward, and who had skills and attributes at least as strong as their own. This was more of a challenge in the early days when the firm's brand to prospective employees was less well developed; the temptation was to fill a vacancy with a candidate who might be 'good enough'. However, experience taught us that being patient and seeking individuals who had qualities that enriched the intellectual and leadership base of the firm was invaluable in achieving business growth.

As well as the recruitment drive we increased the investment in the development of staff. This was supported in principle by the partners of the business, although in practice there were two main challenges. The first was that most of the existing partners were self-starters, who had generally sought little support in their own careers to date, and thus were unsure as to what level of support others needed. The second challenge was the differing development priorities articulated by the various practice areas. One initiative that successfully navigated both such challenges was the introduction of a coaching culture. The business, led by the HR director, had already started reviewing existing policies – such as the reward scheme, which included the remuneration structure, pension arrangements and flexible benefits – in order to ensure that the business continued to attract strong candidates and to retain staff. We also invested in training, focusing on the commercial areas of business development and client engagement as well as on general leadership development.

Coaching is complementary to training; it is about change at a personal level – enhancing awareness of one's strengths and weaknesses and following through on actions that drive positive behavioural change. A few of the longer-serving partners had been introduced to coaching by the HR team, but otherwise it was neither widely recognized nor understood across the business. The drive to cascade coaching throughout the organization was championed by a professional learning and development (L&D) manager and was designed to encourage those more experienced partners who had worked with coaches to actively promote coaching. They talked about coaching with their staff and presented it as a 'badge of honour' for those who wished to develop their skills further, rather than something offered as a remedial intervention. In parallel, the L&D manager created a bespoke coaching framework for the organization and increased the number of internal and external coaches. Not only was this infrastructure necessary to support a coaching culture, it also clearly demonstrated to all partners and staff that coaching was an important personal development tool. Over time, coaching has become embedded in the organization and has played an important role in helping individuals to hone their leadership and commercial skills.

Leadership development

Training and development interventions need to be targeted at specific populations, such as leaders. Pernod Ricard – a French company that produces distilled beverages – have a university where leadership development programmes are held. They also have an i-Share portal that is intended to inform and grow leadership values and foster a mindset of conviviality. Apple – the technology corporation – also has a corporate university. In an interview with Rick Tetzeli and Brent Schlender (2015), the successor to Steve Jobs as CEO of Apple – Tim Cook – says that Jobs wanted to use Apple's university to grow the company's next generation of leaders and to make sure that the lessons of the past were not forgotten. Such corporate universities can provide bespoke leadership development programmes, which are popular in organizations.

Lynne Chambers and colleagues (2010) describe a leadership development intervention implemented in Sony, the electronics manufacturer. The programme was developed in response to a major downturn in sales in mature markets and a lack of expected growth due to recession and intensified price competition. This impacted on the requirements of leaders in a number of ways. More decisions had to be made on a global business basis. There was a greater need for doing things in completely different ways, such as partnering with other organizations, new ways of interacting with customers, and balancing the longer-term vision with what the company needed to do in the short term. In response, leaders had to be open to new ideas, include others in decision making, listen to individuals and show more trust in what employees suggested. To address these needs Sony launched its Senior Leadership Development Programme (SLDP). The core elements of the programme included visionary leadership, emotional intelligence and coaching for potential. The programme followed an inside/out approach by starting to look inside at individual leaders' values and purpose, then focused on the impact of their leadership style on their staff, peers and customers. The programme was visibly supported by the CEO, who attended the launch of each event, as well as events at the end of the programme. Chambers and colleagues (2010) outline the considerable impact of the programme. First, participants from the programme were promoted to senior positions. Second, they continued to identify and lead initiatives to help the company get closer to customers.

An approach to development programmes, such as Sony's, will work only if participants recognize the need for them. One way to achieve this is to involve employees in the design of an intervention rather than just imposing it on them. For instance, in an article in in the *Financial Times*, Andrew Hill (2013) writes about 'Bankers back in the classroom'. Hill describes how Antony Jenkins, the former chief executive at Barclays, set out to change the bank's culture through the 'Transform' (an acronym for Turnaround; Return acceptable numbers; Sustain For Momentum) programme, after the Libor interest rate-rigging scandal undermined his predecessor Bob Diamond's early efforts at post-crisis culture change. Workshops for senior management were led by leaders from across the bank (Jenkins was sacked from his role, however, when stakeholders criticized the progress of the change as being too slow).

Development programmes, such as Barclays's, where employees are involved in the design and delivery of them, can help to create buy-in to the intervention and its content, thus ensuring that capabilities are learnt and applied.

To be sustainable, any effort to develop leaders must be deeply entwined with the organization's talent and performance management processes, as well as with its

broader vision, norms and strategy. In this way, a leadership engine can be built into the fabric of the organization, which is much more powerful than an outsourced, detached training programme. Boris Ewenstein and colleagues (2010) provide the example of an oil and gas company that built such a leadership engine. Ewenstein and colleagues describe how the company started by collaboratively defining a four-part leadership model, which was an explicit articulation of the behaviours needed from their leaders. The four elements of the model – delivering results, driving change, developing people and demonstrating passion – were translated into observable behaviours, and then fleshed out with detailed examples of what 'poor', 'solid' and 'outstanding' practice against each would look like. This provided the basis for designing a leadership programme and coaching sessions to help leaders develop behaviours in line with the model. The company monitored the impact of the intervention by tracking both observable shifts in leadership behaviours and the business outcomes associated with better leadership.

Leadership development interventions need to bring learning into work. This means focusing on real business issues during formal learning events and bringing the conditions of the workplace environment more directly into formal learning interventions. This is especially important in a business environment that requires an improved ability to cope with the ambiguity and complexity of change. Simulating the business environment in learning interventions helps to prepare learners for the challenges they will face. This can also be done through action learning.

Action learning

The purpose of action learning, according to Mike Pedler and colleagues (2005), is that a group of peers, each seeking to bring about change, meet regularly to discuss where they are each experiencing difficulty and then test in action the ideas that arise from the discussion. In organizations, action learning is usually practised through action learning groups or sets. The groups tend to consist of a small number of people, usually four to seven, and working on separate projects, who meet regularly to discuss the problems they are each encountering, the objective being to learn with and from one another. At each meeting the time is usually split equally so that everyone can focus on the issues of each person in turn. The group meetings, however, are only one part of the process. The other part is the testing of the ideas in action, which happens during the time between the group meetings. The group helps each individual in turn to reflect on the outcomes of his or her recent actions and to develop ideas for overcoming obstacles that are getting in the way of progress. In this way, action learning is about experimenting with the application of existing and new ideas in a safe yet challenging environment. Each meeting of an action learning group is a unique experience. To help you to structure an action learning meeting you can use the framework provided in Appendix 9.2.

Sustain and monitor how the learning is being applied

The challenge with training and development for change and transformation initiatives is not whether individuals complete the training but whether they absorb enough of the lessons to avoid the pitfalls that they may have fallen into in the past, and also that they acquire the skills and knowledge that will give them confidence to adapt to the changes. It is therefore important to measure the impact and effectiveness of training and development interventions, and to identify the benefits that have been achieved, as well as to identify any further gaps that need to be addressed. The most common survey method used for training and development is Donald Kirkpatrick's four-level evaluation model, originating in 1959 and further developed since then. The four levels of evaluation are:

- *Level one – reaction*
  Evaluation at this level measures how learners feel about the training and is often measured with attitude questionnaires that are distributed at the end of events. Such questionnaires are called 'happy sheets' as they measure only how satisfied participants feel at the end of an event.

- *Level two – learning*
  This is the extent to which participants' attitudes, knowledge and skills are improved as a result of participating in the development intervention. This learning evaluation requires some type of post-event testing to ascertain what skills were learnt or improved during the event. Evaluating the learning that has taken place typically focuses on such questions as: what knowledge was acquired or increased? What skills were developed or enhanced? What attitudes were changed?

- *Level three – performance (behaviour)*
  This level involves testing the participants' abilities to apply the knowledge and skills learnt on the job rather than merely in the classroom. This is often done formally through testing, or informally through observation.

- *Level four – business results*
  This level measures the effectiveness of the programme in terms of the impact on the organization and the benefits it receives from the intervention.

The strengths of Kirkpatrick's model are that it is a simple, practical and well-established one that is popular in many organizations. It is, however, open to a number of criticisms in that it is too simple. Levels one and two are the most common methods of evaluation used but are open to personal interpretation, which may result in inaccurate conclusions. Levels three and four are not always applied, which breaks the chain-like connection of the levels. The model also fails to take into account the return on investment (ROI) for training and development activities. To address such criticisms Anthony Hamblin (1974) built on Kirkpatrick's model and extended it to comprise five levels, including Kirkpatrick's first three levels plus the following two levels:

- *Level four – functioning*
  This level determines the effect of the intervention on the organization as a whole in terms of a cost/benefit analysis.

- *Level five – return on investment*
  This level evaluates the value that the training and development contributes to the organization and to the individual.

Robert Brinkerhoff (2006) has taken Hamblin's model a step further and included a sixth level termed 'wider contribution', which involves the extent to which an individual's long-term potential has increased as a result of the intervention. According to Homayoun Hatami and colleagues (2015) the best-performing companies develop dashboards to track progress, which include basic financial-performance metrics, and indicators of changes in behaviour. Such companies, Hatami and colleagues say:

> Also actively track capability metrics, such as the training courses employees have taken, whether they passed or failed, and how that correlates with performance in the field. They then use those calculations to adjust their capability-building efforts and zero in on performers who need more or different training.

To be most effective, measurement must start before a transformation kicks in, so as to create a baseline. Then, at regular intervals, metrics can be assessed again in order to understand what progress has been made in developing capabilities at both the organizational and individual levels.

Activity

Identify with your colleagues the experiences you have had of development programmes that have focused explicitly on organizational change and discuss:

1 What did the programme aim to achieve?

2 How did it aim to do so?

3 How well did it achieve its aims?

4 What could have been done differently to improve the programme?

5 What did you learn and apply from the programme?

In the following case study Tom Ivison outlines the challenges of training and development interventions.

CASE STUDY Training for an IT configuration management system

Written by Tom Ivison, configuration manager

I was the project manager responsible for delivering a configuration management system in a program development environment. I had complete autonomy and thought that I was well acquainted with change management, having been involved in the editing of a book on the topic, one of the series in the IT infrastructure Library Service Management Series. However, whilst I was well versed in the theory and the need for simple processes that dealt with the mechanics of change management, I completely underestimated the impact of the change on the people who were being asked to change.

The overall project required a completely new design of a major financial system and the introduction of new business processes. The computer system was at the heart of the project and, in particular, the software on which it was based. A Belgian company won this part of the contract and introduced its own methods of working. However, there were problems with integrating their processes and our processes, and it was soon apparent that the newly developed software was not meeting the quality standards. In effect, software modules were being amended by more than one person. Although they passed their initial system testing they often crashed when integrated into the live suite. A method had to be found to improve the quality of the software being developed.

Everyone agreed the need for change and could see the benefits of the proposals that were being promoted. So I thought it was a simple matter of arranging training courses in four locations: Scotland, the north-east of England, the north-west of England and London. Unfortunately, very few of the key stakeholders (the programmers) who were meant to attend the courses actually did so. The programmers involved were mainly Belgian but all had the same excuse: 'We are too busy fixing problems.' This necessitated a rethink on my part. I hired a training consultant, who pointed out that together with my team I had adopted the classic attitude that we knew best and that the merits of our system (PVCS Dimensions) would carry forward the change. The training consultant had experience of similar situations and recommended a solution. This entailed undoing the damage created by our original approach, which had alienated the programmers we were trying to help. The new method aimed to engender trust by engaging with the stakeholders and leading them to identify problems that could be resolved in accordance with their requirements. In short, we delivered what they wanted, not what they perceived as our solution. Once the training consultant joined the team we began our detailed planning on how to manage both the change and the stakeholders' perceptions, in the following way:

- Stage one:
  - A list of all programmers was compiled so that none of them would miss the workshops that were being planned.
  - Workshops were arranged in each location to facilitate the identification of the issues faced by the programmers.
  - Each programmer was allocated to a workshop.

- Stage two:
  - Each workshop followed the same approach with the same content.
  - We managed perceptions by making a point of publicly valuing the programmers' expertise and appreciating their help in identifying their specific requirements.
  - A list of their requirements was compiled.
  - Their input was evaluated against what we could deliver.

- Stage three:
  - The workshops were rerun.

- We demonstrated that our solution met their requirements in a way that they understood.

- Stage four:
The workshops were rerun in such a way that the stakeholders were given what they needed to do their job better. This approach worked well: all courses were fully booked, and ultimately the project was delivered on time and under budget. However, we did face a number of challenges along the way, including:

  - Entrenched working practices: the programmers had their own way of doing things and found it difficult to conform to different working practices.

  - There was uncertainty initially about the change, due to past experiences that led to individuals clinging to what they knew.

  - A new and unfamiliar system with many interlinked modules was introduced with interfaces that were not always fully documented.

  - Multiple system crashes occurred following the integration of the developed code into the live environment as a result of multiple amendments to the same code by different members of staff who knew nothing of the earlier amendments.

  - There were teams of different nationalities, culture and practices working together without an understanding of the differences that they each brought.

  - Timescales were tight and put a lot of people, especially the programmers, under pressure.

The change was eventually sustained because all the stakeholders understood that their individual needs were being met, that they had ownership of the new procedures, and that the change was not being forced upon them. They were able to appreciate the benefits of identifying:

  - each piece of code, each of which was given a reference number and this meant that no code was overlooked;

  - who amended the code and when – programmers were aware of what had been done in earlier amendments and by whom so that they were mindful that their input did not cancel earlier amendments;

  - the other configuration items affected by the amendment – very important so that no linked item would be missed and future amendments would be cascaded as required;

  - the impact of any amendment, which enabled management to identify minor and major amendments and schedule them accordingly.

Discussion questions

How might commitment to the workshops have been achieved prior to bringing in the training consultant?

What are the lessons that can be learnt from this case?

Summary

Leaders and managers need to build the organizational capability to anticipate, prepare for, cope with and survive the effects of transformations. This means that they need to have the ability to adapt, modify and transform organizational structures, systems and processes, and engage with and gain commitment from people as they transition through change.

Training and development are important contributors to building capabilities for change for employees across the organization at all levels. This can be done through a variety of interventions, including formal development programmes, field and forum events, and action learning. Such interventions can help employees to learn new habits and unlearn old habits that are no longer required.

Leaders can play an active role as faculty in leadership programmes. In this way, development becomes an integral part of how the organization works, not a detached exercise. To be effective, training and development interventions should respond to the specific circumstances and requirements of the organization and individuals, based on the diagnosis and analysis of the capability gaps. Specifically for leaders there is a requirement for a range of multiple intelligences. These intelligences include contextual, cognitive, emotional, social, cultural, moral, spiritual, behavioural and political intelligences. Such intelligences can be developed by leaders and can be applied when appropriate to lead people effectively through change.

When individuals without the relevant training, experience or skills are given responsibility and ownership for any part of the change process, this can have a significant detrimental impact on the outcome of the change as it may result not only in benefits not being achieved, but also normal operations – business as usual – suffering. Providing employees with adequate training and development can give them both the knowledge and the skills necessary to adapt to new ways of working and to reinforce the intended behaviour and thus help to sustain the change. Building capabilities for change is therefore imperative for sustaining change through people.

Implications for leaders and managers

From this chapter there are some practical implications for managers and leaders for building capability for change:

- *Encourage learning from failure*
  Hold washup/review sessions not only at the end of a transformation programme but also at intervals during its implementation. Ask the programme team and staff affected by the changes: what is going well? What do we have to do differently?

- *Conduct a capability audit*
  Conduct a capability audit in order to find out if the organization has the ability to deliver transformation and realize benefits from it. The audit should provide a framework for critically evaluating the skills, experience and knowledge that will be needed to implement and sustain change.

- *Ensure appropriate development interventions are designed and delivered*
  Design development interventions so that people can work on real business issues. Giving people the opportunity to apply their learning to a specific issue will help them to retain their learning. Learning cannot be sustained if it happens only in the classroom – otherwise people will be learning but not *doing*.

- *Introduce a mentoring scheme*
  Consider a mentor for all senior managers, either an internal from a different department or an external with whom they can have honest conversations and maintain perspective.

- *Align development interventions with performance management objectives*
  Embedding and sustaining the learning from development programmes requires a concerted effort. One way this can be encouraged is to align development interventions with performance management objectives. Agree with direct reports, prior to them attending an intervention, what they want to learn from it and work with them to create a development plan with SMART objectives.

- *Monitor the impact of capability-building programmes*
  Monitor the impact of capability-building programmes, tracking both observable shifts in behaviours and the outcomes associated with the change.
  After an individual has attended a development event, follow up with them to their development objectives. If individuals are struggling to apply the learning, work with them to identify what will help.

Note

1 Shortened version of 'The Serenity Prayer' by Reinhold Niebuhr, the US protestant theologian (1892–1971), according to the *Oxford Dictionary of Modern Quotations* and to *Bartlett's Familiar Quotation*.

References

Aguirre, D and Alpern, M (2014) [accessed 16 October 2015] 10 Principles of Leading Change Management [Online] http://www.strategy-business.com/article/00255?gko=9d35b

Aitken, P and Higgs, M (2010) *Developing Change Leaders: The principles and practices of change leadership development*, Butterworth-Heinemann, Oxford

Ang, S, Van Dyne, L, Koh, C, Ng, K Y, Templer, K J, Tay, C and Chandrasekar, N A (2007) Cultural intelligence: its measurement and effects on cultural judgment and decision making, cultural adaptation and task performance, *Management and Organization Review*, 3 (3), pp 335–71

Bass, B (2001) Cognitive, social, and emotional intelligence of transformational leaders, in *Multiple Intelligences and Leadership*, LEA's Organization and Management series, ed R Riggio, S E Murphy and F J Pirozzolo, pp 105–17, Lawrence Erlbaum Associates Publishers, New Jersey

Battilana, J, Gilmartin, M, Sengul, M, Pache, A-M and Alexander, J A (2010) Leadership competencies for implementing planned organizational change, *The Leadership Quarterly*, 21, pp 422–38

Benson-Armer, R, Otto, S and van Dam, N (2015) [accessed 16 October 2015] Do Your Training Efforts Drive Performance, *McKinsey Quarterly*, March [Online] http://www.mckinsey.com/insights/organization/do_your_training_efforts_drive_performance

Boal, K B and Hooijberg, R (2001) Strategic leadership research: moving on, *Leadership Quarterly*, 11 (4), pp 515–49

Borba, M (2001) *Building Moral Intelligence*, Jossey-Bass, London

Brinkerhoff, R O (2006) Increasing impact of training investments: an evaluation strategy for building organizational learning capability, *Industrial and Commercial Training*, 38 (6), pp 302–07

Caldwell, R (2003), Change leaders and change managers: different or complementary? *Leadership & Organization Development Journal*, 24 (5), pp 285–93

Chambers, L, Drysdale, J and Hughes, J (2010) The future of leadership: a practitioner view, *European Management Journal*, 28 (4), pp 260–68

Coutu, D (2002) How resilience works, *Harvard Business Review*, May, pp 46–56

Evans, J (2012) Facilitating organizational change with a network of change champions, *Training & Development*, ASTD, 8 June

Ewenstein, B, Gurdjian, P, Lane, K and Webb, C (2010) [accessed 16 October 2015] How Do I Build Leadership Capabilities to Drive Business Performance, *McKinsey* [Online] https://hcexchange.conference-board.org/attachment/How-do-I-build-leaders-mo6.pdf

Gauthier, V (2014) *Leading with Sense: The intuitive power of savoir-relier*, Stanford University Press, Stanford

Gilley, A, McMillan, H and Gilley, J W (2009) Organizational change and characteristics of leadership effectiveness, *Journal of Leadership & Organizational Studies*, **16** (1), pp 38–47

Gladwell, M (2008) *Outliers*, Allen Lane, London

Goleman, D (1998) *Working with Emotional Intelligence*, Bantam Books, New York

Goleman, D (2006) *Social Intelligence: The new science of human relationships*, Bantam Books, New York

Hamblin, A C (1974) Evaluation and control of training, *Industrial Training International*, **9** (5), pp 154–56

Hatami, H, McLellan, K, Plotkin, C L and Schulze, P (2015) [accessed 16 October 2015] Six Steps to Transform Your Marketing and Sales Capabilities, *McKinsey* [Online] http://www.mckinsey.com/insights/marketing_sales/six_steps_to_transform_your_marketing_and_sales_capabilities

Heifetz, R and Linsky, M (2002) A survival guide for leaders, *Harvard Business Review*, June

Hill, A (2013) Bankers back in the classroom, *Financial Times*, 16 October 2013

Hitt, W D (1995) The learning organization: some reflections on organizational renewal, *Leadership and Organization Development Journal*, **16** (8), pp 17–25

Hodges, J and Gill, R (2015) *Sustaining Change in Organizations*, Sage, London

Hoffman, B J and Frost, B C (2006) Multiple intelligences of transformational leaders: an empirical examination, *International Journal of Manpower*, **27** (1), pp 37–51

Hogan, J, Hogan, R and Kaiser, R B (2010) Management derailment, in *American Psychological Association Handbook of Industrial and Organizational Psychology*, vol 3, ed S Zedeck, pp 555–75, American Psychological Association, Washington DC

Huczynski, A A and Buchanan, D A (2010) *Organizational Behaviour*, 7th edn, Pearson, Essex

Krummaker, S and Vogel, B (2013) An in-depth view of the facets, antecedents, and effects of leaders change competency: lessons from a case study, *The Journal of Applied Behavioral Science*, **49** (3), pp 279–307

LaClair, J and Rao, R (2002) [accessed 16 October 2015] Helping employees embrace change, *McKinsey Quarterly* [Online] http://www.mckinsey.com/insights/organization/helping_employees_embrace_change

Lennick, D and Kiel, F (2011) *Moral Intelligence*, Pearson Education, New Jersey

Livermore, D (2009) *Leading with Cultural Intelligence: The new secret to success*, Amacom, New York

Mayer, J D and Salovey, P (1997) What is emotional intelligence?, in *Emotional Development and Emotional Intelligence: Educational implications*, ed P Salovey and D Sluyter, pp 3–31, Basic Books, New York

McGill, L and Beatty, I (2013) *Action Learning: A practitioner's guide*, 3rd edn, Routlege, London

Moorhouse Consulting (2014) [accessed 16 October 2015] Barometer on Change 2014, *Moorhouse* [Online] http://www.moorhouseconsulting.com/news-and-views/publications-and-articles/barometer-on-change

Nye Jr, J S (2014) Transformational and transactional presidents, *Leadership*, **10** (1), pp 118–24

Pedler, M, Burgoyne, J and Brook, C (2005) What has action learning learned to become? *Action Learning*, **2** (1), pp 49–68

Proctor, A (2014) [accessed 16 October 2015] Increase your Resilience to Change [Online] https://www.linkedin.com/pulse/20141209100529-8521084-increase-your-resilience-to-change

Proudfoot, J G, Corr, P J, Guest, D E and Dunn, G (2009) Cognitive-behavioural training to change attributional style improves employee well-being, job satisfaction, productivity, and turnover, *Personality and Individual Differences*, **46** (2), pp 147–53

Randell, G and Tolpis, J (2014) *Towards Organizational Fitness: A guide to diagnosis and treatment*, Gower, London

Reffo, G and Wark, V (2014) *Leadership PQ: How political intelligence sets successful leaders apart*, Kogan Page, London

Richards, S (2002) Habits of successful change leaders in the modern public sector, quoted by Ewart Wooldridge (2002) Modern times: public sector modernization, *People Management*, **8** (7), pp 28–30

Senge P M (1990) *The Fifth Discipline: The art and practice of the learning organisation*, Random House Business Books, London

Seo, M-G, Taylor, M S, Hill, N S, Zhang, X, Tesluk, P E and Lorinkova, N M (2012) The role of affect and leadership during organizational change, *Personnel Psychology*, **65**, pp 121–65

Smollan, R and Parry, K (2011) Follower perceptions of the emotional intelligence of change leaders: a qualitative study, *Leadership*, **7** (4), pp 435–62

Tetzeli, R and Schlender, B (2015) [accessed 16 October 2015] Tim Cook on Apple's Future: Everything Can Change Except Values, *Fastcompany.com* [Online] http://www.fastcompany.com/3042435/steves-legacy-tim-looks-ahead

Watkins, M D and Bazerman, M H (2003) Predictable surprises: the disasters you should have seen coming, *Harvard Business Review*, **81** (3), pp 72–85

Wicks, R (2015) Personal and professional development, in *The Effective Change Manager's Handbook*, ed R Smith, D King, R Sindhu and D Skelsey, pp 492–534, Kogan Page, London

Wilcox, M and Jenkins, M (2015) *Engaging Change: A people-centred approach to business transformation*, Kogan Page, London

Zaccaro, S J (2002) Organizational leadership and social intelligence, in *Multiple Intelligences and Leadership*, ed R Riggio, Lawrence Erlbaum Mahwah, New Jersey

Zohar, D and Marshall, I (2012) *Spiritual Intelligence: The ultimate intelligence*, Bloomsbury Publishing, London

Further reading

Helfat, C, Finkelstein, S and Mitchell, W (2007) *Dynamic Capabilities: Understanding strategic change in organizations*, Blackwell, London

Roth, G L and DiBella, J (2015) *Systemic Change Management: The five capabilities for enterprise change*, Palgrave, London

Appendix 9.1 – High-level training and development audit: training needs analysis template

This template can be used to conduct a training needs analysis.

Change initiative (brief description of the proposal)	
Timescales (summary of phases of activity)	

High-level objectives (what are the critical capabilities we need to develop?)	Target audience (who and how big is the audience?)	Proposed delivery method (most appropriate delivery approach such as workshop, on the job)	Key resource requirement (people, technology, infrastructure required for development and delivery)	Timing (when will training and development be needed to support implementation plans?)	Budget (how much will it cost to develop and deliver?)

Appendix 9.2 – Structuring action-learning group meetings

Each meeting of an action learning group is a unique experience. This framework can be used to help each member of the group to gain from the process.

Initial meeting

The first meeting of an action learning group should focus on the agreement of the ground rules and the opportunity to understand the background and experience that each member brings to the group. It is also useful at this meeting to discuss the change initiative that will be used as the key vehicle for learning.

Subsequent meetings

As the process evolves, a different format is necessary. The following is a suggested approach (adapted from McGill and Beatty, 2013) to guide the way in which each member and the group might present and reflect on progress.

Looking back:

- What actions did you take following the meeting?
  - Did you do what you planned?
  - If not, why? What might be the blockage/s?
- What are your reflections on the actions and their effectiveness?
  - If your actions were successful – why?
  - If your actions were unsuccessful – why?
  - What could you have done differently?
  - How did you feel about the outcomes?

Looking forward:

- What do you want from the group at this meeting?

Looking forward – actions:

- What actions do you plan to take before the next meeting?

Reflections on learning:

- What have you learnt about the change?
- What have you learnt about your organization?
- What have you learnt about your colleagues?

- What have you learnt about yourself?
- What have you learnt about leadership and management in your time in the action-learning group?
- What have other members of the group learnt about leadership and management from the group-meeting discussions?

Reflections on process:

- What could you do to make the operation of the group more effective?

Reflections on norms and dynamics:

- What might you find it hard to talk about in the group?
- What might we be avoiding discussing in the group? Why?

To provide a basis for the closure of an action-learning group, it is helpful to spend some time consolidating the learning that has taken place during the process. The following questions are helpful in conducting a review:

- What impact has action learning had on the project?
- What have you gained from the process?
- What do you still require?
- How have you changed during the process?
- What (if anything) has been a surprise?
- How have your personal and career aspirations changed?
- What areas of development have you identified to work on over the next year?

PART FIVE
Ethics, sustainability and change

10
Sustaining change

KEY POINTS

- Leading and managing people through change in an ethical way is a necessity in managing for sustainable change in terms of the intentions, methods, results and consequences of the change process.

- Any attempt to change an organizational culture raises ethical issues relating to attempting to change individuals' attitudes, values and beliefs.

- Change needs to be sustained in an organization in order to ensure that benefits are realized. The key influences on ensuring that change is sustained are leadership, management and individuals.

- The way that change is led and managed is changing. The process approach, which has dominated transformation efforts and traditional change management, is making way for a more people-centric approach.

Introduction

Managing and leading people ethically, responsibly and effectively through change so that it is sustainable is not an altruistic 'nice to have' but a business imperative. Leaders and managers have a responsibility to engage in behaviour that is not only efficient and effective but also ethical.

Ethics are a vital part of organizational change and, as such, leaders need to recognize and act in an ethical way. Yet set against events in recent corporate history – such as: the exposure of Bernie Madoff's fraudulent Ponzi scheme; the supermarket Tesco's false financial statements; GlaxoSmithKline's bribery in China; and the manipulation of the LIBOR rate by UK bankers – it would appear that we are still living in an era where business leaders are allowed to, and are even rewarded for, putting their own egos and self-interests ahead of the interests of others, often with disastrous results and consequences. Joseph Stiglitz (2010) observes of leaders in the banking sector prior to the 2007–08 crash that the short-term performance incentives of mortgage salespeople and those of the corporate leaders, who were supposed to supervise them, were not aligned with the long-term interests of the institutions for which they worked. Stiglitz concludes that the long-term, sustainable interests of the many are sacrificed to the short-term greed and arrogance of the few.

There may, however, be signs that this is starting to change, especially with developments such as those at Harvard Business School, where there has been a public commitment made to the MBA Oath (mbaoath.org) – a voluntary pledge for graduating MBAs to create value responsibly and ethically. Companies as diverse as Chevron and Coca-Cola have produced their own ethical code of conduct. This is a positive step forward. However, to avoid repeating the leadership errors of past decades and the considerable damage that has been done to organizations, and especially to the people within them, there is a need to focus on the ethical implications of sustaining change. It is also important to consider how change can be ethically sustained in order to realize benefits from it.

This chapter focuses on the two key factors of ethics and the sustainability of change. The first part of the chapter discusses the importance of the ethical dimension of change as a means of ensuring that managers and leaders act in the interests of the people within the organization. The key ethical issues in carrying out change, especially culture change, are explored. The implications for leaders and managers and what they need to do in order to pursue an ethical approach to change are also considered. The second part of the chapter examines how change can be sustained and the benefits realized from it. It focuses on the leadership, management and individual influences on sustaining change. The chapter concludes by reviewing the traditional process approach and the emerging people approach to change, in the context of ethics and sustainability.

Key questions are addressed such as: what do we mean by ethical and sustainable change? How can we ethically lead and manage people through transformations? How can managers implement change in a way that is both effective and ethical? What are the key influences for sustaining change?

LEARNING OUTCOMES

By the end of this chapter you will be able to:

- appreciate the importance of the ethical aspects of leading and managing change;
- evaluate the ethical and moral issues that arise in change initiatives and how they may be resolved;
- identify ways to improve the ethical dimensions of organizational change;
- implement factors that will enable change to be sustained through people.

Ethical standards of behaviour

What do we mean by ethical and unethical? Most people would agree that child labour is clearly unethical, but would they recognize which change practices are unethical? If leaders and managers are to be able to monitor the ethical dimensions of change, they must have measures for judging whether it is potentially ethical or not.

Ethics are not set in stone – there is no rulebook for them. Ethics can be defined as a code of conduct or behaviour that reflects a set of moral values or beliefs to be applied in certain circumstances. Moral values are values that reflect what is right versus what is wrong and what is good versus what is bad. Values are principles or standards of behaviour that are felt to be important or have worth or merit. Ethics are also highly individual beliefs, some of which may be perceived as being universal, and distinguishing between what is right or wrong, good or bad. These beliefs provide a basis for judging the appropriateness of motivation and the consequences of behaviour, and they guide people in their dealings with other individuals, groups and organizations. Nearly one-third of the 1,600 workers and managers in the UK questioned for the Management Agenda (2015) survey told researchers that they had felt under pressure to compromise their organization's ethical standards in order to meet business objectives. This was found to be especially true in the public sector, where it was felt by 40 per cent of respondents, against 27 per cent in the commercial world and 31 per cent in the not-for-profit sector. The need for employees to compromise their ethical standards in favour of business objectives is highlighted by Carly Chynoweth (2015) in an article in the *Times* newspaper entitled 'Ethics v profit: the fight goes on'. Chynoweth says that employees feel that they sometimes have to choose between doing the right thing and doing the right thing by their boss. It is a matter of whether an individual is willing to choose to behave in an ethical manner.

Ethical standards of behaviour in organizations, according to George Steiner (1975: 217–22), arise from several value systems:

- *Religious values* of right and wrong emphasize human dignity and worth and the need to recognize the rights and obligations of other people, such as employees, customers, shareholders and the general public.

- *Philosophical ideas*, through reasoning, produce ethical norms, such as the Aristotelian 'Golden Rule' that we should behave to others as we would wish them to behave towards us.

- *Culture* – organizational or national – is associated with values that maintain or advance people's interests and well-being.

- *The legal system* codifies customs, ideas, beliefs and behavioural standards that society wishes to preserve and enforce, such as employment protection, and health and safety at work.

- *Professional and business codes of practice* promote ethical corporate behaviour, for example in appointing people to new jobs or roles and in consultation procedures about proposed changes.

To be clear on what precisely constitutes unethical behaviours during change, organizations need to move beyond general statements of ethics, such as those found in corporate social responsibility (CSR) statements and policies. They need to evaluate the ethical values of leaders and their actions, and determine whether they are compatible with those of the organization and its stakeholders. This requires an understanding of the ethics of change in policy and practical terms, and clarity about the ethical basis of different approaches to change. A leader is acting in an unethical way if they pursue organizational change or transformation for their own self-interest; act outside of the law or their delegated authority in planning or implementing change; coerce employees into certain behaviour; or use manipulative tactics that involve deceit, threats, fear, secrecy or dishonesty to gain commitment to change. How leaders and managers behave ethically (or not) will be reflected in the culture of the organization.

An ethical culture is a culture of ethical shared values and individual responsibility to act ethically. It is characterized by people's attitudes and behaviours that display a desire to act ethically. An ethical culture is vital for achieving sustainable change in organizations. The risk of not having developed an ethical culture for organizational change is much greater than the risks of not having developed other areas of business, leadership and management. So ethics are a vital part of an organization's culture for leading and managing change.

Ethical aspects of managing change

Managing people through change in a responsible way involves ensuring that the purpose, goals, processes, actions, outcomes and consequences are ethical. Ethical transitions contribute to the well-being of all people internal and external to the organization, through both how the change is managed and the benefits realized. Key to this is how decisions are made.

Ethical decision making

Before and during a transition process employees need to assess whether or not a particular change is 'the right thing to do' and whether not changing will have serious consequences. Raytheon, a major US defence contractor and an industrial corporation with core manufacturing concentrations in weapons and in military and commercial electronics, is in an industry challenged by ethical issues and dilemmas. Raytheon's ethics process, 'Take an Ethics Check', enables employees to pause when they are confronted with a work problem and to consider it from an ethical point of view; then to contact the company's ethics helpline and speak to a manager or a subject specialist before deciding what to do next. This approach, according to Dayton Fandray (2000), offers employees an opportunity to ask questions concerning the ethics of a problem, without fear of reprisal.

Ethics is not just about policy and procedures; there also has to be a process such as the one used by Raytheon for people to use in order to ensure that decisions made are ethical. To help understand and appreciate the ethical dimensions of change, the following questions need to be considered:

- Is the change legal?
- Is it right?
- Who will be affected?
- Does it fit with the organization's values?
- How would it look in the newspaper or on social media?
- Will it reflect poorly on the company?

To help address such questions and to raise awareness among employees of the ethical dimensions of change, training and education in ethics is beneficial.

Training and education in ethics

Training and education in ethics is of value in managing and leading people through change. Patti Ellis (2013), a vice-president of Raytheon, says that an effective ethics education programme not only reinforces a company's code of conduct and corporate values but also shows how to engage ethically at multiple levels both internally and externally, which is vital for transformations. Having a current, evolving and interactive ethics education programme, Ellis says, serves to uphold a company's principles of compliance, ethics and governance. This view is supported by Carillon, a construction services company that retrained 30,000 employees in order to make sure that they understood the company's policy on ethics. Osama Al Jayousi, the compliance manager at Carillon, says:

> We needed to make sure [people] were aware of our policies, where to go if there are issues, where to go to raise concerns, and also to know they won't be victimized if they raise genuine concerns. (Cited in Chynoweth, 2015)

Education and training in ethics is therefore undoubtedly a worthwhile investment in order to help ensure an ethical approach to change.

Discussion question

Who is ethically responsible for what in leading and managing people through change?

Ethical aspects of leading change

Leadership is all about change – and no change is value free. Bernard Burnes and Phil Jackson (2011) say that all approaches to leadership and change are underpinned by a set of ethical values that influence the actions of leaders and the outcomes/consequences of change initiatives – for good or ill. These values impact not only on the economic impact and outcome of the change but also the well-being and satisfaction of people who are involved in the change and affected by it. Meeting this challenge is at the heart of an approach to leading people through change. Pushing too hard for change can alienate people, disengaging rather than engaging them. Yet how do leaders rock the boat without falling out of it? Debra Meyerson (2001) responds to this question by saying that those who quietly challenge prevailing wisdom and stimulate change are 'tempered radicals'. Meyerson says that such people exercise a form of leadership within organizations that is more localized, more diffuse, more modest and less visible than traditional forms, yet no less significant. Meyerson says that such people typically display several behaviours:

- Disruptive self-expression: demonstrating their values through their language, dress, office décor or behaviour.
- Verbal jujitsu: redirecting negative statements or actions into positive change.
- Variable-term opportunism: capitalizing on unexpected opportunities for change as well as orchestrating deliberate, longer-term change.
- Strategic alliance building: gaining influence by working with allies, thereby enhancing their legitimacy and implementing change more quickly and directly than by working alone, and treating opponents not as enemies but as a source of support and resources.

Such 'quiet' leadership creates incremental change, which Meyerson says is gentle, decentralized and, over time, produces a broad and lasting shift with less upheaval, in other words, sustainable change. There is, however, a view that 'being nice' is no way to pursue change that is a groundbreaking transformational innovation. Consultant Simon Rucker (2012), quoting Steve Jobs of Apple as a positive example, says: 'the lack of a singular, visionary – and frankly autocratic – someone in charge is one of the biggest reasons why transformational initiatives lose focus, seek the lowest common denominator, and ultimately fall short'. In contrast, Peter Stokes and Phil Harris (2012) say that consistent 'good' behaviour and 'good' character displayed by individuals in the responsible and ethical choices that they make, and the actions that they take from moment to moment, are central to ensuring sustainable change, and that 'bad' behaviour and character undermine it unless corrected. So the impact of individuals in effecting or preventing ethical sustainable change is important. This is especially relevant for leaders.

Ethical leadership

Ethical leadership is interpreted in much the same way across the public, private and non-profit/third-sector organizations, but with some differences that are cultural. Leonie Heres and Karin Lasthuizen (2012) found that leaders operating in public and non-profit/third-sector organizations in the Netherlands place more importance on being altruistic, showing concern for the common good, and being responsive, transparent and accountable to society at large than do leaders in the private sector. They also consider explicit and frequent communication about ethics to be intrinsic to leadership, while private-sector leaders tend to prefer communication strategies that embed ethics in business practices, such as the business model and customer relationships. Such differences are likely, according to Heres and Lasthuizen, to determine or influence the leadership of organizational change.

Ethical leaders display a desire to benefit others in the organization or in society at large. Their behaviour reflects the values of empathy, care, concern and respect for others. They take an altruistic rather than egotistical stance. Ethical leaders model pro-social and altruistic behaviour; they behave, according to Micha Popper and Ofra Mayseless (2003), like good parents. Ethical leadership is, however, about more than just being authentic. It is also about sacrificing some values when generally applicable moral requirements legitimately compete with them (Price, 2003). Ethical leadership behaviour demonstrates social responsibility, the key to which is the empowerment of employees. In the view of Anita Roddick, founder of The Body Shop: 'There are not many motivating forces more potent than giving your staff an opportunity to exercise and express their idealism to influence change' (Roddick, 2000: 26).

Addressing ethical issues

The key leadership tasks to help address ethical issues during transformations include:

- Providing a clear purpose and vision for the change initiative: 'Why do we want to change?' 'What do we want to be as a result of the change?' 'How will we achieve it in an ethical way?'
- Recognizing employees' values and beliefs in the company's core values that guide change efforts.
- Empowering employees to voice their opinions and influence change.

Ethical leadership is therefore of crucial importance for organizational change and transformation.

Ethical checkpoints

Steps or checkpoints that can help when managing the ethical dimensions of change include the following:

- *Identify that there is an issue.* This involves acknowledging that there is a problem that needs to be addressed. It can help separate ethical questions from disagreements about manners and social conventions. For example, an individual not attending a kick-off meeting to discuss changes to operating processes may be bad manners and violate peer and team expectations. However, this is not a moral problem involving right or wrong. On the other hand, deciding whether to make someone's job redundant during a restructuring exercise because you do not like him or her is an ethical issue.

- *Determine who is responsible.* Once it has been agreed that there is an ethical issue, the person/s responsible need to be identified, as well as who is responsible for addressing the problem. For example, you might be concerned that one of your suppliers is exploiting child labour and therefore need to decide what you should do.

- *Gather the relevant facts.* Adequate, accurate and current information is important for making effective decisions of all kinds, including ethical ones. For instance, in deciding whether it is fair to suspend a colleague for being rude and aggressive about a proposed new IT system, before you make a decision you will need to discuss the issue with the individual's colleagues, line manager and the offender in order to determine the seriousness of the offence and the reason why they criticized the system.

- *Review right-versus-wrong issues.* To decide whether an issue or course of action is right or wrong consider if the decision violates any of the following: it gives you a negative reaction; it would make you uncomfortable if it appeared on a social medial site; or it would violate the ethical code of the organization.

- *Apply the ethical standards and perspectives.* Apply the ethical code of conduct, standards and perspectives of the organization that is most relevant and useful to the specific issue.

- *Make the decision.* At some point you need to make the decision. This requires, as Rushworth Kidder says:

  > Moral courage, an attribute essential to leadership and one that, along with reason, distinguishes humanity most sharply from the animal world. Little wonder, then, that the exercise of ethical decision making is often seen as the highest fulfilment of human kind. (1995: 186)

- *Revisit and reflect on the decision.* Finally, review the learning from the decision you have taken and reflect on it. What lessons emerged from this case that you can apply to future decisions? What ethical issues were raised? Did you address them in the right way?

Identify with colleagues any examples of unethical leadership during organizational change that you have witnessed. What were the problems with the examples you have identified? Why do you think the ethical issue(s) arose?

The ethics of culture change

Any attempt to change an organizational culture raises ethical concerns relating to attempting to change individuals' attitudes, values and beliefs. This assumes that people are malleable and open to change, if not in their values then at least in their behaviour. Jean Woodall summarizes the issues in culture change as being surrounded by ethical dilemmas, which she says: 'do not just concern the inherent worth of the exercise or its benefit to the organization. They also include the impact on individual motivation to comply and above all the infringement of individual autonomy, privacy, self-esteem and equitable treatment (1996: 35).

The ethical issues in changing an organization's culture are further highlighted by Gareth Morgan (2006), who advocates that although leaders and managers can influence the evolution of culture by being aware of the symbolic consequences of their actions and by attempting to foster desired values, they should never attempt to control culture, as individuals are not passive recipients of managerial cultural interventions. Furthermore, if the essence of culture change is to change what is inside people's heads, without requesting the explicit consent of individuals, Tony Watson (2002: 267) asks: 'What right do managers have to engage with the deeper beliefs and conceptions of right and wrong held by organizational employees?'

There are therefore ethical issues to consider when attempting to change a culture. Andrew Brown (1998) highlights these as: 1) if organizations are developing their own ethical codes, there may be overlaps between tangible statements in an ethical code and the intangibility of an organizational culture; 2) ethical choices may be implied by the values and assumptions that exist in an organization; and 3) there may be a morally dubious third-order control function over individuals. This may take the form of power being exercised over individuals without them becoming aware of it. Such views on culture change and ethics draw attention to the dark side of culture change.

By attempting to change culture, leaders may be encouraging people to suppress or suspend independent thought and action. This raises ethical questions about whether leaders deliberately set out to change the meanings associated with organizational artefacts in ways that have consequences for employees' meanings and identities. If this is the case then individuals risk being treated as objects to be manipulated through the commodification of artefacts, which separates them from the meanings they represent for individuals. Any attempt at culture change therefore needs to take into account individuals' own values and has to be participative, collaborative and interactive.

In sum, the ethical principles, moral values and integrity of leaders and managers are a key factor for the success or failure of organizational change. It is the leader's moral principles and integrity, as Manuel Mendonca rightly says, that 'give legitimacy and credibility to the vision and sustain it' (2001: 266).

Sustaining change

Changes need to be sustained in an organization in order to ensure that benefits are realized. In reviewing the literature on leadership and sustainable change, Dave Ulrich and Norm Smallwood (2013) distil their conclusions into seven drivers of sustainable change that concern both leadership and management:

1 *Simplicity*: focusing on the behaviours that will make the most difference to the most important issues; moving from analysis to action with a determination to act; framing complex phenomena into simple patterns; and sequencing change.

2 *Time*: matching behaviour to intentions in prioritizing action; devoting the appropriate amount of time, with whom time is spent, what it is spent on, where it is spent and how it is spent.

3 *Accountability*: taking personal responsibility for doing what is promised and accounting for what was or was not accomplished and sustained – and why.

4 *Resources*: ensuring the practice of ongoing coaching so that desired behavioural change is enacted.

5 *Tracking*: monitoring behaviour and actions, progress and results using appropriate metrics.

6 *Melioration* (also known as 'amelioration'): making things better by learning from mistakes and failures and displaying resilience in the ups and downs of the journey of change.

7 *Emotion*: sustained change is not merely an intellectual phenomenon but an emotional one too: 'Action without passion will not long endure, nor will passion without action.' Such emotion – passion – draws on one's deep values, sense of purpose and the meaningfulness of the work that is done.

Management consultants Ashley Harshak and colleagues (2010) from Strategy&, define the following success factors for managing change that is sustainable:

- Understanding and spelling out the impact of change on people, including roles and responsibilities; skills and knowledge; behaviours; and performance management.

- Building the emotional and rational case for change by addressing the following questions: why are we changing? What is changing? What are the benefits? What is staying the same? 'What's in it for me?' 'What's against my interests?'

- Role modelling the change as a leadership [and management] team that involves: displaying the new behaviours; holding one another to account for their successful adoption; explaining what the top management were discussing and doing; and progress being made.

- Mobilizing people to own and accelerate the change. This involves: leveraging the informal organization, such as the network of peer-to-peer interaction; and focusing on shared values, communities and pride.

- Embedding the change in the organization by: continuing to engage and involve employees over the long term; identifying lessons that have been learnt; institutionalizing best practices to capture the full benefit of the change and any future changes; and aligning HR systems, structures, processes and incentives with the goals of the transformation, such as performance management, recruitment and selection, learning and development, and the workforce strategy.

Realizing benefits

Sustaining change is vital in order to realize the benefits enabled by the change. Benefits realization depends on the process of organizing and managing so that potential benefits, arising from investment in change, are actually achieved. It should be a core management process of any change initiative (Hodges and Gill, 2015: 377). To realize benefits Moorhouse Consulting (2012) propose the following:

- A clear framework providing a common language and a route map to follow.

- Available staff resources with the relevant skills, tools and techniques.

- Clear and consistent benefits, defined in detail at the outset of the initiative and agreed within the business.

- Performance management using accurate and timely data.

- A clear strategic linkage shaping the change programme to ensure that the business strategies are delivered.

- Full engagement of the change programme by the business, facilitated by a business change manager.

To this list can be added: stakeholder management; developing a business case, clear purpose and rationale for change; identifying and managing risks; communicating benefits achieved; and monitoring and evaluating benefits (each of these is discussed further in Chapters 4 and 5).

Influences on sustaining change

In my book *Sustaining Change in Organizations* (Hodges and Gill, 2015) I identify the following influences on sustaining change: leadership, management and individual. I expand upon these influences below.

Leadership influences

Sustaining change starts with the intentions and actions of leaders. In more detail, effective leaders sustain change through:

- Recognizing the need for change, as well as the what, how and when of change.
- Ensuring that the purpose and vision for change are clear for everyone.
- Identifying and personally displaying, promoting and reinforcing values that inform and support the purpose and strategies for transformation.
- Recognizing that change is emotional and appreciating why people react as they do.
- Gaining engagement and commitment from people.
- Maintaining commitment to transformation throughout its journey, until it becomes business as usual.
- Not declaring victory too soon – give change time to embed.
- Encouraging learning, reflection and development throughout the transformation.
- Being cognizant of the power and politics of stakeholders and of any conflict.
- Identifying and managing key internal and external stakeholders.
- Working in partnership with HR to ensure that people transition successfully through the transformation.
- Modelling and promoting a code of ethics for change, outlining what is and what is not acceptable in the organization.
- Gaining input from others into decisions about change.
- Ensuring that any decisions made are ethical.
- Appreciating the impact of decisions and the consequences of the actions of people involved in the transformation.
- Maintaining the sponsorship and profile of the transformation.

Management influences

Managers play a key influence in sustaining change by:

- Fostering support, trust and participation among employees.
- Recognizing and addressing the emotional impact of change.
- Encouraging dialogue across teams, groups and the organization.
- Identifying whether or not there is readiness for change.
- Involving employees in the decision-making process.
- Managing the benefits and costs of the implementation.
- Managing the timing, sequence and pace of change.
- Working with HR to provide support to address the stress, anxiety and uncertainty that change may cause.
- Being highly proactive and constantly reminding all involved about the aims of the change and what steps should be taken next in order to keep the change progressing.
- Providing training and development to build capability for change across the organization.
- Having a champion within each department who will ensure that there is constantly someone monitoring the improvement within that department.

Individual influences

The individual influences on sustaining change include:

- Active commitment and involvement in the change in order to help to create a sense of ownership and responsibility.
- Raising any concerns and issues that may impact on the success of the change.
- Engaging in dialogue about the change and sharing creative ideas.
- Recognizing that change is emotional – and where you are on the change curve.

All the above factors will help to sustain change. The key is to maintain commitment and energy and not to let the momentum gradually wane, because once people begin to forget the why and how of the change, then it can eventually fade.

In conclusion, there is no one right way to sustain change, because the success of any initiative is to a great extent dependent on its context and the commitment of people. What may fail in one situation is likely to be a success in another and vice versa. When transformations fail or fade over time, people will often drift back to their previous ways of working and behaving. This is often referred to as change decay or improvement evaporation. To prevent the benefits from change being lost and the new practices and behaviours being abandoned, change must transition from being something separate to become part of the way that an organization/team/individual operates – it needs to become business as usual. This means that it is no longer labelled as change or something different. Unless this happens, and the change is injected into the bloodstream of the organization, it may remain just a passing idea that is costly and creates no benefits.

The challenge for organizations is to build a cadre of leaders, managers and individuals with the capability and capacity to collectively accomplish what is needed to survive, thrive and sustain change, in an ethical way.

Moving forward

Change is changing. The process approaches to change are being transformed in order to ensure that change is successful and sustained through people. Table 10.1 illustrates the differences between the 'process' and the 'people' approach to change. On the left-hand side is the 'process approach' to change. This is the approach that has traditionally dominated transformation efforts. It is in contrast to the 'people approach' that is emerging and is outlined in this book. These approaches are not set out as a 'from/to' or with any value judgement of 'good versus bad'. For whilst the people approach will become more important, the process approach will remain strong.

In the process approach, the power to create change comes through positional authority. The leaders in the most senior roles have the greatest positional power. In the people approach, power comes from relationships and the ability to influence through networks. The process approach focuses

TABLE 10.1   Process and people approaches

Process Approach	People Approach
Power through position	Power through relationships
Mission and vision	Shared purpose
Making sense through logic, linear tasks	Making sense through emotions
Leadership-driven innovation	People connectivity
Traditional, based on experience	Open approaches
Transactional	Relationships
Getting things done	Capability

on change to achieve the mission and vision of the organization. This comes from the traditional view that change is driven from the top down, where leaders cascade their vision for change down to people in the organization and automatically expect them to accept and comply with it. On the people side, the emphasis is on a shared purpose of the rationale and decisions for change. On the process side change approaches are driven by logical, linear tasks, whereas the people approach emphasizes the connection with the emotional aspects of change.

On the process side it is leaders who drive the passion and energy for creativity and innovation, as part of a corporate approach to change and improvement. In the people approach, the drive for creativity and innovation is sparked by people across the organization at different levels, often via virtual networks and social media.

Much of the traditional planning and improvement methodologies of the process approach are well established and validated in practice. These include methods such as lean, Six Sigma and TQM. In the people approach, account is taken of the increasingly open and connected world, where there are many new opportunities to share ideas, compare data and co-create novel approaches to change, such as crowd wisdom.

In the process approach many of the levers for change are transactional, such as compliance. People are accountable through transaction performance targets. In the people approach, change is about commitment and ownership. People are accountable through shared commitments and to how they work together.

Finally, the process approach focuses on getting things done, completing them and moving on; while on the people side the emphasis is on capabilities and building capabilities for change that will be of benefit to the organization in the longer term.

Many transformation initiatives prefer to use the process approach, often described as diagnosis by analysis whereby leaders focus on process, measurement and execution, and ignore the people and the emotional dimensions. Organizations that embrace the people approach by building a shared purpose, connectivity, innovation, relationships, empathy and change capabilities will, as discussed in this book, tend to get better outcomes when it comes to sustaining change.

Summary

Organizational change is unlikely to be sustainable unless it is ethical. The danger of not only allowing but encouraging unethical change can be reduced where there is openness about and alignment of values and objectives, and transparency in decision making, carried out in a way that avoids coercion and manipulation, and listens to the views of the people in the organization. Individuals will have their own perceptions about the change. For instance, they may perceive it as threatening their status or adding extra work to their already overloaded work schedule. Individuals may then appear to oppose the change and, as a result, be viewed in negative terms as 'resistors'. Too often managers fail to understand how people feel about change. They tend to frame the situation in ways that make the misunderstandings and so-called 'resistance' worse. Managers need to recognize the impact of change on individuals and why they respond as they do. They need to be aware of where individuals are on the change curve. The reality is that many people will be optimistic and react positively to change. They will embrace rather than resist change if the outcome is important to them and they have been convinced that they will be better rather than worse off, as well as being given the opportunity to participate in the decision-making process about the change. People will want to have a warning of the need for the change and to know how the change is being managed, the reasons for the change, and what training and development will be provided to help them make the transition. Providing the opportunities for people to be involved in decisions and ideas about the change, and in its implementation and sustainability, will help to create an ethical approach to change.

It is therefore vital to ensure that ethics and sustainability are at the heart of leading and managing people through change.

Implications for managers and leaders

There are a number of key practical implications for managing and leading change in an ethical and sustainable way, based on the issues discussed in this chapter:

- *Provide clear ethical guidelines*
  Staff need to be given clear, formal ethical guidelines, and training on how to apply the guidelines during transformations. They also need to be confident that they will not be penalized when making an ethical decision.

- *Ensure ethical principles are understood and applied*
  An understanding and acceptance of ethical principles, including the organization's espoused core values and behaviours, in leading and managing change is vital. It is particularly important for each leader and manager involved in the change process to accept such responsibility in their own actions, methods, intentions and behaviours.

- *Address unethical behaviours*
  If you have a corporate policy on values and behaviours, reiterate it clearly throughout a period of change and live up to it. Manage quickly – and be seen to manage quickly – any inappropriate behaviour that is not in line with corporate policy.

- *Identify the benefits of the change*
  The key factors that will enable the benefits from change to be realized and sustained should be identified. This should be done early

on in a transformation to ensure that the factors identified are measured and monitored throughout the transformation.

- *Acknowledge when the change becomes business as usual*
  Do not go straight from one transformation to the next or people will stop seeing any benefit. Be clear when the change has ended – so people get a sense that there is an end.

References

Brown, A (1998) *Organisational Culture*, 2nd edn, Financial Times/Prentice Hall, London

Burnes, B and Jackson, P (2011) Success and failure in organizational change: an exploration of the role of values, *Journal of Change Management*, **11** (2), pp 133–62

By, R T, Burnes, B and Oswick, C (2012) Change management: leadership, values and ethics, *Journal of Change Management*, **12** (1), pp 1–5

Chynoweth, C (2015) Ethics v profit: the fight goes on, *The Times*, 25 January

Ciulla, J B (ed) (2014) *Ethics, the heart of leadership*, 3rd edn, ABC-CLIO, California

Ellis, P (2013) Corporate ethics education yields rewards, *National Defense Magazine*, USA, 8 August

Fandray, D (2000) [accessed 16 October 2015] The Ethical Company, *Workforce* [Online] http://www.workforce.com/articles/the-ethical-company

Harshak, A, Aguirre, D and Brown, A (2010) *Making Change Happen, and Making It Stick: Delivering sustainable organizational change*, Booz & Company, New York

Heres, L and Lasthuizen, K (2012) What's the difference? Ethical leadership in public, hybrid and private sector organizations, *Journal of Change Management*, **12** (4), pp 441–66

Hodges, J and Gill, R (2015) *Sustaining Change in Organizations*, SAGE, London

Hughes, M (2006) *Change Management: A critical perspective*, CIPD, London

Kidder, R M (1995) *How Good People Make Tough Choices: Resolving the dilemmas of ethical living*, Fireside, New York

Mendonca, M (2001) Preparing for ethical leadership in organizations, *Canadian Journal of Administrative Sciences/Revue Canadienne des Sciences de l'Administration*, **18** (4), pp 266–76

Meyerson, D (2001) Radical change, the quiet way, *Harvard Business Review*, October

Moorhouse Consulting (2012) *Start With the End in Mind and You'll Head in the Right Direction: The benefits of organisational change*, Moorhouse, London, September

Morgan, G (2006) *Images of Organization*, 4th edn, Sage, London

Popper, M and Mayseless, O (2003) Back to basics: applying a parenting perspective to transformational leadership, *The Leadership Quarterly*, **14** (1), pp 41–65

Price, T L (2003) The ethics of authentic transformational leadership, *The Leadership Quarterly*, **14** (1), pp 67–81

Roddick, A (2000) *Business as Usual*, 2nd edn, Thorsons, London

Rucker, S (2012) [accessed 16 October 2015] Why you won't get breakthrough innovation by being nice, *Harvard Business Review*, 17 April [Online] http://blogs.hbr.org/cs/2012/04/why_you_wont_get_breakthrough.html?cm_mmc=em

Steiner, G A (1975) *Business and Society*, 2nd edn, Random House, New York

Stiglitz, J E (2010) *Freefall: Free market and the sinking of the global economy*, Allen Lane, London

Stokes, P and Harris, P (2012) Micro-moments, choice and responsibility in sustainable organizational change and transformation, *Journal of Organizational Change Management*, 25 (4), pp 595–611

Ulrich, D and Smallwood, N (2013) *Leadership Sustainability: Seven disciplines to achieve the changes great leaders know they must make*, McGraw Hill Professional, London

Watson, T (2002) *Organising and Managing Work*, FT/Prentice Hall, Harlow

Woodall, J (1996) Managing culture change: can it ever be ethical?, *Personnel Review*, 25 (6), pp 26–40

Further reading

Kitson, A and Campbell, R (2008) *The Ethical Organisation*, Palgrave McMillan, Basingstoke

Todnem By, R and Burnes, B (2014) *Organizational Change, Leadership and Ethics: Leading organizations toward sustainability*, Routledge Studies in Organizational Change & Development, Routledge, London

GLOSSARY

action learning   When a group of peers, each seeking to bring about change, meet to discuss where they are each experiencing difficulty and then test in action the ideas that arise from the discussion.

behavioural intelligence   How an individual physically behaves, consisting of the skills of both using and responding to emotion.

benefits realization   The process of organizing and managing so that potential benefits, arising from investment in change, are actually achieved.

capabilities for change   Competencies that comprise individual and collective knowledge, skills, attitudes and experience as well as structural, cultural and contextual factors.

change   Change is any adjustment or alteration in an organization that has the potential to influence the organization's stakeholders' physical or psychological experience. It is an opportunity to make or become different through new ways of organizing and working.

cognitive intelligence   Or thinking, includes aptitudes such as dealing with abstract concepts and complex problem solving, visionary capacity, mental ability and the ability to cope with complexity, and to express ideas clearly.

commitment   Where people actively want to change.

compliance   Where people will change because they are instructed to do so.

contextual intelligence   An intuitive diagnostic skill that helps a leader to understand change, interpret the outside world, set objectives, and align strategies and tactics with objectives.

content of change   The content is *what* actually changes in the organization, such as the operations, structure and systems. The process is *how* the change occurs, which includes the pace of the change, the sequence of activities, the way decisions are made and communicated, and how people are engaged in change initiatives and respond to transition.

context of change   The context is about the environment in which the organization is operating and the situation in which the change is being implemented. Hence the need for an awareness of the internal and external drivers for change and for the content and process of change to be adapted to the context in which an organization is operating.

cultural intelligence   The capability to connect and interact with people in different cultures and to cope effectively with cultural diversity.

culture   The most popular definition of culture is the one by Edgar Schein that describes organizational culture as consisting of artefacts, espoused values, beliefs and basic assumptions.

dialogue In the context of organizational change dialogue is about people engaging in crucial conversations about the why, how, what and when of change. Dialogue has two components to it: listening and voicing.

drivers of change The forces that are driving the need for change arise from the external and internal environment in which an organization operates.

emergent change Iterative, unpredictable and often unintentional, emergent change can come from anywhere, and involves informal self-organizing groups.

emotions Intense, short-lived reactions that are linked to a specific cause such as an event, issue, relationship or object. They can be classified as positive or negative.

emotional balancing Working with your own and your employees' feelings, so that change and continuity are achieved.

emotional contagion Emotions can spread to teams and other organizational members much like a virus, and this contagion can have an impact on the emotions and behaviours of employees.

emotional intelligence The ability of managers and leaders to recognize and manage emotions in themselves and in other people. It comprises four elements: 1) emotional awareness, 2) emotional facilitation, 3) emotional knowledge, and 4) emotional regulation.

emotional labour Describes when individuals manage their emotions within an organization in exchange for a salary.

ethics Can be defined as a code of conduct or behaviour that reflects a set of moral values or beliefs to be applied in certain circumstances.

ethical leadership Displaying a desire to benefit others in the organization or in society at large The behaviour of an ethical leader reflects the values of empathy, care, concern and respect for others They take an altruistic rather than egotistical stance.

ethical or moral intelligence The capacity to understand right from wrong, to have strong ethical convictions and to act on them to behave in the right and honourable way. In the simplest terms, moral intelligence is the ability to differentiate right from wrong as defined by universal principles that include empathy, responsibility, reciprocity, respect for others and caring for others.

impact analysis A technique designed to unearth the unexpected negative effects of a change on an organization. It provides a structured approach for looking at a proposed change, so that managers can identify as many of the negative impacts or consequences of the change as possible.

incremental changes The outcome of the everyday process of management, which tend to be when individual parts of an organization deal increasingly and separately with one problem and one objective at a time. Incremental change can include changing a product formula in such a way that customers would not notice any difference.

leadership A process whereby an individual influences a group of individuals to achieve a common goal. It is the process that translates into acts. It is in his or her acts of leadership that the leader exists.

management Ensuring that processes and people are working efficiently and effectively, which concerns not only maintaining the status quo but also changing it.

mindfulness An enhanced attention to awareness of current experiences or present reality.

organizational learning Concerned with continuous improvement and development; it enables an organization to build the capability to change and adapt.

organizational structure The structure is the way in which the organization divides tasks and establishes reporting lines to make up a chain of command, so that individuals are accountable at various stages of a process.

pattern break A series of abrupt interruptions that permanently break a habit or state In the context of change this can be translated to mean that something has to happen to shatter the status quo and let people know, especially supporters of the existing culture, that there is a need for change.

political intelligence The ability to effectively understand others at work and to use such knowledge to influence others to act in ways that enhance one's personal and/or organizational objectives.

process of change The process is 'how' the change occurs, which includes the pace of the change, the sequence of activities, the way decisions are made and communicated, and how people are engaged in change initiatives and respond to transition. The process of change is critical not only for recipients, given that their acceptance and engagement is a key determinant of success, but also for managers and leaders, since they are responsible for shaping and implementing strategy in order to affect required changes.

planned change An intentional intervention for bringing about change to an organization; best characterized as deliberate, structured and linear, with leaders and managers as the pivotal instigators of the change.

politics Politics is power in action, people exercising their power in overt and covert ways that can be difficult to understand or navigate. Change can trigger and intensify political behaviour.

power An individual's formal position in the organization but also their personal characteristics and experience.

readiness for change This refers to organizational members' beliefs, attitudes and intentions regarding the extent to which changes are needed, and the extent to which employees have positive views about the need for change and believe that these changes have positive implications for themselves and the wider organization, as well as the organization's capacity to successfully make those changes.

relational intelligence The ability to understand and collaborate with others and facilitate the development of relationships between individuals, cultures and ideas.

resilience A critical capability for coping with change, and that is required by all people in all organizations.

resistance Resistance to change is productive energy to discuss what is being proposed and to explore alternative approaches.

sense making   The process whereby people give meaning to experience. It is a retrospective process that uses evidence from past events to construct a storyline that makes sense in the present.

sense building   A process that contains a notion of construction and looks to the future. It involves setting a goal by connecting the sources of knowledge, including sensory data.

social intelligence   The ability to read and adapt to diverse social situations.

spiritual intelligence   Concerns the quest for meaning and a sense of worth or value in what leaders seek and do.

stakeholder   Any individual or group with an interest or involvement in the change and its outcomes.

transformation   The marked change in nature, form or appearance of something. Transformational or strategic change and everyday incremental change can be viewed as different, not just in terms of their objectives but also in terms of their processes and size, scope and breadth, and what they demand of individuals.

transition   The process or period of adapting to the change. It involves moving from the current state or phase to another: for example, an individual changing from one role to another, a team changing from one process for dealing with customer complaints to another, or an organization going from one structural arrangement to another.

trust   Fundamentally, a judgement of confidence in either a person or an organization. Employees who perceive their leader as being able to lead change effectively, who perceive their manager as trustworthy and supportive, and who feel respected are more willing to accept and support change.

ZOUD   Gaining engagement and commitment to change at times means that managers (and leaders) need to get into a 'zone of uncomfortable debate' (ZOUD) with other people. The ZOUD focuses on conversations and communication about complex or hard-to-resolve change issues, whether they involve a team, a business unit or an individual.

INDEX

360° feedback   138

ABC model of emotions   58
Abrahamson, Eric   24–25
action learning   312
adaptive leadership   118
ADKAR model of engagement assessment
     130–31
Adobe   194
Aegon Asset Management (case study)   304
ageing global population   17
Agness, Lindsey   232–33
Aitken, Carolyn   122, 137–38, 253
Aitken, Paul   287
Al Jayousi, Osama   333
Allen, Woody   133
Amarant, John   87
Amazon (case study)   233–34
American Express Travel Related Services
     (TRS)   24–25
analogies, use in communications   200
Andriopoulos, Constantine   219–20, 235
Ang, S   296
Antonacopoulou, Elena   57
Appalatch outdoor apparel company   22
Apple   28, 132, 193, 299, 310, 334
Asch, David   226
Ashcroft, John   29
Asian model of planned change   30
AstraZeneca   285
Atlassian   91
authentic leadership   118
autonomy at work as motivator   90, 91–92
availability bias   198
Avey, James   53
Avon Products   200, 267
Ayling, Bob   136

Balmer, Steve   39–40
bandwagon effect   198
BankCo Group (case study)   305–07
banking sector crash (2007–08)   330–31
Barclays   311
Barrett, Deborah   193
Barsh, Joanna   133, 200, 237
Bartunek, Jean   37
Bass, Bernard   296
Bate, Paul   216, 221

Battilana, Julie   139–40, 287
Bazerman, M H   300
Beaujon, Andrew   266
Beer, Michael   38–39
Beer's model of planned change   30–32
behavioural intelligence   298–99
benevolence   102
Benson-Armer, Richard   301
Best Buy   91
best-practice traps   9
Beyer, Janie   59
Bhatt, Om Prakash   122
biased thinking   197–98
biological theory of emotions   54–55
Birchenhough, Mark   274
Blanchard, Ken   198
Blanchard, Scott   198
Blyton, Paul   62
Boal, Kimberley   300
body language   298
Boerner, Sabine   117
Bohm, Daniel   201
Borba, Michele   297
Bordia, Prashant   150, 196
Borland, Russell   307–10
Bratton, John   59
Bremmer, Ian   16
BRIC economies   15
Bridges, William, transition model
     80–83
bridging networks   140
Brin, Sergey   132
Brinkerhoff, Robert   314
Brown, Andrew   337
Buchanan, David   34
Buckler, Sheldon   236
Burger King   61
Burnes, Bernard   36, 334
Busby, Nicola   100
Bush, Mirabai   66
business continuity   291
By, Rue Todnem   178

Cadbury   267–68
Cagni, Pascal   299
Caldwell, Raymond   115, 255, 288
Callahan, Jaime   59
Callaway, Travis   205–07

capabilities for change   284–319
    action learning   312
    approach to building   284–85
    assessment tools   302–03
    building capabilities   301–19
    capability gap analysis   302–03
    capability matrix   304
    identifying capability gaps   302
    identifying development needs   304–05
    implications for leaders and managers
        318–19
    intelligences for leading people
        292–301
    intervention design and
        development   305–10
    key leadership capabilities   285–91
    leadership development
        interventions   310–12
    monitoring how learning is being applied
        312–14
    nature of   284–85
    psychometric tests   302–03
    resilience   291–92
    sustaining learning   312–14
    training and development interventions
        (case study)   314–17
Carillon   333
Carlyle, Thomas   116
Carolan, Brian   140
Casciaro, Tiziana   139–40
centred leadership   287–88
Chambers, John   264
Chambers, Lynne   310–11
Chambers, Thomas   67–69
change
    definitions   21–27
    disruptive nature of   1–2
    nature of   27–39
    recognising the need for   39–42
change curve   78–79
change fatigue   152–53
change leadership   see   leading change
change management   see   managing
        change
charismatic leadership   116
Chevron   330
Chynoweth, Carly   331, 333
'circle of fire' process   138
Cisco   60, 203, 264
climate change   16–17
Coca-Cola   16, 330
cognitive appraisal theory of emotions
        55–56
cognitive intelligence   293
cohesive networks   140
collaboration as enabler of change   125–26

commitment   83, 86–89, 123–24
    as means to achieve change   154–55
communication during change
    actions and symbolism   199–200
    addressing rumours   196–97
    analogies and metaphors   200
    biased thinking   197–98
    creating compelling stories   200
    effective communication   192–93
    employee concerns   190–91
    goals of communication   193
    human dimension of
        communication   197–98
    impact of lack of communication
        (case study)   194–96
    impact of communications   193
    impact on emotions   198–200
    importance as a change practice
        194–96
    importance to the process   190–91
    needs of employees   198–99
    practical implications   211–12
    use of e-mail   191, 192
    ZOUD (zone of uncomfortable debate)
        209–10
    see also   dialogue
competence and trustworthiness   102
competitive environment, changing
        nature of   1–2
compliance, as means to achieve change
        154–55
confirmation bias   197
conflict management   164–69
conflict resolution approaches   165–69
consultancy
    expert consultancy   270–71
    external consultants   272–74
    HR consultants   270–74
    internal consultants   272–73
    process consultancy   270–71
consumer markets in emerging economies
        15–16
content of change   25
context of change   14–15, 25
contextual intelligence   293–94
contingency model of change   37–38
continuous improvement   21–22
Cook, Tim   310
Cornelissen, Joep   200
corporate scandals   120, 329
corporate social responsibility (CSR)
        statements   332
corporate universities   310
Cosack, Sabine   269
Coutu, Diane   291
Coyle-Shapiro, Jacqueline   99

Crail, Mark 260
creativity, and culture change 234–37
cross-border transformations 265
crowdsourcing 208
cultural intelligence 296
culture *see* organizational culture
Cunha, Miguel 37
Cunha, Rita 37
cynicism 83, 85–86, 87, 88, 125, 196

Darwin, Charles 24, 54
Davis, James 102
Dawson, Patrick 36, 219–20
decision making
    challenges for leaders 136–37
    ethical issues 332–33
deep acting 61, 62
demographic shifts 17–18
dialogue
    barriers to engaging in 202–03
    creating effective dialogue 203
    feedback 204–05
    feedback (case study) 205–07
    listening and voicing 201–02
    planning dialogue 204–07
    strategy 204
    the art of 200–07
    using social media to create 208–09
    ZOUD (zone of uncomfortable debate) 209–10
    see also communication during change
Diamond, Bob 311
Dibadj, Ali 267
Dietz, Graham 102–03
Dinwoodie, David 151
Direct Line Group 132
disaster recovery 291
Disney 226
disruptive technologies 18–19
distributed leadership 118–19
distributive justice 98
divergent change 139–40
Dollard, Maureen 62
Dragons' Den TV show 86
drivers of change 15–21
    climate change 16–17
    demographic shifts 17–18
    external environment 15–21
    ideologically-driven conflicts 19
    internal factors 20–21
    legislative changes 19–20
    resource scarcity 16–17
    shifts in global economic power 15–16
    technological breakthroughs 18–19
    urbanization 17–18

Dunphy, Dexter 37
DuPont 132, 133, 266

e-finance revolution 18
E7 countries 15
economic globalization and change 15–16
Edgley-Pyshorn, Charlotte 256
Ellis, Albert 58
Ellis, Patti 333
Elop, Stephen 192
Elster, John 51
emergent change 29, 35–37
emerging economies, purchasing power 15–16
emotion theories 54–58
    ABC model 58
    biological perspective 54–55
    cognitive appraisal perspective 55–56
    learned experience perspective 57
    social constructivist perspective 56–57
emotional alignment 136
emotional awareness 64, 65
emotional balancing 63–64
emotional contagion 63
emotional dissonance 62
emotional facilitation 64, 65
emotional harmony 62
emotional intelligence 64–66, 294–95
emotional knowledge 64, 65
emotional labour 61–62
emotional regulation 64, 65
emotional schemata 56
emotions
    and organizational culture 59–60
    changes over time 53
    definitions 52
    effects of change at work 51–52
    experiences at work 51–52
    impact of communications on 198–200
    impact on work performance 54
    implications for change managers and leaders 70–72
    negative emotions 52–53
    positive emotions 52–53
    reactions to change 50
    role during organizational change 66–70
    suppressing and expressing 61–62
    ties between leaders and individuals 140–41
    types of reaction to organizational change 52–53
employee assistance programmes (EAPs) 270
employee retention, role of HR 269

employees
    effects on health and well-being   152–54
    emotional labour   61–62
energy-investment model   86–89
energy required to sustain change   126–29
engagement
    measurement of   130–31
    of middle managers   130–31
Enron   300
Ericsson, Anders   284
ethical aspects of change
    culture change   337–38
    leading change   334–37
    managing change   332–33
    practical implications   344–45
ethical behaviour
    corporate scandals   329–30
    defining unethical behaviours   332
    ethical standards   331–32
    training and education   333
ethical checkpoints   336
ethical codes of conduct   330
ethical decision making   332–33
ethical intelligence   297
ethical leadership   119, 335
    addressing ethical issues   335
    ethical values of leaders   331–32
ethical organizational culture   332
European Union (EU) legislation   19–20
Evans, James   283–84
Ewenstein, Boris   287–88, 307, 311–12
expectancy theory   89–90
expert consultancy   270–71
external consultants   272–74
external drivers of change   15–21
extrinsic motivation   90

F7 countries   15
Facebook   208
failure of change initiatives
    failure rate   2, 253–54
    learning from   133–34, 283–84
    reasons for   35
fairness   102
    perceptions of   98–99
Fandray, Dayton   332
Fineman, Stephen   56, 59, 69
Fiorina, Carly   221–22
focus groups   205
Ford, Jeffrey   96
Ford, Laura   96
Forster, Nick   60
French, Robert   50
Frost, Brian   300
Fugate, Mel   53
Furnham, Adrian   137

G7 countries   15
Gabriel, Yiannis   57
Gandhi, Mahatma   138
Gates, Bill   284
Gauthier, Valerie   123, 131–32, 299
Gaymard, Clara   299
General Electric (GE)   39, 221, 299
Georgens, Tom   201–02
Gersick, Connie   24
Gerstner, Lou   24–25
Ghafoor, Mohsin   208–09
Gillespie, Nicole   102–03
Gilley, Ann   286
Gladwell, Malcolm   284
GlaxoSmithKline   329
global level transformations   265
globalization
    and change   15–16
    impacts of global recession   16
Glocer, Tom   136
goals, establishment of   121, 264
Goleman, Daniel   64, 294, 295
Google   1, 91, 132, 133
Gotsi, Manto   235
Gould, Stephen   24
Grant, Adam   93
Gratton, Linda   120, 133, 201
Great Man theory   116
Griffin, Michael   274–75
groupthink   140
Gurjar, Nandita   202–03
Gyurjyan, Gayane   153

Hall, Gene   198
Hamblin, Anthony   313–14
Hameed, Imran   158
Handy, Charles   1
Hardy, Cynthia   130
Harris, Phil   334
Harshak, Ashley   338–39
Hasegawa, Yasuchika   233
Hatami, Homayoun   314
Hatch, Mary   35
Heifetz, Ronald   285
Hendry, Chris   3
Heres, Leonie   335
Hewlett-Packard   60, 222
Higgs, Malcolm   287
Hill, Andrew   311
Hitt, William   283
Hochschild, Arlie   61
Hoffman, Brian   300
Hofman, Debra   36
Hogan, Joyce   299
holacracy   266
Holliday, Steve   121

honesty 102
Hooijberg, Robert 300
Hooper, Alan 136
Hornung, Severin 94
Horth, David 132
Howieson, Brian 118–20
HR (human resources)
    capability for transformations 274–75
    cross-border transformations 265
    diagnosis of potential change issues 257
    employee assistance programmes (EAPs) 270
    global level transformations 265
    implementation role 259–60
    key activities during change 256–63
    monitoring role 259–60
    people dimension of change 253–55
    performance management 264–65
    practical implications of change 276–77
    preparation for change 257–59
    retention of key employees 269
    role during mergers and acquisitions 267–68
    role during organizational change 252–53
    role during restructuring 266–68
    strategic role 255–56
    supporting change (case study) 261–63
    sustaining change 260–61
    use of HR consultants 270–74
HRM (human resources management) 252 *see also* HR
Hüttermann, Hendrik 117
Huisman, Jeroen 256
human dimension of communication 197–98
human resources *see* HR
Huy, Quy 62, 63–64
Hymans Robertson LLP (case study) 307–10

IBM 162
ideologically-driven conflicts 19
impact analysis of change on people 176–77
implementing change with impact 163–64
incremental change 21–22, 24, 28, 117
individual interviews 205
individual responses to change 76–77
    helping people make sense of change 103–04
    influence on sustaining change 341
    implications for managers and leaders 104–07

individual sense-making, helping to make sense of change 103–04
informational justice 98
Infosys 125, 126, 137–38, 202–03
innovation 83, 86
    and culture change 234–37
    as enabler of change 131–33
Insights Inventory 303
intelligences for leading people through change 292–301
internal consultants 272–73
internal drivers of change 20–21
interpersonal justice 98
intrinsic motivation 90–93
Isabella, Lynn, transition model 80
Isern, Josep 126
Ivison, Tom 314–17

Jackson, Phil 334
Jackson, Susan 268
James, William 55
James–Lange theory of emotions 55
Jenkins, Antony 311
Jenkins, Mark 288
Jimmieson, Nerina 193
job autonomy as motivator 90, 91–92
job satisfaction, and emotions at work 54, 62
Jobs, Steve 132, 193, 310, 334
Johansen, Svein 101
Johnson, Gerry 224–25
Johnson, Yulia 172–76
Jung, Andrea 200
Jung, Carl 303
justice, perceptions of 98–99

kaizen (continuous improvement) 21
Kanter, Rosabeth 199
    model of planned change 31–32
Katen, Karen 233
Kaynar, Or 261–63
Keen shoe company 22
Kegan, Robert 96–97
Keller, Scott 122, 137–38, 253
Kennedy, Robert 85
Kessler, Ian 99
Kevlar 132
KFC 16
Kidder, Rushworth 336
Kiel, Fred 297
Kilmann, Ralph 165–66
King Jr, Martin Luther 141
Kirkland, Rik 60
Kirkpatrick, Donald 313
Kleiner, Art 216
Kodak (case study) 40–41

Kolb's model of learning styles   303
Konovsky, Mary   98
Kotter, John   139
    accelerator model of planned change
        33–34
    model of planned change   31–32
    reasons for failure of planned change   35
Kowitt, Beth   267
Kraft Foods   267–68
Krummaker, Stefan   286
Kübler-Ross, Elisabeth, transition model
        78–80
Kurzweil, Ray   1

LaClair, Jennifer   285
Lafley, Alan G   122, 133–34
Lahey, Lisa   96–97
LaMarsh, Jeanne   256, 257
Lange, Carl   55
Larsen & Toubro   124
Lasthuizen, Karin   335
Lawrence, Paul   130, 194, 203
Lazarus, Richard   55
leadership challenges, role-modelling desired
        behaviour   137–38
leadership development interventions
        310–12
leadership enablers of change   120–34
    collaboration   125–26
    commitment   123–24
    effects of bad attitudes   120
    energy   126–29
    engagement of middle managers   130–31
    innovation   131–33
    learning from failure   133–34
    Northumbrian Water Group (case study)
        127–29
    sense building   123
    sense of purpose   121–23
    sponsorship   124–25
leadership philosophies   118–20, 298
leadership theories   116–18
leading change   113–14, 115
    building adaptability   136
    challenges of   135–38
    changing your mind   137
    comparison with managing change   115
    connect with the disconnected   139–40
    definitions of leadership   116
    development of a learning organization
        284
    emotional ties with employees   140–41
    ensuring emotional alignment   136
    ethical aspects   334–37
    inspiring others to change   138–39
    intelligences for leading people   292–301

key leadership capabilities   285–91
    people-centred approach   138–41
    power and politics in organizations
        134–35
    practical implications   142
    sustaining change   340
    taking bold decisions   136–37
    use of networks   140
lean methodology   343
    implementation (case study)   159–61
learned experience theory of emotions   57
learning anxiety   95–96
learning organization   see   organizational
        learning
learning styles   303
legislative changes   19–20
Lego   28–29
Lennick, Doug   297
Lewig, Kerry   62
Lewin, Kurt   2, 27
    model of planned change   30
lifespan of companies   14–15
Linsky, Marty   285
listening effectively   201–02
Liu, Yi   91
Livermore, David   296
Livne-Tarandach, Reut   37
Lloyds pharmacy group   254
Ludema, James   115
Luecke, Richard   257
Luecke's model of planned change   31–32
Lunar Design   235, 237

M-Pesa mobile money service   18
Madoff, Bernie   329
Magnus, George   17
management-theory fads   9, 149
managing change   146–47
    comparison with leading change   115
    conflict management   164–69
    defining activities   162–63
    defining change management tasks
        171–72
    definition of change management   148
    effects on people's health and well-being
        152–54
    engagement of middle managers   130–31
    engaging teams   162–63
    ensuring readiness for change   157–61
    ethical aspects   332–33
    how change is mismanaged   148–50
    impact analysis of change on people
        176–77
    implementing change with impact
        163–64
    involving people at every level   162

key capabilities 287–91
navigating change 151–52
Nissan (case study) 172–76
ownership of change 156–63
practical implications 179–80
role of managers 150–52
stakeholder analysis 169–72
stress during change 153–54
sustaining change 340
using commitment or compliance 154–55
managing organizational culture, views on 220–22
Margerison, Charles 303
Marshak, Robert 30
Marshall, Ian 297–98
Martin, Trinity 208–09
Mast, Marianne 134
mastery as a motivator 90, 92
Mayer, J D 294
Mayer, John 64–65
Mayer, Marissa 132, 222–24
Mayer, Roger 102
Mayseless, Ofra 335
MBA Oath 330
McCalman, James 34, 148
McCann, Dick 303
McDonald's 61, 227
McDonough, Geoff 117
McGuire, John 120
McIntosh, Perry 257
McLagan, Patricia 138–39
Meaney, Mary 156
Mendonca, Manuel 338
Mento, Jones and Dirndorfer's model of planned change 31–32
Mercedes 226
mergers and acquisitions, role of HR 267–68
metaphors, use in communications 200
Meyerson, Debra 334
micromanagement 91
Microsoft 39–40, 192, 284
middle managers, engagement of 130–31
Miller, Claire 223–24
mindfulness 65–66
models of planned change 30–34
Moeller, Scott 267–68
moral intelligence 297
Morgan, Fiona 254
Morgan, Gareth 26–27, 222, 337
Morgan Stanley 291
Morning Star 125
motivating people to change 89–93
expectancy theory 89–90
motivators for change 90–93

Muir, James 127–29
Mullins, Laurie 148
Murthy, N R Narayana 126, 137–38
Myers Briggs Type Inventory (MBTI) 303

Nadella, Satya 192
Nadler, David 40
Nahavandi, Afsaneh 115
Narayen, Shantanu 194
National Health Service (NHS) UK 36, 139–40, 274
Natriello, Guy 140
negative emotions 52–53
negotiation 164–65
NetApp 201
networks 140
Nino, David 59
Nissan (case study) 172–76
Nohria, Nitin 38–39
non-divergent change 139–40
non-verbal communication 298
Noon, Mike 62
Northouse, Peter 116, 119
Northumbrian Water Group (case study) 127–29
Nye Jr, Joseph 117, 294, 297

old-age dependency ratio 17
Oliver, Jamie 229–31
one-off surveys 205
openness 102
organizational change
emotional responses to 51–52
failure rate of change initiatives 2
people dimension 2–3
perceptions of justice and fairness 98–99
power and politics in organizations 134–35
resistance to 93–97
role of emotions 66–70
see also organizational culture change
organizational culture
and emotions 59–60
artefacts 217
basic assumptions 218
characteristics of 219–20
cultural paradigm 225
definitions 217–18
diagnosing 224–25
elements of the cultural web 224–25
espoused beliefs and values 218
ethical culture 332
perspectives on 219–20
Schein's model 217–18
views on managing 220–22

organizational culture change
    Amazon (case study) 233–34
    approaches to change 226–28
    call centre culture change (case study)
        227–28
    challenges of 229–31
    creating a culture for change 233–37
    decision to change or not 226–27
    delivering sustainable culture change
        237–39
    emotional responses to 60
    ethical issues 337–38
    implications for leaders and managers
        240–41
    manufacturing (case study) 241–46
    pattern breaks 231–33
    possible approaches 240
    reasons for changing 222–24
    stimulating creativity and
        innovation 234–37
    symbolic management 226–28
    views on changing culture 216
    Yahoo! culture change (case study)
        222–24
organizational learning 283–84
organizations
    nature of 26–27
    power and politics in 134–35
    trap of success 40–41
Orlikowski, Wanda 36
ownership of change 156–63
    assessing readiness for change 158–59
    defining activities 162–63
    DUCO Ltd (case study) 159–61
    engaging teams 162–63
    ensuring readiness for change 157–61
    involving people at every level 162
    levels of stakeholder control 156–57

Page, Larry 132
Parry, Ken 295
passion, and purpose 122–23
Paton, Robert 34, 148
pattern breaks 231–33
Pedler, Mike 312
Penman, Danny 65, 66
people, transition and change 22
people approach to change 2–3, 342–43
people-centred leadership 138–41
people-driven change 38–39
perceptions of justice and fairness 98–99
performance management, role of HR
        264–65
Perlroth, Nicole 223–24
Pernod Ricard 310
Pettigrew, Andrew 220

Pfizer 16
Pink, Daniel 90–93
planned change 29–30
    criticisms and limitations 34–35
    models of 30–34
Poilâne, Apollonia 299
policy changes 19–20
political behaviour in organizations 135
political intelligence 299–300
Polyakov, Audrey 172–76
Ponzi schemes 329
Popper, Micha 335
positive emotions 52–53
Potter, John 136
power and politics in organizations 134–35
proactive change 28–29
procedural justice 98
process approach to change 342–43
process consultancy 270–71
process-driven change 38–39
process of change 25
Procter & Gamble (P&G) 122, 132–34,
        235, 237
Proctor, Audra 291–92
Proudfoot, Judith 292
psychological contract, impacts of change
        99–100
pulse surveys 204–05
punctuated equilibrium 24–25
Pung, Caroline 126
purpose
    and goals 121
    and passion 122–23
    as a motivator 90, 93
    clarity of 121
    connection to the past and present 121
    sense of 121–23
    statement of 121
    use of stories 122

RACI chart 162–63
Rafferty, Alannah 158
Randell, Gerry 298
Rao, Ravi 285
Rational-Emotive Therapy (RET) 58
Raytheon 332–33
reactive change 28–29
Redford, Robert 142
Reffo, Gerry 299
reflective learning 283–84
Reilly, Peter 274
relational intelligence (savoir-relier) 299
resilience 291–92
resistance to change 93–97
    as a positive reaction 96–97
resource scarcity 16–17

restructuring, role of HR   266–68
Richards, Susan   286
Robbins, Stephen   164
Robertson, Bryan   132
Roddick, Anita   335
role-modelling desired behaviour   137–38
Rousseau, Denise   94
Royal Dutch Shell   201
Rubin, Robert   85
Rucker, Simon   334
rumours, dealing with   196–97

Sakson, Steven   259
Salaman, John   226
Salovey, Peter   64–65, 294
Sandvik Materials Technology   121
Schein, Edgar   59, 60, 95
      model of organizational culture   217–18
Scherer, Klaus   56
Schlender, Brent   310
Schmidt, Warren   156
Schuler, Richard   268
Schultz, Howard   84, 217, 218
Selart, Marcus   101
Senge, Peter   283
sense building   123
sense making   75–76, 123
Seo, Myeong-Gu   294–95
servant leadership   119
shared leadership   119
Sharer, Kevin   138
Shaw, Robert   40
Sherman, Stanford   51
Shield's model of planned change   30, 31
Sidhu, Ranji   197–98
silent veto power   135
silo behaviour   140
Singh, Nupur   125–26
Six Sigma   343
      implementation (case study)   159–61
Smallwood, Norm   338
SMART goals   121, 264
Smith, Richard   27, 124–25
Smollan, Ray   295
Sobi   117
social constructivist theory of emotions
      56–57
social intelligence   295–96
social media
      emergent change related to   35–36
      using to create dialogue   208–09
Sony   310–11
Spears, Larry   119
spiritual intelligence   297–98
sponsorship of transformational change
      124–25

Stace, Doug   37
stakeholder analysis   169–72
stakeholder management   135
stakeholders, levels of control during change
      156–57
Starbucks   16, 84, 217, 218
status quo bias   197–98
Steiner, George   331–32
Stern, Tom   194–96
Stiglitz, Joseph   329–30
Stokes, Peter   334
Storey, John   34
stories
      communicating purpose   122
      use in communications   200
Stoughton, Anne   115
stress during change   153–54
Styhre, Alexander   37
success, trap of   40
surface acting   61, 62
surveys   204–05
survival anxiety   95
sustainable culture change   237–39
sustainable development   17–18, 22
sustaining change   126–29, 338–45
      individual influences   341
      influences on   340–42
      leadership influences   340
      management influences   340
      moving forward   342–43
      practical implications   344–45
      realizing benefits   339–40
      role of HR   260–61
sustaining learning   312–14

Takeda   233
Talwar, Jennifer   61
Tannenbaum, Robert   156
Tata, Ratan   133
Tata Group   125–26, 133
Taurel, Sidney   233
technology-driven change   18–19
temporal aspect of emotions   53
Tesco   329
Tetzeli, Rick   310
The Beatles   284
The Body Shop   335
Theory E (process-driven change)   38–39
Theory O (people-driven change)
      38–39
Thomas, Kenneth   165–66
Thomas, Robyn   130
Tichy, Noel   51
Time Inc   266
TMS (Team Management System)   303
Tolpis, John   298

Tosti, Donald   87
TQM (Total Quality Management)   343
Transactional Analysis   303
transactional leadership   117
transformation stories   122
transformational change   23–24, 28–29
transformational leadership   116–18
transition, definition   22
transition curve   83–89
    ability and willingness to change
        83, 86–89
    anxiety   83, 84–85
    commitment   83, 86–89
    cynicism   83, 85–86
    innovation   83, 86
    recommitment   83, 86–89
    reconciliation   83, 84
    reorientation   83, 85–86
    uncertainty   83, 84
transition models   78–89
trap of success   40
trust
    building   101–03
    repairing   102–03
trustworthiness   101–02
Tucci, Joseph M   137
Turnbull, Sharon   62
Turner, Richard   159–61
Twitter   208, 266

Ulrich, Dave   338
uncertainty and stress   153–54
UPS   291
urbanization and city growth   17–18

Vehar, Jonathan   132
visionary leadership   116
Vogel, Bernd   286

voicing   201, 202
Volkswagen   329
Vorhauser-Smith, Sylvia   16

W L Gore   235
Walker, Simon   136
Wark, Valerie   299
Watkins, M D   300
Watson, Tony   337
Weick, Karl   35, 123
Welch, Jack   39, 221
White, Katherine   193
Whitmore, George   259
Wicks, Ray   291
Wilcox, Mark   288
Wileman, Gwen   255
Williams, Mark   65, 66
Williams, Tony   274
Wilson, Tony   241–46
Woodall, Jean   337
Woodward, Sally   3
work, changing nature of   17, 19
work performance, impact of emotions   54

Yahoo! culture change (case study)   222–24
Yamada, Tachi   233
Yammer   208
Yong Kim, Dr Jim   17
Yukl, Gary   116, 118
Yum! Brands Inc   220

Zaccaro, Stephen   293, 295
Zappo   266
Zien, Karen Ann   236
Zohar, Danah   297–98
ZOUD (zone of uncomfortable debate)
        209–10
Zumwinkel, Klaus   122

CPSIA information can be obtained
at www.ICGtesting.com
Printed in the USA
BVHW041704160119
537992BV00007

3 4711 00230 5086